Quantum Artificial Intelligence with Qiskit

Quantum Artificial Intelligence (QAI) is a new interdisciplinary research field that combines quantum computing with Artificial Intelligence (AI), aiming to use the unique properties of quantum computers to enhance the capabilities of AI systems. *Quantum Artificial Intelligence with Qiskit* provides a cohesive overview of the field of QAI, providing tools for readers to create and manipulate quantum programs on devices as accessible as laptop computers.

Introducing symbolical quantum algorithms, sub-symbolical quantum algorithms, and quantum Machine Learning (ML) algorithms, this book explains each process step by step with associated Qiskit listings. All examples are additionally available for download at https://github.com/andrzejwichert/qai.

Allowing readers to learn the basic concepts of quantum computing on their home computers, this book is accessible to both the general readership as well as students and instructors of courses relating to computer science and AI.

Quantum Artificial Intelligence with Qiskit

Andreas Wichert

CRC Press
Taylor & Francis Group
Boca Raton London New York

CRC Press is an imprint of the
Taylor & Francis Group, an **informa** business

A CHAPMAN & HALL BOOK

First edition published 2024
by CRC Press
2385 NW Executive Center Drive, Suite 320, Boca Raton FL 33431

and by CRC Press
4 Park Square, Milton Park, Abingdon, Oxon, OX14 4RN

CRC Press is an imprint of Taylor & Francis Group, LLC

ISBN: 978-1-032-44897-8 (hbk)
ISBN: 978-1-032-44898-5 (pbk)
ISBN: 978-1-003-37440-4 (ebk)

DOI: 10.1201/9781003374404

Typeset in LM Roman
by KnowledgeWorks Global Ltd.

Publisher's note: This book has been prepared from camera-ready copy provided by the authors.

Access the Support Material: https://github.com/andrzejwichert/qai.

For my son André and my wife Manuela

Contents

Preface

Quantum artificial intelligence (QAI) is a new interdisciplinary research field that combines quantum computing with artificial intelligence (AI). It aims to use the unique properties of quantum computers, which leverage quantum mechanical effects (such as superposition and entanglement) to enhance the capabilities of AI systems. In QAI, progress is being made quickly. What was a scientific dream some years ago is becoming more real, and you are now (by reading this book) at the forefront of the revolution in QAI.

Quantum algorithms for AI have been proposed, including a quantum tree search algorithm and a quantum production system that will be demonstrated by *qiskit* simulation step by step. *Qiskit* is an open-source software development kit (SDK) for working with quantum computers at the level of circuits and algorithms [21], IBM Quantum, *https://quantum-computing.ibm.com/*. It provides tools for creating and manipulating quantum programs and running them on prototype quantum devices on IBM Quantum Experience or on simulators on a local computer. It follows the quantum circuit model for universal quantum computation and can be used for any quantum hardware that follows this model. *Qiskit* is based on Python and you can find all information about it at *https://qiskit.org*.

This book provides tools for creating and manipulating quantum programs and running them on prototype quantum devices or simulators on a local computer, such as a simple personal laptop. It follows the quantum circuit model for universal quantum computation and can be used with any quantum hardware that follows this model. You can download all the examples (Jupyter notebooks) from the book *https://github.com/andrzejwichert/qai.*[1]

In the book, we will introduce quantum computation and its application to AI. AI can be divided into different areas: symbolical artificial intelligence and machine learning (ML), the same is true for the QAI.

Artificial Intelligence – Chapter 1

AI is a subfield of computer science that models the mechanisms of intelligent human behavior. This approach is accomplished via simulation with the help of artificial artifacts, typically with computer programs on a machine that performs calculations. However, the terms "intelligence" and "intelligent human behavior" are not very well defined and understood. That is why over the years the definition of AI

---

[1]The author acknowledges the use of IBM Quantum services for this work. The views expressed are those of the author and do not reflect the official policy or position of IBM or the IBM Quantum team.

changed following the development of more powerful computers. For example, it is now common to identify AI with deep learning.

We divide the present AI domain into two main branches: symbolic AI and statistical ML. Symbolic AI deals with symbolic representations and problem solving, and statistical ML is based on distributed representations.

We first give a short history of AI, and then we describe the principles of the two main branches of AI, symbolic AI and ML.

Quantum Physics and Quantum Computation – Chapter 2

Statistical laws govern the totality of observations in physics. An object can be described in classical mechanics by a vector which describes the position and its momentum. Classical mechanics is usually valid at the macro scale. The changes in the position and the momentum of the object over time are described by the Hamiltonian equation of motion. The state of the object is described by the Hamiltonian function. At a micro scale the observations are described by quantum physics. Light appears only in chunks that can be quantized. An individual chunk is called quantum and a quantum of light is called a photon [27]. Quantum theory gets its name from this property, which it attributes to all measurable physical quantities. A photon can be described by a wave function if it is isolated from its environment. The wave function in quantum mechanics, if unobserved, evolves into a smooth and continuous way according to the Schrödinger equation, which is related to the Hamiltonian equation of motion. This equation describes a linear superposition of different states at time. During the observation (measurement by the observer, by us), the wave collapses into one definite state with a certain probability.

The mathematical framework of quantum theory is based on linear algebra in Hilbert space. A two-state quantum system is described by a two-dimensional Hilbert space. Thus, a two-state quantum system corresponds to a qubit. A register is composed of several qubits and is defined by the tensor product. We describe the principles of computation with one and m qubits, and we introduce the principles of entanglement, cloning, and the matrix representation of quantum Boolean gates, as well as an example of a simple quantum Boolean circuit.

Qiskit – Chapter 3

We describe how to install *qiskit* and demonstrate the two main backend simulator functions we will use. We demonstrate the working principles of the *qiskit* software development kit on the simple example of a quantum coin. We indicate how to represent simple quantum circuits by unitary matrices using the *qiskit* get unitary command. We indicate step by step how to define quantum circuits on an example of a four-bit conjunction. The concept of un-computation is introduced since in quantum computing we cannot reset qubits to zero. The Deutsch algorithm determines if an unknown function $f:\mathbf{B}^1 \to \mathbf{B}^1:f(x) = y$ of one bit is constant or not by calling the function one time. The Deutsch algorithm was the first algorithm (1985) that demonstrated a quantum advantage: it is a proof of concept that, in certain settings, quantum computers are strictly more powerful than classical ones by reduction in query complexity compared to the classical case. Finally, we give an example how to run the Deutsch algorithm on a real small quantum computer.

Quantum Gates – Chapter 4

Quantum gates are the building blocks of quantum circuits, like classical logic gates are for conventional digital circuits. Unlike classical logic gates, quantum logic gates are reversible and can be described by unitary matrices. First, we introduce Boolean quantum gates that allow us to map any Boolean circuit in such a way that the circuit becomes reversible. Such a circuit represents a permutation in Hilbert space and can be represented by a permutation matrix composed of the unitary matrices representing the quantum gates. Then we describe quantum gates for one qubit, like for example, Clifford gates that are the elements of the Clifford group and can be efficiently simulated with a classical computer. Parameterized gates play an important role in quantum ML. A parameterized rotation gate is a parameterized gate with the parameter being the amount of rotation to be performed around the three axes. We introduce the controlled-U gates and introduce the unitary decomposition and formulate the process of transpilation. Translation is a complex problem of finding an optimal decomposition into the present quantum gates for a quantum computer.

Grover's Amplification – Chapter 5

We describe the Grover's amplification algorithm. We represent n state by a super-position; each state has the same real positive amplitude. A parallel computation is applied to all the n states, and the state with the solution is marked by a minus sign, and the amplitude is now negative. We then apply a linear operation based on the Householder reflection, and by the reflection, the value of the marked amplitude grows linearly. For dimensions higher than four, the operations of marking and the Householder reflection must be repeated $\sqrt{n}$ times, since at each step the amplitude only grows linearly. After $\sqrt{n}$ steps we measure the solution. The algorithm guarantees us a quadratic speed up over a classical computer that would require n steps. The Grover's amplification algorithm is optimal and one can prove that a better algorithm cannot exist. We will demonstrate the principles of Grover's amplification using the matrix notation *NumPy*. Then we explain how to represent the algorithm with quantum gates by a *qiskit* example of three qubits representing eight states using one and two rotations.

SAT Problem – Chapter 6

The Boolean satisfiability problem (SAT problem) is the problem of determining if there exists an interpretation that satisfies a given Boolean formula, whether the formula evaluates true [22]. Each variable of the formula can have the values true (one) or false (zero). We formulate the formula satisfiability problem and indicate an example step by step. Then we discuss the relation between the SAT problem and the time complexity. Computational complexity theory addresses questions regarding which problems can be solved in a finite amount of time on a computer. A decision problem is a computational problem with instances formulated as a question with a binary answer. An example is the question of whether a certain number n is a prime number. Most problems can be converted into a decision problem. The time complexity describes the amount of computer time it takes to run an algorithm. Time complexity is commonly estimated by counting the number of elementary operations performed by the algorithm. The amount of time taken is linearly related to the number of elementary operations performed by the algorithm. A problem is easy if an algorithm on a computer can determine the instances related to the input for the answer in polynomial time. Polynomial-time algorithms are said to be fast since they can be executed in an acceptable time on a computer. Otherwise, we state that the problem is hard, meaning the time required grows exponentially and cannot be executed in an acceptable time on a computer. We describe a simple SAT problem with a Boolean formula with three Boolean variables and indicate it step by step using the *qiskit* framework of how to solve the problem using Grover's amplification algorithm by a quantum circuit.

Symbolic State Representation – Chapter 7

An economic symbolic representation of objects and attributes that can represent a state during problem solving is introduced. This representation is motivated by the biological *what where* principle and requires a low number of bits. Such an economical symbolical representation is ideal for the current generation of quantum computers. We describe the tree search on which problem solving is based. Nodes and edges represent a search tree. Each node represents a state, and each edge represents a transition from one state to the following state. The path descriptors is the basis idea of quantum tree search. In a quantum tree search we represent all possible path descriptors simultaneously and can use Grover's amplification algorithm to determine the solution.

Quantum Production System – Chapter 8

A production system is a model of human problem solving. It is composed of long-term memory and working memory, which is also called the short-term memory. Problem-solving can be modeled by a production system that implements a search algorithm. The search defines a problem space and can be represented as a tree. Using Grover's algorithm, we search through all possible paths and verify, for each path, whether it leads to the goal state.

A pure production system has no mechanism for recovering from an impasse. We describe an example of a simple pure production systems for sorting of a string and indicate how to port this simple pure production systems into the quantum production system. Then we indicate that a quantum production system can be the basis of a unified theory of cognition.

3 Puzzle – Chapter 9

We demonstrate the working principles of quantum production system and the quantum tree search by a *qiskit* implementation of a toy example from symbolical AI, the

3-puzzle. The goal is to find a series of moves that changes the board from the initial configuration to a desired configuration. We describe the representation of the rules (productions) of the long-term memory and describe the search of depth one, two and three. The search of depth three results in eight possible states. The solution is marked by an oracle and a Grover's amplification is applied once. To increase the probability value of the solution we will apply two Grover's amplification. The solution corresponds to the path descriptor that indicates the sequence of rules (productions) that changes the board from the initial configuration to a desired configuration.

8 Puzzle – Chapter 10

The n puzzle is a classical problem for modeling algorithms. For n-puzzle there are $n + 1$ different objects: n cells and one empty cell. Each object can be coded by $\rho = \lceil \log_2 n + 1 \rceil$ qubits and a configuration of $n + 1$ objects can be represented by a register of $z := \rho \cdot (n + 1)$ qubits $|x\rangle$. The function $g(x)$ is represented a unitary operator T. T acts on the $z + 1$ qubits with $x \in B^z$ and $c \in B^1$

$$T \cdot |x\rangle |c\rangle = |x\rangle |f(x) \oplus c\rangle.$$

We indicate how to extend the 3-puzzle to the 8-puzzle resulting in a non-constant branching factor. We show that the branching factor is reduced by Grover's amplification to the square root of the average branching factor and not to the maximal branching factor. Simple experiments of the search of the depth one requires already 49 qubits. The experiments indicate that the presented methods can be extended to a search of any depth, given that more qubits are present.

Blocks World – Chapter 11

The blocks world is a planning domain in AI [73]. The blocks can be placed at the table and picked up and set down on a table or another block, and the goal is to build one or more vertical stacks of blocks. Only one block may be moved at a time and any blocks that are under another block cannot be moved. There are three different types of blocks. They differ by attributes such as color (red, green, and blue) or marks, but not by form. In AI, they are traditionally called A, B, C blocks [61]. The simplicity of this toy problem allows to compare classical approach with quantum computing approach. We indicate how the binding of the stats is achieved through the entanglement. We indicate how to represent the states with a class descriptor and the position descriptor (adjective) and perform a search of depth one. The A, B, C blocks planning problem results in a non-constant branching factor. We show again that the branching factor is reduced by Grover's amplification to the square root of the average branching factor and not to the maximal branching factor.

Five Pennies Nim Game – Chapter 12

Games involving two players represent one of the classic applications of symbolic problem solving. Starting with some initial game position, the algorithm explores the tree of all legal moves down to the requested depth. An example is the *nim* game in which two players take turns removing objects from distinct piles. A simplified version is the *nim* game with no piles, the five pennies *nim* game. Two players alternate remove either one, two, or three pennies from a stack that initially contains five pennies. The player who pick up last penny loses. The five pennies *nim* game is a zero game where neither player has any legal options. The first player loses, and the second-player wins if correct moves are chosen.

We indicate the architecture for the five pennies *nim* game and indicate that a quantum tree search cannot implement the minimax-algorithm. We can determine the search path, but we cannot model the behavior of the player that choses the best move since we cannot compare different states that are described by different path descriptors.

Basis Encoding of Binary Vectors – Chapter 13

Quantum encoding is a process to transform classical information into quantum states. It plays a crucial role in using quantum algorithm. Basis encoding is the most intuitive way to encode classical binary vectors into a quantum state. It encodes n dimensional binary vector to an n-qubit quantum state represented computational basis state. We will describe two possible approaches, a method that was developed by Ventura and Martinez and the method of entanglement of binary patterns vectors with index qubits in superposition.

Quantum Associative Memory – Chapter 14

Quantum associative memory (QuAM) in the domain of quantum computation is a model with a capacity exponential in the number of neurons. Quantum Nearest Neighbor (QNN) is related to the QuAM. In QNN the binary patterns are stored by entanglement with index qubits. For Grover's amplification to the index qubits, we have to un-compute the entanglement of index qubits with the patterns. In QNN we need to un-compute. However, in QuAM we do not un-compute. In the QuAM as proposed by Venture and Martinez, a modified version of Grover's search algorithm is applied to determine the answer vector to a query vector so that instead of un-computing one can apply Grover's algorithm to all qubits. Most quantum ML algorithms including quantum associative memory suffer from the input destruction problem where the classical data must be read and after the measurement the superposition collapses. However, the input destruction problem is not solved until today, and usually theoretical speed ups are analyzed. We will demonstrate a simple QNN model, and a modified version of Grover's search algorithm as proposed by Venture and Martinez. Then we analyze the input destruction problem.

Quantum Lernmatrix – Chapter 15

We introduce quantum Lernmatrix based on where n units are stored in the quantum superposition. Lernmatrix is an associative-memory-like architecture. During the retrieval phase, quantum counting of ones based on Euler's formula is used for the pattern recovery as proposed by Trugenberger. We demonstrate how to represent the quantum Lernmatrix by a quantum circuit and preform experiments using *qiskit*. Then we introduce a tree-like structure that increases the measured value of correct answers. During the active phase the quantum Lernmatrices are queried and the results are estimated efficiently. The required time is much lower compared to the conventional approach or Grover's algorithm.

Amplitude Encoding – Chapter 16

Amplitude encoding encodes a real or complexed value vector of the length one into the amplitudes of a quantum state. We describe the top-down strategy and indicate the algorithm step by step. Then we describe the combining states strategy. Instead of representing the binary tree by multi-control rotation gates, we can use controlled SWAP operators with simple rotation gates. The resulting circuits depth is less than the top-down divide strategy; however, we require the same number of qubits as the number of rotation gates, and the qubits are entangled after the operation. Then we describe the possibility of initializing the desired states using *qiskit* commands. We cannot access the amplitudes that represent vectors, but we estimate the value of the scalar product between them using the swap test. We give two examples of the swap test.

Quantum Kernels – Chapter 17

A quantum computer can estimate a quantum kernel, and the estimate can be used by a kernel method on a classical computer. This is because the exponential quantum advantage in evaluating inner products allows us to estimate the quantum kernel directly in the higher dimensional space. We give an example of quantum kernels and the swap test. Then we describe quantum kernels and the inversion test. Quantum feature maps encode classical data into quantum data via a parametrized quantum circuit. Parameterized quantum circuits are based on superposition and entanglement. They are hard to simulate classically and could lead to an advantage over the classical ML approach. The inversion test is based on the usual idea of estimating the fidelity (similarity) between two states. We describe an example using the *qiskit* command *ZZFeatureMap*. Then we indicate how the quantum kernel is plugged into classical kernel methods like support vector machines.

qRAM – Chapter 18

Quantum memory is proposed as an analogue to classical computer memory, like the random-access memory (RAM). RAM is a form of computer memory that can be read and changed in any order, typically used to store working data. In a quantum ML domain, the usage of quantum random access memory $(qRAM)$ is proposed to avoid the input destruction problem. We demonstrate the bucket brigade architecture of $qRAM$. The method of $qRAM$ is related to the entanglement of the index qubits that are in the superposition with the patterns. We demonstrate an example of binary patterns and indicate why the representation of amplitude coding leads to the same complexity as a recall operation on a classical RAM.

Quantum Fourier Transform – Chapter 19

A periodic function can be represented in the frequency space. The frequency is the number of occurrences of a repeating event per one unit of time. If something changes rapidly, then we say that it has a high frequency. If it does not change rapidly, i.e., it changes smoothly, we say that it has a low frequency. The discrete Fourier transform converts discrete time-based or space-based data into the frequency domain.

We describe the discrete Fourier transforms (DFT) and indicate the relation to the quantum Fourier transform (QFT). The we indicate how the QFT can be factored into the tensor product of m single-qubit operations and implemented by basic quantum gates. We demonstrate examples of QFT for two, three, and four qubits. Then we indicate that the circuit for m qubits can be imported from the *qiskit* library. We analyze the QFT costs and give a simple example of its operation.

Phase Estimation – Chapter 20

The Kitaev's Phase Estimation Algorithm (also referred to as a quantum eigenvalue estimation algorithm), is a quantum algorithm to estimate the phase (or eigenvalue) of an eigenvector of a unitary operator. We explain the algorithm and indicate an example of the determination of the eigenvalue of the T gate. Then we introduce the quantum counting algorithm based on the quantum phase estimation algorithm and on the Grover's search algorithm. The quantum counting algorithm is a quantum algorithm for counting the number of solutions for a given search problem.

Quantum Perceptron – Chapter 21

The classical perceptron describes an algorithm for supervised learning that considers only linearly separable problems in which groups can be separated by a line or hyperplane. The quantum perceptron does not usually include learning, but instead computes the output of a binary unit (neuron) efficiently. It is based on the Kitaev's phase estimation algorithm. A quantum perceptron can be used as a building block of larger systems and it can process an arbitrary number of input vectors in parallel. We present a simple example of the quantum perceptron for two-dimensional input.

HHL – Chapter 22

The quantum algorithm for linear systems of equations is one of the main fundamental algorithms expected to provide a speedup over their classical counterparts. In the honor of its inventors Aram Harrow, Avinatan Hassidim, and Seth Lloyd, it is called the HHL algorithm. HHL is going to be one of the most useful subroutines for any quantum ML algorithm because almost all ML uses some form of a linear system of equations. For example, in support vector machines and quantum support vector machines, maximizing the objective function with the optimum values of the Lagrange multipliers are based on solving linear equations. We describe the HHL algorithm, give an example step by step using *qiskit* command $HamiltonianGate$, and indicate the constrains of the algorithm.

Hybrid Approaches – Variational Classification – Chapter 23

Variational approaches are characterized using a classical optimization algorithm to iteratively update a parameterized quantum trial solution also called an *ansatz* (from the German word Ansatz which means approach). The parameterized quantum trial solution is defined by a parametrized quantum circuit, for example, the *ZZFeatureMap*. We indicate the basic principles of a variational classifier by a simple example. Then we describe the cross entropy loss function and the Simultaneous Perturbation Stochastic Approximation (SPSA). The optimizer performs stochastic gradient approximation, which requires only two measurements of the loss function. *Qiskit* implements the variational quantum classifier (VQC) that can be embedded in classical ML tasks. We indicate a simple example of the VQC classifier whose learning is based on SPSA.

Conclusion – Chapter 24

We conclude our journey with quantum artificial intelligence (QAI). A quantum computer is a computer that exploits quantum mechanical phenomena such as superposition and entanglement. The quantum advantage is based on two principles related to Grover's algorithm and the phase estimation algorithm. Quantum computing is still in its early stages, and there are many technical challenges that must be overcome before it can be used to implement QAI. However, for the quantum computing race is on; what was a scientific dream some years ago, is becoming more real. You are now at the forefront of the revolution in quantum computing.

Author

Andreas Wichert studied computer science at the University of Saarland, where he graduated in 1993. He studied philosophy and computer science at Ulm University. In 1999, he completed his bachelor in philosophy and in 2000 his PhD in computer science. He is an assistant professor with habilitation in the Department of Computer Science and Engineering, University of Lisbon, where he is also lecturing on machine learning and quantum computation. His research focuses on neuronal networks, cognitive systems, and quantum computation. He published 6 books and over 100 scientific articles.

## CHAPTER 1

Artificial Intelligence

Artificial intelligence (AI) is a subfield of computer science that models the mechanisms of intelligent human behavior (intelligence). This approach is accomplished via simulation with the help of artificial artifacts, typically with computer programs on a machine that performs calculations. However, the term "intelligence" and "intelligent human behavior" are not very well-defined and understood. That is why over the years the definition of AI changed following the development of more powerful computers. For example, it is now common to identify AI with deep learning.

We divide the present AI domain into two main branches: symbolical AI and statistical machine learning (ML). Symbolic AI deals with symbolic representations and problem solving, and statistical (ML) is based on distributed representations.

We first give a short history of AI, and then we describe the principles of the two main branches of AI, symbolic AI and statistical ML.

1.1 A SHORT HISTORY OF AI

1.1.1 Cybernetics

Cybernetics has its origins in the intersection of the fields of control systems, electrical network theory, mechanical engineering, logic modeling, fuzzy logic, evolutionary biology, neuroscience, anthropology, and psychology [123]. In 1943, McCulloch, a neuroscientist, and Walter Pitts, a logician, developed the artificial neuron, a mathematical model that mimics the functionality of a biological neuron [67]. This model is called the McCulloch-Pitts model of a neuron. The perceptron algorithm was invented in 1957 by Frank Rosenblatt [86] and was inspired by the McCulloch-Pitts model of a neuron. Perceptron describes a simple algorithm for supervised learning. In the 1960s, an active research program concerning ML with artificial neural networks was carried out by Rosenblatt.

During the early years analog computers were predominant. They were developed in the years 1930–1950. An analog computer represents information by analog means, such as voltage. In such a computer, information is represented by a voltage wave and the algorithm is represented by an electrical circuit. Such a circuit is composed of resistors and capacitors that are connected together. An algorithm represents a mathematical model of a physical system, which can be described, for example, by

DOI: 10.1201/9781003374404-1

specific differential equations. The input and output of the computation are voltage waves that can be observed by an oscilloscope. The represented values are usually less accurate than digitally represented values. The results of each computation can vary due to external influences. For this reason, each result of the computation is unique.

1.1.2 Symbolic Artificial Intelligence

Analog computers started to decline with the advent of the development of the microprocessor, which led to the development of digital computers and a possible reproduction of a calculation without an error. The Electronic Numerical Integrator and Calculator (ENIAC) was a digital computer build and developed (1943–1944) by John Mauchly and J. Presper Eckert. They proposed the EDVAC's (Electronic Discrete Variable Automatic Computer) construction in August 1944. Unlike its predecessor the ENIAC, it was binary rather than decimal, and was designed to be a stored-program computer [116], [9]. A digital computer is a device that processes information represented in discrete means such as symbols. Usually, the symbols are represented in binary form. In a digital circuit, the information is represented by binary digits. Due to a digital representation, the exact values of each computation can be reproduced since there is no external influences. The computation can be repeated, and the result remains the same. Binary digits are represented by the minimal unit of information, the bit with the values 0 or 1. The binary information is manipulated by Boolean digital circuits.

With the rise of digital computers, AI was founded as a distinct discipline at the Dartmouth workshop in 1956. The term itself was invented by the American computer scientist John McCarthy and used in the title of the conference. During this meeting, programs were presented that played chess and checkers, proved theorems and interpreted texts. Arthur Samuel developed ML algorithms for checkers. Checkers requires intelligence when the algorithm for playing is unknown. As soon as the algorithm is known, playing checkers no longer requires intelligence. AI is a subfield of computer science that models the mechanisms of intelligent human behavior (intelligence). Problems of this kind are solved by algorithms studied by AI. The key idea behind these algorithms is the symbolic representation of the domain in which the problems are solved. Usually symbolical algorithms requires less computational power as ML algorithms that require expensive vector operations.

1.1.3 Connectionist Movement

The simple perceptron describes an algorithm for supervised learning that considers only linearly separable problems in which groups can be separated by a line or hyperplane [68]. These limitations do not apply to feedforward networks with nonlinear units, also called multilayer perceptrons. Such networks can be trained by the backpropagation learning algorithm. The algorithm itself was invented independently several times [19], [117], [77], [65]. However, it became popular with the books Parallel Distributed Processing (PDP) published by David Rumelhart and his colleagues,

[65], [66], [64]. The authors returned to perceptrons and claimed that the pessimism about learning in perceptrons during the raise of symbolical AI was misplaced. The books consist of three volumes, foundations, psychological and biological models and a handbook of models, programs, and exercises that included software on a diskette written in the programming language C. With the development of the personal computer in 1980–1986 by Apple and IBM lead to the popularization of the backpropagation algorithm through the PDP books. The popularization led to a connectionist movement that resulted in the "symbol wars" with the old symbolic AI school. The symbol wars describe the emotional discussion of the two camps around the question as to whether the departure from the symbolic approach leads to something new and worthwhile.

1.1.4 Deep Learning

GPUs (Graphics Processing Units) were originally designed to accelerate the rendering of 3D graphics. Over time, they became more flexible and programmable, enhancing their capabilities. Nvidia was the very first company to bring GPUs into the world in 1999. The first GPU in history was known as the Geforce 256.

With more computer power by GPUs, it is possible to train huge data by deep artificial networks (Deep Learning) that use many hidden layers to increase the model's power in statistical learning. The models achieved tremendous results in handling vision, speech recognition, speech synthesis, image generation, and machine translation. It is now common to identify AI with deep learning and not with symbol manipulating systems, assuming that the symbolic approach is no longer relevant. However, the downside of the deep learning (DL) approach is requirement of huge computing power, large data sets, and the lack of comprehensibility and explanation contrary to the symbolic approach.

1.1.5 Quantum Artificial Intelligence

With the appearance of first small quantum computers by IBM, Google, Microsoft and developing quantum artificial intelligence (QAI) emerged. The quantum computers execute some quantum circuits with a certain error, their capacity varies from 5 qubit to 127 qubit, but the race is set up. One of the most popular software development kits (SDK) for working with quantum computers is *Qiskit* [21], IBM Quantum, *https://quantum-computing.ibm.com/*. It provides tools for creating and manipulating quantum programs and running them on prototype quantum devices or on simulators on a local computer, like your own simple laptop. It follows the quantum circuit model for universal quantum computation and can be used for any quantum hardware that follows this model. This allows to investigate the possibilities for the realization of AI by means of quantum computation through computer experiments [118]. If we relate qubits to bits, it becomes clear that the symbolic approach is an ideal candidate for quantum computation since the algorithms requirs much lower capacity compared to the ML algorithms. We will discuss first symbolic quantum artificial AI, and only in the second part we cover the quantum ML [119].

1.2 SYMBOLICAL ARTIFICIAL INTELLIGENCE

Logical symbolical representation is motivated by philosophy and mathematics [53, 109, 61]. Predicates are functions that map objects' arguments into true or false values. They describe the relation between objects in a world which is represented by symbols. Whenever a relation holds with respect to some objects, the corresponding predicate is true when applied to the corresponding object symbols.

Predicates can be negated by the function ¬ (not) and combined by the logical connectives ∨ (disjunction), ∧ (conjunction), and the implies (→) operator. ¬, ∨, ∧, and → determine the predicate's value. To signal that an expression is universally true, the universal quantifier and a variable standing for possible objects is used.

$$\forall \, x[\text{Feathers}(x) \rightarrow \text{Bird}(x)].$$
An Object having feathers is a bird.

Some expressions are true only for some objects. This is represented by an existential quantifier and a variable.

$$\exists \, x[\text{Bird}(x)].$$
There is at least one object which is a bird.

An interpretation is an accounting of the correspondence between objects and object symbols and between relations and predicates. An interpretation can be only either true or false. These are some basic ideas about representation in predicate calculus, which is a subset of formal logic.

Symbols in general are defined by their occurrence in a structure and by a formal language (for example predicate calculus), which manipulates these structures [101, 71] (see Figure 1.1).

In this context, symbols do not, by themselves, represent any utilizable knowledge. For example, they cannot be used for a definition of similarity criteria between themselves. The use of symbols in algorithms which imitate human intelligent behavior led to the famous physical symbol system hypothesis by Newell and Simon (1976) [70]: "The necessary and sufficient condition for a physical system to exhibit intelligence is that it be a physical symbol system". Symbols are not present in the world; they are the constructs of a human mind and simplify the process of representation used in communication and problem solving.

1.2.1 Bits

The symbols are represented in a computer by bits. The smallest information unit is called a binary digit, or bit. To represent n symbols we require $\lceil \log_2 n \rceil$. For example, to represent 9 symbols we require four bits with $16 = 2^4$ possible generated codes $16 = 2^4$. For 7 bits, there are $128 = 2^7$ alternative symbols that can represent different characters. A set of 128 different characters is described by the American Standard Code for Information Interchange, the ASCII character set, is the most popular code. It was developed based on the English alphabet around 1963. In addition to all

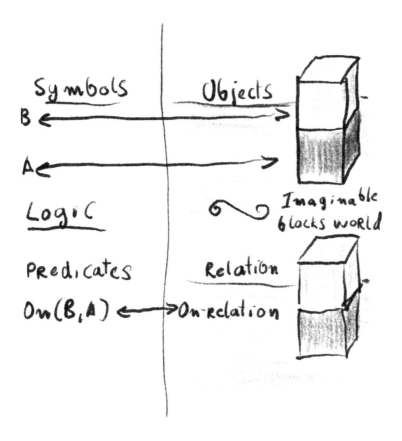

Figure 1.1 Object represented by symbols and relation represented by predicate.

normal alphabetic characters, numeric characters and printable characters, the set also includes a number of control characters. The character set was extended to 8 bits by adding additional character definitions after the first 128 characters.

1.2.2 Rules and Operators

A world state can be described including properties and relations using predicate calculus. This kind of description can be used to define operators like those used in the STRIPS computer science approach (see Figure 1.2) [29, 73, 33]. ABC block world has been a popular planning domain in AI research exemplified using three blocks named A, B, and C. Three blocks lie arranged in some initial configuration over a table (as in Figure 1.2). Each may have at most one block over it, and each may be either over the table or another block. A robot arm can stack, unstack, and move the blocks on the table.

$$ontable(A).$$
$$ontable(C).$$
$$on(B,A).$$
$$clear(B).$$
$$clear(C).$$
$$gripping().$$

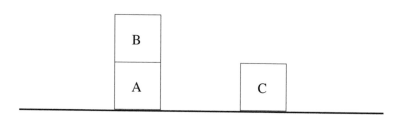

Figure 1.2 ABC block world.

Using the block examples, four operations "pickup", "putdown", "stack", and "unstack" can be defined [73]. The expressions are always universally true, and therefore the universal quantifier ∀ is omitted.

$$pickup(x) \begin{cases} P: & gripping() \wedge clear(x) \wedge ontable(x) \\ A: & gripping(x) \\ D: & ontable(x) \wedge gripping() \end{cases}$$

$$putdown(x) \begin{cases} P: & gripping(x) \\ A: & ontable(x) \wedge gripping() \wedge clear(x) \\ D: & gripping(x) \end{cases}$$

$$stack(x,y) \begin{cases} P: & gripping(x) \wedge clear(x) \\ A: & on(x,y) \wedge gripping() \wedge clear(x) \\ D: & clear(y) \wedge gripping(x) \end{cases}$$

$$unstack(x,y) \begin{cases} P: & gripping() \wedge clear(x) \wedge on(x,y) \\ A: & gripping(x) \wedge clear(y) \\ D: & on(x,y) \wedge gripping() \end{cases}$$

Each of the operators is represented as triples of description. The first element is the precondition, the world state that must be met for an operator to be applied. It can be true or false when variables become identified with the values, which describe the state. The second element is the additions to the state description that are a result of applying the operator. The last element is the items that are removed from the state description to create a new state when the operator is applied. These operators obey the frame axiom since they specify what is true in one state of the world and what exactly has changed by performing some action by an operator. The problem of specifying which part of the description should change and which should not is called the frame problem [125].

$$ontable(A).$$
$$clear(A)$$
$$ontable(C).$$
$$clear(C).$$
$$gripping(B).$$

The state after the operator *pickup(B)* was applied to the state of Figure 1.2 (see Figure 1.3).

Instead of operators, we can as well use simple rules. A rule [125, 88, 61] contains several "if" patterns and one or more "then" patterns. A pattern in the context of rules is an individual predicate which can be negated together with arguments. The rule can establish a new assertion by the "then" part, the conclusion whenever the "if" part, the premise, is true.

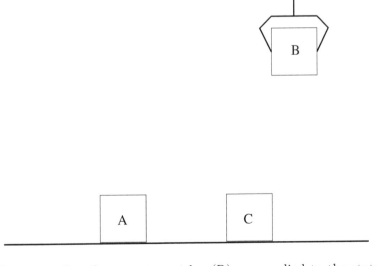

Figure 1.3 The state after the operator *pickup(B)* was applied to the state of Figure 1.2.

1.2.3 Production Systems

Problems in symbolical AI are often described by the representation of a problem space and a search procedure [73]. Problem-solving can be modeled by a production system that implements a search algorithm. The search defines a problem space and can be represented by a tree. The production system in the context of classical AI and Cognitive Psychology is one of the most successful computer models of human problem solving. The production system theory describes how to form a sequence of actions, which lead to a goal, and offers a computational theory of how humans solve problems [7].

Production systems are composed of if-then rules that are also called productions. A production system is composed of [17, 61]:

- The long-term memory is modeled by a set of productions.

- The short-term memory or working memory that represents the states. This memory contains a description of the state in a problem solving process. The state is described by logically structured representation and is simply called a pattern. Whenever a premise is true, the production (the rule) fires (is executed). It means that the conclusions of the productions change the contents of the working memory.

- The focus of attention, also called the recognize-act cycle. If several productions can be applied to the working memory, conflict resolution chooses a production from the conflict set for firing. There are different conflict resolution strategies, such as choosing a random production from the set, or selecting a production using some function.

The computation is done in the following steps. The working memory is initialized with the initial state description. The patterns in working memory are matched against the premise of the production. The premise of the productions that match the patterns in working memory produces a set, which is called the conflict set. One of the productions of this set is chosen using the conflict resolution and the conclusion of the production changes the content of the working memory. This process is denoted as firing of the production. This cycle is repeated on the modified working memory until a goal state is reached or no productions can fire. An example of a production system is the 8-puzzle. The 8-puzzle is composed of eight numbered movable tiles in a 3×3 frame. One cell of the frame is empty; as a result, tiles can be moved around to form different patterns. The goal is to find a series of moves off tiles into the blank space that changes the board from the initial configuration to a goal configuration.

The long-term memory is specified by four productions [61]:

- **If** the empty cell is not on the top edge, **then** move the empty cell up;

- **If** the empty cell is not on the left edge, **then** move the empty cell left;

- **If** the empty cell is not on the right edge, **then** move the empty cell right;

- **If** the empty cell is not on the bottom edge, **then** move the empty cell down.

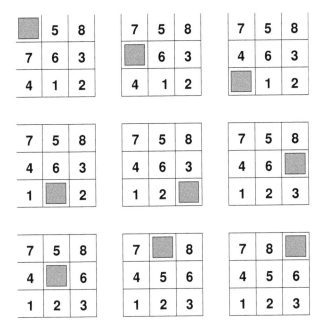

Figure 1.4 The first pattern (upper left) represents the initial configuration and the last (low right) the goal configuration. The series of moves describe the solution to the problem.

The control strategy for the search would be:

- Halt when goal is in the working memory.

- Chose a random production.

- Do not allow loops.

In Figure 1.4, we see an example representing a sequence of states that lead form the initial configuration to the goal configuration.

Production system implements a search algorithm that defines a problem space and can be represented as a tree.

1.2.4 Tree Search

The search represented by a search tree is performed from an initial state through the following states until a goal state is reached. A search tree is represented by nodes and edges. Each node represents a state, and each edge represents a transition from one state to the following state. The initial state defines the root of the tree. From each state v, either B_v states can be reached or the state is a leaf. B_v represents the branching factor of the node v. A leaf represents either the goal of the computation or an impasse when no valid transition to a succeeding state exists. In contrast to a real tree in computer science, the root of a tree structure is at the top of the tree and the leaves are at the bottom. Every node besides the root has a unique node from which it was reached, called the parent. The parent is the node above it and is connected by an edge. Each parent ν has B_ν children. The depth of a node ν is the number of edges to the root node. Nodes with the same depth k define the level k. For a tree with a constant branching factor B, each node at each level k has B children, and at each level k, there are $B \cdot k$ nodes [73], [60], [87]. Breadth-first search performs a level-wise search. All nodes at a level have to be visited before visiting a node at the next level. Depth-first search always expands the deepest node in the search tree until a goal is reached or all nodes are impasse states.

1.2.5   Informed Tree Search

Heuristic search is based on a heuristic function $h(\nu)$ that estimates the cheapest cost from the node ν to the goal.

We will demonstrate the principles of heuristic function $h(\nu)$ on the 8-puzzle example. Two common heuristics for this task are the number of misplaced tiles, and the "city-block distance" [73, 78, 61]. The first heuristic counts the number of misplaced tiles out of place in each state compared to the desired goal. However, this heuristic fails to take into account all available information such as the distance the tiles must be moved. The "city-block distance" sums all the distances by which the tiles are out of place, with one count for each square a tile must be moved to reach a position of the desired state. The "city-block distance", also called the "Manhattan distance", is often better than the "number of misplaced tiles".

Greedy best-first search expands the node ν that is closest to the goal according to a heuristic function $h(\nu)$. Out of the B children the node ν_i is chosen with

$$\min_{1 \leq i \leq B} \left(h(\nu_i) \right). \tag{1.1}$$

Like depth-first search it follows a single path to the goal. It always expands the deepest node in the search tree according to $h(\nu)$ until a goal is reached or all nodes are impasse states. The A search evaluates the nodes through a function $f(\nu)$ that estimates the cheapest solution that passes through the node ν. The function $f(\nu)$ is composed out of the heuristic function $h(\nu)$ and the function $g(\nu)$ that indicates the cheapest costs of reaching the node ν from the root node representing the initial state. Finally the A^* search is equivalent to the A search with the constraint that the function $h(\nu)$ is an admissible heuristic, it never overestimates the cost to reach the goal. Generally the invention of heuristic functions is difficult.

1.3   MACHINE LEARNING

Many of the ML techniques are derived from the efforts of psychologists and biologists to make more sense of human learning through computational models [7],[121]. There are some parallels between humans and ML. During learning, humans attempt to gain some knowledge, which involves some modification of behavioral tendencies by experience. In ML, we can distinguish between supervised learning and unsupervised learning. In supervised learning, the algorithm is presented with examples of inputs and their desired outputs. The goal is to learn a general rule that maps inputs to outputs. Supervised learning is frequently referred to as learning with a teacher because the desired outputs are indicated by some kind of a teacher. Consequently, unsupervised learning is referred to as learning without a teacher. In unsupervised learning, the algorithm groups information that is primarily represented by vectors into groups. The algorithm attempts to find the hidden structure of unlabeled data; clustering is an example of such an algorithm [121]. Statistical ML is mostly based on distributed representation using vector representation.

1.3.1 Vector Representation

In ML a sub-symbolical or distributed representation is used. One form of distributed representation corresponds to vectors. A vector $\mathbf{x}$ of dimension D is represented as

$$\mathbf{x} = \begin{pmatrix} x_1 \\ x_2 \\ \vdots \\ x_D \end{pmatrix} = (x_1, x_2, \cdots, x_D)^T,$$

with each dimension x_i representing a value like for example a real number. One can measure the distance between two D dimensional vectors by a distance function like the Euclidean distance function

$$d(\mathbf{x}, \mathbf{y}) = \|\mathbf{x} - \mathbf{y}\| = \sqrt{|x_1 - y_1|^2 + |x_2 - y_2|^2 + \cdots + |x_D - y_D|^2},$$

or the Taxicab or Manhattan metric d_1 with

$$d_1(\mathbf{x}, \mathbf{y}) = \|\mathbf{x} - \mathbf{y}\|_1 = |x_1 - y_1| + |x_2 - y_2| + \cdots + |x_D - y_D|. \tag{1.2}$$

The dot product or scalar product is represented as,

$$\langle \mathbf{x} | \mathbf{y} \rangle = \sum_{i=1}^{D} y_j \cdot x_j.$$

The scalar product is commutative

$$\langle \mathbf{x} | \mathbf{y} \rangle = \mathbf{x}^T \cdot \mathbf{y} = \mathbf{y}^T \cdot \mathbf{x} = \langle \mathbf{y} | \mathbf{x} \rangle.$$

However, matrix multiplication between vectors is not commutative, since

$$\mathbf{x}^T \cdot = \langle \mathbf{x} | \mathbf{y} \rangle = \begin{pmatrix} y_0 & y_1 \end{pmatrix} \cdot \begin{pmatrix} x_0 \\ x_1 \end{pmatrix} = y_0 \cdot x_0 + y_1 \cdot x_1$$

is very different from

$$\mathbf{x} \cdot \mathbf{y}^T = |\mathbf{y}\rangle\langle\mathbf{x}| = \begin{pmatrix} y_0 \\ y_1 \end{pmatrix} \cdot \begin{pmatrix} x_0 & x_1 \end{pmatrix} = \begin{pmatrix} y_0 \cdot x_0 & y_0 \cdot x_1 \\ y_1 \cdot x_0 & y_1 \cdot x_1 \end{pmatrix}.$$

In quantum physics, a shorthand notation for a column vector and a vector is used which is less confusing. Related to the scalar product $\langle \mathbf{x} | \mathbf{y} \rangle$, row vectors $\mathbf{x}^T$ are $\langle \mathbf{x} |$ "bra" and column vectors $\mathbf{y}$ are $|\mathbf{y}\rangle$ "kets" from bra(c)kets.

1.3.2 Nearest Neighbor

The Nearest Neighbors (NN) classifier works under the assumption that objects represented by a feature vector that share similar features will likely have the same class [69]. With that, if we represent every example as a feature vector, we can, for instance, compute the Euclidean distance between a new example and some known training data to find out what previously seen examples are similar to the new one. We can then use that information to perform classification.

Let DB be a database of s objects $\mathbf{x}_k$ represented by vectors of dimension n in which the index k is an explicit key identifying each object,

$$\{\mathbf{x}_k \in DB \mid k \in \{1..s\}\},$$

with

$$\mathbf{x}_1, \mathbf{x}_2, \mathbf{x}_3, \cdots, \mathbf{x}_s.$$

The NN-similarity is defined for one solution. For a query vector $\mathbf{y}$ *one vector* $\mathbf{x}_j$ is NN-similar to $\mathbf{y}$ according to the distance function d with

$$x_i = \min_j d(\mathbf{x}_j, \mathbf{y}). \tag{1.3}$$

Since in quantum computation we cannot simply compare vectors, the ϵ-similarity is more useful. The ϵ-similarity is defined for a range queries. For a query vector $\mathbf{y}$ *all* vectors $\mathbf{x}_j$ are ϵ-similar to $\mathbf{y}$ according to the distance function d with

$$d(\mathbf{x}_j, \mathbf{y}) < \epsilon. \tag{1.4}$$

The search is sensitive to the value of ϵ, too big ϵ results in the whole dataset, too small value in no solution.

1.3.3 Associative Memory

A complex system that is based on self-organization is the associative memory that is modeled by interacted neurons.

The associative memory incorporate the following abilities in a natural way [75, 44, 7, 49]:

- The ability to correct faults if false information is given.

- The ability to complete information if some parts are missing.

- The ability to interpolate information. In other words, if a sub-symbol is not currently stored, the most similar stored sub-symbol is determined.

When an incomplete pattern is given, the associative memory is able to complete it by a dynamical process.

Human memory is based on associations with the memories it contains. Just a snatch of well-known tune is enough to bring the whole thing back to mind. A forgotten

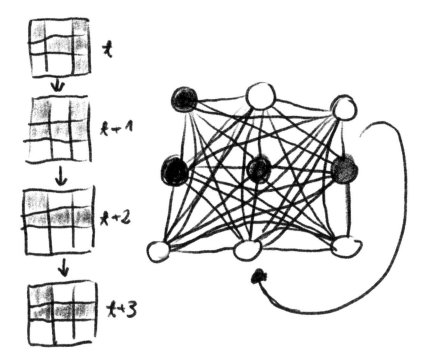

Figure 1.5 In a Hopfield network all units are connected to each other by the weights. Each unit has a value -1 indicated by white pixel or 1 indicated by black pixel. All the activation of the units represent a pattern at a state t. Usually the units are updated asynchronously, updated them one at the time t. After the training we start with some configuration and the network will converge after several steps using the update rule to an attractor if the state at t is the same at $t + 1$.

joke is suddenly completely remembered when the next-door neighbor starts to tell it again. This type of memory has previously been termed content-addressable, which means that one small part of the particular memory is linked - associated -with the rest. Cited from [18], page 104.

The Hopfield network represents a model of the associative memory [46], [44]. In a Hopfield network all units are connected to each other by the weights, see Figure 1.5. Patterns that the network uses for training (called retrieval states) become attractors of the system. After the training we start with some configuration and the network will converge after several steps using the update rule to an attractor representing a fixed point (a vector), see Figure 1.6.

1.3.4 Artificial Neuron

With two vectors of the same dimension D, the vector $\mathbf{x}$ represents an input pattern (signals incoming from other neurons) and the vector $\mathbf{w}$ represents a stored pattern (in the weights of each synapse). We can define a scalar product also called the dot

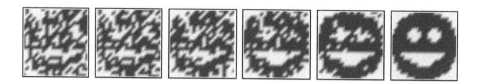

Figure 1.6 Example how Hopfield network restores distorted pattern. The network will converge after several steps using the update rule to an attractor representing the stored pattern or a spurious state composed of a linear combination of an odd number of stored patterns.

product

$$\langle \mathbf{x} | \mathbf{w} \rangle = \sum_{j=1}^{D} w_j \cdot x_j = \cos \omega \cdot \|\mathbf{x}\| \cdot \|\mathbf{w}\|, \tag{1.5}$$

that measures the projection of one vector onto another. The dot product is a linear representation usually represented by the value net,

$$net = \sum_{j=1}^{D} w_j \cdot x_j.$$

The components w_j are called weights, they model the synapses representing the traces of memory. Nonlinearity of the linear representation can be achieved by a threshold operation in which the threshold T has a certain value with

$$o = \begin{cases} 1 & \text{if} \quad net \geq T \\ -1 & \text{if} \quad net < T \end{cases}, \tag{1.6}$$

being the output of the artificial neuron. This threshold operation can be described by a nonlinear transfer function like sgn for $T = 0$

$$o = sgn(net) = \begin{cases} 1 & \text{if} \quad net \geq 0 \\ -1 & \text{if} \quad net < 0 \end{cases}, \tag{1.7}$$

The $sgn(net)$ operation is related to the threshold operation of a real biological neuron with -1 meaning not firing and 1 firing. Firing indicates that the neuron sends output information to other neurons to which it is connected. Not firing indicates that no information is sent. The transfer function is also called the activation function, with o being the output of the artificial neuron

$$o = sgn(net) = sgn(\langle \mathbf{x} | \mathbf{w} \rangle) = sgn \left(\sum_{j=1}^{D} w_j \cdot x_j \right). \tag{1.8}$$

This model is also known as the linear threshold unit (LTU).

1.3.5 Perceptron

Perceptron describes an algorithm for supervised learning that considers only linearly separable problems in which groups can be separated by a line or hyperplane [67], [86]. Defining $x_0 = 1$ [42, 44], the perceptron implements the mathematical function $sgn(net)$ with

$$net := \sum_{j=0}^{D} w_j \cdot x_j = \sum_{j=1}^{D} w_j \cdot x_j + w_0 = \langle \mathbf{x} | \mathbf{w} \rangle + w_0 \cdot x_0 \tag{1.9}$$

and o being the output of the artificial neuron with

$$o := sgn(net) = \begin{cases} 1 & \text{if} \quad net \geq 0 \\ -1 & \text{if} \quad net < 0 \end{cases}, \tag{1.10}$$

The value w_0 is called the "bias", it is a constant value that does not depend on any input value. The goal of the perceptron is to learn how to correctly classify patterns into one of two classes $C_1 = 1$ and $C_2 = -1$. To achieve this task, the model needs examples of correct associations between patterns and their respective classes.

$$Data = \{(\mathbf{x}_1, t_1), (\mathbf{x}_2, t_2), \cdots, (\mathbf{x}_N, t_N)\}$$

with

$$t_k \in \{-1, 1\},$$

the output for class C_1 is $o = -1$ and for C_2 is $o = 1$ with

$$o = sgn\left(\sum_{j=0}^{D} w_j \cdot x_j\right) = sgn\left(\langle \mathbf{x} | \mathbf{w} \rangle + w_0 \cdot x_0\right) \tag{1.11}$$

and $x_0 = 1$.

Simplified, the perceptron tries to learns the function $f(\mathbf{x})$

$$f(\mathbf{x}) = \begin{cases} 1 & \text{if} \quad \langle \mathbf{x} | \mathbf{w} \rangle + w_0 \geq 0 \\ -1 & \text{otherwise.} \end{cases} \tag{1.12}$$

With this approach, the perceptron is only able to solve linearly separable problems (see Figure 1.7), that is, ones that can be separated by a line or hyperplane.

The hyperplane is described by the model weights $\mathbf{w}$ and w_0. The correct weights can be determined by a supervised learning algorithm.

Before learning, the weight values w_j are initialized to some small random values, so, the hyperplane is placed randomly in the space. Then, the perceptron learning algorithm verifies whether, for a given input $\mathbf{x}_k$, the output value o_k belongs to the desired class represented by t_k. If the output matches the class, the algorithm does not touch the boundary, if it does not, then, the algorithm moves the boundary in a direction where the input $\mathbf{x}_k$ is closer to being correctly classified. This movement corresponds to the following updated rule

$$\Delta w_j = \eta \cdot (t_k - o_k) \cdot x_j, \tag{1.13}$$

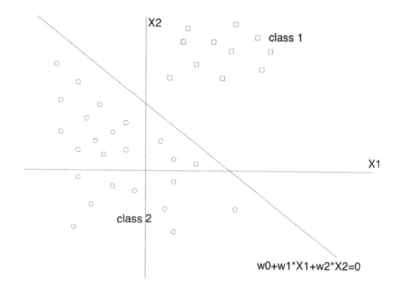

Figure 1.7 The hyperplane is described by $\mathbf{w}$ and w_0, in two dimensions by a line $w_0 + w_1 \cdot x_1 + w_2 \cdot x_2 = 0$. The perceptron only solves linearly separable problems, in our example *class* 1 and *class* 2.

and

$$w_j^{new} = w_j^{old} + \Delta w_j, \tag{1.14}$$

where η is called the learning rate that defines the size of the movement that is applied to the boundary with

$$0 < \eta \le 1.$$

The algorithm converges to the correct classification if the training data are linearly separable, and η is sufficiently small. When assigning a value to η, we must consider two conflicting requirements: averaging of past inputs to provide stable weight estimates, which requires small η; however, fast adaptation with respect to real changes in the underlying distribution of the process responsible for generating the input vector $\mathbf{x}$, which requires a large η.

This simple algorithm is the basis for many supervised ML algorithms.

If the training set is not linearly separable, then no solution exists. In this setting, after several epochs, the weights begin to oscillate. To get an approximate solution, the learning rate η has to decrease slowly to zero as the epochs go by.

1.3.6 Support Vector Machine

Given a training set $\{\mathbf{x}_i, t_i\}_{i=1}^{N}$, with $t_i \in \{-1, +1\}$ of linearly separable patterns we have

$$\mathbf{w}^T \cdot \mathbf{x}_i + w_0 \ge 0, \quad for \ \ t_i = +1$$

$$\mathbf{w}^T \cdot \mathbf{x}_i + w_0 < 0, \quad for \ \ t_i = -1$$

with a hyperplane

$$\mathbf{w}^T \cdot \mathbf{x} + w_0 = \mathbf{w}^T \cdot \mathbf{x} + b = 0$$

We want to have a margin between each class and the boundary, we want to find the parameters $\mathbf{w}_{opt}$ and b_{opt} such that

$$\mathbf{w}_{opt}^T \cdot \mathbf{x}_i + b_{opt} \geq 1, \quad for \ t_i = +1 \tag{1.15}$$

$$\mathbf{w}_{opt}^T \cdot \mathbf{x}_i + b_{opt} \leq -1, \quad for \ t_i = -1 \tag{1.16}$$

for the hyperplane

$$\mathbf{w}_{opt}^T \cdot \mathbf{x}_i + b_{opt} = 0. \tag{1.17}$$

The value of 1 is set for convenience because we can always rescale $\mathbf{w}_{opt}$ and b_{opt} correspondingly [24]. The data points that are closest to the boundary, that is, those points $\{\mathbf{x}_i, t_i\}$ for which

$$\mathbf{w}_{opt}^T \cdot \mathbf{x}_i + b_{opt} = \pm 1 \tag{1.18}$$

are called support vectors $\mathbf{x}^{(s)}$. That is why the algorithm is called a support vector machine. All the remaining examples in the training sample are really **irrelevant** to determine where to place the hyperplane. After some optimization, we get

$$\mathbf{w} = \sum_{i=1}^{N} \alpha_i \cdot t_i \cdot \mathbf{x}_i, \quad \sum_{i=1}^{N} \alpha_i \cdot t_i = 0, \tag{1.19}$$

and we define the dual optimization problem that depends entirely on the training data and the Lagrange multipliers. Given the training sample $\{\mathbf{x}_i, t_i\}_{i=1}^{N}$, with $t_i \in \{-1, +1\}$ of linearly separable patterns, we want to find the Lagrange multipliers $\{\alpha_i\}_{i=1}^{N}$ that maximize

$$Q(\alpha) = \sum_{i=1}^{N} \alpha_i - \frac{1}{2} \cdot \sum_{i=1}^{N} \sum_{j=1}^{N} \alpha_i \cdot \alpha_j \cdot t_i \cdot t_j \cdot \mathbf{x}_i^T \mathbf{x}_j \tag{1.20}$$

subject to the usual constraints

$$\sum_{i=1}^{N} \alpha_i \cdot t_i = 0 \tag{1.21}$$

and adding a new constraint

$$0 \leq \alpha_i \leq C, \quad i = 1, 2, \cdots, N \tag{1.22}$$

where C is a user specified positive parameter. Having determined the optimum Lagrange multipliers $\alpha_{opt,i}$ (not equal to zero) by solving a system of $N \times N$ linear equations, we may recover

$$\mathbf{w}_{opt} = \sum_{i=1}^{N} \alpha_{opt,i} \cdot t_i \cdot \mathbf{x}_i, \tag{1.23}$$

$$\mathbf{w}_{opt}^T \cdot \mathbf{x}_i + b_{opt} = \pm 1 \tag{1.24}$$

and

$$b_{opt} = 1 - \mathbf{w}_{opt}^T \cdot \mathbf{x}^{(s)}, \quad for \ t^{(s)} = 1 \tag{1.25}$$

since

$$b_{opt} = 1 - \left(\sum_{i=1}^{N} \alpha_{opt,i} \cdot t_i \cdot \mathbf{x}_i^T\right) \cdot \mathbf{x}^{(s)}, \quad for \ t^{(s)} = 1. $$

1.3.7   Support Vector Machine as a Kernel Machine

Let $\mathbf{x}$ be a vector from the input space of dimension D and let $\{\phi_j(\mathbf{x})\}_{j=1}^{\infty}$ be a set of nonlinear functions, from D dimension to infinite dimension. In that feature space, the hyperplane would be defined as

$$\mathbf{w}^T \cdot \Phi(\mathbf{x}) + b = 0 \tag{1.26}$$

with $\Phi(\mathbf{x})$ being a feature vector with infinite dimension and $\mathbf{w}$ being the wight vector with infinite dimension. With N_s being the number of support vectors, we can represent the weight vector as

$$\mathbf{w} = \sum_{i=1}^{N_s} \alpha_i \cdot t_i \cdot \Phi(\mathbf{x}_i). \tag{1.27}$$

We do not need the weight vector itself, all we need is the boundary or decision surface and we can represent it by

$$\sum_{i=1}^{N_s} \alpha_i \cdot t_i \cdot \Phi^T(\mathbf{x}_i)\Phi(\mathbf{x}) = 0. \tag{1.28}$$

All we need are inner products between support vectors $\langle\Phi(\mathbf{x}_i)|\Phi(\mathbf{x})\rangle$. We can look at these inner products as the result of a kernel function

$$k(\mathbf{x}, \mathbf{x}_i) = \Phi^T(\mathbf{x}_i)\Phi(\mathbf{x}) = \langle\Phi(\mathbf{x}_i)|\Phi(\mathbf{x})\rangle \tag{1.29}$$

Specifying the kernel $k(\mathbf{x}, \mathbf{x}_i)$ is sufficient, we need never explicitly compute the weight vector $\mathbf{w}_{opt}$ [98]. Having the kernel we can take full advantage of the fact that

$$\sum_{j=1}^{\infty} w_j \cdot \phi_j(\mathbf{x}) + b = \sum_{i=1}^{N_s} \alpha_i \cdot t_i \cdot k(\mathbf{x}, \mathbf{x}_i) + b = 0. \tag{1.30}$$

We can compute kernel matrix or Gram matrix where $k(\mathbf{x}_i, \mathbf{x}_j)$ is the ij-th element of the $N \times N$ matrix. Resulting in something like

$$K = \begin{pmatrix} k(\mathbf{x}_1, \mathbf{x}_1) & k(\mathbf{x}_1, \mathbf{x}_2) & k(\mathbf{x}_1, \mathbf{x}_3) & \cdots & k(\mathbf{x}_1, \mathbf{x}_N) \\ k(\mathbf{x}_2, \mathbf{x}_1) & k(\mathbf{x}_2, \mathbf{x}_2) & k(\mathbf{x}_2, \mathbf{x}_3) & \cdots & k(\mathbf{x}_2, \mathbf{x}_N) \\ \vdots & \vdots & \ddots & \vdots \\ k(\mathbf{x}_N, \mathbf{x}_1) & k(\mathbf{x}_N, \mathbf{x}_2) & k(\mathbf{x}_N, \mathbf{x}_3) & \cdots & k(\mathbf{x}_N, \mathbf{x}_N) \end{pmatrix} \tag{1.31}$$

In the dual problem, we replace the scalar multiplication

$$\mathbf{x}_i^T \mathbf{x}_j = \langle \mathbf{x}_i | \mathbf{x}_j \rangle$$

by the kernel

$$k(\mathbf{x}_i, \mathbf{x}_j),$$

everything else stays the same. So, given the training sample $\{\mathbf{x}_i, t_i\}_{i=1}^N$, with $t_i \in \{-1, +1\}$ we want to find the Lagrange multipliers $\{\alpha_i\}_{i=1}^N$ that maximize

$$Q(\alpha) = \sum_{i=1}^N \alpha_i - \frac{1}{2} \cdot \sum_{i=1}^N \sum_{j=1}^N \alpha_i \cdot \alpha_j \cdot t_i \cdot t_j \cdot k(\mathbf{x}_i, \mathbf{x}_j) \tag{1.32}$$

subject to constraints

$$\sum_{i=1}^N \alpha_i \cdot t_i = 0 \tag{1.33}$$

$$0 \leq \alpha_i \leq C, \quad i = 1, 2, \cdots, N \tag{1.34}$$

where C is a user specified positive parameter. To compute the output

1. First we determine the bias

$$b = \frac{1}{N_s} \sum_{i=1}^{N_s} \left(t_i - \sum_{j=1}^{N_s} \alpha_j \cdot t_j \cdot k(\mathbf{x}_i, \mathbf{x}_j) \right), \tag{1.35}$$

2. then the output

$$o = sgn \left(\sum_{i=1}^{N_s} \alpha_i \cdot t_i \cdot k(\mathbf{x}, \mathbf{x}_i) + b \right). \tag{1.36}$$

1.3.7.1 Example: XOR Problem

The XOR Problem is described by four vectors [41], instead of 0 we will use (-1)

$$\mathbf{x}_1 = \begin{pmatrix} -1 \\ -1 \end{pmatrix}, \mathbf{x}_2 = \begin{pmatrix} 1 \\ 1 \end{pmatrix}, \mathbf{x}_3 = \begin{pmatrix} 1 \\ -1 \end{pmatrix}, \mathbf{x}_4 = \begin{pmatrix} 1 \\ 1 \end{pmatrix},$$

and the corresponding target of the two classes is indicated as

$$t_1 = -1, t_2 = 1, t_3 = 1, t_4 = -1.$$

We will use a polynomial kernel

$$k(\mathbf{x}_i, \mathbf{x}_j) = (1 + \mathbf{x}_i^T \mathbf{x}_j)^2$$

with

$$k(\mathbf{x}_i, \mathbf{x}_j) = 1 + x_{i1}^2 \cdot x_{j1}^2 + 2 \cdot x_{i1} \cdot x_{i2} \cdot x_{j1} \cdot x_{j2} + x_{i2}^2 \cdot x_{j2}^2 + 2 \cdot x_{i1} \cdot x_{j1} + 2 \cdot x_{i2} \cdot x_{j2}$$

with the feature vectors (not required, indeed for certain kernels the vector can have an infinite dimension)

$$\Phi(\mathbf{x}_i) = \begin{pmatrix} 1 \\ x_{i1}^2 \\ \sqrt{2} \cdot x_{i1} \cdot x_{i2} \\ x_{i2}^2 \\ \sqrt{2} \cdot x_{i1} \\ \sqrt{2} \cdot x_{i2} \end{pmatrix}, \quad \Phi(\mathbf{x}_j) = \begin{pmatrix} 1 \\ x_{j1}^2 \\ \sqrt{2} \cdot x_{j1} \cdot x_{j2} \\ x_{j2}^2 \\ \sqrt{2} \cdot x_{j1} \\ \sqrt{2} \cdot x_{j2} \end{pmatrix}$$

We obtain the Gram

$$K = \begin{pmatrix} k(\mathbf{x}_1, \mathbf{x}_1) & k(\mathbf{x}_1, \mathbf{x}_2) & k(\mathbf{x}_1, \mathbf{x}_3) & k(\mathbf{x}_1, \mathbf{x}_4) \\ k(\mathbf{x}_2, \mathbf{x}_1) & k(\mathbf{x}_2, \mathbf{x}_2) & k(\mathbf{x}_2, \mathbf{x}_3) & k(\mathbf{x}_2, \mathbf{x}_4) \\ k(\mathbf{x}_3, \mathbf{x}_1) & k(\mathbf{x}_3, \mathbf{x}_3) & k(\mathbf{x}_3, \mathbf{x}_3) & k(\mathbf{x}_4, \mathbf{x}_3) \\ k(\mathbf{x}_4, \mathbf{x}_1) & k(\mathbf{x}_4, \mathbf{x}_4) & k(\mathbf{x}_4, \mathbf{x}_3) & k(\mathbf{x}_4, \mathbf{x}_4) \end{pmatrix} = \begin{pmatrix} 9 & 1 & 1 & 1 \\ 1 & 9 & 1 & 1 \\ 1 & 1 & 9 & 1 \\ 1 & 1 & 1 & 9 \end{pmatrix}$$

The objective function for the dual form of optimization is

$$Q(\alpha) = \sum_{i=1}^{4} \alpha_i - \frac{1}{2} \cdot \sum_{i=1}^{4} \sum_{j=1}^{4} \alpha_i \cdot \alpha_j \cdot t_i \cdot t_j \cdot k(\mathbf{x}_i, \mathbf{x}_j)$$

$$Q(\alpha) = \alpha_1 + \alpha_2 + \alpha_3 + \alpha_4 - \frac{1}{2} \cdot (9\alpha_1^2 - 2\alpha_1\alpha_2 - 2\alpha_1\alpha_3 + 2\alpha_1\alpha_4$$

$$9\alpha_2^2 + 2\alpha_2\alpha_3 - 2\alpha_2\alpha_4 + 9\alpha_3^2 - 2\alpha_3\alpha_4 + 9\alpha_4^2)$$

We maximize the objective function $Q(\alpha)$ by determining the partial derivatives

$$\frac{\partial Q(\alpha)}{\partial \alpha_1} = 1 - 9 \cdot \alpha1 + \alpha2 + \alpha3 - \alpha4 = 0$$

$$\frac{\partial Q(\alpha)}{\partial \alpha_2} = 1 - +\alpha1 - 9 \cdot \alpha2 - \alpha3 + \alpha4 = 0$$

$$\frac{\partial Q(\alpha)}{\partial \alpha_3} = 1 + \alpha1 - \alpha2 - 9 \cdot \alpha3 + \alpha4 = 0$$

$$\frac{\partial Q(\alpha)}{\partial \alpha_4} = 1 - \alpha1 + \alpha2 + \alpha3 - 9 \cdot \alpha4 = 0$$

that lead to four equations that can be solved by

$$\begin{pmatrix} 9 & -1 & -1 & 1 \\ -1 & 9 & 1 & -1 \\ -1 & 1 & 9 & -1 \\ 1 & -1 & -1 & 9 \end{pmatrix} \cdot \begin{pmatrix} \alpha_1 \\ \alpha_2 \\ \alpha_3 \\ \alpha_4 \end{pmatrix} = \begin{pmatrix} 1 \\ 1 \\ 1 \\ 1 \end{pmatrix}$$

with the optimum values of the Lagrange multipliers

$$\alpha_{opt,1} = \alpha_{opt,2} = \alpha_{opt,3} = \alpha_{opt,4} = \frac{1}{8}$$

with all input vectors being support vectors.

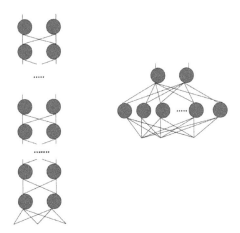

Figure 1.8 Empirical experiments indicate that "deep" neural networks (left) give better results than "fat" neural networks (right).

1.3.8 Deep Learning

The limitations of a perceptron do not apply to feedforward networks with nonlinear units, also called multilayer perceptrons trained by the backpropagation learning algorithm. According to the universality theorem, a neural network with a single nonlinear hidden layer trained by backpropagation is capable of approximating any continuous function. Attempting to build a network with only one layer to approximate complex functions often requires a very large number of nodes ("fat" neural networks). The immediate solution to this is to build networks with more hidden layers. Empirical experiments indicate that "deep" neural networks give better results than "fat" neural networks, see Figure 1.8. The term "Deep Learning" was introduced to the ML community by Rina Dechter in 1986 [25] and to artificial neural networks by Igor Aizenberg and colleagues in 2000 [4]. Deep artificial network uses many hidden layers to increase the model's power in statistical learning, see Figure 1.9.

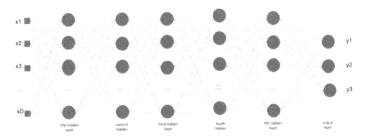

Figure 1.9 A feed forward network many hidden layers is called a deep network, in our example the network has five hidden layers. They are referred to as hidden layers because the outputs of the units in the hidden layer is not the output of the network. The input of the network is $x_1, x_2, \cdots X_D$ and the output y_1, y_2, and y_3 that indicates a presence of a classified object.

These layers are trained by backpropagation. As a result, after the training during the classification no explanation can be given why a certain input was mapped to a certain class. Deep learning enables high-level abstractions in data by architectures composed of multiple nonlinear transformations. It offers a natural progression from low-level structures to high-level structures, as demonstrated by natural complexity. [56, 84, 85, 83].

By increasing the number of layers we can increase the number of parameters faster. By doing so, we can add enough degrees of freedom to model large training sets. This is extremely helpful since nowadays a really large amount of data is collected for specific tasks.

The models achieved tremendous results, however they requires high computational resources of very large training sets which is a bottleneck in current quantum ML applications. However, quantum basic linear algebra subroutines can be to speed up the deep learning algorithms, a kind of "mathematical" quantum coprocessor that can be used with a conventional computer.

## CHAPTER 2

Quantum Physics and Quantum Computation

Statistical laws govern the totality of observations in physics. An object can be described in classical mechanics by a vector which describes the position and its momentum. Classical mechanics is usually valid at the macro scale. The changes in the position and the momentum of the object over time are described by the Hamiltonian equation of motion. The state of the object is described by the Hamiltonian function. At micro scale the observations are described by quantum physics. Light appears only in chunks that can be quantized. An individual chunk is called quantum, a quantum of light is called a photon [27]. Quantum theory gets its name from this property, which it attributes to all measurable physical quantities. A photon can be described by a wave function if it is isolated from its environment. The wave function in quantum mechanics, if unobserved, evolves in a smooth and continuous way according to the Schrödinger equation, which is related to the Hamiltonian equation of motion. This equation describes a linear superposition of different states at time. During the observation (measurement by the observer, by us), the wave collapses into one definite state with a certain probability.

The mathematical framework of quantum theory is based on linear algebra in Hilbert space. A 2-state quantum system is described by a two-dimensional Hilbert space. Such a 2-state quantum system corresponds to a qubit. A register is composed of several qubits and is defined by the tensor product. We describe the principles of computation with one and m qubits, introduce the principles of entanglement, cloning and the matrix representation of quantum Boolean gates, and an example of a simple quantum Boolean circuit.

2.1 QUANTUM MEASUREMENT

The wave function in quantum mechanics, if unobserved, evolves in a smooth and continuous way according to the Schrödinger equation, which is related to the Hamiltonian equation of motion. This equation describes a linear superposition of different states at time t. A general solution of the Schrödinger equation represents the unitary (linear) evolution that is deterministic and reversible. Reversible means that no information is lost. According to Susskind this is the "Zero law" of physics [105]. The vector $\mathbf{x}(t)$ (for simplicity we will call it as well a wave) describes the probability of the presence of certain states at time t. A dimension represents each state, and the value of the vector is related to the probability of the state being present. This evolution is done in parallel over all states of the vector $\mathbf{x}(t)$. During the observation (measurement by the observer, by us), the wave collapses into one definite state with a certain probability. This state corresponds to one dimension of the vector $\mathbf{x}(t)$. The measurements always find the physical system to be in a definite state. It does something to the wave function represented by the vector $\mathbf{x}(t)$. This something is not explained by quantum theory. The best known example of this type kind of this "something" is the Schrödinger's cat paradox [93] and it tells us that our universe is non-deterministic. A Geiger counter measures the decay of a radioactive substance. There is a fifty percent chance that, in a given time frame, decay is measured. The Geiger counter is connected to a device that kills the cat, if decay is measured. Because the cat and the Geiger counter are in a closed room, we do not know whether the cat is dead or alive. Each of these possibilities is associated with a specific fifty percent probability. The cat is dead and alive at the same time. One can think that there is one world where the cat is alive and another where the cat is dead. They are at the same time present in the closed room. The two states are "really" present at the same time, one says that the cat is in a superposition state. A measurement always finds either an alive cat or a dead cat with a probability of fifty percent.

2.1.1 Interpretations of Quantum Mechanics

During the observation (measurement by the observer, by us), the wave collapses into one definite state with a certain probability. A quantum system that is perfectly isolated maintains its wave representation, its coherence. If it is not perfectly isolated, during interaction with the environment the wave representation of an event is lost, this is called the quantum decoherence. Quantum decoherence happens during the measurement. Decoherence is usually viewed as the loss of information from a system into the environment. However, the quantum decoherence provides us only with a framework for apparent wave-function collapse and it does not explain the collapse itself. Since quantum systems are not isolated in a the large scale (macro scale), the effects are mostly present at the scale of atoms and subatomic particles (micro scale). During the measurement true randomness is present, but after the measurement the physical system is always in a definite state. Measurement doses something to the wave function. This something is not explained by quantum theory itself, however there are two common interpretations:

- The most popular interpretation, the Copenhagen interpretation, claims that quantum mechanics is a mathematical tool that is used in the calculation of probabilities and has no physical existence; all other questions are metaphysical [43] and should be avoided.

- The many-worlds is less popular due to some philosophical difficulties. The many-worlds theory views reality as a many-branched tree in which every possible quantum outcome is realized [28], [20]. Every possible outcome to every event exists in its own world. In one world, randomness exists, but not in the universe (multiverse) that describes all possible worlds [27].

2.2 PRINCIPLES OF QUANTUM COMPUTATION

Richard Feynman asked in the early eighties whether a quantum system can be simulated on an imaginary quantum computer. Today, 40 years later first small quantum computers begin to appear. A quantum computer represents information by qubits. A qubit can be represented by the spin state of a particle, either spin down or spin up. Several qubits to represent different states at the same time. The qubits need to be coherent for a long enough time so that a computation can take place. During recent years a huge progress was achieved in keeping the quits perfectly isolated (coherent), opening the road to a universal quantum computer.

2.2.1 Qubits

A qubit is represented abstractly by a two-dimensional vector. The first dimension of the vector corresponds to zero and the second to a one. The values of the two dimensions correspond to the probabilities that when measured, one of the two states is present. We can combine a qubit to several qubits by a tensor operation. Two qubits have four possible states, the first dimension represents the state zero-zero, the second zero-one, the third one-zero, and the fourth one-one. They are described by a four-dimensional vector. Four qubits would represent 16 different combinations, eight 256 combinations, represented by a 256-dimensional vector, and so on. The number of possible states grows exponentially in relation to the number of qubits, with the number of states being equal to two power the number of represented qubits [119]. In a vector representing several possible states, each dimension corresponds to the probabilities of measuring a state. The probabilities values are represented by amplitudes. The relation between an amplitude and the probability is the absolute value of the amplitudes power two. For example the probability value 0.25 corresponds to an amplitude 0.5, since $|0.5|^2$ is 0.25. The amplitude can be negative, since $|-0.5|^2$ is 0.25 or even imaginary numbers since $|-0.5*i|^2 = 0.25$. As a consequence of this relation, the Euclidean length of the vector representing the probabilities is always one, all probabilities sum to one. If a dimension of the state vector represents the probability zero, the corresponding state will be never measured. If one dimension of the state vector represents the probability one, all other dimensions represent the probabilities zero, and the corresponding dimension will be measured for sure. If the represented probabilities are bigger than zero or smaller than one, they will be measured with certain probability. Repeating the same experiment several times the measured values converge to the represented probability values, the individual measurement is random. A qubit with the probability values 0.5 (amplitude $\sqrt{0.5}$) and 0.5 (amplitude $\sqrt{0.5}$) represents a true random process when measured, True random numbers are generated during the measurement.

2.2.2 Representation

A quantum mechanical description of a physical system is related to a probabilistic representation; it is described by a vector in Hilbert space. This description extends the two- or three-dimensional Euclidean space into spaces that have any finite or infinite number of dimensions. In such a space, the Euclidean norm is induced by the inner product

$$\|\mathbf{x}\| = \sqrt{\langle \mathbf{x}|\mathbf{x} \rangle}. \tag{2.1}$$

Without a scalar product there is no **orthogonality**. In a Hilbert space, two vectors are orthogonal if and only if the scalar product is zero. A basis of n dimensional Hilbert space $\mathcal{H}_n$ is chosen. A 2-state system is described by a two-dimensional Hilbert space $\mathcal{H}_2$. For the basis

$$\mathbf{e}_1 = \begin{pmatrix} 1 \\ 0 \end{pmatrix}, \mathbf{e}_2 = \begin{pmatrix} 0 \\ 1 \end{pmatrix} \tag{2.2}$$

the system is described by a vector $\mathbf{x}$ with complex numbers ω_1, ω_2 that represent the amplitude of each dimension

$$\mathbf{x} = \omega_1 \cdot \mathbf{e}_1 + \omega_2 \cdot \mathbf{e}_2 = \begin{pmatrix} \omega_1 \\ \omega_2 \end{pmatrix}. \tag{2.3}$$

The probabilities are real numbers between 0 and 1. The probability that the system is in e_1 and e_2 is $|\omega_1|^2$ and $|\omega_2|^2$. This is because the product of complex number with is conjugate is always a real number

$$\omega^* \cdot \omega = (x - y \cdot i) \cdot (x + y \cdot i) = x^2 + y^2 = |\omega|^2. \tag{2.4}$$

The vector representing a state is normalized. Its length is one. The amplitudes correspond to the probability with

$$|\omega_1|^2 + |\omega_2|^2 = 1.$$

Paul Dirac introduced the following notation for a vector $\mathbf{x}$ describing a state

$$|x\rangle = \omega_1 \cdot |e_1\rangle + \omega_2 \cdot |e_2\rangle = \omega_1 \cdot |x_1\rangle + \omega_2 \cdot |x_2\rangle = \begin{pmatrix} \omega_1 \\ \omega_2 \end{pmatrix} \tag{2.5}$$

with

$$|e_1\rangle = |x_1\rangle, |e_2\rangle = |x_2\rangle.$$

It is a shorthand notation for a column vector. Related to the scalar product $\langle x|x \rangle$ row vector are $\langle x|$ "bra" and column vectors are $|x\rangle$ "kets" from bra(c)kets. A state vector is just a particular instance of a ket vector. It is specified by a particular choice of basis and refers to observable that can have some system properties.

2.2.3 Linear Operators

The computation on the coherent qubits (before the measurement) is described by linear operators that change the distribution of the quantum probabilities represented by amplitudes in a linear way [119]. The operators are represented by orthogonal matrices for real amplitudes (inverse of the matrix is the transpose of the matrix), for complex amplitudes by unitary matrices (inverse matrix is the conjugate transpose of the matrix).

Operators represented by a square matrix give mathematical description how something changes in the quantum world. For a 2-state quantum system, an operator that acts on the memory register would be represented by a 2×2 dimensional unitary matrix. In Unitary matrices, its conjugate transpose is equal to its inverse.

$$U^* = U^{-1}. \tag{2.6}$$

For example a quantum coin is a system with two basis states 0 and 1 with

$$|0\rangle = \begin{pmatrix} 1 \\ 0 \end{pmatrix}, |1\rangle = \begin{pmatrix} 0 \\ 1 \end{pmatrix}. \tag{2.7}$$

The mapping is represented as

$$|0\rangle \rightarrow \frac{1}{\sqrt{2}} \cdot |0\rangle + \frac{1}{\sqrt{2}} \cdot |1\rangle \tag{2.8}$$

and

$$|1\rangle \rightarrow \frac{1}{\sqrt{2}} \cdot |0\rangle - \frac{1}{\sqrt{2}} \cdot |1\rangle. \tag{2.9}$$

The corresponding operator is indicated by the following unitary matrix,

$$H = \begin{pmatrix} \frac{1}{\sqrt{2}} & \frac{1}{\sqrt{2}} \\ \frac{1}{\sqrt{2}} & -\frac{1}{\sqrt{2}} \end{pmatrix} = \frac{1}{\sqrt{2}} \cdot \begin{pmatrix} 1 & 1 \\ 1 & -1 \end{pmatrix}. \tag{2.10}$$

called a Hadamard or Hadamard Walsh, matrix. If the system starts in state $|0\rangle$ and undergoes the time evolution, the probability of observing 0 or 1 is $\left| \frac{1}{\sqrt{2}} \right|^2 = \frac{1}{2}$. If we do not preform a measurement and repeat the mapping, the probability of observing 0 becomes 1 and observing 1 becomes zero. This is due to the fact, that the amplitudes of $|1\rangle$ cancel each other. This effect is called destructive interference and cannot occur in the probability distribution since all its coefficients are non-negative real numbers.

2.3 COMPOUND SYSTEMS

A 2-state quantum system (qubit) is described by a two-dimensional Hilbert space $\mathcal{H}_2$,

$$|x_1\rangle = \begin{pmatrix} 1 \\ 0 \end{pmatrix}, |x_2\rangle = \begin{pmatrix} 0 \\ 1 \end{pmatrix} \tag{2.11}$$

is described by a vector $|x\rangle$ with complex numbers ω_1, ω_2 that represent the amplitude of each dimension.

$$|x\rangle = \omega_1 \cdot |x_1\rangle + \omega_2 \cdot |x_2\rangle = \begin{pmatrix} \omega_1 \\ \omega_2 \end{pmatrix}. \tag{2.12}$$

Such a 2-state quantum system corresponds to a qubit with the basis

$$|0\rangle = |x_1\rangle, \quad |1\rangle = |x_2\rangle.$$

The qubit is described by a vector $|x\rangle$ with complex numbers ω_1, ω_2 that represent the amplitude of each dimension

$$|x\rangle = \omega_0 \cdot |0\rangle + \omega_1 \cdot |1\rangle. \tag{2.13}$$

The vector has length one with

$$|\omega_0|^2 + |\omega_1|^2 = 1 \rightarrow |||x\rangle|| = 1.$$

The unitary matrix H (Hadamard matrix) performs the following mapping in the ket notation

$$H \cdot |0\rangle = \frac{1}{\sqrt{2}} \cdot |0\rangle + \frac{1}{\sqrt{2}} \cdot |1\rangle$$

with the vector notation

$$\frac{1}{\sqrt{2}} \cdot \begin{pmatrix} 1 & 1 \\ 1 & -1 \end{pmatrix} \cdot \begin{pmatrix} 1 \\ 0 \end{pmatrix} = \begin{pmatrix} \frac{1}{\sqrt{2}} \\ \frac{1}{\sqrt{2}} \end{pmatrix}.$$

Applying H again results in

$$H \cdot \left(\frac{1}{\sqrt{2}} \cdot |0\rangle + \frac{1}{\sqrt{2}} \cdot |1\rangle \right) = H \cdot \frac{1}{\sqrt{2}} \cdot |0\rangle + W \cdot \frac{1}{\sqrt{2}} \cdot |1\rangle = |0\rangle$$

with the vector notation

$$\frac{1}{\sqrt{2}} \cdot \begin{pmatrix} 1 & 1 \\ 1 & -1 \end{pmatrix} \cdot \begin{pmatrix} \frac{1}{\sqrt{2}} \\ \frac{1}{\sqrt{2}} \end{pmatrix} = \begin{pmatrix} 1 \\ 0 \end{pmatrix}.$$

How can we represent a register composed of two qubits? Such a register would represent 2^2 possible states and would be represented in a Hilbert space $\mathcal{H}_4$. The first qubit is represented by a two-dimensional Hilbert space $\mathcal{H}_2$,

$$|x\rangle = \omega_0 \cdot |0\rangle + \omega_1 \cdot |1\rangle = \begin{pmatrix} \omega_0 \\ \omega_1 \end{pmatrix}$$

and the second as

$$|y\rangle = \omega_0 \cdot |0\rangle + \omega_1 \cdot |1\rangle = \begin{pmatrix} \omega_0 \\ \omega_1 \end{pmatrix}.$$

The register of two qubits is represented as a direct product of $|x\rangle$ and $|y\rangle$

$$|x\rangle \otimes |y\rangle = |x\rangle |y\rangle = |xy\rangle = \begin{pmatrix} \omega_0 \\ \omega_1 \end{pmatrix} \otimes \begin{pmatrix} \omega_0 \\ \omega_1 \end{pmatrix} = \begin{pmatrix} \omega_0 \cdot \omega_0 \\ \omega_0 \cdot \omega_1 \\ \omega_1 \cdot \omega_0 \\ \omega_1 \cdot \omega_1 \end{pmatrix} = \begin{pmatrix} \omega_0 \\ \omega_1 \\ \omega_2 \\ \omega_3 \end{pmatrix} \tag{2.14}$$

or

$$|xy\rangle = (\omega_0 \cdot |0\rangle + \omega_1 \cdot |1\rangle) \otimes (\omega_0 \cdot |0\rangle + \omega_1 \cdot |1\rangle)$$

$$|xy\rangle = \omega_0 \cdot |00\rangle + \omega_1 \cdot |01\rangle + \omega_2 \cdot |10\rangle + \omega_3 \cdot |11\rangle \tag{2.15}$$

with the new basis

$$|00\rangle = \begin{pmatrix} 1 \\ 0 \\ 0 \\ 0 \end{pmatrix}, |01\rangle = \begin{pmatrix} 0 \\ 1 \\ 0 \\ 0 \end{pmatrix}, |10\rangle = \begin{pmatrix} 0 \\ 0 \\ 1 \\ 0 \end{pmatrix}, |11\rangle = \begin{pmatrix} 0 \\ 0 \\ 0 \\ 1 \end{pmatrix}. \tag{2.16}$$

A register of three qubits represents 2^3 different states represented in a Hilbert space $\mathcal{H}_8$.

$$|xyz\rangle = |x\rangle \otimes |y\rangle \otimes |z\rangle =$$

$$\omega_0 \cdot |00\rangle + \omega_1 \cdot |001\rangle + \omega_2 \cdot |010\rangle + \omega_3 \cdot |011\rangle +$$

$$+\omega_4 \cdot |100\rangle + \omega_5 \cdot |001\rangle + \omega_6 \cdot |110\rangle + \omega_7 \cdot |111\rangle. \tag{2.17}$$

A quantum register of length m represents m qubits in a Hilbert space of dimension $n = 2^m$. A state in a n-dimensional Hilbert space $\mathcal{H}_n$ is defined by an orthonormal basis

$$|x_1\rangle, |x_1\rangle, \cdots |x_n\rangle$$

and is represented as a unit-lengt vector

$$\omega_1 \cdot |x_1\rangle + \omega_2 \cdot |x_2\rangle + \cdots + \omega_n \cdot |x_n\rangle$$

that determines the probability of distribution of the states. Each dimension correspond to a possible combination. The state is in a basis state $|x_i\rangle$ with a probability $|\omega_i|^2$.

The compound system of the Hilbert space $\mathcal{H}_n$ and a w-dimensional Hilbert space $\mathcal{H}_w$ defined by a orthonormal basis $|y_1\rangle, |y_1\rangle. \cdots |y_w\rangle$ is defined by the tensor product

$$\mathcal{H}_{n\cdot w} = \mathcal{H}_n \otimes \mathcal{H}_w \tag{2.18}$$

According to this definition we can apply an operator on two qubits as

$$H \cdot (\omega_0 \cdot |0\rangle + \omega_1 \cdot |1\rangle) \otimes H \cdot (\omega_0 \cdot |0\rangle + \omega_1 \cdot |1\rangle) =$$

$$\left(H \cdot \begin{pmatrix} \omega_0 \\ \omega_1 \end{pmatrix} \right) \otimes \left(H \cdot \begin{pmatrix} \omega_0 \\ \omega_1 \end{pmatrix} \right) \tag{2.19}$$

$$(H \otimes H) \cdot (\omega_0 \cdot |0\rangle + \omega_1 \cdot |1\rangle) \otimes (\omega_0 \cdot |0\rangle + \omega_1 \cdot |1\rangle) = (H \otimes H) \cdot \begin{pmatrix} \omega_0 \\ \omega_1 \\ \omega_2 \\ \omega_3 \end{pmatrix} \quad (2.20)$$

it follows

$$\left(H \cdot \begin{pmatrix} \omega_0 \\ \omega_1 \end{pmatrix} \right) \otimes \left(H \cdot \begin{pmatrix} \omega_0 \\ \omega_1 \end{pmatrix} \right) = (H \otimes H) \cdot \begin{pmatrix} \omega_0 \\ \omega_1 \\ \omega_2 \\ \omega_3 \end{pmatrix}. \quad (2.21)$$

The tensor product between matrix is defined as

$$A \otimes B = \begin{pmatrix} a_{11} \cdot B & a_{12} \cdot B \\ a_{21} \cdot B & a_{22} \cdot B \end{pmatrix} = \begin{pmatrix} a_{11} \cdot b_{11} & a_{11} \cdot b_{12} & a_{12} \cdot b_{11} & a_{12} \cdot b_{12} \\ a_{11} \cdot b_{21} & a_{11} \cdot b_{22} & a_{12} \cdot b_{21} & a_{12} \cdot b_{22} \\ a_{21} \cdot b_{11} & a_{21} \cdot b_{12} & a_{22} \cdot b_{11} & a_{22} \cdot b_{12} \\ a_{21} \cdot b_{21} & a_{21} \cdot b_{22} & a_{22} \cdot b_{21} & a_{22} \cdot b_{22} \end{pmatrix}.$$

For example $H \otimes H$ is

$$H \otimes H = \frac{1}{\sqrt{2}} \cdot \begin{pmatrix} 1 & 1 \\ 1 & -1 \end{pmatrix} \otimes \frac{1}{\sqrt{2}} \cdot \begin{pmatrix} 1 & 1 \\ 1 & -1 \end{pmatrix} = \frac{1}{2} \cdot \begin{pmatrix} 1 & 1 & 1 & 1 \\ 1 & -1 & 1 & -1 \\ 1 & 1 & -1 & -1 \\ 1 & -1 & -1 & 1 \end{pmatrix}.$$

2.4 MEASUREMENT

After a unitary information processing starting form an initial basis state the result of the algorithm is determined by the measurement. The measurement corresponds to the collapse of the state vector, a projection into a basis state. The projection is not reversible and it is not consistent with the unitary time evolution. For a state represented by a unit-length vector

$$\omega_1 \cdot |x_1\rangle + \omega_2 \cdot |x_2\rangle + \cdots + \omega_n \cdot |x_n\rangle$$

in a n-dimensional Hilbert space $|x_k\rangle$ is observed. After the measurement (observation) the state is in a basis state

$$1 \cdot |x_k\rangle.$$

The state of a compound system is projected to the subspace that corresponds to the observed state and the vector representing the state is renormalized to the unit length. An observable describes a subspace for some dimensions with a special case of one dimension. A part of the system can be observed by a projection in a subspace with a dimension higher one. The compound system of n-dimensional Hilbert space $|x\rangle \in \mathcal{H}_n$ and a w-dimensional Hilbert space $|y\rangle \in \mathcal{H}_w$ defined by a orthonormal basis $|xy\rangle \in \mathcal{H}_{n \cdot w}$. A state of the system is represented as

$$|xy\rangle = \sum_{i=1}^{n} \sum_{j=1}^{w} \omega_{ij} |x_i\rangle |y_j\rangle. \quad (2.22)$$

For example

$$|xy\rangle = \sum_{i=1}^{2} \sum_{j=1}^{2} \omega_{ij} |x_i\rangle |y_j\rangle =$$

$$= \omega_{11} \cdot |x_1\rangle|y_1\rangle + \omega_{12} \cdot |x_1\rangle|y_2\rangle + \omega_{21} \cdot |x_2\rangle|y_1\rangle + \omega_{22} \cdot |x_2\rangle|y_2\rangle.$$

For simplicity we use the following notation for a qubit register

$$|xy\rangle = \omega_0 \cdot |00\rangle + \omega_1 \cdot |01\rangle + \omega_2 \cdot |10\rangle + \omega_3 \cdot |11\rangle$$

The probability of observing x_k is $\sum_{j=1}^{w} |\omega_{kj}|^2$. If we observe x_k, the system after the observation is projected into

$$|xy\rangle = \frac{1}{\sqrt{\sum_{j=1}^{w} |\omega_{kj}|^2}} \sum_{j=1}^{w} \omega_{kj} |x_k\rangle|y_j\rangle.$$

Suppose the two qubits are in the following state

$$\sqrt{0.25} \cdot |00\rangle + \sqrt{0.25} \cdot |01\rangle + \sqrt{0.25} \cdot |10\rangle + \sqrt{0.25} \cdot |11\rangle = \begin{pmatrix} \frac{1}{2} \\ \frac{1}{2} \\ \frac{1}{2} \\ \frac{1}{2} \end{pmatrix}.$$

The observed first qubit is $|0\rangle$. The probability of the observation is

$$|\omega_{00}|^2 + |\omega_{01}|^2 = |\omega_0|^2 + |\omega_1|^2 = |\sqrt{0.25}|^2 + |\sqrt{0.25}|^2 = 0.25 + 0.25 = 0.5$$

the system after the observation is projected into

$$\frac{\sqrt{0.25} \cdot |00\rangle + \sqrt{0.25} \cdot |01\rangle}{\sqrt{0.5}} = \sqrt{0.5} \cdot |00\rangle + \sqrt{0.5} \cdot |01\rangle = \begin{pmatrix} \sqrt{\frac{1}{2}} \\ \sqrt{\frac{1}{2}} \\ 0 \\ 0 \end{pmatrix}.$$

2.5 COMPUTATION WITH ONE QUBIT

A unitary operator on a qubit is called an unary quantum gate. It is described by a unitary matrix of the dimension 2×2. For the qubit with the basis

$$|0\rangle = \begin{pmatrix} 1 \\ 0 \end{pmatrix}, |1\rangle = \begin{pmatrix} 0 \\ 1 \end{pmatrix}$$

the quantum not gate X does the not operation on a qubit

$$X|0\rangle = |1\rangle, X|1\rangle = |0\rangle$$

and is represented by the unitary matrix

$$X = \begin{pmatrix} 0 & 1 \\ 1 & 0 \end{pmatrix}. \tag{2.23}$$

The not operation can be written using $XOR = \oplus$ for $x \in \mathbf{B}^1$ ($\mathbf{B}^m$ stands for binary string of length m representing a binary number)

$$X|x\rangle = |x \oplus 1\rangle$$

$$X|0\rangle = |0 \oplus 1\rangle = |0\rangle, \quad X|1\rangle = |1 \oplus 1\rangle = |1\rangle.$$

The square root of the not gate $X = \sqrt{X} \cdot \sqrt{X}$ is represented by the unitary matrix

$$\sqrt{X} = \begin{pmatrix} \frac{1+i}{2} & \frac{1-i}{2} \\ \frac{1-i}{2} & \frac{1+i}{2} \end{pmatrix} \tag{2.24}$$

with

$$X = \begin{pmatrix} \frac{1+i}{2} & \frac{1-i}{2} \\ \frac{1-i}{2} & \frac{1+i}{2} \end{pmatrix} \cdot \begin{pmatrix} \frac{1+i}{2} & \frac{1-i}{2} \\ \frac{1-i}{2} & \frac{1+i}{2} \end{pmatrix} = \begin{pmatrix} 0 & 1 \\ 1 & 0 \end{pmatrix} \tag{2.25}$$

and it is unitary because

$$\begin{pmatrix} \frac{1+i}{2} & \frac{1-i}{2} \\ \frac{1-i}{2} & \frac{1+i}{2} \end{pmatrix} \cdot \begin{pmatrix} \frac{1-i}{2} & \frac{1+i}{2} \\ \frac{1+i}{2} & \frac{1-i}{2} \end{pmatrix} = \begin{pmatrix} 1 & 0 \\ 0 & 1 \end{pmatrix} \tag{2.26}$$

with

$$X|0\rangle = \frac{1+i}{2} \cdot |0\rangle + \frac{1-i}{2} \cdot |1\rangle$$

and

$$X|1\rangle = \frac{1-i}{2} \cdot |0\rangle + \frac{1+i}{2} \cdot |1\rangle.$$

The probability of measuring $|0\rangle$ and $|1\rangle$ is 0.5, because

$$\left| \frac{1-i}{2} \right|^2 = \left| \frac{1+i}{2} \right|^2 = \frac{1}{2}.$$

$-\sqrt{X}$ has the same behavior with

$$X = -\sqrt{X} \cdot -\sqrt{X}.$$

The identity gate preforms no operation on a qubit, it is defined as the identity matrix

$$I_1 = \begin{pmatrix} 1 & 0 \\ 0 & 1 \end{pmatrix}. \tag{2.27}$$

The square root of the identity matrix is the identity I matrix is I and $-I$

$$-I_1 = \begin{pmatrix} -1 & 0 \\ 0 & -1 \end{pmatrix}. \tag{2.28}$$

$-I_1$ changes the sign of the amplitude but not the probabilities. The introduced Hadamard matrix H maps a basis state in a superposition.

$$|0\rangle \rightarrow \frac{1}{\sqrt{2}} \cdot |0\rangle + \frac{1}{\sqrt{2}} \cdot |1\rangle$$

$$|1\rangle \rightarrow \frac{1}{\sqrt{2}} \cdot |0\rangle - \frac{1}{\sqrt{2}} \cdot |1\rangle$$

The probability of measuring $|0\rangle$ and $|1\rangle$ is 0.5.

2.6 COMPUTATION WITH M QUBIT

The register of m qubits is represented as a direct product of m qubits. It defines $n = 2^m$ dimensional Hilbert space $\mathcal{H}_n$ with an orthonprmal basis $|x_1\rangle, |x_1\rangle, \cdots |x_n\rangle$. For example, four qubits define a 16 dimensional Hilbert space $\mathcal{H}_{16}$ with the basis

$$|0000\rangle = \begin{pmatrix} 1 \\ 0 \\ 0 \\ 0 \\ 0 \\ 0 \\ 0 \\ 0 \\ 0 \\ 0 \\ 0 \\ 0 \\ 0 \\ 0 \\ 0 \\ 0 \end{pmatrix}, |0001\rangle = \begin{pmatrix} 0 \\ 1 \\ 0 \\ 0 \\ 0 \\ 0 \\ 0 \\ 0 \\ 0 \\ 0 \\ 0 \\ 0 \\ 0 \\ 0 \\ 0 \\ 0 \end{pmatrix}, |0010\rangle = \begin{pmatrix} 0 \\ 0 \\ 1 \\ 0 \\ 0 \\ 0 \\ 0 \\ 0 \\ 0 \\ 0 \\ 0 \\ 0 \\ 0 \\ 0 \\ 0 \\ 0 \end{pmatrix}, \cdots, |1111\rangle = \begin{pmatrix} 0 \\ 0 \\ 0 \\ 0 \\ 0 \\ 0 \\ 0 \\ 0 \\ 0 \\ 0 \\ 0 \\ 0 \\ 0 \\ 0 \\ 0 \\ 1 \end{pmatrix}. \quad (2.29)$$

It is difficult to simulate more than few of tens bits on an ordinary computer because the dimension of the Hilbert space grows exponentially in relation to the number of represented qubits. For example 16 qubits are represented by a 65536 dimensional Hilbert space $\mathcal{H}_{65536}$.

The Hadamard matrix H on one qubit has the dimension 2×2 is also called a Hadamard gate and is indicated as H_1. A Hadamard operator for m qubits H_m is represented by a $2^m \times 2^m$ dimensional matrix built by a direct product of m H_1 matrices. The complexity of the operator H_m corresponds to m Hadamard gates H_1.

$$H_m = \bigotimes^m H_1 = H_1 \otimes H_1 \cdots \otimes H_1 \quad (2.30)$$

The Hadamard matrix is also called the Hadamard transform and can be defined recursively with $H_0 = 1$ and

$$H_m = \frac{1}{\sqrt{2}} \cdot \begin{pmatrix} H_{m-1} & H_{m-1} \\ H_{m-1} & -H_{m-1} \end{pmatrix} \quad (2.31)$$

with H_3

$$H_3 = H_1 \otimes H_1 \otimes H_1$$

$$H_3 = \frac{1}{\sqrt{2}} \cdot \begin{pmatrix} H_2 & H_2 \\ H_2 & -H_2 \end{pmatrix} = \frac{1}{\sqrt{2^3}} \cdot \begin{pmatrix} 1 & 1 & 1 & 1 & 1 & 1 & 1 & 1 \\ 1 & -1 & 1 & -1 & 1 & -1 & 1 & -1 \\ 1 & 1 & -1 & -1 & 1 & 1 & -1 & -1 \\ 1 & -1 & -1 & 1 & 1 & -1 & -1 & 1 \\ 1 & 1 & 1 & 1 & -1 & -1 & -1 & -1 \\ 1 & -1 & 1 & -1 & -1 & -1 & -1 & 1 \\ 1 & 1 & -1 & -1 & -1 & -1 & 1 & 1 \\ 1 & -1 & -1 & 1 & -1 & 1 & 1 & -1 \end{pmatrix}.$$

The Hadamard operator H_m maps m qubits $|z\rangle$ representing a basis state in a Hilbert space $\mathcal{H}_{2^m}$ with $z \in B^m$ ($\mathbf{B}^m$ stands for binary string of length m representing a binary number)

$$H_m|z\rangle = \frac{1}{\sqrt{2^m}} \sum_{x \in B^m} (-1)^{\langle z|x \rangle} \cdot |x\rangle \qquad (2.32)$$

with a scalar product ($\langle z|x\rangle$) over the binary field with two elements corresponding to the bits 0 and 1. The multiplication of two bits is equal to the AND operation with

$$0 \cdot 0 = 0 \wedge 0 = 0, \quad 0 \cdot 1 = 0 \wedge 1 = 0, \quad 1 \cdot 0 = 1 \wedge 0 = 0, \quad 1 \cdot 1 = 1 \wedge 1 = 1$$

and the addition is equal to the XOR operation $\oplus$

$$0 + 0 = 0 \oplus 0 = 0, \quad 0 + 1 = 0 \oplus 1 = 1,$$

$$1 + 0 = 1 \oplus 0 = 1, \quad 1 + 1 = 1 \oplus 1 = 0.$$

For the state zero represented by m qubits

$$|0\rangle^{\otimes m} = |0\rangle|0\rangle|0\rangle \cdots |0\rangle = \begin{pmatrix} 1 \\ 0 \\ \vdots \\ 0 \\ 0 \end{pmatrix}$$

the Hadamard operator H_m maps a basis state into a superposition of all possible states with no negative sign,

$$H_m|0\rangle^{\otimes m} = \frac{1}{\sqrt{2^m}} \sum_{x \in B^m} |x\rangle. \qquad (2.33)$$

For example

$$H_3|0\rangle^{\otimes 3} = H_3|000\rangle = \frac{1}{\sqrt{2^3}} \sum_{x \in B^3} |x\rangle$$

$$H_3|000\rangle =$$

$$= \frac{1}{\sqrt{2^3}} \left(|000\rangle + |001\rangle + |000\rangle + |010\rangle + |011\rangle + |100\rangle + |101\rangle + |111\rangle \right).$$

It can be expressed as

$$H_3|000\rangle = H_1|0\rangle \otimes H_1|0\rangle \otimes H_1|0\rangle = \left(\frac{|0\rangle + |1\rangle}{\sqrt{2}}\right) \cdot \left(\frac{|0\rangle + |1\rangle}{\sqrt{2}}\right) \cdot \left(\frac{|0\rangle + |1\rangle}{\sqrt{2}}\right)$$

and

$$H_3 \cdot H_3|000\rangle = |000\rangle.$$

This is because $H_m = H_m^*$ so that $I_m = H_m \cdot H_m$. The basis states $|11\rangle$ is mapped into

$$H_2|11\rangle = H_1|1\rangle \otimes H_1|1\rangle = \left(\frac{|0\rangle - |1\rangle}{\sqrt{2}}\right) \cdot \left(\frac{|0\rangle - |1\rangle}{\sqrt{2}}\right)$$

$$H_2|11\rangle = \frac{1}{2} \cdot (|00\rangle - |01\rangle - |10\rangle + |11\rangle).$$

2.6.1 Matrix Representation of Serial and Parallel Operations

A serial computation corresponds to a multiplication of matrices that represent the gates. The multiplication of matrices is usually not commutative, for example $H_1 \cdot X \neq X H_1$

$$\left(\begin{array}{cc} \frac{1}{\sqrt{2}} & \frac{1}{\sqrt{2}} \\ \frac{1}{\sqrt{2}} & -\frac{1}{\sqrt{2}} \end{array}\right) \cdot \left(\begin{array}{cc} 0 & 1 \\ 1 & 0 \end{array}\right) \neq \left(\begin{array}{cc} 0 & 1 \\ 1 & 0 \end{array}\right) \cdot \left(\begin{array}{cc} \frac{1}{\sqrt{2}} & \frac{1}{\sqrt{2}} \\ \frac{1}{\sqrt{2}} & -\frac{1}{\sqrt{2}} \end{array}\right)$$

$$\left(\begin{array}{cc} \frac{1}{\sqrt{2}} & \frac{1}{\sqrt{2}} \\ -\frac{1}{\sqrt{2}} & \frac{1}{\sqrt{2}} \end{array}\right) \neq \left(\begin{array}{cc} \frac{1}{\sqrt{2}} & -\frac{1}{\sqrt{2}} \\ \frac{1}{\sqrt{2}} & \frac{1}{\sqrt{2}} \end{array}\right),$$

it means

$$H_1 \cdot X \cdot |0\rangle = H_1 \cdot |1\rangle = \frac{|0\rangle - |1\rangle}{\sqrt{2}}$$

and

$$X \cdot H_1 \cdot |0\rangle = X \cdot \left(\frac{|0\rangle + |1\rangle}{\sqrt{2}}\right) =$$

$$= \frac{X \cdot |0\rangle + X \cdot |1\rangle}{\sqrt{2}} = \frac{|1\rangle + |0\rangle}{\sqrt{2}} = \frac{|0\rangle + |1\rangle}{\sqrt{2}}$$

and it follows

$$X \cdot H_1 \cdot |0\rangle = H_1 \cdot |0\rangle.$$

Only the multiplication with the identity matrix and the inverse matrix are commutative operations. Parallel operations correspond to the direct product, also called the tensor product or Kronecker product when dealing with matrices. For example with

$$X \otimes I_1 \otimes H_1 \cdot |000\rangle = (X \cdot |0\rangle) \otimes (I_1 \cdot |0\rangle) \otimes (H_1 \cdot |0\rangle) =$$

$$|10\rangle \cdot \frac{|0\rangle + |1\rangle}{\sqrt{2}} = \frac{|100\rangle + |101\rangle}{\sqrt{2}}$$

in vector representation as

$$\left(\left(\begin{array}{cc} 0 & 1 \\ 1 & 0 \end{array}\right) \cdot \left(\begin{array}{c} 1 \\ 0 \end{array}\right)\right) \otimes \left(\left(\begin{array}{cc} 1 & 0 \\ 0 & 1 \end{array}\right) \cdot \left(\begin{array}{c} 1 \\ 0 \end{array}\right)\right) \otimes \left(\left(\begin{array}{cc} \frac{1}{\sqrt{2}} & \frac{1}{\sqrt{2}} \\ \frac{1}{\sqrt{2}} & -\frac{1}{\sqrt{2}} \end{array}\right) \cdot \left(\begin{array}{c} 1 \\ 0 \end{array}\right)\right) =$$

$$\begin{pmatrix} 0 & 0 & 0 & 0 & \frac{1}{\sqrt{2}} & \frac{1}{\sqrt{2}} & 0 & 0 \\ 0 & 0 & 0 & 0 & \frac{1}{\sqrt{2}} & -\frac{1}{\sqrt{2}} & 0 & 0 \\ 0 & 0 & 0 & 0 & 0 & 0 & \frac{1}{\sqrt{2}} & \frac{1}{\sqrt{2}} \\ 0 & 0 & 0 & 0 & 0 & 0 & \frac{1}{\sqrt{2}} & -\frac{1}{\sqrt{2}} \\ \frac{1}{\sqrt{2}} & \frac{1}{\sqrt{2}} & 0 & 0 & 0 & 0 & 0 & 0 \\ \frac{1}{\sqrt{2}} & -\frac{1}{\sqrt{2}} & 0 & 0 & 0 & 0 & 0 & 0 \\ 0 & 0 & \frac{1}{\sqrt{2}} & \frac{1}{\sqrt{2}} & 0 & 0 & 0 & 0 \\ 0 & 0 & \frac{1}{\sqrt{2}} & -\frac{1}{\sqrt{2}} & 0 & 0 & 0 & 0 \end{pmatrix} \cdot \begin{pmatrix} 1 \\ 0 \\ 0 \\ 0 \\ 0 \\ 0 \\ 0 \\ 0 \end{pmatrix} = \begin{pmatrix} 0 \\ 0 \\ 0 \\ 0 \\ \frac{1}{\sqrt{2}} \\ \frac{1}{\sqrt{2}} \\ 0 \\ 0 \end{pmatrix}.$$

Matrices representing quantum operators can be decomposed, for example

$$H_4 = H_2 \otimes H_2 = H_1 \otimes H_1 \otimes H_1 \otimes H_1.$$

There are however matrices representing quantum operators that can be not decomposed easily.

2.7 ENTANGLEMENT

It can happen that we cannot decompose a register into individual qubits after certain linear operations. For example a register of two qubit is decomposable if it can be represented as a tensor product of two qubits. A state that is not decomposable is called entangled. If two qubits are entangled in a state, then observing one of them will result in the same value of the other one. Both qubits behave as one unit and are called an *ebit*. The two qubits in an *ebit* behave as one unit, even if the qubits are separated. Once either qubit of an ebit is measured, the states of both qubits become definite. Experiments have shown that this correlation can remain even if the qubits are separated over a distance of several kilometers. It is possible to teleport a qubit from one location to another using an *ebit* [12]. More than two qubits can be entangled.

The following operator cX is unitary and defends an injective mapping on two qubits that is reversible

$$cX|00\rangle = |00\rangle, \quad cX|01\rangle = |01\rangle,$$

$$cX|10\rangle = |11\rangle, \quad cX|11\rangle = |10\rangle.$$

The operator cX is called a controlled not gate. The first qubit counting from the left is not changed. The second qubit is only flipped in the case that the first qubit is 1. In this case a not operation X on the second qubit is executed. The control not gate can as well perform the fan-out operation. For this operation the second qubit has to be zero. In this case the value of the first qubit is copied into the second one. The cX operator can be represented by a matrix

$$CX = \begin{pmatrix} 1 & 0 & 0 & 0 \\ 0 & 1 & 0 & 0 \\ 0 & 0 & 0 & 1 \\ 0 & 0 & 1 & 0 \end{pmatrix}. \tag{2.34}$$

CX cannot be expressed as a tensor product of 2×2 matrices. Suppose we start with the state $|00\rangle$ and map the first qubit bit into the superposition using the Hadamard gate

$$H_1 \otimes I \cdot |00\rangle = (H_1 \cdot |0\rangle) \otimes |0\rangle = \frac{|0\rangle + |1\rangle}{\sqrt{2}} \otimes |0\rangle = \frac{|00\rangle + |10\rangle}{\sqrt{2}}.$$

To this state represented by the two qubit we apply CX gate

$$CX \cdot \left(\frac{|00\rangle + |10\rangle}{\sqrt{2}} \right) = \frac{CX \cdot |00\rangle + CX \cdot |10\rangle}{\sqrt{2}} = \frac{|00\rangle + |11\rangle}{\sqrt{2}}.$$

A register of two qubit is decomposable if it can be represented as a direct product of two qubits. For example the state

$$\frac{|00\rangle + |01\rangle + |10\rangle + |11\rangle}{2} = \left(\frac{|0\rangle + |1\rangle}{\sqrt{2}} \right) \otimes \left(\frac{|0\rangle + |1\rangle}{\sqrt{2}} \right)$$

is decomposable. In vector notation it is represented as

$$\begin{pmatrix} \frac{1}{2} \\ \frac{1}{2} \\ \frac{1}{2} \\ \frac{1}{2} \end{pmatrix} = \begin{pmatrix} \frac{1}{\sqrt{2}} \\ \frac{1}{\sqrt{2}} \end{pmatrix} \otimes \begin{pmatrix} \frac{1}{\sqrt{2}} \\ \frac{1}{\sqrt{2}} \end{pmatrix}.$$

However, the state of two qubits

$$\frac{|00\rangle + |11\rangle}{\sqrt{2}} \tag{2.35}$$

is not decomposable. We preform a proof by contradiction. From the assumption that the state is decomposable follows a contradiction,

$$\frac{|00\rangle + |11\rangle}{\sqrt{2}} = (a_o \cdot |0\rangle + a_1 |1\rangle) \otimes (b_o \cdot |0\rangle + b_1 |1\rangle) = \tag{2.36}$$

$$= a_0 \cdot b_0 \cdot |00\rangle + a_0 \cdot b_1 \cdot |01\rangle + a_1 \cdot b_0 \cdot |10\rangle + a_1 \cdot b_1 \cdot |11\rangle$$

$$\rightarrow \quad a_0 \cdot b_0 = \frac{1}{\sqrt{2}}, \quad a_0 \cdot b_1 = 0, \quad a_1 \cdot b_0 = 0, \quad a_1 \cdot b_1 = \frac{1}{\sqrt{2}}$$

that is a contradiction.

A state that is not decomposable is called entangled. If two qubits are entangled in a state $\frac{|00\rangle + |11\rangle}{\sqrt{2}}$, then observing one of them will result in either $|0\rangle$ or $|1\rangle$ with probability $\frac{1}{2}$. However, it is not possible to observe a different value on the other, non-observed qubit. Both qubits behave as one unit and are called an *ebit*. There are four known *ebits*:

$$\frac{|00\rangle + |11\rangle}{\sqrt{2}}, \quad \frac{|00\rangle - |11\rangle}{\sqrt{2}}, \quad \frac{|01\rangle + |10\rangle}{\sqrt{2}}, \quad \frac{|01\rangle - |10\rangle}{\sqrt{2}}. \tag{2.37}$$

Quantum collapse during measurement is a non-local force. A non-local interaction is not limited by the speed of light, and its strength is not mediated with distance. This arrangement conflicts with Einstein's theory of special relativity, which states that nothing can travel faster than light. The conflict is resolved by the fact that one cannot use an ebit to send any information. If two qubits of an ebit are separated over a distance in two places, A and B, and there are no other means of communication, then measuring the qubit on place A determines the outcome on place B, but at place B, the outcome is unknown. Measuring at place B is a random process without the knowledge of the results of place A. Also to preform teleportation we need a conventional channel to send an information how to map the teleported qubit in a correct state.

2.8 CLONING

A linear operation that would produce a copy of an arbitrary quantum state is not possible. We cannot copy an unknown amplitude distribution of a state. This has profound implications in the field of quantum computing, since we cannot reuse an arbitrary quantum state.

To preform this task we define a copy machine. We chose one orthonormal basis state of the orthonormal basis, for example $|x_1\rangle$ and define a unitary copy operator that copies an state $|x\rangle \in H_n$ as

$$U_{copy}(|x\rangle, |x_1\rangle) = |x\rangle|x\rangle. \tag{2.38}$$

Does U_{copy} exist? For basis states U_{copy} is defined. It can be realized for example by CX with $|x_1\rangle = |0\rangle$ and $|x_2\rangle = |1\rangle$,

$$U_{copy}(|x_1\rangle, |x_1\rangle) = |x_1\rangle|x_1\rangle, \quad U_{copy}(|x_2\rangle, |x_1\rangle) = |x_2\rangle|x_2\rangle.$$

If the state is in a superposition

$$|x\rangle = \frac{|x_1\rangle + |x_2\rangle}{\sqrt{2}}$$

it implies that

$$U_{copy}(|x\rangle, |x_1\rangle) = |x\rangle|x\rangle = \left(\frac{|x_1\rangle + |x_2\rangle}{\sqrt{2}}\right) \otimes \left(\frac{|x_1\rangle + |x_2\rangle}{\sqrt{2}}\right) =$$

$$\frac{1}{2} \cdot (|x_1\rangle|x_1\rangle + |x_1\rangle|x_2\rangle + |x_2\rangle|x_1\rangle + |x_2\rangle|x_2\rangle).$$

Because of the linearity of U_{copy} it follows,

$$U_{copy}(|x\rangle, |x_1\rangle) = U_{copy}\left(\frac{|x_1\rangle + |x_2\rangle}{\sqrt{2}}, |x_1\rangle\right) =$$

$$U_{copy}(|x\rangle, |x_1\rangle) = U_{copy}\left(\frac{|x_1\rangle|x_1\rangle + |x_2\rangle|x_1\rangle}{\sqrt{2}}\right) =$$

$$\frac{U_{copy}(|x_1\rangle|x_1\rangle) + U_{copy}(|x_2\rangle|x_1\rangle)}{\sqrt{2}} = \frac{1}{\sqrt{2}} \cdot (|x_1\rangle|x_1\rangle + |x_2\rangle|x_2\rangle)$$

it leads to a contradiction. An operation that would produce a copy of an arbitrary quantum state is not possible and we cannot copy an unknown amplitude distribution of a state. For example we cannot copy an unknown qubit $\alpha \cdot |0\rangle + \beta \cdot |1\rangle$. The amplitude distribution is specified by the values of α and β.

2.9   PHASE KICK-BACK

If we apply CX gate to the target value $\frac{|0\rangle - |1\rangle}{\sqrt{2}}$ with the control qubit $|1\rangle$ we get

$$CX|1\rangle \cdot \left(\frac{|0\rangle - |1\rangle}{\sqrt{2}}\right) = |1\rangle \cdot \left(\frac{X \cdot |0\rangle - X \cdot |1\rangle}{\sqrt{2}}\right)$$

$$CX|1\rangle \cdot \left(\frac{|0\rangle - |1\rangle}{\sqrt{2}}\right) = |1\rangle \cdot \left((-1) \cdot \left(\frac{|0\rangle - |1\rangle}{\sqrt{2}}\right)\right)$$

$$CX|1\rangle \cdot \left(\frac{|0\rangle - |1\rangle}{\sqrt{2}}\right) = -|1\rangle \cdot \left(\frac{|0\rangle - |1\rangle}{\sqrt{2}}\right).$$

For the control qubit $|0\rangle$ nothing happens,

$$CX|0\rangle \cdot \left(\frac{|0\rangle - |1\rangle}{\sqrt{2}}\right) = |0\rangle \cdot \left(\frac{|0\rangle - |1\rangle}{\sqrt{2}}\right).$$

We say that the target value (phase) is being "kicked back" to the control register.

2.10   QUANTUM BOOLEAN GATES

A reversible circuit that is composed of m bits corresponds to a unitary mapping that represents a permutation on m bits, defining an injective mapping $\mathbf{B}^m \to \mathbf{B}^m$. A unitary permutation matrix can represent this unitary mapping. A more elegant method is to map the reversible circuit into the quantum Boolean gates. Such a mapping allows us to determine the complexity of the circuit by the number of gates. The following quantum gates are Boolean quantum gates: the identity gate I, the not gate X and the control not gate cX. The control not gate performs the essential fan-out operation. What is missing are the AND and OR operations. These operations can be represented by the universal reversible. A reversible Toffoli gate ccX is a unitary mapping. It defines a quantum gate on three qubits and can be represented by a unitary matrix CCX in Hilbert space $\mathcal{H}_8$

$$CCX = \begin{pmatrix} I_1 & 0 & 0 & 0 \\ 0 & I_1 & 0 & 0 \\ 0 & 0 & I_1 & 0 \\ 0 & 0 & 0 & X \end{pmatrix} = \begin{pmatrix} 1 & 0 & 0 & 0 & 0 & 0 & 0 & 0 \\ 0 & 1 & 0 & 0 & 0 & 0 & 0 & 0 \\ 0 & 0 & 1 & 0 & 0 & 0 & 0 & 0 \\ 0 & 0 & 0 & 1 & 0 & 0 & 0 & 0 \\ 0 & 0 & 0 & 0 & 1 & 0 & 0 & 0 \\ 0 & 0 & 0 & 0 & 0 & 1 & 0 & 0 \\ 0 & 0 & 0 & 0 & 0 & 0 & 0 & 1 \\ 0 & 0 & 0 & 0 & 0 & 0 & 1 & 0 \end{pmatrix}. \tag{2.39}$$

The unitary matrix CCX can be decomposed in several ways using non-Boolean quantum gates. However each decomposition involves the CX matrix, indicating that an entanglement may arise when applying a quantum Toffoli gate. With the basis of three qubits of the Hilbert space $\mathcal{H}_8$

$$|000\rangle = \begin{pmatrix} 1 \\ 0 \\ 0 \\ 0 \\ 0 \\ 0 \\ 0 \\ 0 \end{pmatrix}, |001\rangle = \begin{pmatrix} 0 \\ 1 \\ 0 \\ 0 \\ 0 \\ 0 \\ 0 \\ 0 \end{pmatrix}, |010\rangle = \begin{pmatrix} 0 \\ 0 \\ 1 \\ 0 \\ 0 \\ 0 \\ 0 \\ 0 \end{pmatrix}, |011\rangle = \begin{pmatrix} 0 \\ 0 \\ 0 \\ 1 \\ 0 \\ 0 \\ 0 \\ 0 \end{pmatrix},$$

$$|100\rangle = \begin{pmatrix} 0 \\ 0 \\ 0 \\ 0 \\ 1 \\ 0 \\ 0 \\ 0 \end{pmatrix}, |101\rangle = \begin{pmatrix} 0 \\ 0 \\ 0 \\ 0 \\ 0 \\ 1 \\ 0 \\ 0 \end{pmatrix}, |110\rangle = \begin{pmatrix} 0 \\ 0 \\ 0 \\ 0 \\ 0 \\ 0 \\ 1 \\ 0 \end{pmatrix}, |111\rangle = \begin{pmatrix} 0 \\ 0 \\ 0 \\ 0 \\ 0 \\ 0 \\ 0 \\ 1 \end{pmatrix}$$

the reversible $ccX(x_1, x_2, x_3) = (x_1, x_2, (x_1 \wedge x_2) \oplus x_3)$ operator corresponds to the unitary mapping

$$CCX \cdot |xyz\rangle = CCX \cdot |x\rangle|y\rangle|z\rangle = |x\rangle|y\rangle|(x \wedge y) \oplus z\rangle. \tag{2.40}$$

For the AND operation, the ancilla bit z is set to 0

$$CCX \cdot |x\rangle|y\rangle|0\rangle = |x\rangle|y\rangle|(x \wedge y)\rangle. \tag{2.41}$$

The OR operation is represented by the unitary mapping according to the De Morgan's laws

$$x_1 \vee x_2 = \neg(\neg x_1 \wedge, \neg x_2)$$

$$((I_2 \otimes X) \cdot CCX \cdot (X \otimes X \otimes I_1)) \cdot |xy0\rangle = xy(x \vee y)\rangle.$$

## CHAPTER 3

Qiskit

We describe how to install *qiskit* and demonstrate the two main backend simulator functions that we will use. We demonstrate the working principles of *qiskit* software development kit on the simple example of a quantum coin. We indicate how to represent simple quantum circuits by unitary matrices using *qiskit* get unitary command. We indicate step by step how to define quantum circuits on an example of four-bit conjunction. The concept of un-computation is introduced since in quantum computing we cannot reset qubits to zero. The Deutsch algorithm determines if a unknown function $f : \mathbf{B}^1 \to \mathbf{B}^1 : f(x) = y$ of one bit is constant or not by calling the function one time. Deutsch's algorithm was the first algorithm (1985) that demonstrated a quantum advantage; it is a proof of concept that, in certain settings, quantum computers are strictly more powerful than classical ones by reduction in query complexity compared to the classical case. Finally, we give an example how to run Deutsch algorithm on a real small quantum computer.

3.1 SOFTWARE DEVELOPMENT KIT

Qiskit is an open-source software development kit (SDK) for working with quantum computers at the level of circuits and algorithms [21], IBM Quantum[1], *https://quantum-computing.ibm.com/*. It provides tools for creating and manipulating quantum programs and running them on prototype quantum devices or on simulators on a local computer. It follows the quantum circuit model for universal quantum computation, and can be used for any quantum hardware that follows this model. *Qiskit* is based on Python, you can find all information about it at *https://qiskit.org*.

3.2 INSTALLATION

Before installing *qiskit* you should either install Anaconda, a cross-platform Python distribution for scientific computing that includes Jupyter. You can as well install Miniconda, a free minimal installer for conda. It is a small, bootstrap version of Anaconda that includes only conda, Python, the packages they depend on, and a small

---

[1]The author acknowledges the use of IBM Quantum services for this work. The views expressed are those of the author, and do not reflect the official policy or position of IBM or the IBM Quantum team.

DOI: 10.1201/9781003374404-3

number of other useful packages. Additionally you could install Visual Studio Code. Visual Studio Code is a code editor redefined to run Jupyter notebooks and automatically recognizes different environments $https://code.visualstudio.com/docs$. You can find installation instruction for *qiskit* at the site:

$$https://qiskit.org/documentation/getting\_started.html.$$

From there you have as well access to online tutorials.

Before installing *qiskit* you have to launch a prompt in Anaconda or a terminal. From there you can call conda. To install *qiskit* execute following commands. Create an environment with the name *qiskit* (or any other name you like)

```
conda create -n qiskit python 3
```

You can list all your environments with command

```
conda-env list
```

You activate the qiskit environment with the name ENV_NAME . Then you can activate it with the command

```
conda activate ENV_NAME
```

You start the installation with the commands

```
pip install qiskit
pip install qiskit[visualization]
```

and for newer versions of macOS

```
pip install 'qiskit[visualization]'
```

We can check the installed *qiskit* version with (see Figure 3.1).

```
import qiskit.tools.jupyter
%qiskit_version_table
%qiskit_copyright
```

3.3 BACKEND SIMULATOR FUNCTIONS

Qiskit provides different backend simulator functions by *Aer* package. We will use use two simulators.

- The *statevector simulator* performs an ideal execution of *qiskit* circuits and returns the final state vector off the simulator after application (all qubits). The state vector of the circuit can represent the probability values (quasi probability in newer version) that correspond to the multiplication of the state vector by the unitary matrix that represents the circuit. The *statevector simulator* will take longer than other simulation methods and requires more computer memory, since the state vector dimension grows exponentially with the number of qubits with $n = 2^m$ (with m number of qubits).

(a)

Version Information

Qiskit Software	Version
qiskit-terra	0.19.2
qiskit-aer	0.10.3
qiskit-ignis	0.7.0
qiskit-ibmq-provider	0.18.3
qiskit	0.34.2
qiskit-machine-learning	0.3.1
System information	
Python version	3.7.11
Python compiler	Clang 10.0.0
Python build	default, Jul 27 2021 07:03:16
OS	Darwin
CPUs	2
Memory (Gb)	8.0

Tue Jun 27 14:17:51 2023 WEST

(b)

Version Information

Qiskit Software	Version
qiskit-terra	0.24.0
qiskit-aer	0.12.0
qiskit-ignis	0.7.1
qiskit-ibmq-provider	0.20.2
qiskit	0.43.0
qiskit-machine-learning	0.5.0
System information	
Python version	3.9.12
Python compiler	Clang 12.0.1
Python build	main, Mar 24 2022 23:24:38
OS	Darwin
CPUs	10
Memory (Gb)	16.0

Thu May 25 09:20:30 2023 WEST

Figure 3.1 (a) *Qiskit* 0.34.2 version running on an older computer with 8 Gb. (b) *Qiskit* 0.43.0 version running on an modern computer with 16 Gb.

- The *qasm simulator* promises to behave like an actual device of today, which is prone to noise resulting from decoherence. It returns count, which is the sampling of the measured qubits that have to be defined in the circuit. It is much smaller in size and will not increase in size exponentially as the number of qubits increases.

3.4   COMPATIBILITY

The presented quantum circuits in the book involve mostly simple quantum circuits using basic quantum gates that can be easily ported to other quantum software development kits. You can download the examples (Jupyter notebooks) from the book from $https://github.com/andrzejwichert/qai$.

The *qiskit* software development kit (SDK) is in constant development and there are some changes between different versions. The programs were tested with *Qiskit* 0.34.2 version running on an older computer with 8 Gb and *Qiskit* 0.43.0 version running on a modern computer with 16 Gb. The main differences concerning the examples is the annotation on the legends of the histograms. In the older version the histogram annotation on the left side is always "Probabilities". In newer version the annotation depends on the used simulator. For the *statevector simulator* the annotation is "Quasi-probability" and for the *qasm simulator* "Count". Quasi-probability concept is introduced in order to apply quantum corrections to classical statistical mechanic. Quasi-probability distribution does not satisfy all the properties of a conventional probability distribution, for example it can take on negative values for states which have no classical model due to quantum-mechanical interference. However, the corresponding effects do not play any role in our simulations as described in this book.

Another difference is present in the *qiskit machine learning algorithms* library. We will use one example in the chapter 23 where two different notebooks for of the variational classifier are present.

3.5   EXAMPLE: QUANTUM COIN

We start with a very simple example, the quantum coin. The quantum coin is a system with two basis states 0 and 1 with

$$|0\rangle = \begin{pmatrix} 1 \\ 0 \end{pmatrix}, |1\rangle = \begin{pmatrix} 0 \\ 1 \end{pmatrix}. \tag{3.1}$$

The mapping is represented as

$$|0\rangle \rightarrow \frac{1}{\sqrt{2}} \cdot |0\rangle + \frac{1}{\sqrt{2}} \cdot |1\rangle \tag{3.2}$$

and

$$|1\rangle \rightarrow \frac{1}{\sqrt{2}} \cdot |0\rangle - \frac{1}{\sqrt{2}} \cdot |1\rangle. \tag{3.3}$$

The corresponding operator is indicated by the following unitary matrix,

$$W = \begin{pmatrix} \frac{1}{\sqrt{2}} & \frac{1}{\sqrt{2}} \\ \frac{1}{\sqrt{2}} & -\frac{1}{\sqrt{2}} \end{pmatrix} = \frac{1}{\sqrt{2}} \cdot \begin{pmatrix} 1 & 1 \\ 1 & -1 \end{pmatrix}. \tag{3.4}$$

If the system starts in state $|0\rangle$ and undergoes the time evolution, the probability of observing 0 or 1 is $\left|\frac{1}{\sqrt{2}}\right|^2 = \frac{1}{2}$. If we do not preform a measurement and repeat the mapping, the probability of observing 0 becomes 1 and observing 1 becomes zero. This is due to the fact, that the amplitudes of $|1\rangle$ cancel each other. This effect is called destructive interference and cannot occur in the probability distribution since all its coefficients are non-negative real numbers.

Either start the Anaconda Navigator or the Visual Studio Code editor (or any other editor that supports Jupyter). Indicate *New file, Jupyeter Notebook*, select the correct channel by indicating the environment name. Hadamard matrix H is represented in *qiskit* by the Hadamard gate $qc.h(qubit)$ where qc is a quantum circuit with the chosen name qc (you can choose as well another name, through the book we use the name qc). The quantum coin is defined with the basis stat as $|0\rangle$

$$H \cdot |0\rangle = \frac{1}{\sqrt{2}} \cdot |0\rangle + \frac{1}{\sqrt{2}} \cdot |1\rangle. \tag{3.5}$$

First we define a quantum circuit with one qubit by

```
qc = QuantumCircuit(1)
```

In a *qiskit* quantum circuit, all qubits are initialized wit the state $|0\rangle$. The Hadamard gate H acts on the qubit zero, the qubits in a circuit are numbered $0, 1, \cdots$. In our circuit we have just one qubit.

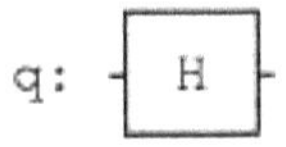

Figure 3.2 Quantum coin represented by a H gate.

```
qc.h(0)
```

The program is defined as,

```
from qiskit import QuantumCircuit, Aer,execute
from qiskit.visualization import plot_histogram

qc = QuantumCircuit(1)
qc.h(0)
qc.draw()
```

First we load the necessary libraries and then we define the circuit and draw it. After typing the program and executing it you should see the drawing of the circuit (see Figure 3.2).

3.5.1 Statevector Evaluation

In the next step we will perform a *statevector* simulation and plot the result in a histogram.

```
simulator = Aer.get_backend('statevector_simulator')
result=execute(qc,simulator).result()
counts = result.get_counts()
print("\nTotal count are:",counts)
plot_histogram(counts)
```

The probability values after the measurement are indicated in the Figure 3.3. We can represent the state vector before the measurement indicating its amplitude values using the build in LaTeX command (when using editor that supports jupyter)

```
final_state = execute(qc,simulator).result().get_statevector()
from qiskit.visualization import array_to_latex
array_to_latex(final_state, prefix="\\text{Statevector} = ")
```

with the output

$$Statevector = \begin{bmatrix} \dfrac{1}{\sqrt{2}} & \dfrac{1}{\sqrt{2}} \end{bmatrix}$$

If Jupyter is not supported replace

`array_to_latex` function by `print(final_state)`.

If we change out quantum circuit to represent the mapping using a NOT gate X, we get different amplitudes

$$H \cdot X \cdot |0\rangle = H \cdot |1\rangle = \frac{1}{\sqrt{2}} \cdot |0\rangle - \frac{1}{\sqrt{2}} \cdot |1\rangle \qquad (3.6)$$

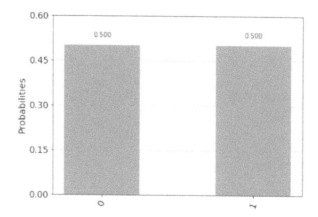

Figure 3.3 Two generated new states represented by one qubit. The state vector of the circuit can represent the probability values that correspond to the multiplication of the state vector by the unitary matrix H. Total count are: $\{'0' : 0.5, '1' : 0.5\}$ indicating the probability values.

Figure 3.4 NOT gate X and a a H gate.

that are represented by the following program. The quantum gate X that changes the initial value of the qubit $|0\rangle$ to $|1\rangle$

```
from qiskit import QuantumCircuit, Aer,execute
from qiskit.visualization import plot_histogram

qc = QuantumCircuit(1)
qc.x(0)
qc.h(0)
qc.draw()
```

See the drawing of the circuit (see Figure 3.4). The probability values after the measurement are still the same, see Figure 3.3. However the state vector before the measurement (using the build in LaTeX command) differs as expected

$$Statevector = \begin{bmatrix} \dfrac{1}{\sqrt{2}} & -\dfrac{1}{\sqrt{2}} \end{bmatrix}.$$

In a real quantum computer we have no direct access to the amplitudes before the measurement.

3.5.2 Qasm Simulator Evaluation

The *qasm simulator* promises to behave like an actual device of today, which is prone to noise resulting from decoherence. It returns count, which is a sampling

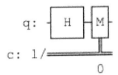

Figure 3.5 Quantum coin represented by a H gate and the measurement of the qubit represented by M. The value of the measurement is represented by one classical bit c.

of the measured qubits that have to be defined in the circuit, the measured values are stored in conventional bits. In our example of quantum coin, we define by the command $qc = QuantumCircuit(1, 1)$ a quantum circuit, the first number indicates the number of quantum qubits, the second of conventional bits.

```
qc = QuantumCircuit(1,1)
qc.h(0)
qc.measure(0,0)
qc.draw()
```

The command $qc.measure(0, 0)$ indicated that we measure the qubit (the counting begins with zero and not one) and store the result of the measurement in the conventional bit c. The quantum circuit is represented in the Figure 3.5.

```
simulator = Aer.get_backend('qasm_simulator')
result=execute(qc,simulator,shots=10).result()
counts = result.get_counts()
print("\nTotal count are:",counts)
plot_histogram(counts)
```

The command $result = execute(qc, simulator, shots = 10).result()$ executes the simulator 10 times, the number of samples (shots) is indicated by the command $qc, simulator, shots = 10$. A histogram represents the frequency of the two states 0 and 1 as measured by one bit is indicated in the Figure 3.6 in relation to the number of shots.

Applying the quantum coin twice

$$H \cdot \left(\frac{1}{\sqrt{2}} \cdot |0\rangle + \frac{1}{\sqrt{2}} \cdot |1\rangle \right) = H \cdot \frac{1}{\sqrt{2}} \cdot |0\rangle + H \cdot \frac{1}{\sqrt{2}} \cdot |1\rangle = |0\rangle$$

```
qc = QuantumCircuit(1,1)
qc.h(0)
qc.h(0)
qc.measure(0,0)
qc.draw()
```

results in the quantum circuit indicated in the Figure 3.7. and in the histogram see Figure 3.8.

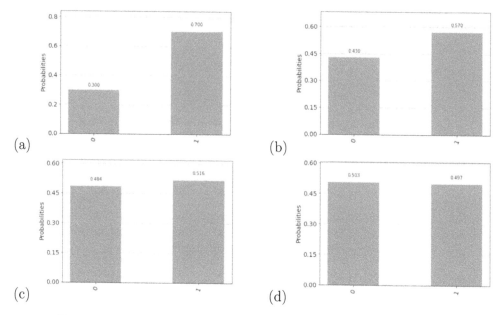

Figure 3.6 Two states 0 and 1 and their frequency of outcome as measured by one bit. The normalized frequencies are represented as probabilities. (a) The number of samples is 10, the total count are: $\{'1' : 6,'0' : 4\}$. (b) The number of samples is 100, the total count are: $\{'1' : 42,'0' : 52\}$. (c) The number of samples is 1000, the total count are: $\{'1' : 502,'0' : 498\}$. (d) The number of samples is 1000, the total count are: $\{'1' : 5026,'0' : 4974\}$. With growing number of samples, the distribution approaches the true values of Figure 3.3.

3.6 MATRIX REPRESENTATION

The Hadamard operator H_3 maps 3 qubits $|000\rangle$ representing a basis state in a Hilbert space $\mathcal{H}_{2^3}$

$$H_3 \cdot |000\rangle = H_1 \cdot |0\rangle \otimes H_1 \cdot |0\rangle \otimes H_1 \cdot |0\rangle =$$

$$\frac{1}{\sqrt{8}} \cdot (|000\rangle + |001\rangle + |010\rangle + |011\rangle + |100\rangle + |101\rangle + |110\rangle + |111\rangle).$$

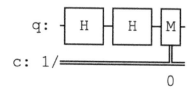

Figure 3.7 Applying quantum coin represented by two H gates and the measurement of the qubit represented by M. The value of the measurement is represented by one classical bit c.

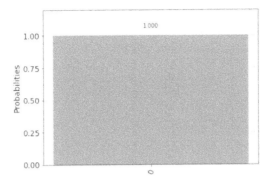

Figure 3.8 One generated new states represented by one qubit.

This corresponds to the simple program of three qubits $0, 1, 2$ using the state vector simulation

```
qc = QuantumCircuit(3)
qc.h(0)
qc.h(1)
qc.h(2)
qc.draw()
```

```
simulator = Aer.get_backend('statevector_simulator')
result=execute(qc,simulator).result()
counts = result.get_counts()
print("\nTotal count are:",counts)
plot_histogram(counts)
```

in the quantum circuit in the Figure 3.9. and in the histogram see Figure 3.10. We can represent the state vector before the measurement indicating its amplitude values using the build in LaTeX command (when using editor that supports jupyter)

```
final_state = execute(qc,simulator).result().get_statevector()
from qiskit.visualization import array_to_latex
array_to_latex(final_state, prefix="\\text{Statevector} = ")
```

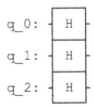

Figure 3.9 The Hadamard operator H_3 maps 3 qubits $|000\rangle$ representing a basis state in a Hilbert space $\mathcal{H}_{2^3}$. This represented by three H gates on the qubits numbered 0, 1 and 2.

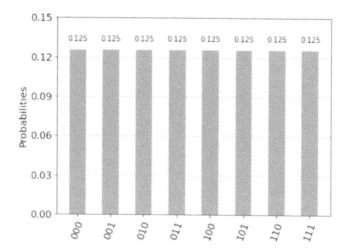

Figure 3.10 Eight generated new states represented by three qubit.

with the output

$$Statevector = \left[\frac{1}{\sqrt{8}} \quad \frac{1}{\sqrt{8}} \quad \frac{1}{\sqrt{8}} \quad \frac{1}{\sqrt{8}} \quad \frac{1}{\sqrt{8}} \quad \frac{1}{\sqrt{8}} \quad \frac{1}{\sqrt{8}} \quad \frac{1}{\sqrt{8}}\right]$$

We can represent the quantum circuit by a matrix with the following commands. We will use *NumPy* that is included in the *qiskit* installation. *NumPy* is a library for the Python programming language, adding support for large, multi-dimensional arrays and matrices that are highly related to MATLAB

```
import numpy as np
from qiskit.visualization import array_to_latex
from qiskit import assemble

simulator = Aer.get_backend('qasm_simulator')
qc.save_unitary()
result = simulator.run(qc).result()
unitary = result.get_unitary(qc)
print("\nSize of the unitary matrix:",np.asarray(unitary).shape)
array_to_latex(unitary, prefix="\\text{Circuit = }\n")
```

with the following output

```
Size of the unitary matrix: (8, 8)
```

$$Circuit = \begin{pmatrix}
\frac{1}{\sqrt{8}} & \frac{1}{\sqrt{8}} & \frac{1}{\sqrt{8}} & \frac{1}{\sqrt{8}} & \frac{1}{\sqrt{8}} & \frac{1}{\sqrt{8}} & \frac{1}{\sqrt{8}} & \frac{1}{\sqrt{8}} \\
\frac{1}{\sqrt{8}} & -\frac{1}{\sqrt{8}} & \frac{1}{\sqrt{8}} & -\frac{1}{\sqrt{8}} & \frac{1}{\sqrt{8}} & -\frac{1}{\sqrt{8}} & \frac{1}{\sqrt{8}} & -\frac{1}{\sqrt{8}} \\
\frac{1}{\sqrt{8}} & \frac{1}{\sqrt{8}} & -\frac{1}{\sqrt{8}} & -\frac{1}{\sqrt{8}} & \frac{1}{\sqrt{8}} & \frac{1}{\sqrt{8}} & -\frac{1}{\sqrt{8}} & -\frac{1}{\sqrt{8}} \\
\frac{1}{\sqrt{8}} & -\frac{1}{\sqrt{8}} & -\frac{1}{\sqrt{8}} & \frac{1}{\sqrt{8}} & \frac{1}{\sqrt{8}} & -\frac{1}{\sqrt{8}} & -\frac{1}{\sqrt{8}} & \frac{1}{\sqrt{8}} \\
\frac{1}{\sqrt{8}} & \frac{1}{\sqrt{8}} & \frac{1}{\sqrt{8}} & \frac{1}{\sqrt{8}} & -\frac{1}{\sqrt{8}} & -\frac{1}{\sqrt{8}} & -\frac{1}{\sqrt{8}} & -\frac{1}{\sqrt{8}} \\
\frac{1}{\sqrt{8}} & -\frac{1}{\sqrt{8}} & \frac{1}{\sqrt{8}} & -\frac{1}{\sqrt{8}} & -\frac{1}{\sqrt{8}} & \frac{1}{\sqrt{8}} & -\frac{1}{\sqrt{8}} & \frac{1}{\sqrt{8}} \\
\frac{1}{\sqrt{8}} & \frac{1}{\sqrt{8}} & -\frac{1}{\sqrt{8}} & -\frac{1}{\sqrt{8}} & -\frac{1}{\sqrt{8}} & -\frac{1}{\sqrt{8}} & \frac{1}{\sqrt{8}} & \frac{1}{\sqrt{8}} \\
\frac{1}{\sqrt{8}} & -\frac{1}{\sqrt{8}} & -\frac{1}{\sqrt{8}} & \frac{1}{\sqrt{8}} & -\frac{1}{\sqrt{8}} & \frac{1}{\sqrt{8}} & \frac{1}{\sqrt{8}} & -\frac{1}{\sqrt{8}}
\end{pmatrix}.$$

Since the size of the matrix grows exponential, it is not possible to represent quantum circuits with a higher number of qubits by a matrix.

3.7 QUANTUM CIRCUITS

The four bit conjunction $x \wedge y \wedge z \wedge v$ requires three quantum Toffoli gates ccX and three additional qubits that are zero. With the input state

$$|x\rangle|y\rangle|0\rangle|z\rangle|0\rangle|v\rangle|0\rangle.$$

First quantum Toffoli gate

$$(CCX \cdot |x\rangle|y\rangle|0\rangle) \otimes (I_4 \cdot |z\rangle|0\rangle|v\rangle|0\rangle) = |x\rangle|y\rangle|x \wedge y\rangle|z\rangle|0\rangle|v\rangle|0\rangle.$$

Second quantum Toffoli gate

$$(I_2 \cdot |x\rangle|y\rangle) \otimes (CCX \cdot |x \wedge y\rangle|z\rangle|0\rangle) \otimes (I_2 \cdot |v\rangle|0\rangle) =$$

$$= |x\rangle|y\rangle|x \wedge y\rangle|z\rangle|x \wedge y \wedge z\rangle|v\rangle|0\rangle.$$

Third quantum Toffoli gate

$$(I_4 \cdot |x\rangle|y\rangle|x \wedge y\rangle|z\rangle) \otimes (CCX \cdot |x \wedge y \wedge z\rangle|v\rangle|0\rangle) =$$

$$= |x\rangle|y\rangle|x \wedge y\rangle|z\rangle|x \wedge y \wedge z\rangle|v\rangle|x \wedge y \wedge z \wedge v\rangle.$$

The circuit corresponds to the following unitary mapping

$$((I_4 \otimes CCX)(I_2 \otimes CCX \otimes I_2) \cdot (CCX \otimes I_4)) \cdot |xy0z0v0\rangle$$

with the result

$$|x\rangle|y\rangle|x \wedge y\rangle|z\rangle|x \wedge y \wedge z\rangle|v\rangle|x \wedge y \wedge z \wedge v\rangle.$$

We define a quantum circuit with seven qubits and name them using the command $QuantumRegister(size, name)$, with $size$ is number of qubits to include in the register and the name of the register as it appears in the drawing of the quantum circuit. We create the register x, y, z v, two auxiliary register and a register r with the name $result$ and generate the quantum circuit with the command $QuantumCircuit(x, y, z, v, aux, r)$. We initialize the qubits x, y, z v to one with the not gate X. Note, we change the order of the aux qubits to make it cleared to read. After the initialization we use the command $qc.barrier()$, it separates the representation in the circuit. It is not a gate and prevents the merging of the gate operations during the computation. Then we use three three quantum Toffoli gates, also called the ccX gate (CCNOT gate – controlled controlled not gate) and the final result or the operation is represented in the quantum qubit r. $Qiskit$ uses the **little endian notation**, it stores the least-significant byte at the smallest address. Qubits are represented from the most significant bit (MSB) on the left to the least significant bit (LSB) on the right (little-endian). This is similar as binary numbers or to bitstring representation on classical computers, in our example we represent we represent x by the first qubit, y by the second qubit and so on representing the state $|r, aux, v, z, y, x\rangle$

```
from qiskit import QuantumCircuit,QuantumRegister, execute
from qiskit.visualization import plot_histogram
from qiskit.quantum_info import Statevector

x = QuantumRegister(1, 'x')
y = QuantumRegister(1, 'y')
z = QuantumRegister(1, 'z')
v = QuantumRegister(1, 'v')
aux =  QuantumRegister(2,'aux')
r = QuantumRegister(1, 'result')
qc = QuantumCircuit(x,y,z,v,aux,r)
qc.x(x)
qc.x(y)
qc.x(z)
qc.x(v)
qc.barrier()
qc.ccx(x,y,aux[0])
qc.ccx(aux[0],z,aux[1])
qc.ccx(aux[1],z,r)

simulator = Aer.get_backend('statevector_simulator')
result=execute(qc,simulator).result()
counts = result.get_counts()
print("\nTotal count are:",counts)
plot_histogram(counts)
```

The quantum circuit is represented in the Figure 3.11. and the results after the statevector "measurement" are indicated in Figure 3.12.

3.7.1 Un-computing

The qubits $aux_0=1$, $aux_1 = 1$ are usually not required for further computation because the result is represented in the output qubit *result*. However they are entangled with the output qubit. It is not possible to reset them to zero. Instead they are un-computed. Because for the matrix $CCX^{-1} = CCX$, we recompute the first and the second quantum Toffoli gate after determining the result. The steps are reversed as indicated in the listing after the command *qc.barrier()*

```
qc.barrier()
qc.ccx(x,y,aux[0])
qc.ccx(aux[0],z,aux[1])
qc.ccx(aux[1],z,r)
#un-computing of the aux registers
qc.ccx(aux[0],z,aux[1])
qc.ccx(x,y,aux[0])
```

as indicated in the Figure 3.13 and the results after the statevector "measurement" are indicated in Figure 3.14.

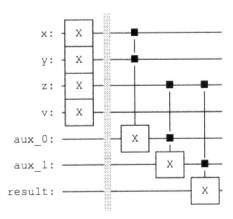

Figure 3.11 We initialize the qubits x, y, z, v to one with the not gate X. After the initialization we use the command $qc.barrier()$ that will separate the representation in the circuit. It is not a gate and prevents the merging of the gate operations during the computation. Then we use three three quantum Toffoli gates, also called the ccX gate (CCNOT gate, controlled controlled not gate) and the result is represented in the quantum qubit r.

3.7.2 General Multi-Controlled X Gate

Instead on can use as well the command $MCXGate(4)$ without the need of defining auxiliary registers. The $MCXGate(n)$ gate is a general, multi-controlled X gate that is controlled by n qubits, in our case by the qubits x, y, z, v, r

```
from qiskit.circuit.library import MCXGate
x = QuantumRegister(1, 'x')
y = QuantumRegister(1, 'y')
z = QuantumRegister(1, 'z')
```

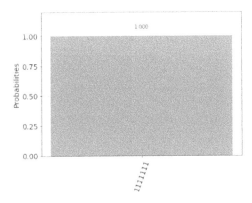

Figure 3.12 After the statevector "measurement" the values of the qubits the qubits are $x = 1$, $y = 1$, $z = 1$, $v = 1$, $aux_0 = 1$, $aux_1 = 1$ and $result = 1$. The total count are: $\{'1111111' : 1.0\}$, 1.0 indicates the probability one.

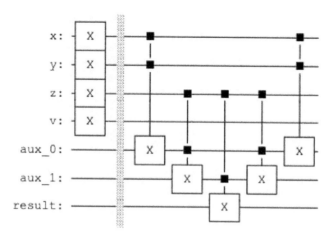

Figure 3.13 Because $CCX^{-1} = CXX$ we recompute the first and the second quantum Toffoli gate ccX after determining the result.

```
v = QuantumRegister(1, 'v')
r = QuantumRegister(1, 'result')
qc = QuantumCircuit(x,y,z,v,r)
qc.barrier()

gate = MCXGate(4)
qc.append(gate,[x,y,z,v,r])
qc.draw()
```

as indicated in the Figure 3.15.

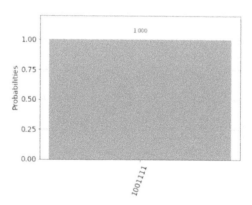

Figure 3.14 After the statevector "measurement", the values of the qubits the qubits are $x = 1$, $y = 1$, $z = 1$, $v = 1$, $aux_0 = 0$, $aux_1 = 0$, and $result = 1$. The total count are (indicated in reverse order): $\{'1001111' : 1.0\}$, 1.0 indicates the probability one of the state $|1001111\rangle$. Total count are: $\{'1001111' : 1.0\}$.

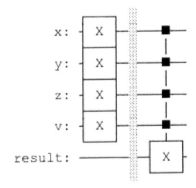

Figure 3.15 One can used as well the command $MCXGate(4)$ without the need of defining auxiliary registers.

3.7.3 OR Operation

The OR operation is represented by the unitary mapping according to the De Morgan's laws

$$x_1 \vee x_2 = \neg(\neg x_1 \wedge, \neg x_2)$$

$$((I_2 \otimes X) \cdot CCX \cdot (X \otimes X \otimes I_1)) \cdot |xy0\rangle = xy(x \vee y)\rangle.$$

```
x = QuantumRegister(1, 'x')
y = QuantumRegister(1, 'y')
r = QuantumRegister(1, 'result')
qc = QuantumCircuit(x,y,r)
#Preparation
qc.x(x)
#qc.x(y)
qc.barrier()
#Or Operation according to De Morgan's law
qc.x(x)
qc.x(y)
qc.x(r)
qc.ccx(x,y,r)
qc.x(x)
qc.x(y)

qc.draw()
```

resulting in the quantum circuit in the Figure 3.16 . For each quantum Boolean AND, OR operation a naive implementation requires an auxiliary (ancilla) bit. These bits can be reused for further computation only by reversing the preceding steps. The complexity of the circuit corresponds to the number of used quantum gates.

3.8   DEUTSCH ALGORITHM

The Deutsch algorithm [26] exploits the superposition of qubits generated by Hadamard gates and is more powerful than any classical algorithm. It determines

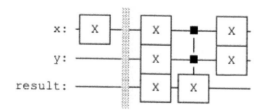

Figure 3.16 The OR operation is represented by the unitary mapping according to the De Morgan's laws $x_1 \vee x_2 = \neg(\neg x_1 \wedge, \neg x_2)$.

if an unknown function $f : \mathbf{B}^1 \to \mathbf{B}^1 : f(x) = y$ of one bit is constant or not by calling the function one time. A classical algorithm requires two calls. A constant function on one bit is either $f(x) = 1$ or $f(x) = 0$. A non-constant function is either the identity function $f(0) = 0$ and $f(1) = 1$ or the flip function $f(0) = 1$ and $f(1) = 0$. The condition of the function being constant $f(0) = f(1)$ implies that the XOR operation $\oplus$ is $f(0) \oplus f(1) = 0$ is zero. On the other hand if the function is not constant $f(0) \neq f(1)$ implies that the XOR operation $\oplus$ is $f(0) \oplus f(1) = 1$ is one. We can define a unitary operator U_f that acts on the two qubits

$$U_f \cdot |xy\rangle = |x\rangle|f(x) \oplus y\rangle.$$

U_f can be implemented by a quantum Boolean circuit including C_{NOT} gate. There are four different cases, for $f(x) = 0$ with the identity mapping

$$i) \quad U_f|00\rangle = |0\rangle|0 \oplus 0\rangle = |00\rangle, \quad U_f|01\rangle = |01\rangle,$$

$$U_f|10\rangle = |10\rangle, \quad U_f|11\rangle = |11\rangle$$

for $f(x) = 1$ with the permutation of all elements.

$$ii) \quad U_f|00\rangle = |0\rangle|1 \oplus 0\rangle = |01\rangle, \quad U_f|01\rangle = |00\rangle,$$

$$U_f|10\rangle = |11\rangle, \quad U_f|11\rangle = |10\rangle$$

and for a non-constant function, $f(x) = x$ corresponds to a permutation of two elements.

$$iii) \quad U_f|00\rangle = |0\rangle|0 \oplus 0\rangle = |00\rangle, \quad U_f|01\rangle = |01\rangle,$$

$$U_f|10\rangle = |11\rangle, \quad U_f|11\rangle = |10\rangle$$

and $f(x) = \neg x$ with a permutation of two elements as well

$$vi) \quad U_f|00\rangle = |0\rangle|1 \oplus 0\rangle = |01\rangle, \quad U_f|01\rangle = |00\rangle,$$

$$U_f|10\rangle = |10\rangle, \quad U_f|11\rangle = |11\rangle.$$

There are two classes:

- No permutation $i)$ or permutation of all elements $ii)$ indicates that the function is constant.

- Permutation of two elements $iii), iv)$ indicates that the function is non-constant.

The algorithm to determine if $f(x)$ is constant or not is composed of four steps. In the first step of the algorithm we build a superposition of two qubits

$$H_2 \cdot |01\rangle = H_1 \cdot |0\rangle \otimes H_1 \cdot |1\rangle = \left(\frac{|0\rangle + |1\rangle}{\sqrt{2}} \right) \otimes \left(\frac{|0\rangle - |1\rangle}{\sqrt{2}} \right) =$$

$$H2 \cdot |01\rangle = \frac{1}{2} \cdot (|00\rangle - |01\rangle + |10\rangle - |11\rangle).$$

```
from qiskit import QuantumCircuit,Aer,execute
from qiskit.visualization import plot_histogram

qc = QuantumCircuit(2)
qc.x(0)
qc.h(0)
qc.h(1)

simulator = Aer.get_backend('statevector_simulator')
final_state = execute(qc,simulator).result().get_statevector()
from qiskit.visualization import array_to_latex
array_to_latex(final_state, prefix="\\text{Statevector} = ")
```

with the output

$$Statevector = \begin{bmatrix} \frac{1}{2} & -\frac{1}{2} & \frac{1}{2} & -\frac{1}{2} \end{bmatrix}.$$

In the second step we apply the U_f, gate.

$$U_f \cdot H_2 \cdot |01\rangle = U_f \left(\frac{1}{2} \cdot (|00\rangle - |01\rangle + |10\rangle - |11\rangle) \right) =$$

$$= \frac{1}{2} \cdot (U_f \cdot |00\rangle - U_f \cdot |01\rangle + U_f \cdot |10\rangle - U_f \cdot |11\rangle).$$

There are four possible outcomes. For constant function

$$i) \quad = \frac{1}{2} \cdot (|00\rangle - |01\rangle + |10\rangle - |11\rangle) = \left(\frac{|0\rangle + |1\rangle}{\sqrt{2}} \right) \otimes \left(\frac{|0\rangle - |1\rangle}{\sqrt{2}} \right),$$

$$ii) \quad = \frac{1}{2} \cdot (|01\rangle - |00\rangle + |11\rangle - |10\rangle) = \frac{1}{2} \cdot (-|00\rangle + |01\rangle - |10\rangle + |11\rangle)$$

$$= \left(\frac{-|0\rangle - |1\rangle}{\sqrt{2}} \right) \otimes \left(\frac{|0\rangle - |1\rangle}{\sqrt{2}} \right) = - \left(\frac{|0\rangle + |1\rangle}{\sqrt{2}} \right) \otimes \left(\frac{|0\rangle - |1\rangle}{\sqrt{2}} \right),$$

and for non-constant function

$$iii) \quad = \frac{1}{2} \cdot (|00\rangle - |01\rangle + |11\rangle - |10\rangle) = \frac{1}{2} \cdot (|00\rangle - |01\rangle |10\rangle + |11\rangle)$$

$$= \left(\frac{|0\rangle - |1\rangle}{\sqrt{2}} \right) \otimes \left(\frac{|0\rangle - |1\rangle}{\sqrt{2}} \right),$$

$iv)$ $\quad = \dfrac{1}{2} \cdot (|01\rangle - |00\rangle + |10\rangle - |11\rangle) = \dfrac{1}{2} \cdot (-|00\rangle + |01\rangle + |10\rangle - |11\rangle)$

$$\left(\frac{-|0\rangle + |1\rangle}{\sqrt{2}} \right) \otimes \left(\frac{|0\rangle - |1\rangle}{\sqrt{2}} \right) = - \left(\frac{|0\rangle - |1\rangle}{\sqrt{2}} \right) \otimes \left(\frac{|0\rangle - |1\rangle}{\sqrt{2}} \right).$$

In the third step a Hadamard gate is applied to the first qubit

$$(H_1 \otimes I_1) \cdot U_f \cdot H_2 \cdot |01\rangle. \tag{3.7}$$

There are four possible outcomes,

$$i) \quad |0\rangle \otimes \left(\frac{|0\rangle - |1\rangle}{\sqrt{2}} \right),$$

$$ii) \quad -|0\rangle \otimes \left(\frac{|0\rangle - |1\rangle}{\sqrt{2}} \right),$$

$$iii) \quad |1\rangle \otimes \left(\frac{|0\rangle - |1\rangle}{\sqrt{2}} \right),$$

$$vi) \quad -|1\rangle \otimes \left(\frac{|0\rangle - |1\rangle}{\sqrt{2}} \right).$$

In the fourth step the first qubit (that is in the basis state) is measured. It is $|0\rangle$ if the function is constant, otherwise $|1\rangle$.

In our simulation, for simplicity we assume the unknown function is the identity mapping $f(x) = 0$

$$i) \quad U_f|00\rangle = |0\rangle|0 \oplus 0\rangle = |00\rangle, \quad U_f|01\rangle = |01\rangle,$$

$$U_f|10\rangle = |10\rangle, \quad U_f|11\rangle = |11\rangle$$

```
qc = QuantumCircuit(2,1)
qc.x(0)
qc.barrier()
qc.h(0)
qc.h(1)
#constant function f(x)=0, do nothing
qc.barrier()
qc.h(1)
#Measure the qubit 1
qc.measure(1,0)
qc.draw()

simulator = Aer.get_backend('qasm_simulator')
result=execute(qc,simulator).result()
counts = result.get_counts()
print("\nTotal count are:",counts)
plot_histogram(counts)
```

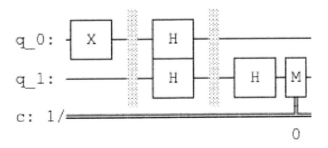

Figure 3.17 The quantum circuit representing the Deutsch algorithm for the unknown function the identity mapping $f(x) = 0$.

see the Figures 3.17 and 3.18. For the non-constant function, $f(x) = x$ corresponds to a permutation of two elements.

$$iii) \ U_f|00\rangle = |0\rangle|0 \oplus 0\rangle = |00\rangle, \quad U_f|01\rangle = |01\rangle,$$

$$U_f|10\rangle = |11\rangle, \quad U_f|11\rangle = |10\rangle$$

This operation can be achieved by the Controlled NOT gate. The CNOT gate flips the second qubit (the target qubit) if and only if the first qubit (the control qubit) is one. In our case the control qubit is q_1 is the target qubit q_1, $qc.cx(1,0)$

```
qc = QuantumCircuit(2,1)

qc.x(0)
qc.barrier()
qc.h(0)
qc.h(1)
#identity function f(x)=x
qc.cx(1,0)
qc.barrier()
```

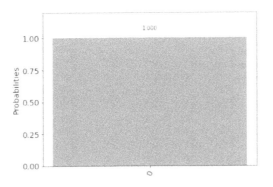

Figure 3.18 In the fourth step the first qubit (that is in the basis state) is measured. It is $|0\rangle$, the function is constant. Total count are: $\{"0' : 1024\}$. By default the number of shots is 1024 if not specified.

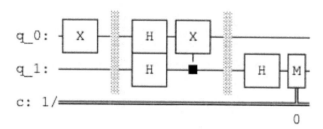

Figure 3.19 The quantum circuit representing the Deutsch algorithm for the unknown function the he non-constant function, $f(x) = x$.

```
qc.h(1)
qc.measure(1,0)

qc.draw()

simulator = Aer.get_backend('qasm_simulator')
result=execute(qc,simulator).result()
counts = result.get_counts()
print("\nTotal count are:",counts)
plot_histogram(counts)
```

see the Figures 3.19 and 3.20.

3.9 DEUTSCH ALGORITHM ON A REAL QUANTUM COMPUTER

Richard Feynman asked in the early eighties whether a quantum system can be simulated on an imaginary quantum computer. Today, 40 years later first small quantum computers begin to appear. During recent years a huge progress was achieved in keeping the quits coherent, opening the road to a universal quantum computer and

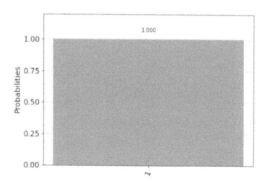

Figure 3.20 In the fourth step the first qubit (that is in the basis state) is measured. It is $|1\rangle$, the function is non-constant. Total count are: $\{"1' : 1024\}$. By default the number of shots is 1024 if not specified.

nairobi				oslo				manila		
		● Online				● Online				● Online	
		Falcon r5.11H				Falcon r5.11H				Falcon r5.11L	
7	32	2.6K		7	32	2.6K		5	32	2.8K	

quito				belem				lima		
		● Online				● Online				● Online	
		Falcon r4T				Falcon r4T				Falcon r4T	
5	16	2.5K		5	16	2.5K		5	8	2.7K	

Figure 3.21 Some free resources for general public access with 5–7 qubits.

the progress will continue. You can access for free (Open Plan) real small quantum computer through the site

https://www.ibm.com/quantum

Figure 3.21 indicates some possible resources and Figure 3.22 for information about a IBM quantum computer with 7 qubits. Follow the instruction and Sign in to IBM Quantum. We perform following changes in the *import* part and execution of the program

```
from qiskit import QuantumCircuit
from qiskit.visualization import plot_histogram

qc = QuantumCircuit(2,1)
qc.x(0)
qc.barrier()
qc.h(0)
qc.h(1)
#identity function f(x)=x
```

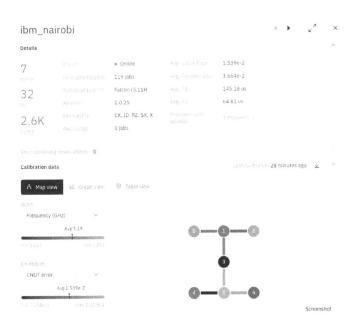

Figure 3.22 IBM quantum computer with 7 qubits and its hardware topology.

```
qc.cx(1,0)
qc.barrier()
qc.h(1)
qc.measure(1,0)

from qiskit import IBMQ, transpile
from qiskit_ibm_provider import IBMProvider, least_busy

provider = IBMProvider()
device=provider.backends(min_num_qubits=5, simulator=False, operational=True)
backend = least_busy(device)
print("least busy backend: ", backend)

# Run our circuit on the least busy backend. Monitor the execution of the
job in the queue from qiskit.tools.monitor import job_monitor
shots = 100
transpiled_bv_circuit = transpile(qc, backend)
job = backend.run(transpiled_bv_circuit, shots=shots)
job_monitor(job, interval=2)

# Get the results from the computation
results = job.result()
counts = results.get_counts()
print("\nTotal count are:",counts)
plot_histogram(counts)
```

First we get the information about the name of the less busy devise and later the status information

```
least busy backend:   <IBMBackend('ibmq_lima')>
Job Status: job has successfully run
```

This can take some time, dependent on how many simulations all over the world are running. The output histogram is represented in Figure 3.23.

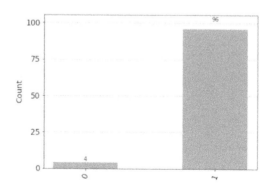

Figure 3.23 In the fourth step the first qubit (that is in the basis state) is measured. It is $|1\rangle$ with "probability" value 0.96 after 100 shots, the function is non-constant with high probability. Total count are: $\{'0' : 4, '1' : 96\}$. The measurements of $|0\rangle$ result from noise through decoherence.

## CHAPTER 4

Quantum Gates

Quantum gates are the building blocks of quantum circuits, like classical logic gates are for conventional digital circuits. Unlike classical logic gates, quantum logic gates are reversible and can be described by unitary matrices. First, we introduce Boolean quantum gates that allow us to map any Boolean circuit in such a way that the circuit becomes reversible. Such a circuit represents a permutation in Hilbert space and can be represented by a permutation matrix composed of the unitary matrices representing the quantum gates. Then we describe quantum gates for one qubit, like for example Clifford gates that are the elements of the Clifford group and can be efficiently simulated with a classical computer. Parameterized gates play an important role in quantum machine learning. A parameterized rotation gate is a parameterized gate with the parameter being the amount of rotation to be performed around the three axes. We introduce the controlled-U gates and introduce the unitary decomposition and formulate the process of transpilation. Translation is a complex problem of finding an optimal decomposition into the present quantum gates for a quantum computer.

4.1 BOOLEAN ALGEBRA AND THE QUANTUM GATES

The following quantum gates are Boolean quantum gates that allow us to map any Boolean circuit in such a way that the circuit becomes reversible. To make a circuit reversible, we must make each of the gates reversible. A necessary condition for a reversible gate is that of a bijective transition function with m inputs and m outputs. For each quantum Boolean AND, OR operation to be reversible an auxiliary qubit is required. The complexity of the circuit corresponds to the number of used quantum gates. A Boolean quantum circuit represents a permutation in Hilbert space and can be represented by a unitary permutation matrix composed of the unitary matrices representing the quantum gates. Such a mapping does not alter the distribution of the amplitudes; the distribution remains unchanged during the execution of the quantum Boolean gates. The probability of measuring certain states is the same before and after the computation.

DOI: 10.1201/9781003374404-4

4.1.1 Identity Gate – I

```
qc.id(qubit)
```

$$I|0\rangle \longrightarrow |0\rangle \qquad I|1\rangle \longrightarrow |1\rangle$$

The identity gate defines a quantum gate on one qubit and can be represented by a unitary matrix I in Hilbert space $\mathcal{H}_2$

$$I = \begin{pmatrix} 1 & 0 \\ 0 & 1 \end{pmatrix}.$$

The identity gate does not perform any operation and does not play any role in *qiskit*. In matrix notation, it indicates which qubits remain when composing a matrix using the tensor product that represents a quantum circuit.

4.1.2 NOT Gate, Pauli X Gate – X

```
qc.x(qubit)
```

$$X|0\rangle \longrightarrow |1\rangle \qquad X|1\rangle \longrightarrow |0\rangle$$

The not gate defines a quantum gate on one qubit and can be represented by a unitary matrix X in Hilbert space $\mathcal{H}_2$

$$X = \begin{pmatrix} 0 & 1 \\ 1 & 0 \end{pmatrix}.$$

The NOT gate is also called the Pauli X-gate.

4.1.3 Toffoli Gate – ccX

```
qc.ccx(control1,control2,target)
```

$$CCX|000\rangle \longrightarrow |000\rangle \qquad CCX|100\rangle \longrightarrow |100\rangle$$
$$CCX|001\rangle \longrightarrow |001\rangle \qquad CCX|101\rangle \longrightarrow |101\rangle$$
$$CCX|010\rangle \longrightarrow |010\rangle \qquad CCX|110\rangle \longrightarrow |111\rangle$$
$$CCX|011\rangle \longrightarrow |011\rangle \qquad CCX|111\rangle \longrightarrow |110\rangle$$

Toffoli Gate, ccX CCNOT gate, controlled controlled not gate also called ccX CCNOT gate – controlled controlled not gate, defines a quantum gate on three qubits and can be represented by a unitary matrix CCX in Hilbert space $\mathcal{H}_8$

$$CCX = \begin{pmatrix} 1 & 0 & 0 & 0 & 0 & 0 & 0 & 0 \\ 0 & 1 & 0 & 0 & 0 & 0 & 0 & 0 \\ 0 & 0 & 1 & 0 & 0 & 0 & 0 & 0 \\ 0 & 0 & 0 & 1 & 0 & 0 & 0 & 0 \\ 0 & 0 & 0 & 0 & 1 & 0 & 0 & 0 \\ 0 & 0 & 0 & 0 & 0 & 1 & 0 & 0 \\ 0 & 0 & 0 & 0 & 0 & 0 & 0 & 1 \\ 0 & 0 & 0 & 0 & 0 & 0 & 1 & 0 \end{pmatrix}.$$

The Toffoli gate does not change the first input qubits x_1 and x_2. The operation is described by the following mapping on three input qubits x_1, x_2, x_3

$$ccX(x_1, x_2, x_3) = (x_1, x_2, (x_1 \wedge x_2) \oplus x_3)$$

A Toffoli gate performs following operations.

- It computes the AND operation, the ancilla (fixed) bit x_3 is set to 0.

$$ccX(x_1, x_2, 0) = (x_1, x_2, x_1 \wedge x_2)$$

- It computes the XOR operation, the bit x_1 is set to 1.

$$ccX(1, x_2, x_3) = (1, x_2, x_2 \oplus x_3)$$

- It computes the NOT operation on x_3.

$$ccX(1, 1, x_3) = (1, 1, \neg x_3)$$

- It computes the $NAND$ operation, the ancilla (fixed) bit x_3 is set to 1.

$$ccX(x_1, x_2, 1) = (x_1, x_2, \neg(x_1 \wedge x_2))$$

- It computes the $FANOUT$ operation (the value of bit x_2 is copied into x_3).

$$ccX(1, x_2, 0) = (1, x_2, x_2)$$

The OR operation follows from the De Morgan's laws

$$x_1 \vee x_2 = \neg(\neg x_1 \wedge, \neg x_2).$$

Because $NAND$ and $FANOUT$ are together universal, we can implement any reversible Boolean quantum circuit using the Toffoli gate.

4.1.4 Controlled NOT Gate – cX

```
qc.cx(qubit1, qubit2)
```

$$CX|00\rangle = |00\rangle \qquad CX|01\rangle = |01\rangle,$$
$$CX|10\rangle = |11\rangle \qquad CX|11\rangle = |10\rangle.$$

The controlled not gate defines a quantum gate on two qubits and can be represented by a unitary matrix CX in Hilbert space $\mathcal{H}_4$

$$CX = \begin{pmatrix} 1 & 0 & 0 & 0 \\ 0 & 1 & 0 & 0 \\ 0 & 0 & 0 & 1 \\ 0 & 0 & 1 & 0 \end{pmatrix}.$$

A controlled not gate performs following operations.

- Controlled not operation. The second qubit is only flipped in the case that the first qubit is 1. In this case a not operation X on the second qubit is executed.

$$cX(1, x) = (1, \neg x_1)$$

$$cX(0, x) = (1, x_1)$$

- Fan-out operation. For this operation the second qubit has to be zero. In this case the value of the first qubit is copied into the second one.

$$cX(x_1, 0) = (x_1, x_1)$$

4.1.5 SWAP Gate – SWAP

```
qc.swap(qubit1, qubit2)
```

$$SWAP|00\rangle = |00\rangle \qquad SWAP|01\rangle = |10\rangle,$$
$$SWAP|10\rangle = |01\rangle \qquad SWAP|11\rangle = |11\rangle.$$

The SWAP gate defines a quantum gate two one qubits and can be represented by a unitary matrix $SWAP$ in Hilbert space $\mathcal{H}_4$

$$SWAP = \begin{pmatrix} 1 & 0 & 0 & 0 \\ 0 & 0 & 1 & 0 \\ 0 & 1 & 0 & 0 \\ 0 & 0 & 0 & 1 \end{pmatrix}.$$

The $SWAP$ gate swaps the two qubits

$$SWAP(x_1, x_2) = (x_2, x_1).$$

4.1.6 Controlled SWAP Gate – cS

```
qc.cswap(control,qubit_1,qubit_2)
```

$$CSWAP|000\rangle \longrightarrow |000\rangle \qquad CSWAP|100\rangle \longrightarrow |100\rangle$$

$$CSWAP|001\rangle \longrightarrow |001\rangle \qquad CSWAP|101\rangle \longrightarrow |110\rangle$$

$$CSWAP|010\rangle \longrightarrow |010\rangle \qquad CSWAP|110\rangle \longrightarrow |101\rangle$$

$$CSWAP|011\rangle \longrightarrow |011\rangle \qquad CSWAP|111\rangle \longrightarrow |110\rangle$$

The Controlled SWAP Gate or Fredkin gate, defines a quantum gate on three qubits and can be represented by a unitary matrix $CSWAP$ in Hilbert space $\mathcal{H}_8$

$$CSWAP = \begin{pmatrix} 1 & 0 & 0 & 0 & 0 & 0 & 0 & 0 \\ 0 & 1 & 0 & 0 & 0 & 0 & 0 & 0 \\ 0 & 0 & 1 & 0 & 0 & 0 & 0 & 0 \\ 0 & 0 & 0 & 1 & 0 & 0 & 0 & 0 \\ 0 & 0 & 0 & 0 & 1 & 0 & 0 & 0 \\ 0 & 0 & 0 & 0 & 0 & 1 & 1 & 0 \\ 0 & 0 & 0 & 0 & 0 & 1 & 0 & 0 \\ 0 & 0 & 0 & 0 & 0 & 0 & 0 & 1 \end{pmatrix}.$$

- If control qubit is zero no swap operation is performed

$$CSWAP(0, x_1, x_2) = (0, x_1, x_2)$$

- If control qubit is one swap operation on is performed

$$CSWAP(1, x_1, x_2) = (1, x_2, x_1).$$

4.2 GATES FOR ONE QUBIT

The corresponding quantum gates for one qubit alter the distribution of the amplitudes that are represented by complex numbers.

4.2.1 Clifford Gates for One Qubit

The Clifford gates are the elements of the Clifford group is generated by three gates, Hadamard, S, and $CNOT$ gates. It is a set of mathematical transformations which affect permutations of the three Pauli gates: X gate, Y gate, and the Z gate. Quantum circuits that consist of only Clifford gates can be efficiently simulated with a classical computer.

4.2.1.1 Hadamard Gate – **H**

`qc.h(qubit)`

$$H|0\rangle \longrightarrow \frac{1}{\sqrt{2}} \cdot |0\rangle + \frac{1}{\sqrt{2}} \cdot |1\rangle \qquad H|1\rangle \longrightarrow \frac{1}{\sqrt{2}} \cdot |0\rangle - \frac{1}{\sqrt{2}} \cdot |1\rangle$$

The Hadamard gate defines a quantum gate on one qubit and can be represented by a unitary matrix H in Hilbert space $\mathcal{H}_2$

$$H = \begin{pmatrix} \frac{1}{\sqrt{2}} & \frac{1}{\sqrt{2}} \\ \frac{1}{\sqrt{2}} & -\frac{1}{\sqrt{2}} \end{pmatrix}$$

The Hadamard gate is also called Hadamard-Walsh gate. If the system starts in state $|0\rangle$ and undergoes the time evolution, the probability of observing 0 or 1 is $\left|\frac{1}{\sqrt{2}}\right|^2 = \frac{1}{2}$. If we do not preform a measurement and repeat the mapping, the probability of observing 0 becomes 1 and observing 1 becomes zero. This is due to the fact, that the amplitudes of $|1\rangle$ cancel each other. This effect is called destructive interference.

4.2.2 Pauli Y Gate – **Y**

`qc.y(qubit)`

$$Y|0\rangle \longrightarrow i|1\rangle \qquad Y|1\rangle \longrightarrow i|0\rangle$$

The Pauli Y gate defines a quantum gate on one qubit and can be represented by a unitary matrix Y in Hilbert space $\mathcal{H}_2$

$$Y = \begin{pmatrix} 0 & -i \\ i & 0 \end{pmatrix}$$

4.2.3 Pauli Z Gate – **Z**

`qc.z(qubit)`

$$Z|0\rangle \longrightarrow |0\rangle \qquad Z|1\rangle \longrightarrow -|1\rangle$$

The Pauli Z gate defines a quantum gate on one qubit and can be represented by a unitary matrix Y in Hilbert space $\mathcal{H}_2$

$$Z = \begin{pmatrix} 1 & 0 \\ 0 & -1 \end{pmatrix}$$

4.2.4   S Gate – **S**

`qc.s(qubit)`

$$S|0\rangle \longrightarrow |0\rangle \qquad S|1\rangle \longrightarrow i|1\rangle$$

The S gate defines a quantum gate on one qubit and can be represented by a unitary matrix S in Hilbert space $\mathcal{H}_2$

$$S = \begin{pmatrix} 1 & 0 \\ 0 & i \end{pmatrix}$$

The S gate is also called the $Z90$ gate.

4.2.5   Sdag Gate – **S**†

`qc.sdg(qubit)`

$$S^\dagger|0\rangle \longrightarrow |0\rangle \qquad S^\dagger|1\rangle \longrightarrow -i|1\rangle$$

The $S^\dagger$ gate defines a quantum gate on one qubit and can be represented by a unitary matrix S in Hilbert space $\mathcal{H}_2$

$$S^\dagger = \begin{pmatrix} 1 & 0 \\ 0 & -i. \end{pmatrix}$$

Clifford gates together with the T gates are universal quantum gates since they can approximate any desired quantum gate with a small error.

4.3   ROTATION GATES

4.3.1   T Gate – **T**

`qc.t(qubit)`

The T gate corresponds to the parameterized RZ gate with $\theta = \pi/4$.

$$T|0\rangle \longrightarrow |0\rangle \qquad T|1\rangle \longrightarrow e^{i\frac{\pi}{4}} \cdot |1\rangle = \left(\frac{1}{\sqrt{2}} + \frac{i}{\sqrt{2}} \right) \cdot |1\rangle$$

The T gate defines a quantum gate on one qubit and can be represented by a unitary matrix T in Hilbert space $\mathcal{H}_2$

$$T = \begin{pmatrix} 1 & 0 \\ 0 & e^{i\frac{\pi}{4}} \end{pmatrix}$$

with T gate being the square root of the S gate

$$S = T^2$$

4.3.2   T† Gate – **T†**

```
qc.tdg(qubit)
```

The T gate corresponds to the RZ with $\theta = -\pi/4$.

$$T^\dagger|0\rangle \longrightarrow |0\rangle \qquad T^\dagger|1\rangle \longrightarrow e^{-i\frac{\pi}{4}} \cdot |1\rangle = \left(\frac{1}{\sqrt{2}} - \frac{i}{\sqrt{2}}\right) \cdot |1\rangle$$

The T gate defines a quantum gate on one qubit and can be represented by a unitary matrix T in Hilbert space $\mathcal{H}_2$

$$T^\dagger = \begin{pmatrix} 1 & 0 \\ 0 & e^{-i\frac{\pi}{4}} \end{pmatrix}$$

with $T^\dagger$ gate being the square root of the S gate

$$S = \left(T^\dagger\right)^2$$

4.4   PARAMETERIZED ROTATION GATES

Parameterized gates play an important role in quantum machine learning. A parameterized rotation gate is a parameterized gate with the parameter being the amount of rotation to be performed around the three axes.

4.4.1   RX Gate – **RX**

```
qc.rx(theta,qubit)
```

The RX gate performs a rotation of one qubit along the x-axis by the rotation angle θ. The rotation angle is in radiants.

With $\theta = \pi$

$$RX|0\rangle \longrightarrow -i|1\rangle \qquad RX|1\rangle \longrightarrow -i|0\rangle$$

With $\theta = \pi/2$

$$RX|0\rangle \longrightarrow \frac{1}{\sqrt{2}} \cdot |0\rangle - \frac{i}{\sqrt{2}} \cdot |1\rangle \qquad RX|1\rangle \longrightarrow -\frac{i}{\sqrt{2}} \cdot |0\rangle + \frac{1}{\sqrt{2}} \cdot |1\rangle$$

The RX gate defines a quantum gate on one qubit and can be represented by a unitary matrix RX in Hilbert space $\mathcal{H}_2$

$$R_X(\theta) = \begin{pmatrix} \cos\left(\frac{\theta}{2}\right) & -i\sin\left(\frac{\theta}{2}\right) \\ -i\sin\left(\frac{\theta}{2}\right) & \cos\left(\frac{\theta}{2}\right) \end{pmatrix}$$

4.4.2 RY Gate – **RY**

`qc.ry(theta,qubit)`

The RY gate performs a rotation of one qubit along the y-axis by the rotation angle θ. The rotation angle is in radiants.

With $\theta = \pi$

$$RY|0\rangle \longrightarrow |1\rangle \qquad RY|1\rangle \longrightarrow -|0\rangle$$

With $\theta = \pi/2$

$$RY|0\rangle \longrightarrow \frac{1}{\sqrt{2}} \cdot |0\rangle + \frac{1}{\sqrt{2}} \cdot |1\rangle \qquad RY|1\rangle \longrightarrow -\frac{1}{\sqrt{2}} \cdot |0\rangle + \frac{1}{\sqrt{2}} \cdot |1\rangle$$

The RY gate defines a quantum gate on one qubit and can be represented by a unitary matrix RX in Hilbert space $\mathcal{H}_2$

$$R_Y(\theta) = \begin{pmatrix} \cos\left(\frac{\theta}{2}\right) & -\sin\left(\frac{\theta}{2}\right) \\ \sin\left(\frac{\theta}{2}\right) & \cos\left(\frac{\theta}{2}\right) \end{pmatrix}$$

4.4.3 RZ Gate – **RZ**

`qc.rz(phi,qubit)`

The RZ gate performs a rotation of one qubit along the z-axis by the rotation angle ϕ. The rotation angle is in radiants.

With $\phi = \pi$

$$RZ|0\rangle \longrightarrow -i|0\rangle \qquad RZ|1\rangle \longrightarrow i|1\rangle$$

With $\phi = \pi/2$

$$RZ|0\rangle \longrightarrow \left(\frac{1}{\sqrt{2}} - \frac{i}{\sqrt{2}}\right) \cdot |0\rangle \qquad RZ|1\rangle \longrightarrow \left(\frac{1}{\sqrt{2}} + \frac{i}{\sqrt{2}}\right) \cdot |1\rangle$$

The RZ gate defines a quantum gate on one qubit and can be represented by a unitary matrix $R_Z(\phi)$ in Hilbert space $\mathcal{H}_2$

$$R_Z(\phi) = \begin{pmatrix} e^{-i\frac{\phi}{2}} & 0 \\ 0 & e^{i\frac{\phi}{2}} \end{pmatrix}$$

4.4.4 U Gate – **U**

U gate is a single-qubit rotation gate with 3 Euler angles.

`qc.u(theata, phi, lambda, qubit)`

The U gate performs a rotation of one qubit along the axes by the rotation angles θ, ϕ, and λ. The rotation angle is in radiants. It can be represented by a unitary matrix RZ in Hilbert space $\mathcal{H}_2$

$$U(\theta, \phi, \lambda) = \begin{pmatrix} \cos\left(\frac{\theta}{2}\right) & -e^{-i\cdot\lambda}\sin\left(\frac{\theta}{2}\right) \\ e^{i\cdot\phi}\sin\left(\frac{\theta}{2}\right) & e^{i\cdot(\phi+\lambda)}\cos\left(\frac{\theta}{2}\right) \end{pmatrix}$$

4.4.5 Phase Gate – P

qc.p(lambda)

the target and the control qubit can be exchanged since the phase is only applied if both values are one

$$P|0\rangle \longrightarrow |0\rangle \qquad P|1\rangle \longrightarrow e^{i\cdot\lambda} \cdot |\rangle$$

The phase gate defines a quantum gate on one qubit and can be represented by a unitary matrix H in Hilbert space $\mathcal{H}_2$

$$P(\lambda) = \begin{pmatrix} 1 & 0 \\ 0 & e^{i\cdot\lambda} \end{pmatrix}.$$

4.5 CONTROLLED U GATES

The controlled-U gates perform a controlled operation described by the a unitary matrix U

$$U = \begin{pmatrix} u_{00} & u_{01} \\ u_{10} & u_{11} \end{pmatrix}.$$

The cU gate defines a quantum gate on two qubits and can be represented by a unitary matrix CU in Hilbert space $\mathcal{H}_4$

$$CU = \begin{pmatrix} 1 & 0 & 0 & 0 \\ 0 & 1 & 0 & 0 \\ 0 & 0 & u_{00} & u_{01} \\ 0 & 0 & u_{10} & u_{11} \end{pmatrix}$$

The controlled-U gates perform the following operations

$$CU|00\rangle \longrightarrow |00\rangle \qquad CU|01\rangle \longrightarrow |01\rangle$$
$$CU|10\rangle \longrightarrow |1\rangle \otimes U|0\rangle \qquad CH|11\rangle \longrightarrow |1\rangle \otimes U|1\rangle$$

The matrix U can be one of three Pauli gates: X gate (resulting in the controlled NOT cX gate) , Y gate, and the Z gate or rotation gates with the syntax

```
qc.cx(control,target)
qc.cy(control,target)
qc.cz(control,target)
qc.crx(theta,control,target)
qc.cry(theta,control,target)
qc.crz(phi,control,target)
qc.cu(theata, phi, lambda,control,target)
```

4.5.1 Controlled Phase Gate

```
qc.cp(lambda, control, target)
```

the target and the control qubit can be exchanged since the phase is only applied if both values are one

$$CP(|00\rangle \longrightarrow |00\rangle \qquad CP|01\rangle \longrightarrow |01\rangle$$
$$CP|10\rangle \longrightarrow |10\rangle \qquad CP|11\rangle \longrightarrow e^{i\cdot\lambda}\cdot|11\rangle$$

The controlled phase gate defines a quantum gate on two qubits and can be represented by a unitary matrix H in Hilbert space $\mathcal{H}_4$

$$CP(\lambda) = \begin{pmatrix} 1 & 0 & 0 & 0 \\ 0 & 1 & 0 & 0 \\ 0 & 0 & 1 & 0 \\ 0 & 0 & 0 & e^{i\cdot\lambda} \end{pmatrix}$$

4.5.2 Controlled Hadamard Gate – **cH**

```
qc.ch(control,target)
```

$$CH|00\rangle \longrightarrow |00\rangle \qquad CH|01\rangle \longrightarrow |01\rangle$$
$$CH|10\rangle \longrightarrow \frac{1}{\sqrt{2}}\cdot|10\rangle + \frac{1}{\sqrt{2}}\cdot|11\rangle \qquad CH|11\rangle \longrightarrow \frac{1}{\sqrt{2}}\cdot|10\rangle - \frac{1}{\sqrt{2}}\cdot|11\rangle$$

The controlled Hadamard gate defines a quantum gate on two qubits and can be represented by a unitary matrix H in Hilbert space $\mathcal{H}_4$

$$CH = \begin{pmatrix} 1 & 0 & 0 & 0 \\ 0 & 1 & 0 & 0 \\ 0 & 0 & \frac{1}{\sqrt{2}} & \frac{1}{\sqrt{2}} \\ 0 & 0 & \frac{1}{\sqrt{2}} & -\frac{1}{\sqrt{2}} \end{pmatrix}$$

4.6 UNIVERSALITY

Unitary decomposition is the process of translating an arbitrary unitary operator into a universal set of single and two-qubit gates. Unitary decomposition is necessary because it is not otherwise possible to execute an arbitrary quantum operator. The Z-Y decomposition theorem [72] provides a way of expressing an unitary operation U on a single qubits by parametrized rotation gates

Z-Y Decomposition Theorem: If u is an unitary operation on single qubit, then there exist real numbers α, β, and γ such that

$$U = e^{i \cdot \alpha} R_Z(\beta) \cdot R_Y(\gamma) \cdot R_Z(\delta) \tag{4.1}$$

For example, in quantum machine learning a Hadamard-like transformation S_p is used to store the patterns.

$$S_p = \begin{pmatrix} \sqrt{\frac{p-1}{p}} & \frac{1}{\sqrt{p}} \\ \frac{-1}{\sqrt{p}} & \sqrt{\frac{p-1}{p}} \end{pmatrix} \tag{4.2}$$

and can be represented by the parametrized U gate with $\phi = \pi, \lambda = \pi$,

$$U(\theta, \pi, \pi) = \begin{pmatrix} \cos\left(\frac{\theta}{2}\right) & \sin\left(\frac{\theta}{2}\right) \\ -\sin\left(\frac{\theta}{2}\right) & \cos\left(\frac{\theta}{2}\right) \end{pmatrix}$$

With

$$\sin\left(\frac{\theta}{2}\right) = \frac{1}{\sqrt{p}}$$

$$\theta = \arcsin\left(\frac{1}{\sqrt{p}}\right) \cdot 2$$

$$\cos\left(\frac{\theta}{2}\right) = \sqrt{\frac{p-1}{\sqrt{p}}}$$

$$U\left(\arcsin\left(\frac{1}{\sqrt{p}}\right) \cdot 2, \pi, \pi\right) = \begin{pmatrix} \sqrt{\frac{p-1}{p}} & \frac{1}{\sqrt{p}} \\ \frac{-1}{\sqrt{p}} & \sqrt{\frac{p-1}{p}} \end{pmatrix}. \tag{4.3}$$

4.7 QUANTUM CIRCUITS

The depth of a quantum circuit indicates the quantum gates that can be executed in parallel to compute the entire circuit. The depth is related to the time to execute the circuit. The depth is indicated with the command *qc.size()*. Either we simulate a quantum circuit or execute it on a real quantum computer. The defined quantum circuit is converted to the target quantum computer for execution. This process is called **transpilation** contrary to the compilation task in classical programing languages. It is a translation problem determined by the available set of operations and the hardware topology. Finding an optimal decomposition of a quantum circuit into the present quantum gates is a complex problem. For example, almost all quantum gates that operate on n qubits require an exponential number of 2 qubits gates by a naive implementation [72]. The transpilation should minimize the circuit's depth and the number of used gates.

## CHAPTER 5

Grover's Amplification

We describe the Grover's amplification algorithm. We represent n state by a super-position, each state has the same real positive amplitude. A parallel computation is applied to all the n states, and the state with the solution is marked by a minus sign, the amplitude is now negative. We then apply a linear operation that is based on Householder reflection, by the reflection the value of the marked amplitude grows linearly. For dimensions higher than four, the operations of marking and Householder reflection must be repeated $\sqrt{n}$ times, since at each step the amplitude only grows linearly. After $\sqrt{n}$ steps we measure the solution. The algorithm guarantees us a quadratic speed up over a classical computer that would require n steps. Grover's amplification algorithm is optimal, one can prove that a better algorithm cannot exist. We will demonstrate the principles of Grover's amplification using the matrix notation using *NumPy*. Then we explain how to represent the algorithm with quantum gates by a *qiskit* example of three qubits representing eight states using one and two rotations.

5.1 SEARCH AND QUANTUM ORACLE

For a function $o(x)$

$$o_\xi(x) = \begin{cases} 1 & if \quad x = \xi \\ 0 & else \end{cases} \tag{5.1}$$

we want to find x for which $o(x) = 1$, $x = \xi$. The task is equivalent to a decision problem with a binary answer $1 = yes$ and $0 = no$ and the instance x. Grover's amplification algorithm implements exhaustive search in $O(\sqrt{n})$ steps in n-dimensional Hilbert space [35], [36], [37], [38], [35], [35]. Hilbert space extends the two- or three-dimensional Euclidean space into spaces that have any finite or infinite number of dimensions. Grover's amplification algorithm is as good as any possible quantum algorithm for exhaustive search due to the lower bound $\Omega(\sqrt{n})$ [2]. The algorithm is based on the Householder reflection of state $|x\rangle$ of m qubits with $n = 2^m$. Grover's amplification algorithm is optimal, one can prove that a better algorithm cannot exist [11], [14]. It follows that using a quantum computer $NP - complete$ problems remain $NP - complete$. The algorithm guarantees us a quadratic speed up over a classical computer that would require n steps.

DOI: 10.1201/9781003374404-5

5.1.1 Quantum Oracle

We represent n states by a superposition, each state has the same real positive amplitude. A parallel computation is applied to all the n states, and the state with the solution $o_\xi(x) = 1$ is marked by a minus sign, the amplitude is now negative. We then apply a linear operation that is based on Householder reflection, by the reflection the value of the marked amplitude grows linearly.

For the function $o(x)$, the solution is encoded by $(-1)^{o(x)}$, the sign of the amplitude. To see why the solution is encoded by $(-1)^{o(x)}$, we indicate the derivative. The unitary operator T represents the **quantum oracle function** $o(x)$ that determines if the configuration is the goal configuration

$$T \cdot |x\rangle|c\rangle = |x\rangle|o(x) \oplus c\rangle.$$

The auxiliary qubit c is set to one, and the state is represented by m qubits $|0^{\otimes m}\rangle$. First, we set qubits representing the states and the auxiliary qubit in superposition by the Hadamard gate for $m + 1$ qubits H_{m+1}, and then we execute the unitary operator T

$$T \cdot H_{m+1} \cdot |0^{\otimes m}\rangle|1\rangle =$$

$$= \frac{1}{\sqrt{2^{m+1}}} \cdot \sum_{x \in B^m} T \cdot |x\rangle|0\rangle - \frac{1}{\sqrt{2^{m+1}}} \cdot \sum_{x \in B^m} T \cdot |x\rangle|1\rangle$$

$$= \frac{1}{\sqrt{2^{m+1}}} \cdot \sum_{x \in B^m} |x\rangle|o(x) \oplus 0\rangle - \frac{1}{\sqrt{2^{m+1}}} \cdot \sum_{x \in B^m} |x\rangle|o(x) \oplus 1\rangle \qquad (5.2)$$

$$= \frac{1}{\sqrt{2^{m+1}}} \cdot \left(\sum_{x \in B^m} |x\rangle|o(x) \oplus 0\rangle - \sum_{x \in B^m} |x\rangle|o(x) \oplus 1\rangle \right).$$

There are four possible cases with the state $|\xi\rangle$ being the solution:

$$T \cdot |x\rangle|0\rangle = |x\rangle|o(x) \oplus 0\rangle = |x\rangle|0\rangle,$$

$$T \cdot |x\rangle|1\rangle = |x\rangle|o(x) \oplus 1\rangle = |x\rangle|1\rangle,$$

$$T \cdot |\xi\rangle|0\rangle = |\xi\rangle|f(\xi) \oplus 0\rangle = |\xi\rangle|1\rangle,$$

$$T \cdot |\xi\rangle|1\rangle = |\xi\rangle|f(\xi) \oplus 1\rangle = |\xi\rangle|0\rangle.$$

It follows that

$$= \frac{1}{\sqrt{2^{m+1}}} \cdot \left(\sum_{x \neq \xi} |x\rangle|0\rangle + |\xi\rangle|1\rangle - \sum_{x \neq \xi} |x\rangle|1\rangle - |\xi\rangle|0\rangle \right)$$

$$\frac{1}{\sqrt{2^{m+1}}} \cdot \left(\sum_{x \neq \xi} |x\rangle \left(|0\rangle - |1\rangle \right) + |\xi\rangle \left(|1\rangle - |0\rangle \right) \right) \qquad (5.3)$$

$$= \frac{1}{\sqrt{m}} \sum_{x \in B^m} (-1)^{o(x)} \cdot |x\rangle \otimes \left(\frac{|0\rangle - |1\rangle}{\sqrt{2}} \right).$$

The value of the function $o(x)$ is encoded by $(-1)^{o(x)}$, the operation is a phase kick-back. We can set the auxiliary qubit $c = \left(\frac{|0\rangle - |1\rangle}{\sqrt{2}} \right)$ to zero by the Hadamard gate.

5.2 HOUSEHOLDER REFLECTION

The Householder reflection reflects one vector $|x\rangle$ to its negative and leaves invariant the orthogonal complement of this vectors. It is described by the Householder matrix Q_x with $\||x\rangle\| = 1$ representing m qubits with $n = 2^m$ and the projection matrix P

$$P = |x\rangle\langle x|$$

and

$$Q_x = I_m - 2 \cdot P \tag{5.4}$$

Suppose P_m is generated by the normalized vector $|x\rangle$ indicating the direction of the bisecting line,

$$|x\rangle = \frac{1}{\sqrt{n}} \cdot |x_1\rangle + \frac{1}{\sqrt{n}} \cdot |x_2\rangle + \cdots + \frac{1}{\sqrt{n}} \cdot |x_n\rangle = \begin{pmatrix} \frac{1}{\sqrt{n}} \\ \vdots \\ \frac{1}{\sqrt{n}} \end{pmatrix} \tag{5.5}$$

then the projection matrix P_m is

$$P_m = |x\rangle\langle x| = \begin{pmatrix} \frac{1}{n} & \frac{1}{n} & \cdots & \frac{1}{n} \\ \frac{1}{n} & \frac{1}{n} & \cdots & \frac{1}{n} \\ \vdots & \vdots & \ddots & \vdots \\ \frac{1}{n} & \frac{1}{n} & \cdots & \frac{1}{n} \end{pmatrix} \tag{5.6}$$

The projection matrix P computes for each dimension the mean value

$$\begin{pmatrix} \frac{\sum_{i=1}^n x_i}{n} \\ \frac{\sum_{i=1}^n x_i}{n} \\ \vdots \\ \frac{\sum_{i=1}^n x_i}{n} \end{pmatrix} = \begin{pmatrix} \frac{1}{n} & \frac{1}{n} & \cdots & \frac{1}{n} \\ \frac{1}{n} & \frac{1}{n} & \cdots & \frac{1}{n} \\ \vdots & \vdots & \ddots & \vdots \\ \frac{1}{n} & \frac{1}{n} & \cdots & \frac{1}{n} \end{pmatrix} \cdot \begin{pmatrix} x_1 \\ x_2 \\ \vdots \\ x_n \end{pmatrix} \tag{5.7}$$

and the Householder reflection

$$Q_x = I_m - 2 \cdot P_m. \tag{5.8}$$

computes the following mapping,

$$x_i^{new} = x_i^{old} - 2 \cdot \frac{\sum_{i=1}^n x_i^{old}}{n}. \tag{5.9}$$

5.3 GROVER'S AMPLIFICATION

Grover's amplification is based on $-Q_x$. It is a unitary operator with

$$G_m := -Q_x = -I_m + 2 \cdot P_m = 2 \cdot P_m - I_m \tag{5.10}$$

the mapping is defined as,

$$x_i^{new} = 2 \cdot \frac{\sum_{i=1}^{n} x_i^{old}}{n} - x_i^{old}. \tag{5.11}$$

Suppose only one amplitude of x_j is negative and the other one are positive. Then the corresponding amplitude grows with

$$x_j^{new} = 2 \cdot \frac{\sum_{i=1}^{n} x_i^{old}}{n} + x_j^{old} \tag{5.12}$$

the other x_i with $i \neq j$ diminish. With $j = 2$ we get

$$\begin{pmatrix} 2 \cdot \frac{\sum_{i=1}^{n} x_i}{n} - x_1 \\ 2 \cdot \frac{\sum_{i=1}^{n} x_i}{n} + x_2 \\ \vdots \\ 2 \cdot \frac{\sum_{i=1}^{n} x_i}{n} - x_n \end{pmatrix} = \begin{pmatrix} \frac{2}{n} - 1 & \frac{2}{n} & \cdots & \frac{2}{n} \\ \frac{2}{n} & \frac{2}{n} - 1 & \cdots & \frac{2}{n} \\ \vdots & \vdots & \ddots & \vdots \\ \frac{2}{n} & \frac{2}{n} & \cdots & \frac{2}{n} - 1 \end{pmatrix} \cdot \begin{pmatrix} x_1 \\ -x_2 \\ \vdots \\ x_n \end{pmatrix}. \tag{5.13}$$

The probability of measuring the solution depending on the size n is

$$p(solution) = \left| \frac{3}{\sqrt{n}} - \frac{4}{n \cdot \sqrt{n}} \right|^2 \tag{5.14}$$

and non-solution

$$p(non - solution) = \left| \frac{1}{\sqrt{n}} - \frac{4}{n \cdot \sqrt{n}} \right|^2. \tag{5.15}$$

5.3.1 Number of Iteration

The probability of seeing one solution should be as close as possible to 1 and the number of iterations [121]. The number of iterations r is the largest integer not greater than t^*,

$$r = \lfloor t^* \rfloor = \left\lfloor \frac{\pi}{4} \cdot \sqrt{\frac{2^m}{k}} - \frac{1}{2} \right\rfloor. \tag{5.16}$$

The value of r depends on the relation of n versus k, with k being the number of solutions. For $n = 4$ and $k = 1$ we need only one rotation, we need as well only one rotation for

$$\frac{n}{4} = k$$

to find **one** of the k solutions. For 16 qubits and one solution, $k = 1$, $n = 65536 = 2^{16}$, with $t^* = 200.562$. In this case we need 201 rotations that corresponds to the complexity $O(\sqrt{n})$, means we get a quadratic speed up to a conventional computer.

When r is unknown (since we do not know k) we can repeatedly chose r randomly between 1 and $\frac{\pi}{4} \cdot \sqrt{2^m}$. This simple strategy leads to success in $O(\sqrt{n}) = O(\sqrt{2^m})$ [82].

A more advanced approach is based on the periodic property of the Grover's amplification (see Figure 5.1). The period is related to k and can be determined by quantum counting algorithm with the complexity $O(\sqrt{n})$. Quantum counting is based on phase estimation algorithm and will be described in chapter 20 about the phase estimation algorithm.

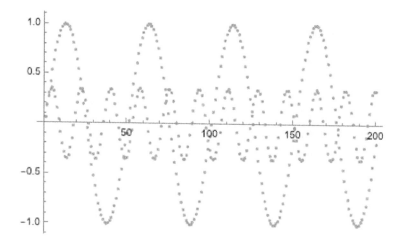

Figure 5.1 Periodic property of the Grover's amplification, y-axis indicates the amplitude of the solution and x-axis the number r of rotation. $m = 8$ representing 256 states. With $k = 1$ the maximal amplitude values is one, with $k = 8$ the maximal amplitude values is $0.3535 = \sqrt{\frac{1}{8}}$, also with a smaller period [121].

5.3.2 Circuit Representation

Grover's amplification (for $m \geq 2$) is based on $G_m = -Q_x$. The unitary operator Λ_m reverses the sign of $|0\rangle$

$$\Lambda_m \cdot |0\rangle = -|0\rangle$$

and for $|x\rangle \neq |0\rangle$

$$\Lambda_m \cdot |x\rangle = |x\rangle.$$

Then we can write

$$G_m = -Q_x = -I_m + 2 \cdot P_m = 2 \cdot P_m - I_m = -(H_m \cdot \Lambda_m \cdot H_m) \tag{5.17}$$

with

$$H_m \cdot \Lambda_m \cdot H_m = \begin{pmatrix} 1 - \frac{2}{n} & -\frac{2}{n} & \cdots & -\frac{2}{n} \\ -\frac{2}{n} & 1 - \frac{2}{n} & \cdots & -\frac{2}{n} \\ \vdots & \vdots & \ddots & \vdots \\ -\frac{2}{n} & -\frac{2}{n} & \cdots & 1 - \frac{2}{n} \end{pmatrix}. \tag{5.18}$$

5.4 NUMPY EXAMPLE WITH MATRIX NOTATION

We will demonstrate the principles of Grover's amplification using the matrix notation before explaining how to represent the algorithm with quantum gates. We will use *Python* and the *NumPy* library that is a part of the *qiskit* installation. We will demonstrate the example of $m = 3$, means $8 = 2^3$ different states. First we will built H_3 matrix by (tensor) Kronecker product operation *kron* of H matrix.

```
import numpy as np
np.set_printoptions(precision=4)
```

```
H=np.matrix([[1, 1], [1, -1]])
H=H*1/np.sqrt(2)
np.matrix.view(H)
print("H=\n",H)
```

Results in the Hadarmard matrix

```
H=
 [[ 0.7071  0.7071]
 [ 0.7071 -0.7071]]
```

and using the Kronecker product operation define H_3

```
H2=np.kron(H,H)
H3=np.kron(H,H2)
print("H3=\n",H3)
```

```
H3=
 [[ 0.3536  0.3536  0.3536  0.3536  0.3536  0.3536  0.3536  0.3536]
 [ 0.3536 -0.3536  0.3536 -0.3536  0.3536 -0.3536  0.3536 -0.3536]
 [ 0.3536  0.3536 -0.3536 -0.3536  0.3536  0.3536 -0.3536 -0.3536]
 [ 0.3536 -0.3536 -0.3536  0.3536  0.3536 -0.3536 -0.3536  0.3536]
 [ 0.3536  0.3536  0.3536  0.3536 -0.3536 -0.3536 -0.3536 -0.3536]
 [ 0.3536 -0.3536  0.3536 -0.3536 -0.3536  0.3536 -0.3536  0.3536]
 [ 0.3536  0.3536 -0.3536 -0.3536 -0.3536 -0.3536  0.3536  0.3536]
 [ 0.3536 -0.3536 -0.3536  0.3536 -0.3536  0.3536  0.3536 -0.3536]]
```

Then we define Λ_m

```
L3=np.matrix([[-1., 0., 0., 0., 0., 0., 0., 0.],
              [0., 1., 0., 0., 0., 0., 0., 0.],
              [0., 0., 1., 0., 0., 0., 0., 0.],
              [0., 0., 0., 1., 0., 0., 0., 0.],
              [0., 0., 0., 0., 1., 0., 0., 0.],
              [0., 0., 0., 0., 0., 1., 0., 0.],
              [0., 0., 0., 0., 0., 0., 1., 0.],
              [0., 0., 0., 0., 0., 0., 0., 1.]])
```

and

```
G=-H3*L3*H3
print("G3=\n",G)
G3=
 [[-0.75  0.25  0.25  0.25  0.25  0.25  0.25  0.25]
 [ 0.25 -0.75  0.25  0.25  0.25  0.25  0.25  0.25]
 [ 0.25  0.25 -0.75  0.25  0.25  0.25  0.25  0.25]
 [ 0.25  0.25  0.25 -0.75  0.25  0.25  0.25  0.25]
 [ 0.25  0.25  0.25  0.25 -0.75  0.25  0.25  0.25]
 [ 0.25  0.25  0.25  0.25  0.25 -0.75  0.25  0.25]
 [ 0.25  0.25  0.25  0.25  0.25  0.25 -0.75  0.25]
 [ 0.25  0.25  0.25  0.25  0.25  0.25  0.25 -0.75]]
```

In the next step we represent the state vector with equally distributed amplitudes and mark the solution with a minus sign

```
a=1/np.sqrt(8)
x1=np.array([a,a,a,a,-a,a,a,a])
print("x1=\n",x1)
x1=
 [ 0.3536  0.3536  0.3536  0.3536 -0.3536  0.3536  0.3536  0.3536]
```

and perform a step in Grover's amplification as with the resulting amplitudes

```
x1=G.dot(x1)
print("x1=\n",x1)
x1=
 [[0.1768 0.1768 0.1768 0.1768 0.8839 0.1768 0.1768 0.1768]]
```

and the second iteration with the resulting amplitudes

```
x2=np.array([0.1768, 0.1768, 0.1768, 0.1768, -0.8839, 0.1768, 0.1768, 0.1768])
x2=G.dot(x2)
print("x2=\n",x2)
x2=
 [[-0.0884 -0.0884 -0.0884 -0.0884  0.9723 -0.0884 -0.0884 -0.0884]].
```

With two rotations we achieved the maximal amplitude value that corresponds to the probability value $0.945367 = |0.9723|^2$. After the third rotation the amplitudes diminish because of the periodic property of Grover's amplification (see Figure 5.1).

5.5 DECOMPOSITION

With the Grove's amplification we have

$$G_m = -(H_m \cdot \Lambda_m \cdot H_m).$$

How can we decompose Λ_m by quantum gates? We note that for one qubit with

$$\frac{1}{\sqrt{2}} \begin{pmatrix} 1 & 1 \\ 1 & -1 \end{pmatrix} \cdot \frac{1}{\sqrt{2}} \begin{pmatrix} 1 & -1 \\ 1 & 1 \end{pmatrix} = \begin{pmatrix} 1 & 0 \\ 0 & -1 \end{pmatrix}.$$

and

$$\begin{pmatrix} 0 & 1 \\ 1 & 0 \end{pmatrix} \cdot \frac{1}{\sqrt{2}} \begin{pmatrix} 1 & 1 \\ 1 & -1 \end{pmatrix} \cdot \frac{1}{\sqrt{2}} \begin{pmatrix} 1 & -1 \\ 1 & 1 \end{pmatrix} \cdot \begin{pmatrix} 0 & 1 \\ 1 & 0 \end{pmatrix} = \begin{pmatrix} -1 & 0 \\ 0 & 1 \end{pmatrix}.$$

For three qubits we can define Λ_3 accordingly with

$$X_3 = X \otimes X \otimes X$$

$$H_0 = I \otimes I \otimes H$$

$$\Lambda_3 = X_3 \cdot H_0 \cdot CCX \cdot H_0 \cdot X_3$$

and for the minus sign operation

$$RZ(2 \cdot \pi)_3 = RZ(2 \cdot \pi) \otimes RZ(2 \cdot \pi) \otimes RZ(2 \cdot \pi)$$

it follows

$$G_m = -(H_3 \cdot \Lambda_3 \cdot H_3) = H_3 \cdot \Lambda_3 \cdot H_3 \cdot RZ(2 \cdot \pi)_3$$

and we can represent it by the following circuit

```python
from qiskit import QuantumCircuit, Aer,execute
from qiskit.visualization import plot_histogram
import numpy as np
from math import pi

qc = QuantumCircuit(3)

#Difusor
qc.h([0,1,2])
qc.x([0,1,2])
qc.h(0)
qc.ccx(1,2,0)
qc.h(0)
qc.x([0,1,2])
qc.h([0,1,2])

#Multiply with (-1)
qc.rz(2*pi,0)
qc.rz(2*pi,1)
qc.rz(2*pi,2)

from qiskit.visualization import array_to_latex
from qiskit import assemble

simulator = Aer.get_backend('qasm_simulator')
qc.save_unitary()
qobj = assemble(qc)
unitary = simulator.run(qobj).result().get_unitary()
print("\nSize of the unitary matrix:",np.asarray(unitary).shape)
array_to_latex(unitary, prefix="\\text{G3 = }\n")
```

resulting in the matrix G_3

$$G3 = \begin{pmatrix}
-\frac{3}{4} & \frac{1}{4} & \frac{1}{4} & \frac{1}{4} & \frac{1}{4} & \frac{1}{4} & \frac{1}{4} & \frac{1}{4} \\
\frac{1}{4} & -\frac{3}{4} & \frac{1}{4} & \frac{1}{4} & \frac{1}{4} & \frac{1}{4} & \frac{1}{4} & \frac{1}{4} \\
\frac{1}{4} & \frac{1}{4} & -\frac{3}{4} & \frac{1}{4} & \frac{1}{4} & \frac{1}{4} & \frac{1}{4} & \frac{1}{4} \\
\frac{1}{4} & \frac{1}{4} & \frac{1}{4} & -\frac{3}{4} & \frac{1}{4} & \frac{1}{4} & \frac{1}{4} & \frac{1}{4} \\
\frac{1}{4} & \frac{1}{4} & \frac{1}{4} & \frac{1}{4} & -\frac{3}{4} & \frac{1}{4} & \frac{1}{4} & \frac{1}{4} \\
\frac{1}{4} & \frac{1}{4} & \frac{1}{4} & \frac{1}{4} & \frac{1}{4} & -\frac{3}{4} & \frac{1}{4} & \frac{1}{4} \\
\frac{1}{4} & \frac{1}{4} & \frac{1}{4} & \frac{1}{4} & \frac{1}{4} & \frac{1}{4} & -\frac{3}{4} & \frac{1}{4} \\
\frac{1}{4} & \frac{1}{4} & \frac{1}{4} & \frac{1}{4} & \frac{1}{4} & \frac{1}{4} & \frac{1}{4} & -\frac{3}{4}
\end{pmatrix}$$

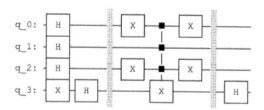

Figure 5.2 Quantum oracle indicating marking the state $|010\rangle$ by writing a one in the qubit 3.

5.6 QISKIT EXAMPLES

In the next step we apply Grover's amplification to a marked state of three qubits. Our solution corresponds to the Boolean formula

$$\neg x \wedge y \wedge \neg z$$

for which it evaluates true, which is the case for $x = 0$, $y = 1$, and $z = 0$. In this case the state determined by the oracle function is $o(010) = 1$ with the solution encoded by $(-1)^{o(x)}$. The unitary operator T

$$T = (X \otimes I \otimes X \otimes I) \cdot MCX \cdot (X \otimes I \otimes X \otimes I)$$

represents the oracle function $o(x)$ that determines if the configuration is the goal configuration

$$T \cdot |x\rangle|c\rangle = |x\rangle|o(x) \oplus c\rangle.$$

with

$$H_0 = I \otimes I \otimes I \otimes H$$

and

$$H_0 \cdot T \cdot H_4 \cdot |0001\rangle = \frac{1}{\sqrt{8}} \sum_{x \in B^3} (-1)^{o(x)} \cdot |x\rangle \otimes |0\rangle$$

the value of the function $o(x)$ is encoded by $(-1)^{o(x)}$, see as well Figure 5.2.

```
import numpy as np
from qiskit import QuantumCircuit, Aer
from qiskit.quantum_info import Statevector
from qiskit.circuit.library import MCXGate
from math import pi

qc = QuantumCircuit(4)
qc.h([0,1,2])
qc.x(3)
qc.h(3)
qc.barrier()
qc.x(0)
qc.x(2)
```

```
gate = MCXGate(3)
qc.append(gate, [0, 1, 2, 3])
qc.x(0)
qc.x(2)
qc.barrier()
qc.h(3)

qc.draw()
```

and we indicate the state vector

```
simulator = Aer.get_backend('statevector_simulator')
final_state = simulator.run(qc).result().get_statevector()

from qiskit.visualization import array_to_latex
array_to_latex(final_state,max_size=16,prefix="\\text{Statevector} = ")
```

$$Statevector = \begin{bmatrix} 0\ 0\ 0\ 0\ 0\ 0\ 0\ 0\ 0\ 0 & \frac{1}{\sqrt{8}} & \frac{1}{\sqrt{8}} & -\frac{1}{\sqrt{8}} & \frac{1}{\sqrt{8}} & \frac{1}{\sqrt{8}} & \frac{1}{\sqrt{8}} & \frac{1}{\sqrt{8}} & \frac{1}{\sqrt{8}} \end{bmatrix}$$

indicating marking the state $|010\rangle$ by a minus sign and perform the Grover's amplification (see Figure 5.3)

```
qc = QuantumCircuit(4)
qc.h([0,1,2])
#Preparation of Aux
qc.x(3)
qc.h(3)
#Oracle
qc.barrier()
qc.x(0)
qc.x(2)
gate = MCXGate(3)
qc.append(gate, [0, 1, 2, 3])
qc.x(0)
qc.x(2)
#Diffusor
qc.barrier()
qc.h(3)
qc.barrier()
qc.h([0,1,2])
qc.x([0,1,2])
qc.h(0)
qc.ccx(1,2,0)
qc.h(0)
qc.barrier()
qc.x([0,1,2])
qc.h([0,1,2])
#Corrrect the sign, not required...
qc.rz(2*pi,0)
qc.rz(2*pi,1)
qc.rz(2*pi,2)
```

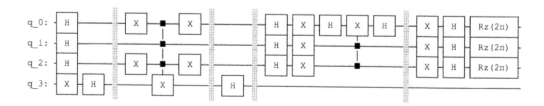

Figure 5.3 Quantum oracle indicating marking the state $|010\rangle$ by a minus sign and the Grover's amplification.

```
qc.draw(fold=140)
```

```
simulator = Aer.get_backend('statevector_simulator')
final_state = simulator.run(qc).result().get_statevector()

from qiskit.visualization import array_to_latex
array_to_latex(final_state,max_size=16,prefix="\\text{Statevector} = ")
```

$Statevector = [0\ 0\ 0\ 0\ 0\ 0\ 0\ 0\ 0\ 0\ 0.1768\ 0.1768\ 0.8839\ 0.1768\ 0.1768\ 0.1768\ 0.1768\ 0.1$

In the next step we will perform two rotations using *qasm simulator*. We do not minus sign operation

$$G_3 = -H_3 \cdot \Lambda_3 \cdot H_3$$

to get the correct result, what changes is the minus sign of over all amplitudes. This has no consequence for the resulting probabilities, so the Grover's amplification can be simplified to (see Figures 5.4 and 5.5)

$$G_3 = H_3 \cdot \Lambda_3 \cdot H_3$$

```
import numpy as np
from qiskit import QuantumCircuit, Aer, execute
from qiskit.visualization import plot_histogram
from qiskit.circuit.library import MCXGate

qc = QuantumCircuit(4,3)
qc.h([0,1,2])
#Preparation of Aux
qc.x(3)
qc.h(3)
#Oracle
qc.barrier()
qc.x(0)
qc.x(2)
gate = MCXGate(3)
qc.append(gate, [0, 1, 2, 3])
qc.x(0)
qc.x(2)
```

```
#Diffusor
qc.barrier()
qc.h(3)
qc.barrier()
qc.h([0,1,2])
qc.x([0,1,2])
qc.h(0)
qc.ccx(1,2,0)
qc.h(0)
qc.x([0,1,2])
qc.h([0,1,2])
qc.barrier()
qc.h(3)
#Oracle
qc.barrier()
qc.x(0)
qc.x(2)
gate = MCXGate(3)
qc.append(gate, [0, 1, 2, 3])
qc.x(0)
qc.x(2)
qc.barrier()
qc.h(3)

#Diffusor

qc.barrier()
qc.h([0,1,2])
qc.x([0,1,2])
qc.h(0)
qc.ccx(1,2,0)
qc.h(0)
qc.x([0,1,2])
qc.h([0,1,2])

qc.barrier()
qc.measure(0,0)
qc.measure(1,1)
qc.measure(2,2)

qc.draw(fold=90)
```

5.7   UN-COMPUTATION

In quantum computation, it is not possible to reset the information to the pattern representing the initial state. Instead, we un-compute the output back to the input. In our oracle

$$T = (X \otimes I \otimes X \otimes I) \cdot MCX \cdot (X \otimes I \otimes X \otimes I)$$

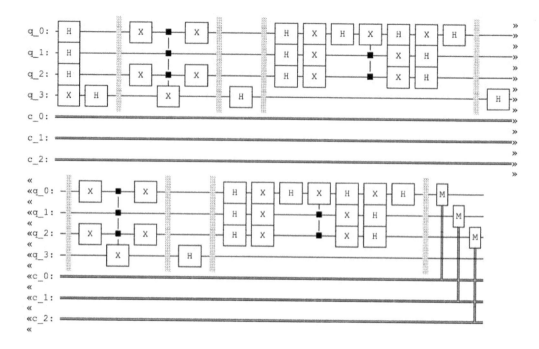

Figure 5.4 Quantum oracle indicating marking the state $|010\rangle$ by a minus sign and two Grover's amplification.

the un-computation is represented by the operations $(X \otimes I \otimes X \otimes I)$. We may ask what would happen if we do not un-compute and define our oracle simply as

$$T = MCX \cdot (X \otimes I \otimes X \otimes I).$$

```
import numpy as np
```

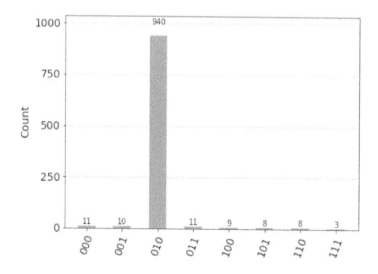

Figure 5.5 Histogram of Counts after two rotations of Grover's amplification.

```
from qiskit import QuantumCircuit, Aer
from qiskit.quantum_info import Statevector
from qiskit.circuit.library import MCXGate
from math import pi

qc = QuantumCircuit(4)
qc.h([0,1,2])
qc.x(3)
qc.h(3)
qc.barrier()
qc.x(0)
qc.x(2)
gate = MCXGate(3)
qc.append(gate, [0, 1, 2, 3])
#No un-computation
#qc.x(0)
#qc.x(2)
qc.barrier()
qc.h(3)
```

In this case the other remaining qubits become entangled and we cannot apply Grover's amplification correctly to the three qubits 0, 1, and 2. The resulting histogram of cost does not indicate the correct solution, see Figure 5.6. We have to un-compute the information to the pattern representing the initial state before applying the Grover's algorithm.

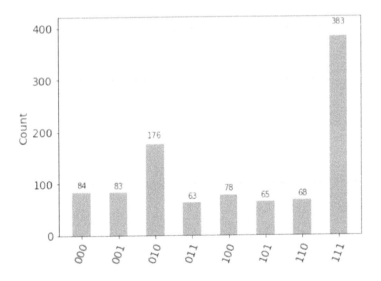

Figure 5.6 Histogram of Counts after two rotations of Grover's amplification without the un-computation of the oracle. The resulting histogram of cost does not indicate the correct solution.

5.8 GENERALIZATION OF Λ_M FOR M QUBITS

For m qubits we can define Λ_m accordingly using the MCX gate

```
gate = MCXGate(m)
qc.append(gate, [0, 1, 2,...., m, m+1])
```

with

$$X_m = \underbrace{X \otimes X \otimes \cdots \otimes X}_{M \text{ times}}$$

$$H_0^m = \underbrace{I \otimes I \otimes \cdots \otimes I}_{M-1 \text{ times}} \otimes H$$

$$\Lambda_m = X_m \cdot H_0^m \cdot MCX \cdot H_0^m \cdot X_m$$

Alternatively Λ_m can be implemented efficiently with $f_0(x)$

$$f_0(x) = \begin{cases} 1 & if \quad x = 0 \\ 0 & else \end{cases} \tag{5.19}$$

as

$$\frac{1}{\sqrt{m}} \sum_{x \in B^m} (-1)^{f_0(x)} \cdot |x\rangle \otimes \left(\frac{|0\rangle - |1\rangle}{\sqrt{2}} \right). \tag{5.20}$$

## CHAPTER 6

SAT Problem

The Boolean satisfiability problem (SAT problem) is the problem of determining if there exists an interpretation that satisfies a given Boolean formula, whether the formula evaluates true [22]. Each variable of the formula can have the values true (one) or false (zero). We formulate the formula satisfiability problem and indicate an example step by step. Then we discuss the relation between the SAT problem and the time complexity. Computational complexity theory addresses questions regarding which problems can be solved in a finite amount of time on a computer. A decision problem is a computational problem with instances formulated as a question with a binary answer. An example is the question of whether a certain number n is a prime number. Most problems can be converted into a decision problem. The time complexity describes the amount of computer time it takes to run an algorithm. Time complexity is commonly estimated by counting the number of elementary operations performed by the algorithm. The amount of time taken is linearly related to the number of elementary operations performed by the algorithm. A problem is easy if an algorithm on a computer can determine the instances related to the input for the answer in polynomial time. Polynomial-time algorithms are said to be fast since they can be executed in an acceptable time on a computer. Otherwise, we state that the problem is hard, means the time required grows exponentially and cannot be executed in an acceptable time on a computer. We describe a simple SAT problem with a Boolean formula with three Boolean variables and indicate it step by step using *qiskit* framework how to solve the problem using Grover's amplification algorithm by a quantum circuit.

6.1 FORMULA SATISFIABILITY

The formula satisfiability problem is as follows, is a formula ϕ composed of

- m Boolean variables: $x_1, x_2, \cdots, x_m$;

- k Boolean connectivities: $\wedge$ (AND), $\vee$ OR $\neg$ (NOT), $\rightarrow$ (implication), $\leftrightarrow$ (if and only if);

- parentheses.

DOI: 10.1201/9781003374404-6

Table 6.1 Truth table for implication ($\rightarrow$).

x	y	$x \rightarrow y$	$\neg x \vee y$
1	1	1	1
1	0	0	0
0	1	1	1
0	0	1	1

with the operation *implication* indicated in the Table 6.1 and the operation *if and only if* indicated in the Table 6.2. For example, the formula [22]

$$\phi = ((x_1 \rightarrow x_2) \vee \neg((\neg x_1 \leftrightarrow x_3) \vee x_4)) \wedge \neg x_2$$

has the interpretation $x_1 = 0$, $x_2 = 0$, $x_3 = 1$, and $x_4 = 1$ that satisfies ϕ with

$$\phi = ((0 \rightarrow 0) \vee \neg((\neg 0 \leftrightarrow 1) \vee 1)) \wedge \neg 0$$

$$\phi = (1 \vee \neg(1 \vee 1)) \wedge 1$$

$$\phi = 1$$

There are 2^m possible assignments in a formula ϕ with m variables, the checking every assignment requires 2^m time on a conventional computer.

6.2 SAT PROBLEM AND NP COMPLETE

A decision problem, like the SAT-problem, is a computational problem with instances formulated as a question with a binary "Yes" or "No" answer [22]. The time complexity describes the amount of conventional computer time it takes to run an algorithm. Time complexity is commonly estimated by counting the number of elementary operations performed by the algorithm. The amount of time taken is linearly related to the number of elementary operations performed by the algorithm. A problem is easy if a conventional computer can determine the instances related to the input for the answer "Yes" in polynomial time. Polynomial-time algorithms are said to be fast since they can be executed in an acceptable time on a conventional computer and are called P.

Otherwise, we state that the problem is hard, means the time required grows exponentially and cannot be executed in an acceptable time on a conventional computer, such a problem is called NP. For such a problem, a conventional computer

Table 6.2 Truth table for if and only if ($\leftrightarrow$).

x	y	$x \leftrightarrow y$	$\neg(x\ XOR\ y)$
1	1	1	1
1	0	0	0
0	1	0	0
0	0	1	1

can verify in polynomial time if one instance of many represents a solution, but no algorithm on a conventional computer exists that determines the solution efficiently in time. A problem is called $NP-complete$ if all possible instances must be examined by the conventional computer. A conventional computer can only solve a problem by checking all possible instances one after the other one. No other algorithm exists, so we cannot speed up the computation. It was not obvious that an $NP-complete$ problem exists. Cook-Levin described the first example of an $NP-complete$ problem, the SAT problem. Until recently, thousands of other problems are known to be $NP-complete$, including the well-known traveling salesman and Hamiltonian cycle problem [23]. Clearly, the class $P \subseteq NP$ is known, and it follows that $NP \neq P$ or $NP = P$; however, other relationships are not known. The class $NP-complete$ is present if the problem is in NP and every other problem in NP can be reduced to the class $NP-complete$.

Despite the fact the saving of Grover's algorithm of $= O(\sqrt{n}) = O(2^{\frac{m}{2}})$ compared to $O(n) = O(2^m)$ is huge, $NP-complete$ problems remain $NP-complete$ on a quantum computer.

6.3   SAT PROBLEM AND GROVER'S ALGORITHM

In the next step we apply Grover's amplification to a marked state of three qubits. Our solution corresponds to the Boolean formula

$$\phi = (x_1 \leftrightarrow x_2) \wedge (x_1 \wedge x_2) \wedge \neg x_3$$

that evaluates true, which is the case for $x_1 = 1$, $x_2 = 1$, and $x_3 = 0$. In this case, the state determined by the oracle function with the solution encoded by $(-1)^{o(x)}$.

6.3.1   Quantum Boolean Circuit

We define the oracle function using the quantum gates and six qubits using the Toffoli gates and NOT gates and six qubits.

The operation $(x_1 \wedge x_2)$ is represented by the AND operation, the ancilla qubit 2 is set to 0, x_1 is represented by qubit 0, and x_2 by qubit 1

$$ccX(x_0, x_1, 0) = (x_0, x_2, x_1 \wedge x_2)$$

```
qc.ccx(0,1,2)
```

and the result of the operation is represented in the qubit 2.
The operation $(x_1 \leftrightarrow x_2)$ is represented by the XOR and NOT operation, x_1 is set to 1 corresponding to the qubit 3. The XOR operation is executed

$$ccX(1, x_2, x_3) = (1, x_2, x_2 \oplus x_3)$$

the result of the XOR operation is written in qubit 1, then the NOT operation is performed

$$X(x_2 \oplus x_3) = \neg(x_2 \oplus x_3)$$

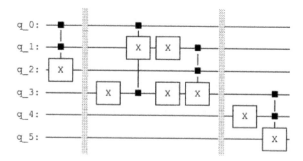

Figure 6.1 The circuit representing the Boolean formula $\phi = (x_1 \leftrightarrow x_2) \wedge (x_1 \wedge x_2) \wedge \neg x_3$. The input are the qubits 0, 1, and 4 and the output is represented in the qubit 5.

```
qc.x(3)
qc.ccx(3,0,1)
qc.x(1)
```

and the result of the operation is represented in the qubit 1. We execute the AND operation of the result represented in the qubit 1 and 2 and write the result in qubit 3. We reset the qubit 3 to zero

```
qc.x(3)
qc.ccx(1,2,3)
```

and write result of the operation in the qubit 3, which corresponds to the Boolean formula $(x_1 \leftrightarrow x_2) \wedge (x_1 \wedge x_2)$. The remaining part of the formula is represented by NOT and AND operation of $\neg x_3$ represented by qubit 4

```
qc.x(4)
qc.ccx(3,4,5)
```

and write result of the operation in the qubit 5, resulting in the circuit indicated in the Figure 6.1

6.3.2 Un-Computation

In quantum computation, it is not possible to reset the information to the pattern representing the initial state. Instead, we un-compute the output back to the input as indicated in the following listing:

```
from qiskit import QuantumCircuit,QuantumRegister, Aer,execute
from qiskit.visualization import plot_histogram
from qiskit.circuit.library import MCXGate
from qiskit.quantum_info import Statevector

qc = QuantumCircuit(6)
#Input 0,1,4
qc.h(0)
qc.h(1)
qc.h(4)
qc.barrier()
```

```
#First And 2 is zero
qc.ccx(0,1,2)
qc.barrier()
#Result in 2

#If AND IF
qc.x(3)
qc.ccx(3,0,1)
qc.x(1)
#Result in 1

#Make 3 zero
qc.x(3)
qc.ccx(1,2,3)
qc.barrier()
#Result in 3

#Input 4
qc.x(4)
qc.ccx(3,4,5)

#Un-compute
qc.barrier()
qc.barrier()
qc.x(4)
qc.barrier()
qc.ccx(1,2,3)
qc.x(3)
qc.barrier()
qc.x(1)
qc.ccx(3,0,1)
qc.x(3)
qc.barrier()
qc.ccx(0,1,2)

qc.draw(fold=120)


simulator = Aer.get_backend('qasm_simulator')
result=execute(qc,simulator,shots=1000).result()
counts = result.get_counts()
print("\nTotal count are:",counts)

plot_histogram(counts)
```

The circuit is represented in the Figure 6.2 and the resulting histogram in the Figure 6.3. The qubit 5 indicates a solution.

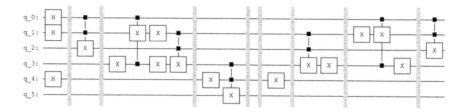

Figure 6.2 The circuit representing the Boolean formula $\phi = (x_1 \leftrightarrow x_2) \wedge (x_1 \wedge x_2) \wedge \neg x_3$. In quantum computation, it is not possible to reset the information to the pattern representing the initial state. Instead, we un-compute the output back to the input. The input are the qubits 0, 1, and 4 mapped in superposition by Hadamard gates. The output is represented in the qubit 5 indicating by the value 1 the presence of the solution. The solution itself is indicated in the qubits 0, 1, and 4.

6.3.3 Grover's Amplification

In the next step we apply the Grover's algorithm with two rotations, see Figures 6.4 and 6.5. The listing of the definition of the circuit:

```
qc = QuantumCircuit(6,3)
```

```
#Input 0,1,4
qc.h(0)
qc.h(1)
qc.h(4)
```

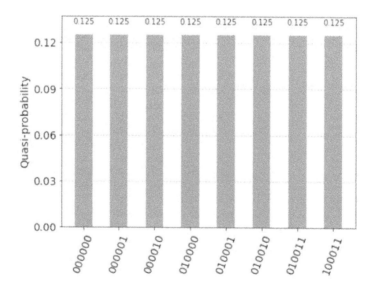

Figure 6.3 The circuit representing the Boolean formula $\phi = (x_1 \leftrightarrow x_2) \wedge (x_1 \wedge x_2) \wedge \neg x_3$. The output is represented in the qubit q_5 indicating by the value 1 the presence of the solution. The solution is indicated in the qubits $q_0 = 1$, $q_1 = 1$, and $q_4 = 0$ by the right column representing the state $|q_5 q_4 q_3 q_2 q_1 q_0\rangle = |100011\rangle$.

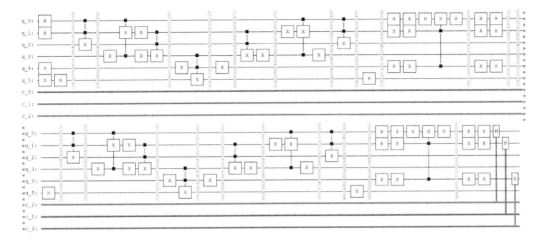

Figure 6.4 The circuit representing the Boolean formula $\phi = (x_1 \leftrightarrow x_2) \wedge (x_1 \wedge x_2) \wedge \neg x_3$ and two rotations of Grover's algorithm. The input are the qubits 0, 1, and 4 is mapped in superposition by Hadamard gates. The rotations itself are separated by two $qc.barrier()$ commands. We could as well simplify the circuit by eliminating the two Hadamard gates of the auxiliary qubit after the first and second rotation, however by doing so the circuit loses its modular structure (less readable) and the redundant operations are simplified during the transpiration process. The qubits 0, 1, and 4 are measured.

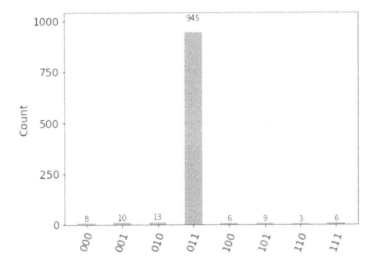

Figure 6.5 The qubits 0, 1, and 4 indicate the eight possible instantiations for x_1, x_2, and x_3 for the $\phi = (x_1 \leftrightarrow x_2) \wedge (x_1 \wedge x_2) \wedge \neg x_3$ SAT problem. The solution after two rotations for the SAT problem has the highest count with the measured state $|011\rangle$.

```
#Preparation of Aux
qc.x(5)
qc.h(5)
qc.barrier()

#First And 2 is zero
qc.ccx(0,1,2)
qc.barrier()
#Result in 2

#If AND IF

qc.x(3)
qc.ccx(3,0,1)
qc.x(1)
#Result in 1

#Make 3 zero
qc.x(3)
qc.ccx(1,2,3)
qc.barrier()
#Result in 3

#Input 4
qc.x(4)
qc.ccx(3,4,5)

#Un-compute
qc.barrier()
qc.x(4)
qc.barrier()
qc.ccx(1,2,3)
qc.x(3)
qc.barrier()
qc.x(1)
qc.ccx(3,0,1)
qc.x(3)
qc.barrier()
qc.ccx(0,1,2)

qc.barrier()
#Preparation of Aux
qc.h(5)
#Diffusor
qc.barrier()
qc.h([0,1,4])
qc.x([0,1,4])
qc.h(0)
qc.ccx(1,4,0)
qc.h(0)
qc.barrier()
```

```
qc.x([0,1,4])
qc.h([0,1,4])


#Second Iteration

#Preparation of Aux
qc.barrier()
qc.barrier()
qc.h(5)
qc.barrier()

#First And 2 is zero
qc.ccx(0,1,2)
qc.barrier()
#Result in 2

#If AND IF

qc.x(3)
qc.ccx(3,0,1)
qc.x(1)
#Result in 1

#Make 3 zero
qc.x(3)
qc.ccx(1,2,3)
qc.barrier()
#Result in 3

#Input 4
qc.x(4)
qc.ccx(3,4,5)

#Un-compute
qc.barrier()
qc.x(4)
qc.barrier()
qc.ccx(1,2,3)
qc.x(3)
qc.barrier()
qc.x(1)
qc.ccx(3,0,1)
qc.x(3)
qc.barrier()
qc.ccx(0,1,2)

qc.barrier()
#Preparation of Aux
qc.h(5)
#Diffusor
```

```
qc.barrier()
qc.h([0,1,4])
qc.x([0,1,4])
qc.h(0)
qc.ccx(1,4,0)
qc.h(0)
qc.barrier()
qc.x([0,1,4])
qc.h([0,1,4])

qc.measure(0,0)
qc.measure(1,1)
qc.measure(4,2)


qc.draw(fold=165)

simulator = Aer.get_backend('qasm_simulator')
result=execute(qc,simulator,shots=1000).result()
counts = result.get_counts()
print("\nTotal count are:",counts)

plot_histogram(counts)
```

6.3.4 No Solution

For the Boolean formula

$$\phi = (x_1 \leftrightarrow x_2) \wedge (\neg x_1 \wedge x_2) \wedge \neg x_3$$

no solution exists, the formula can never evaluate to the value true. We change our circuit correspondingly with

```
#First And 2 is zero
qc.x(0)
qc.ccx(0,1,2)
qc.x(0)
qc.barrier()
#Result in 2
```

In the next step we apply Grover's amplification; however no state is marked. In Figure 6.6 the distribution of the eight possible instantiations for x_1, x_2, and x_3 after one Grover's amplification and two Grover's amplifications are indicated.

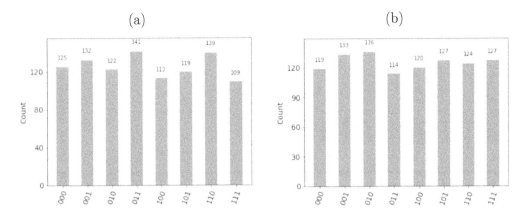

Figure 6.6 For the Boolean formula $\phi = (x_1 \leftrightarrow x_2) \wedge (\neg x_1 \wedge x_2) \wedge \neg x_3$ no solution exists. The qubits 0, 1, and 4 indicate the eight possible instantiations for x_1, x_2, and x_3. (a) The distribution of the eight possible instantiations for x_1, x_2, and x_3 after one rotation. (b) The distribution after two rotations. Each instantiation has nearly the same count, no solution exists.

The qubits 0, 1, and 4 indicate the eight possible instantiations for x_1, x_2 and x_3 for the $\phi = (x_1 \leftrightarrow x_2) \wedge (x_1 \wedge x_2) \wedge \neg x_3$ SAT problem. Each instantiation has nearly the same count after applying Grover's amplification and no solution exists.

## CHAPTER 7

Symbolic State Representation

An economic symbolic representation of objects and attributes that can represent a state during problem solving is introduced. This representation is motivated by the biological *what where* principle and requires a low number of bits. Such an economical symbolical representation is ideal for the current generation of quantum computers. We describe the tree search on which problem solving is based. Nodes and edges represent a search tree. Each node represents a state, and each edge represents a transition from one state to the following state. The path descriptors is the basis idea of quantum tree search. In a quantum tree search we represent all possible path descriptors simultaneously and can use Grover's amplification algorithm to determine the solution.

7.1 BIT REPRESENTATION OF OBJECTS AND ATTRIBUTES

We can represent n symbols with $\lceil \log_2 n \rceil$ bits. To represent four symbols A, B, C, D we require two bits with the following code: $A = 00$, $B = 01$, $C = 10$, $D = 11$. To represent a string $B\ A\ D\ C$ we code each symbol at a corresponding position: 01 00 11 10. In this representation the attribute is fixed, and the code descriptors of the object moves. Each symbol can represent an object. Each object can have one or more attributes (adjectives), like position in one or two dimensions. In our case the attribute corresponds to the position in the representation. Instead of coding symbols we could alternatively code the positions, for four positions we could code the first position by 00, second position by 01, third position by 10 and the fourth position by 11. A symbol would be represented by the order, to represent a string $D\ B\ A\ C$ we code 10 01 11 00, A at position 10 (fourth position in the string), B at position 01 (second position in the string), C at position 11 (fourth position in the string), and D at position 00 (first position in the string). In this representation the code descriptors of the object are fixed, and the attribute moves. In the case several attributes are present, it is more economical to represent the code descriptors of the object fixed since some attributes may change while the other remain fixed. During the problem solving the number of objects remains fixed, only the values of the attributes change.

Objects cannot disappear or appear. A state is of object and attributes is described by fixed number of bits that change its position, a rule corresponds to the permutation of bits. This kind of representation is related to the biological what where principle.

7.1.1 "What" and "Where"

Gross and Mishkkin [34] suggested that the brain includes two mechanisms for visual categorization: one for the representation of the object and the other for the representation of the localization [57, 52, 79]. The first mechanism is called the "what" pathway and is composed of the temporal lobe. The second mechanism is called the "where" pathway and is composed by the partial lobe [52, 79]. According to this division, the identity of a visual object can be coded apart from the location and the size of the object.

7.2 TREE SEARCH AND THE PATH DESCRIPTORS

Nodes and edges represent a search tree. Each node represents a state, and each edge represents a transition from one state to the following state. The initial state defines the root of the tree. From each state, either $B \in \mathbb{N}$ states can be reached, or the state is a leaf. From a leaf, no other state can be reached. B represents the branching factor of the node, the number of possible choices. A leaf represents either the goal of the computation or an impasse when there is no valid transition to a succeeding state. Every node besides the root has a unique node from which it was reached, which is called the parent. Each node and its parent are connected by an edge. Each parent has B children. If $B = 2$, each of the m questions has a reply of either "yes" or "no" and can be represented by a bit (see Figure 7.1). The m answers are represented by a binary number of length m. There are $n = 2^m = B^m$ possible binary numbers of length m. Each binary number represents a path from the root to a leaf. For each goal, a certain binary number indicates the solution. For a constant branching factor $B > 2$, each question has B possible answers. The m answers can be represented by m digits. For example, with $B = 8$, the number is represented by 2^3 bits. These numbers represent all paths from the root to the leaves.

7.3 QUANTUM TREE SEARCH

In a quantum computation, we can simultaneously represent all possible path descriptors. There is one path descriptor for each leaf of the tree. Using Grover's algorithm, we search through all possible paths and verify whether each path leads to the goal state. This type of procedure is called a quantum tree search [107, 119]. For $n = B^m$ possible paths, the costs are (approximately) $\sqrt{n} = B^{\frac{m}{2}}$ (see Figure 7.2). A constraint of this approach is that we must know the depth m of the search tree in advance. The constraint can be overcome by iterative deepening in an iterative deepening search. During the iterative deepening search, the states are generated multiple times [51, 87]. The time complexity of the iterative deepening search is of the same order of magnitude as a search to the maximum depth [51], as explained by Richard E. Korf: *Since the number of nodes on a given level of the tree grows*

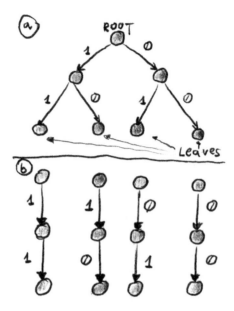

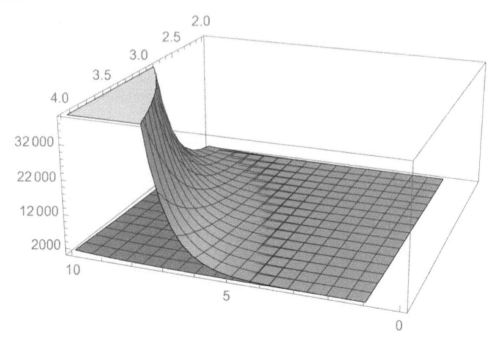

Figure 7.1 (a) Search tree for $B = 2$ and $m = 2$. (b) Each question can be represented by a bit. Each binary number (11, 10, 01, 00) represents a path from the root to the leaf.

Figure 7.2 For branching factor B from 2 to 4 and the depth of the tree search m from 1 to 10. The cost on a conventional computer are $n = B^m$, upper plane. On a quantum computer we need only $\sqrt{n} = B^{\frac{m}{2}}$ steps, plane below.

exponentially with depth, almost all time is spent in the deepest level, even though shallower levels are generated an arithmetically increasing number of times. The paradox can be explained using the arithmetic–geometric sequence. A quantum iterative deepening search is equivalent to the iterative deepening search [108]. For each limit max, a quantum tree search is performed from the root, where max is the maximum depth of the search tree. The possible solutions are determined using a measurement. We gradually increase the limit of the search from one, to two, three and four and continue to search until the goal is found. For each limit m, a quantum tree search is performed from the root, with m being the maximum depth of the search tree. The possible solutions are determined by a measurement. The time complexity of an iterative deepening search has the same order of magnitude as the quantum tree search. The total costs of m iterations with m measurements are

$$O(1) + O(B^{\frac{1}{2}}) + O(B^{\frac{2}{2}}) + O(B^{\frac{3}{2}}) + \cdots + O(B^{\frac{m}{2}}) = O(B^{\frac{m}{2}}), \qquad (7.1)$$

the equation is based on the geometric series [108].

A second constraint is represented by the constant branching factor. If the branching factor is not constant, the maximal branching factor B_{max} must be used for the quantum tree search [107]. It turns out in the chapters 10 and 11 that this problem may be overcome elegantly.

## CHAPTER 8

Quantum Production System

A production system is a model of human problem solving. It is composed of long-term memory and working memory, which is also called the short-term memory. Problem-solving can be modeled by a production system that implements a search algorithm. The search defines a problem space and can be represented as a tree. Using Grover's algorithm, we search through all possible paths and verify, for each path, whether it leads to the goal state.

A pure production system has no mechanism for recovering from an impasse. We describe an example of a simple pure production systems for sorting of a string and indicate how to port this simple pure production systems into the quantum production system. Then we indicate that a quantum production system can be the basis of a unified theory of cognition.

8.1 PURE PRODUCTION SYSTEMS

The pure production system model has no mechanism for recovering from an impasse [80]. The system halts if no production can fire. It is composed of the set of productions L (the long-term memory) and control system C. A pure production system is a sextuple:

$$(\Sigma, L, W, \gamma_i, \gamma_g, C) \tag{8.1}$$

with

- Σ is a finite alphabet;

- W is the working memory. It represents a state $\gamma \in \Sigma$.

- L is the long-term memory. It is the set of B productions. A production p has the form $(precondition, conclusion) \in \Sigma$. The precondition is matched against the contents of the working memory. If the precondition is met then the conclusion is preformed and changes the contents of the working memory;

- $\gamma_i \in \Sigma$ is the initial state. The working memory is initialized with the initial state γ_i;

- $\gamma_g \in \Sigma$ is the goal state;

DOI: 10.1201/9781003374404-8

- δ is the control function of the form $\Sigma \to L \times \Sigma \times h$. It chooses a production and fires it or halts h.

If $C(\gamma) = (p, \gamma', h)$, then the working memory contains symbol γ. It is substituted by a production p by γ' or the computation halts h. The computation halts if the goal state γ_g is reached or an impasse is present, means no production can be applied. An impasse is solved during tree search by backtracking to a previous state.

Production systems are closely related to the approach of Markov algorithms [62]; similar to these approaches, production systems are equivalent in power to a Turing machine [113]. A Turing machine can also be easily simulated by a production system; thus, a production system is a complete model of computation. The search represented by a search tree is performed from an initial state through the following states until a goal state is attained.

8.1.1 Quantum Production Systems

Quantum production systems are related to pure production systems since the computation is not continued in the branch if an impasse is present, no backtracking to a previous state is done. Contrary to the pure production systems no control system C exists since all productions are executed simultaneously.

Quantum production system can operate independently of whether the computation terminates; in the case of non-termination, the computation continues forever, and the iterations do not terminate. The quantum production system also provides a maximal speedup of $O(\sqrt{n})$ if the Turing machine simulation allows n multiple computational branches [108].

A future quantum computer based on a quantum production system will involve classical artificial-intelligence programing languages, such as OPS5 [17]. OPS5 programs are executed by matching the working memory elements with productions in the long-term memory [30]. Thus, the programmer is not required to contend with quantum gates, nor is he or she required to address the principles of quantum computation. It is equivalent to current programmers who specify their algorithms in high-level languages, such as Java or Python, without the requirement of understanding the nature of electronic circuits or semiconductor devices, such as a transistor.

8.2 EXAMPLE: SORTING A STRING

We demonstrate a simple pure production systems for sorting of a string with:

- Σ: a, b, c, d composed of four letters

- W is the working memory. It represents a state $\gamma \in \Sigma$ by a string of five letters

- The long-term memory L, the set of $B = 6$ productions

  1. $ab \to ba$
  2. $ac \to ca$
  3. $ad \to da$

Table 8.1 Execution of a simple pure production system or sorting a string.

Iteration	Working Memory	Conflict Set	Rule Fired
0	$cdcab$	1, 6	1
1	$cdcba$	6	6
2	$dccba$		Halt

    4. $bc \rightarrow cb$

    5. $bd \rightarrow db$

    6. $cd \rightarrow dc$

The production (rule) can fire if the precondition matches portion of the string in the working memory.

- $\gamma_i \in \Sigma$ is the initial state: $cdcab$

- $\gamma_g \in \Sigma$ is the goal state: $dccba$

- δ is the control function: random choice of a production

The execution is indicated in the Table 8.1.

8.2.1 Quantum Production System for Sorting a String

To port this simple pure production systems into the quantum production system, we represent first the finite alphabet Σ by two qubits and approximate a problem by reformulation of the rules without a precondition that has to be tested.

- Σ: $a = |00\rangle$, $b = |01\rangle$, $c = |10\rangle$, $d = |11\rangle$

- W is the working memory. It represents a state of teen qubits $\gamma \in \Sigma$, two qubits represent a position p_i

$$|x_7 x_6 x_5 x_4 x_3 x_2 x_1 x_0\rangle = |p_5 p_4 p_3 p_2 p_1\rangle$$

- The long-term memory L, the set of $B = 4$ productions that manipulate the position of the string, indexed by two qubits that represent the path descriptor. Each precondition determines the rule, each rule can be always applied

    - index $|11\rangle$: $p_2 p_1 \rightarrow p_1 p_2$

    - index $|10\rangle$: $p_3 p_2 \rightarrow p_2 p_3$

    - index $|01\rangle$: $p_4 p_3 \rightarrow p_3 p_4$

    - index $|00\rangle$: $p_5 p_4 \rightarrow p_4 p_5$

At each search step all four rules can be applied in parallel.

- $\gamma_i \in \Sigma$ is the initial state: $cdcab = |1011100001\rangle$

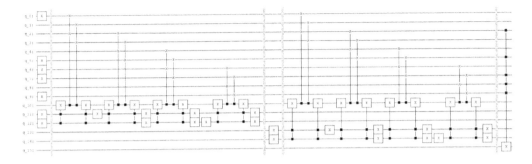

Figure 8.1 The working memory W and the long-term memory L are represented in the quantum circuit by teen qubits 0 to 9. The qubit 10 is used as an internal flag to mark the execution of the rule in relation to the path descriptor. The marking of the flag is implemented by the Toffoli gate, also called the ccX gate, it recognizes the corresponding index represented by the path descriptor. Since we are searching for the depth two we require two path descriptors represented by the qubits 11 to 14, since each index has four values. The path descriptor is indexes are indicated by the NOT gates. To implement the oracle that marks the solution we will use the $MCXGate$, a multi-controlled X (Toffoli) gate. The auxiliary qubit 14 indicates by one the presence of a solution $|1110100100\rangle$ by the oracle function.

- $\gamma_g \in \Sigma$ is the goal state is represented by the oracle : $dccba = |1110100100\rangle$

The working memory W and the long-term memory L are represented in the quantum circuit by teen qubits 0 to 9. The qubit 10 is used as an internal flag to mark the execution of the rule in relation to the path descriptor. The marking of the flag is implemented by the Toffoli gate, also called the ccX gate (CCNOT gate, controlled controlled not gate), it recognizes the corresponding index represented by the path descriptor. The long-term memory L and γ_g are represented by the following circuit with the path descriptor that index the four rules. Since we are searching for the depth two, two path descriptors are required represented by the qubits 11 to 14, since each index has four values. The path descriptor is indexes are indicated by the NOT gates.

The oracle that marks the solution is implemented bz the $MCXGate$, a multi-controlled X (Toffoli) gate. A multi-controlled X gate is composed in of simple (Toffoli) gate and temporary working registers. It is represented in the qiskit circuit library. The auxiliary qubit 14 indicates by one the presence of a solution $|1110100100\rangle$ by the oracle function, see Figure 8.1

```
from qiskit import QuantumCircuit, Aer,execute
from qiskit.visualization import plot_histogram
from qiskit.quantum_info import Statevector
from qiskit.circuit.library import MCXGate

qc = QuantumCircuit(16)

#State Preparation 0-9
```

```
#Working Memory for Flag bit 10
#1St Path descriptor 11-12
#1th Path descriptor 13-14

#Initial state b,a,c,d,c
#First Position 01 is b 01
qc.x(0)
#Second Position 23 is a 00
#Third Position 45 is c 10
qc.x(5)
#Fourth Position 67 is d 11
qc.x(6)
qc.x(7)
#Fifth Position 89 is c 10
qc.x(9)

#Path Descriptor
qc.h(11)
qc.h(12)
qc.barrier()

#First Rule
#Set flag 10 dependent on the path descriptor
qc.ccx(11,12,10)
# Move
qc.cswap(10,0,2)
qc.cswap(10,1,3)
#Reset flag
qc.ccx(11,12,10)
#Second Rule
#Set flag 10 dependent on the path descriptor
qc.x(11)
qc.ccx(11,12,10)
# Move
qc.cswap(10,2,4)
qc.cswap(10,3,5)
#Reset flag
qc.ccx(11,12,10)
qc.x(11)
#Third Rule
#Set flag 10 dependent on the path descriptor
qc.x(12)
qc.ccx(11,12,10)
# Move
qc.cswap(10,4,6)
qc.cswap(10,5,7)
#Reset flag
qc.ccx(11,12,10)
qc.x(12)
#Fourth Rule
#Set flag 10 dependent on the path descriptor
```

```
qc.x(11)
qc.x(12)
qc.ccx(11,12,10)
# Move
qc.cswap(10,6,8)
qc.cswap(10,7,9)
#Reset flag
qc.ccx(11,12,10)
qc.x(12)
qc.x(11)
qc.barrier()


#Depth two: 2th Path Descriptor
qc.h(13)
qc.h(14)
qc.barrier()
#First Rule
#Set flag 10 dependent on the path descriptor
qc.ccx(13,14,10)
# Move
qc.cswap(10,0,2)
qc.cswap(10,1,3)
#Reset flag
qc.ccx(13,14,10)
#Second Rule
#Set flag 10 dependent on the path descriptor
qc.x(13)
qc.ccx(13,14,10)
# Move
qc.cswap(10,2,4)
qc.cswap(10,3,5)
#Reset flag
qc.ccx(13,14,10)
qc.x(13)
#Third Rule
#Set flag 10 dependent on the path descriptor
qc.x(14)
qc.ccx(13,14,10)
# Move
qc.cswap(10,4,6)
qc.cswap(10,5,7)
#Reset flag
qc.ccx(13,14,10)
qc.x(14)
#Fourth Rule
#Set flag 10 dependent on the path descriptor
qc.x(13)
qc.x(14)
qc.ccx(13,14,10)
# Move
qc.cswap(10,6,8)
```

```
qc.cswap(10,7,9)
#Reset flag
qc.ccx(13,14,10)
qc.x(14)
qc.x(13)
qc.barrier()

#Oracle
gate = MCXGate(5)
#Mark the goal state
#Initial state a,b,c,c,d
qc.append(gate, [2,5,7,8,9,15])
```

We will use the *qiskit def* function to reduce the complexity of the quantum circuit. Using the *def* function we define the circuit that represents the four rules.

```
def rules():
    qc = QuantumCircuit(15)
    #First Rule
    #Set flag 10 dependent on the path descriptor
    qc.ccx(11,12,10)
    # Move
    qc.cswap(10,0,2)
    qc.cswap(10,1,3)
    #Reset flag
    qc.ccx(11,12,10)
    #Second Rule
    #Set flag 10 dependent on the path descriptor
    qc.x(11)
    qc.ccx(11,12,10)
    # Move
    qc.cswap(10,2,4)
    qc.cswap(10,3,5)
    #Reset flag
    qc.ccx(11,12,10)
    qc.x(11)
    #Third Rule
    #Set flag 10 dependent on the path descriptor
    qc.x(12)
    qc.ccx(11,12,10)
    # Move
    qc.cswap(10,4,6)
    qc.cswap(10,5,7)
    #Reset flag
    qc.ccx(11,12,10)
    qc.x(12)
    #Fourth Rule
    #Set flag 10 dependent on the path descriptor
    qc.x(11)
    qc.x(12)
    qc.ccx(11,12,10)
    # Move
```

```
 qc.cswap(10,6,8)
 qc.cswap(10,7,9)
 #Reset flag
 qc.ccx(11,12,10)
 qc.x(12)
 qc.x(11)
#depth two
 #First Rule
 #Set flag 10 dependent on the path descriptor
 qc.ccx(13,14,10)
 # Move
 qc.cswap(10,0,2)
 qc.cswap(10,1,3)
 #Reset flag
 qc.ccx(13,14,10)
 #Second Rule
 #Set flag 10 dependent on the path descriptor
 qc.x(13)
 qc.ccx(13,14,10)
 # Move
 qc.cswap(10,2,4)
 qc.cswap(10,3,5)
 #Reset flag
 qc.ccx(13,14,10)
 qc.x(13)
 #Third Rule
 #Set flag 10 dependent on the path descriptor
 qc.x(14)
 qc.ccx(13,14,10)
 # Move
 qc.cswap(10,4,6)
 qc.cswap(10,5,7)
 #Reset flag
 qc.ccx(13,14,10)
 qc.x(14)
 #Fourth Rule
 #Set flag 10 dependent on the path descriptor
 qc.x(13)
 qc.x(14)
 qc.ccx(13,14,10)
 # Move
 qc.cswap(10,6,8)
 qc.cswap(10,7,9)
 #Reset flag
 qc.ccx(13,14,10)
 qc.x(14)
 qc.x(13)
 qc.name="RULES"
 return qc
```

In quantum computation it is not possible to reset the information to the pattern representing the initial state. Instead we un-compute the output back to the input before applying the amplification step of the Grover's algorithm. We use the *qiskit* inverse command *inverse()* to define the inverse operation by a function.

```
def rules_inv():
    qc=rules()
    qc_inv=qc.inverse()
    qc_inv.name="RULES_INV"
    return qc_inv
```

A search of depth two is described by a path descriptor of four qubits, 11, 12, 13, and 14. The Grover amplification act on the qubits 13, 18, and 23 that describe the path descriptor resulting in 16 states and we use the *qiskit def* function.

```
def Grover():
    qc = QuantumCircuit(15)
    #Diffusor 11, 12, 13, 14
    qc.h([11,12,13,14])
    qc.x([11,12,13,14])
    qc.h(11)
    gate = MCXGate(3)
    qc.append(gate, [12,13,14,11])
    qc.h(11)
    qc.x([11,12,13,14])
    qc.h([11,12,13,14])
    qc.name="G"
    return qc
```

We apply the Grover's algorithm with two rotations (see Figure 8.2).

```
qc = QuantumCircuit(16,4)

#State Preparation 0-9
#Working Memory for Flag bit 10
#1St Path descriptor 11-12
#1th Path descriptor 13-14

#Initial state b,a,c,d,c

#First Position 01 is b 01
qc.x(0)
#Second Position 23 is a 00

#Third Position 45 is c 10
qc.x(5)

#Fourth Position 67 is d 11
qc.x(6)
qc.x(7)

#Fifth Position 89 is c 10
```

```
qc.x(9)


#Path Descriptor
qc.h(11)
qc.h(12)
qc.h(13)
qc.h(14)

#Preparation of Aux
qc.x(15)
qc.h(15)

qc.append(rules(),range(15))
#Oracle
gate = MCXGate(5)
#Mark the goal state
#Initial state a,b,c,c,d
qc.append(gate, [2,5,7,8,9,15])

qc.append(rules_inv(),range(15))
qc.barrier()
qc.h(15)
qc.barrier()
qc.append(Grover(),range(15))

qc.barrier()

qc.h(15)

qc.append(rules(),range(15))
#Oracle
gate = MCXGate(5)
#Mark the goal state
#Initial state a,b,c,c,d
qc.append(gate, [2,5,7,8,9,15])

qc.append(rules_inv(),range(15))
qc.barrier()
qc.h(15)
qc.barrier()
qc.append(Grover(),range(15))

qc.measure(11,0)
qc.measure(12,1)
qc.measure(13,2)
qc.measure(14,3)

qc.draw(fold=220)

simulator = Aer.get_backend('qasm_simulator')
```

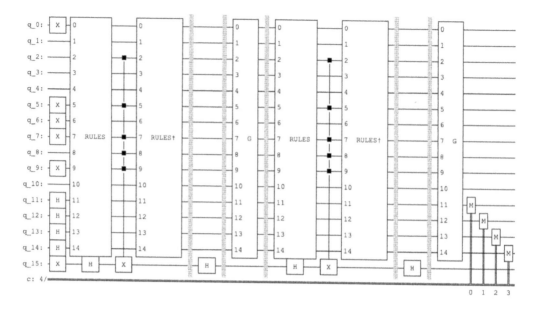

Figure 8.2 Quantum circuit for a simple quantum production systems for sorting of a string. We apply the Grover's algorithm with two rotations.

```
result=execute(qc,simulator,shots=1000).result()
counts = result.get_counts()
print("\nTotal count are:",counts)
plot_histogram(counts)
```

Two marked state results after two iterations are indicated in the histogram of Figure 8.3. The two solutions correspond to the path descriptor $|1100\rangle$ and the symmetric path descriptor $|0011\rangle$.

The solution of the path descriptor $|1100\rangle$ corresponds to:

- index $|11\rangle$: $p_2 p_1 \rightarrow p_1 p_2$, working memory: $cdcab \rightarrow cdcba$
- index $|00\rangle$: $p_5 p_4 \rightarrow p_4 p_5$, working memory: $cdcba \rightarrow dccba$

The solution of the path descriptor $|0011\rangle$ corresponds to:

- index $|00\rangle$: $p_5 p_4 \rightarrow p_4 p_5$, working memory: $cdcab \rightarrow dccab$
- index $|11\rangle$: $p_2 p_1 \rightarrow p_1 p_2$, working memory: $dccab \rightarrow dccba$

8.2.2 Number of Iteration

The number of iterations r is

$$r = \lfloor t^* \rfloor = \left\lfloor \frac{\pi}{4} \cdot \sqrt{\frac{2^m}{k}} - \frac{1}{2} \right\rfloor. \tag{8.2}$$

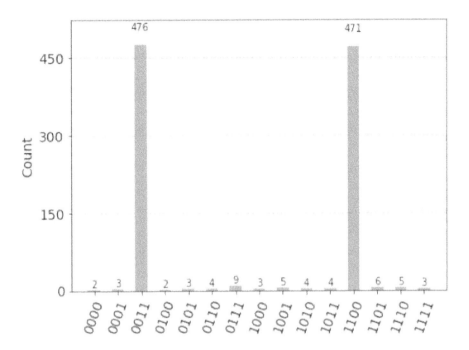

Figure 8.3 Two solutions correspond to the path descriptor $|0011\rangle$ and the symmetric path descriptor $|1100\rangle$.

The value of r depends on the relation of n versus k, with k being the number of solutions. When r is unknown we can repeatedly chose r randomly between 1 and $\frac{\pi}{4} \cdot \sqrt{2^m}$. This simple strategy leads to success in $O(\sqrt{n}) = O(\sqrt{2^m})$ [82].

A more advanced approach is the quantum counting algorithm with the complexity $O(\sqrt{n})$. Quantum counting is based on phase estimation algorithm and will be described later.

8.3 COGNITIVE ARCHITECTURE

A quantum production system can be the basis of a unified theory of cognition. Unified theories of cognition is a theory that attempts to unify all of the theories of the mind in a single framework. Allen Newell proposed the SOAR cognitive architecture [55], [71], [31]. SOAR is an architecture of the mind: a fixed structure underlying the flexible domain of cognitive processing as well as an architecture for intelligent agents. All problem solving activity is formulated as the selection and application of productions to a state, to achieve some goal. The decision takes place in the context of earlier decisions. Those decisions are rated utilizing preferences and added by chosen rules. Preferences are determined together with the rules by an observer using knowledge about a problem. SOAR models the psychological phenomena of chunking, the association of expressions, or symbols (chunks) into a new single expression or symbol (chunk). Chunking represents a theory of learning. A chunk is a new rule (production) that describes the processing that was present due to lack of applicable knowledge [54], [71]. A lack of applicable knowledge is present if it cannot be decided which rule to use or no rule can be applied for a certain mental state represented in the working memory.

An extension of the proposed SOAR cognitive architecture by a quantum production system would lead to a hybrid architecture. The quantum production system would be invoked if an impasse were present. Such a hybrid approach would speed up the learning process without a need for domain-specific control knowledge. Quantum SOAR architecture described by a quantum computer would allow faster planning of actions, like for example flying a plane or support better face-to-face dialogues with humans.

8.4 CONTROL FUNCTION

In the following chapters 9–11 we will give examples how quantum production systems may be used to solve popular artificial intelligence applications and describe the implementation in more details. In these applications all productions cannot fire at the same time, instead several instantiations of certain productions can be executed. The control function determines if a production can fire or not. The preconditions are matched against the contents of the working memory. If the preconditions are met, then the productions can fire at the same time. All the productions that can fire are mapped in superposition and are instantiated. In the next step all instantiated productions fire and change the contents of the working memories in the superposition.

## CHAPTER 9

3 Puzzle

We demonstrate the working principles of quantum production system and the quantum tree search by a *qiskit* implementation of a toy example from symbolical artificial intelligence, the 3-puzzle. The goal is to find a series of moves that changes the board from the initial configuration to a desired configuration. We describe the representation of the rules (productions) of the long-term memory and describe the search of depth one, two, and three. The search of depth three results in eight possible sates. The solution is marked by an oracle and a Grover's amplification is applied once. To increase the probability value of the solution we will apply two Grover's amplification. The solution corresponds to the path descriptor that indicates the sequence of rules (productions) that changes the board from the initial configuration to a desired configuration.

9.1   3 PUZZLE

The 3-puzzle is composed of three numbered movable tiles in a 2×2 frame (see Figure 9.1).

One cell of the frame is empty, and because of this, tiles can be moved around to form different patterns [119]. The goal is to find a series of moves of tiles into the blank space that changes the board from the initial configuration to a desired configuration. There are 12 possible configurations (see Figure 9.2). For any of these configurations, only two movements are possible. The movement of the empty cell is either a clockwise or counter-clockwise movement.

The 3-puzzle is tractable and requires fewer qubits to encode. There are four different objects: three cells and one empty cell. Each object can be coded by two qubits (2^2) and a configuration of the four objects can be represented by a register of eight qubits $|x\rangle$. In this representation, position description (adjective) is fixed and the class descriptors moves. The control function of the quantum production system needs to fulfill two requirements [106]:

- For a given board, configuration and a production rule determine the new board configuration.

- To determine if the configuration is the goal configuration.

DOI: 10.1201/9781003374404-9

Figure 9.1 The desired configuration of the 3-puzzle.

The new board configuration is determined by productions that are represented by the function p. There are four possible positions of the empty cell. The input of the function p is the current board configuration and a bit m that indicates whether the blank cell should perform a clockwise ($m = 1$) or counter-clockwise movement ($m = 0$). Together, there are 8 possible mappings, which are represented by 8 productions. There are four possible positions of the empty cell times two possible moves. For simplicity, we represent the mappings of the function p by a unitary permutation matrix $L(1)$. For each mapping, the empty tile can have three different neighbors. It follows that, in total, there are $24 = 8 \times 3$ instantiated rules. They correspond to permutations in the unitary permutation matrix $L(1)$. The matrix acts on the $8 + 1$ qubits with $m \in B^1$ and $x \in B^8$

$$L(1) \cdot |m\rangle|x\rangle = |m\rangle|\gamma\rangle. \tag{9.1}$$

The $L(1)$ matrix represents the long-term memory of our production system.

The function $o(x)$, called oracle, determines if the configuration is the goal configuration.

$$o(x) = o(\underbrace{x_0, x_1, x_2, x_3, x_4, x_5, x_6, x_7}_{board\ configuration}) = \begin{cases} 1 & \text{if goal} \\ 0 & \text{otherwise.} \end{cases} \tag{9.2}$$

Function $o(x)$ oracle is represented by a unitary operator T (for target). T acts on the $8 + 1$ qubits, with $x \in B^8$ and $c \in B^1$ being the auxiliary qubit

$$T \cdot |x\rangle|c\rangle = |x\rangle|o(x) \oplus c\rangle. \tag{9.3}$$

An important open question is whether the permutation matrix $L(1)$ of dimension $512 = 2^9$ can be decomposed. It is possible to determine if a permutation is tensor decomposable and to choose an efficient tensor decomposition if present [50, 119]. An alternative less costly representation of the long-term memory can be realized by a uniformly polynomial circuit that describes the function p.

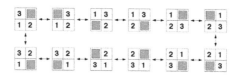

Figure 9.2 There are 12 possible configurations. For any of this configuration only two movements are possible. The movement of the empty cell are either a clockwise or counter-clockwise movement.

3 10 7 6	**X** 11 5 4
1 00 3 2	**2** 01 1 0

Figure 9.3 3-puzzle coding representing the state of the Figure 9.1. The four objects are by a register of eight qubits. We indicate the state, its representation and below the position of the 8 qubits. In this representation, position description (adjective) is fixed and the class descriptors moves.

9.2 REPRESENTATION

There are four different objects: three cells and one empty cell. Each object can be coded by two qubits (2^2), and a configuration of the four objects can be represented by a register of eight qubits $|x\rangle$. The object 1 is represented by 00, 2 is represented by 01, 3 is represented by 10, and empty space x is represented by 11. The state is represented by 8 qubits $x_0, x_1, x_2, x_3, x_4, x_5, x_6, x_7$, and the state of the Figure 9.1 is represented by the qubits 10 11 00 01, see Figure 9.3.

In this representation, position description (adjective) is fixed and the class descriptors moves. In the *qiskit* circuit, all qubits before the computation are in the state 0, so the state of the Figure 9.3 is prepared with the *NOT* gate with the following commands of the qubits 0 to 7:

```
qc.x(0)
qc.x(4)
qc.x(5)
qc.x(7)
```

In the 3-puzzle task, we have four different rules defined by the position of the empty space. Each of the rules has two instantiations, either moving the empty space clockwise or a counter-clockwise movement. We recognize the four rules and indicate the presence of a rule by a qubit. We use four qubits that indicate the presence of the four rules and call them the trace. We need the trace represented by the four qubits, since we cannot delete the information and we cannot un-compute the output back. By un-computing, we would redo the rules. Additionally, we require a flag represented by a qubit that indicates to us if the rule with the corresponding instantiation can be executed or not. Finally, we need a qubit that represents the path descriptor that will be present by superposition using a Hadamard gate. Altogether, we need 14 qubits, and we define the following circuit:

```
qc = QuantumCircuit(14,8)
#State Preparation 0-7
qc.x(0)
qc.x(4)
qc.x(5)
```

```
qc.x(7)
#Flag represented by qubit 8
#1St Trace represented by qubits 9-12
#1St Path descriptor in superposition
qc.h(13)
qc.barrier()
```

QuantumCircuit(14, 8) defines a quantum circuit with the name *qc* that uses 14 qubits and measures 8 qubits.

9.2.1 Rules and Trace

The *if part* of the rules is implemented by the Toffoli gate, also called the ccX gate (CCNOT gate, controlled controlled not gate), it recognizes the position of the empty space and indicates it by setting one qubit of the four qubits 9 to 11 to one.

```
#If part of rules marked in trace (empty state)
qc.ccx(0,1,9)
qc.ccx(2,3,10)
qc.ccx(4,5,11)
qc.ccx(6,7,12)
```

The execution of the rules uses the Fredkin gate, also called controlled swap (CSWAP) gate, using the trace information and the path descriptor setting the flag qubit (qubit 8) to indicate if the rule is going to be executed. The reset is performed by uncomputing, by repeating the operation to set the flag again in the state zero. We change the path descriptor by the NOT gate and execute the second instantiation of the rule depending on the trace value; the *qc.barrier*() will separate the representation in the circuit, resulting in the quantum circuit indicated in the Figure 9.4.

```
#If then rule (1) for empty at 0, 1  -> 4 , 5  or 2, 3
#Search empty state with the descriptor
qc.ccx(9,13,8)
#Execute 1st then part by moving the empty space clockwise
qc.cswap(8,0,4)
qc.cswap(8,1,5)
#Secod then part with changed descriptor
#Reset Flag
qc.ccx(9,13,8)
#Fetch second superposition
qc.x(13)
qc.ccx(9,13,8)
#Execute 2th then part  by moving the empty space anti-clockwise
qc.cswap(8,0,2)
qc.cswap(8,1,3)
#Reset Flag
qc.ccx(9,13,8)
#Restore descriptor
qc.x(13)
qc.barrier()
```

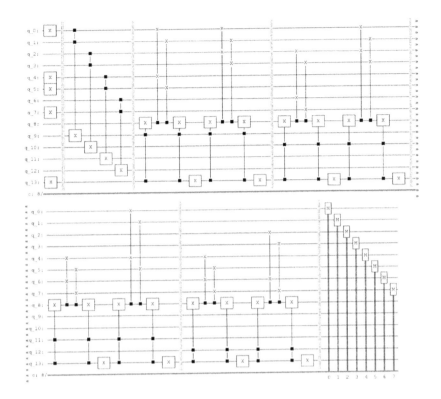

Figure 9.4 Quantum circuit representing the generation of two instantiations of rules
in the 3-puzzle task of one depth search.

The second rule is represented accordingly.

```
#If then rule (2) for empty at 2, 3  -> 6 , 7  or 0, 1
#Search empty state with the descriptor
qc.ccx(10,13,8)
#Execute 1st then part
qc.cswap(8,2,6)
qc.cswap(8,3,7)
#Secod then part with changed descriptor
#Reset Flag
qc.ccx(10,13,8)
#Fetch second superposition
qc.x(13)
qc.ccx(10,13,8)
#Execute 2th then part
qc.cswap(8,0,2)
qc.cswap(8,1,3)
#Reset Flag
qc.ccx(10,13,8)
#Restore descriptor
qc.x(13)
qc.barrier()
```

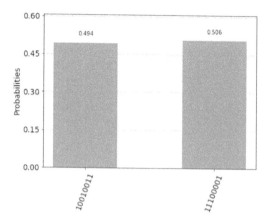

Figure 9.5 Two generated new states represented by eight qubits using the *qasm simulator*.

The third and the fourth rules are represented in the same way. Finally we measure the state represented by the 8 qubits

```
qc.measure(0,0)
qc.measure(1,1)
qc.measure(2,2)
qc.measure(3,3)
qc.measure(4,4)
qc.measure(5,5)
qc.measure(6,6)
qc.measure(7,7)
```

resulting in the quantum circuit indicated in the Figure 9.4.

By performing the simulation

```
simulator = Aer.get_backend('qasm_simulator')
result=execute(qc,simulator).result()
counts = result.get_counts()
plot_histogram(counts)
```

we get the following representation of the two generated new states represented by the histogram represented in the Figure 9.5.

9.3   SEARCH OF DEPTH TWO

Grover's amplification cannot be applied to fewer than four states. A search of depth one for the 3-puzzle results in two states and a search of depth two in four states. The operator $L(2)$ that describes the search of depth two is represented as

$$L(2) \cdot |m_2, m_1\rangle|x\rangle = |m_2, m_1\rangle|\gamma\rangle, \tag{9.4}$$

using two qubits, m_2, m_1, representing the path descriptor. The unitary operator T represents the oracle function $o(x)$ that determines if the configuration is the goal configuration

$$T \cdot |x\rangle|c\rangle = |x\rangle|o(x) \oplus c\rangle.$$

For the function $o(x)$, the solution is encoded by $(-1)^{o(x)}$, the sign of the amplitude. If the path descriptor is represented by m qubits, it can represent $n = 2^m$ states. To see why the solution is encoded by $(-1)^{o(x)}$, we indicate the derivative. The auxiliary qubit c is set to one, and the path descriptor is represented by m qubits $|0^{\otimes m}\rangle$. First, we set the path descriptor and the auxiliary qubit in superposition by the Hadamard gate for $m+1$ qubits H_{m+1}, and then we execute the unitary operator T

$$T \cdot H_{m+1} \cdot |0^{\otimes m}\rangle|1\rangle =$$

$$= \frac{1}{\sqrt{2^{m+1}}} \cdot \sum_{x \in B^m} T \cdot |x\rangle|0\rangle - \frac{1}{\sqrt{2^{m+1}}} \cdot \sum_{x \in B^m} T \cdot |x\rangle|1\rangle$$

$$= \frac{1}{\sqrt{2^{m+1}}} \cdot \sum_{x \in B^m} |x\rangle|o(x) \oplus 0\rangle - \frac{1}{\sqrt{2^{m+1}}} \cdot \sum_{x \in B^m} |x\rangle|o(x) \oplus 1\rangle \qquad (9.5)$$

$$= \frac{1}{\sqrt{2^{m+1}}} \cdot \left(\sum_{x \in B^m} |x\rangle|o(x) \oplus 0\rangle - \sum_{x \in B^m} |x\rangle|o(x) \oplus 1\rangle \right).$$

There are four possible cases with the path descriptor $|\xi\rangle$ being the solution:

$$T \cdot |x\rangle|0\rangle = |x\rangle|o(x) \oplus 0\rangle = |x\rangle|0\rangle,$$

$$T \cdot |x\rangle|1\rangle = |x\rangle|o(x) \oplus 1\rangle = |x\rangle|1\rangle,$$

$$T \cdot |\xi\rangle|0\rangle = |\xi\rangle|f(\xi) \oplus 0\rangle = |\xi\rangle|1\rangle,$$

$$T \cdot |\xi\rangle|1\rangle = |\xi\rangle|f(\xi) \oplus 1\rangle = |\xi\rangle|0\rangle.$$

It follows that

$$= \frac{1}{\sqrt{2^{m+1}}} \cdot \left(\sum_{x \neq \xi} |x\rangle|0\rangle + |\xi\rangle|1\rangle - \sum_{x \neq \xi} |x\rangle|1\rangle - |\xi\rangle|0\rangle \right)$$

$$\frac{1}{\sqrt{2^{m+1}}} \cdot \left(\sum_{x \neq \xi} |x\rangle\,(|0\rangle - |1\rangle) + |\xi\rangle\,(|1\rangle - |0\rangle) \right) \qquad (9.6)$$

$$= \frac{1}{\sqrt{n}} \sum_{x \in B^m} (-1)^{o(x)} \cdot |x\rangle \otimes \left(\frac{|0\rangle - |1\rangle}{\sqrt{2}} \right).$$

The value of the function $o(x)$ is encoded by $(-1)^{o(x)}$, (phase kick-back). We can set the auxiliary qubit $c = \left(\frac{|0\rangle - |1\rangle}{\sqrt{2}} \right)$ to zero by the Hadamard gate. For simplicity, we ignore the trace and the flag qubit and we obtain

$$(I_2 \otimes T) \cdot (L(2) \otimes I_1) \cdot (L(2) \otimes I_1) \cdot |m_2, m_1, x_0, x_1, x_2, x_3, x_4, x_5, x_6, x_7, c\rangle$$
$$(I_2 \otimes T) \cdot (L(2) \otimes I_1)^2 \cdot |m_2, m_1, x_1, x_2, x_3, x_4, x_5, x_6, x_7, x_8, c\rangle. \qquad (9.7)$$

The operator that describes the application of the production rules for the 3-puzzle for the depth search t, and a test condition in order to determine if the final board is a target configuration board, is represented with

$$L(t) \cdot |m_t, \cdots, m_1\rangle|x\rangle = |m_t, \cdots, m_1\rangle|\gamma\rangle$$

and

$$|\kappa^t\rangle = |m_t, \cdots, m_1\rangle$$

as

$$(I_t \otimes T) \cdot (L(t) \otimes I_1)^t \cdot |\kappa^t, x_1, x_2, x_3, x_4, x_5, x_6, x_7, x_8, c\rangle. \tag{9.8}$$

With depth search $t = 2$ additional four qubits are needed to represent the new trace, one additional qubit for the path descriptor of the depth two and one auxiliary qubit for the oracle operation. The quantum circuit is represented by 20 qubits. We will measure the path descriptor represented by two qubits 13 and 18.

```
qc = QuantumCircuit(20,2)
#State Preparation 0-7
# Flag bit 8
#1St Trace 9-12
#1St Path Descriptor in superposition
qc.h(13)
#1St Trace 14-17
#2th Path Descriptor in superposition
qc.h(18)
#Aux Bit c indicating the solution is negated and put in superposition
qc.x(19)
qc.h(19)
```

In the following we will use the *qiskitdef* function to define the oracle using the *MCXGate* command. The *MCXGate* is a multi-controlled X (Toffoli) gate. A multi-controlled X gate is composed in of simple (Toffoli) gate and temporary work registers. It is represented in the *qiskit* circuit library.

```
def oracle():
    qc = QuantumCircuit(20)
    gate = MCXGate(4)
  #Goal Configurations
    qc.append(gate,[2, 3, 4, 7, 19])
    #Alternative Goal Configurations
    #qc.append(gate,[0, 2, 3, 5, 19])
    #Grover in depth two cannot resolve this since
      two solutions out of four  are marked.
    #qc.append(gate,[0, 4, 5, 7, 19])
    qc.name="0"
    return qc
```

We define rules for the depth one and rules for the depth two using the *qiskit def* function.

```
def rules1():

    qc = QuantumCircuit(14)

    #If part of rules marked in trace (empty state)
    qc.ccx(0,1,9)
    qc.ccx(2,3,10)
    qc.ccx(4,5,11)
```

```
qc.ccx(6,7,12)

qc.barrier()

#Rules

#If then rule (1) for empty at 0, 1  -> 4 , 5  or 2, 3

#Search empty state with the descriptor
qc.ccx(9,13,8)

#Execute 1st then part
qc.cswap(8,0,4)
qc.cswap(8,1,5)

#Secod then part with changed descriptor
#Reset WM
qc.ccx(9,13,8)
#Fetch second superposition
qc.x(13)
qc.ccx(9,13,8)

#Execute 2th then part
qc.cswap(8,0,2)
qc.cswap(8,1,3)

#Reset WM
qc.ccx(9,13,8)
#Restore descriptor
qc.x(13)
qc.barrier()

#If then rule (2) for empty at 2, 3  -> 6 , 7  or 0, 1

#Search empty state with the descriptor
qc.ccx(10,13,8)

#Execute 1st then part
qc.cswap(8,2,6)
qc.cswap(8,3,7)

#Secod then part with changed descriptor
#Reset WM
qc.ccx(10,13,8)
#Fetch second superposition
qc.x(13)
qc.ccx(10,13,8)

#Execute 2th then part
qc.cswap(8,0,2)
qc.cswap(8,1,3)
```

```
#Reset WM
qc.ccx(10,13,8)
#Restore descriptor
qc.x(13)
qc.barrier()

#If then rule (3) for empty at 4, 5  -> 6 ,7  or 0, 1

#Search empty state with the descriptor
qc.ccx(11,13,8)

#Execute 1st then part
qc.cswap(8,4,6)
qc.cswap(8,5,7)

#Secod then part with changed descriptor
#Reset WM
qc.ccx(11,13,8)
#Fetch second superposition
qc.x(13)
qc.ccx(11,13,8)

#Execute 2th then part
qc.cswap(8,0,4)
qc.cswap(8,1,5)

#Reset WM
qc.ccx(11,13,8)
#Restore descriptor
qc.x(13)
qc.barrier()

#If then rule (4) for empty at 6, 7  -> 4 ,5  or 2, 3

#Search empty state with the descriptor
qc.ccx(12,13,8)

#Execute 1st then part
qc.cswap(8,4,6)
qc.cswap(8,5,7)

#Secod then part with changed descriptor
#Reset WM
qc.ccx(12,13,8)
#Fetch second superposition
qc.x(13)
qc.ccx(12,13,8)

#Execute 2th then part
qc.cswap(8,2,6)
```

```
    qc.cswap(8,3,7)

    #Reset WM
    qc.ccx(12,13,8)
    #Restore descriptor
    qc.x(13)

    qc.name="R1"
    return qc

    qc.name="R1"
    return qc
```

and

```
def rules2():

    qc = QuantumCircuit(19)

    #If part of rules marked in trace (empty state)
    qc.ccx(0,1,14)
    qc.ccx(2,3,15)
    qc.ccx(4,5,16)
    qc.ccx(6,7,17)

    qc.barrier()

    #Rules

    #If then rule (1) for empty at 0, 1  -> 4 , 5  or 2, 3

    #Search empty state with the descriptor
    qc.ccx(14,18,8)

    #Execute 1st then part
    qc.cswap(8,0,4)
    qc.cswap(8,1,5)

    #Secod then part with changed descriptor
    #Reset WM
    qc.ccx(14,18,8)
    #Fetch second superposition
    qc.x(18)
    qc.ccx(14,18,8)

    #Execute 2th then part
    qc.cswap(8,0,2)
    qc.cswap(8,1,3)

    #Reset WM
    qc.ccx(14,18,8)
    #Restore descriptor
```

```
qc.x(18)
qc.barrier()


#If then rule (2) for empty at 2, 3  -> 6 , 7  or 0, 1

#Search empty state with the descriptor
qc.ccx(15,18,8)

#Execute 1st then part
qc.cswap(8,2,6)
qc.cswap(8,3,7)

#Secod then part with changed descriptor
#Reset WM
qc.ccx(15,18,8)
#Fetch second superposition
qc.x(18)
qc.ccx(15,18,8)

#Execute 2th then part
qc.cswap(8,0,2)
qc.cswap(8,1,3)

#Reset WM
qc.ccx(15,18,8)
#Restore descriptor
qc.x(18)
qc.barrier()

#If then rule (3) for empty at 4, 5  -> 6 ,7  or 0, 1

#Search empty state with the descriptor
qc.ccx(16,18,8)

#Execute 1st then part
qc.cswap(8,4,6)
qc.cswap(8,5,7)

#Secod then part with changed descriptor
#Reset WM
qc.ccx(16,18,8)
#Fetch second superposition
qc.x(18)
qc.ccx(16,18,8)

#Execute 2th then part
qc.cswap(8,0,4)
qc.cswap(8,1,5)

#Reset WM
```

```
qc.ccx(16,18,8)
#Restore descriptor
qc.x(18)
qc.barrier()

#If then rule (4) for empty at 6, 7  -> 4 ,5  or 2, 3

#Search empty state with the descriptor
qc.ccx(17,18,8)

#Execute 1st then part
qc.cswap(8,4,6)
qc.cswap(8,5,7)

#Secod then part with changed descriptor
#Reset WM
qc.ccx(17,18,8)
#Fetch second superposition
qc.x(18)
qc.ccx(17,18,8)

#Execute 2th then part
qc.cswap(8,2,6)
qc.cswap(8,3,7)

#Reset WM
qc.ccx(17,18,8)
#Restore descriptor
qc.x(18)

qc.name="R2"
return qc
```

In quantum computation it is not possible to reset the information to the pattern representing the initial state. Instead we un-compute the output back to the input before applying the amplification step of the Grover's algorithm. Because of the unitary evolution it follows that

$$((L(t) \otimes I_1)^*)^t \cdot (I_t \otimes T) \cdot (L(t) \otimes I_1)^t \cdot |\kappa^t, x, c\rangle \tag{9.9}$$

the computation can be undone and the corresponding path is marked by a negative sign using the auxiliary qubit c.

We use the *qiskit* inverse command *inverse()* to perform the inverse operation

```
def rules1_inv():
    qc=rules1()
    qc_inv=qc.inverse()
    qc_inv.name="R1_INV"
    return qc_inv
```

```
def rules2_inv():
    qc=rules2()
    qc_inv=qc.inverse()
    qc_inv.name="R2_INV"
    return qc_inv
```

The Grover's amplification is applied to the two qubits 13 and 16 representing the path descriptor

```
def Grover():
    qc = QuantumCircuit(19)
    #Diffusor
    qc.h([13,18])
    qc.z([13,18])
    qc.cz(13,18)
    qc.h([13,18])
    qc.name="G"
    return qc
```

The quantum circuit using the defined functions is represented as

```
qc = QuantumCircuit(20,2)
#State Preparation 0-7
# Flag bit 8
#1St Trace 9-12
#1St Path Descriptor in superposition
qc.h(13)
#1St Trace 14-17
#2th Path Descriptor in superposition
qc.h(18)
#Aux Bit c indicating the solution is negated and put in superposition
qc.x(19)
qc.h(19)
qc.barrier()
#Preperation of state
qc.append(state_A(),range(8))
#Depth1
qc.append(rules1(),range(14))
#Depth2
qc.append(rules2(),range(19))
#Oracle
qc.append(oracle(),range(20))
#Depth2
qc.append(rules2_inv(),range(19))
#Depth1
qc.append(rules1_inv(),range(14))
#Redo Preperation
qc.append(state_A(),range(8))
qc.barrier()
#Redo Superposition of Aux Bit
qc.h(19)
qc.barrier()
```

```
qc.append(Grover(),range(19))
qc.measure(13,0)
qc.measure(18,1)
```

The quantum circuit is indicated in the Figure 9.6.

9.4 SEARCH DEPTH THREE

A search of depth three is described by a path descriptor of three qubits. We define rules for the depth three using the *qiskit def* function and use the *qiskit* inverse command *inverse()* to perform the inverse operation in the same way as before. The Grover amplification act on the qubits 13, 18, and 23 that describe the path descriptor resulting in eight states.

```
def Grover():
    qc = QuantumCircuit(24)
    #Diffusor
    qc.h([13,18,23])
    qc.x([13,18,23])
    qc.h(13)
    qc.ccx(18,23,13)
    qc.h(13)
    qc.x([13,18,23])
```

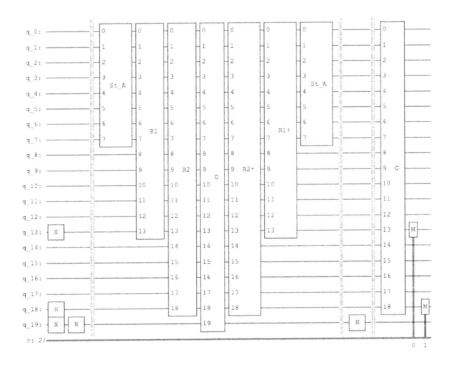

Figure 9.6 The quantum circuit of 3-puzzle task of the depth search 2. The circuits depth in the number of quantum gates is 12. The path descriptor has four possible states represented by two qubits. One marked state results in a certain solution 01 after one iteration, since for one marked qubit one requires only one rotation.

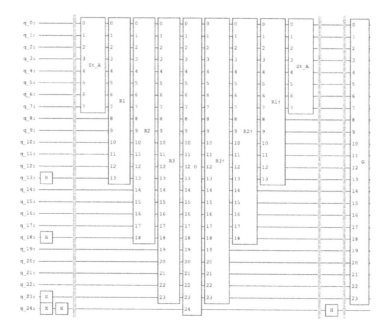

Figure 9.7 The quantum circuit for the 3-puzzle task of the depth search 3. Since we are using the *statevector simulator*, we do not need any measurement since the simulator determines the exact probabilities of each qubit. The circuits depth in the number of quantum gates is 13. The depth of a circuit is a metric that calculates the longest path between the data input and the output. The path descriptor has eight possible states represented by three qubits. One marked state results in a solution after one iteration indicated in the histogram of Figure 9.8.

```
qc.h([13,18,23])
qc.name="G"
return qc
```

The circuit is indicated in Figure 9.7. The *statevector simulator* without any measurements represent all probabilities of all qubits.

```
simulator = Aer.get_backend('statevector_simulator')
result=execute(qc,simulator).result()
counts = result.get_counts()
plot_histogram(counts)
```

The circuit's depth in the number of quantum gates is 13. The depth of a circuit is a metric that calculates the longest path between the input data and the output data. The path descriptor has eight possible states represented by three qubits. One marked state results after one iteration is indicated in the histogram of Figure 9.8. One marked state resulted after one iteration is indicated with a probability value 0.781 and the path descriptor 001. The path descriptor can be verified by measurement using the *qasm simulator* as well.

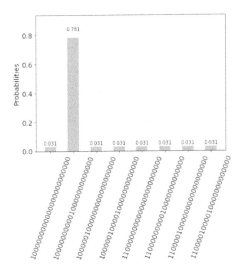

Figure 9.8 One marked state results after one iteration is indicated with a probability value 0.781 and the path descriptor 001 represented by the qubits 13, 18, and 23 by the *statevector simulator*. All other states are zero due to un-computation. The path descriptor can be verified by measurement using the *qasm simulator* of the qubits representing the path descriptor as well.

9.5 SEARCH DEPTH THREE WITH TWO ITERATIONS

We apply the $U_{3-puzzle}$ operator ignoring the trace for simplicity for the depth t resulting in 2^t states represented by the path descriptor

$$U_{3-puzzle} = ((L(t) \otimes I_1)^*)^t \cdot (I_t \otimes T) \cdot (L(t) \otimes I_1)^t \qquad (9.10)$$

With Grover amplification on t qubits representing the path descriptor by the unitary operator G_t

$$\Gamma_t := (G_t \otimes I_{10}) \cdot U_{3-puzzle}. \qquad (9.11)$$

With r iterations

$$\Gamma_t^r = \prod_{t=1}^{r} \Gamma_t \qquad (9.12)$$

and determine the solution by the measurement of the register that represents the path descriptor. In our case $t = 3$ and $r = 2$, with Γ_3^2 resulting in the circuit represented in the Figure 9.9.

```
qc = QuantumCircuit(25)

#State Preparation 0-7
#Working Memory for Flag bit 8
#1St Trace 9-12
#1St Descriptor in superposition
qc.h(13)
#1St Trace 14-17
```

```
#2th Descriptor in superposition
qc.h(18)
#1St Trace 19-22
#2th Descriptor in superposition
qc.h(23)
#Aux Bit
qc.x(24)
qc.h(24)
qc.barrier()

qc.append(state_A(),range(8))
#Depth1
qc.append(rules1(),range(14))
#Depth2
qc.append(rules2(),range(19))
#Depth3
qc.append(rules3(),range(24))
#Oracle
qc.append(oracle(),range(25))
#Depth 3
qc.append(rules3_inv(),range(24))
#Depth2
qc.append(rules2_inv(),range(19))
#Depth1
qc.append(rules1_inv(),range(14))
#Redo Preperation
qc.append(state_A(),range(8))
qc.barrier()

#Redo Aux Bit
qc.h(24)
qc.barrier()
qc.append(Grover(),range(24))
qc.barrier()

#Second Iteration!!!!
#Aux Bit in Superposition
qc.h(24)
qc.barrier()

qc.append(state_A(),range(8))
#Depth1
qc.append(rules1(),range(14))
#Depth2
qc.append(rules2(),range(19))
#Depth3
qc.append(rules3(),range(24))
#Oracle
qc.append(oracle(),range(25))
#Depth 3
qc.append(rules3_inv(),range(24))
```

```
#Depth2
qc.append(rules2_inv(),range(19))
#Depth1
qc.append(rules1_inv(),range(14))
#Redo Preperation
qc.append(state_A(),range(8))

qc.barrier()

#Redo Aux Bit
qc.h(24)
qc.barrier()
qc.append(Grover(),range(24))

print("\nCirquit depth:",qc.depth())

Cirquit depth: 25
```

One marked state results after two iterations are indicated in the histogram of Figure 9.10. One marked state results after two iterations are indicated with a probability value of 0.945 and the path descriptor 001.

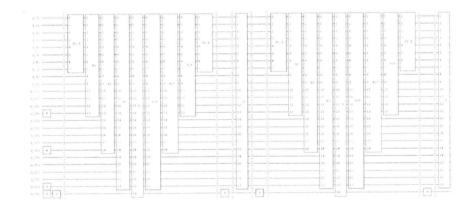

Figure 9.9 The quantum circuit for the 3-puzzle task of the depth search three with two iterations. Since we are using *statevector* simulator we do not need any measurement since the simulator determines the exact probabilities of each qubit. The circuits depth in the number of quantum gates is 25. The path descriptor has eight possible states represented by three qubits. An important operation before the second iteration is the setting of the auxiliary qubit 24 in superposition by a Hadamard gate. We could simplify the circuit by eliminating the two Hadamard gates of the auxiliary qubit 24 after the first and second iteration, however by doing so the circuit loses its modular structure (less readable) and the redundant operations are simplified during the transpilation process. One marked state results in a solution after two iteration indicated in the histogram of Figure 9.10.

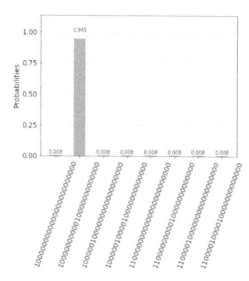

Figure 9.10   One marked state results after two iterations is indicated with a probability value 0.945 by the *statevector simulator*. This is the optimum theoretical value for one marked solution using Grover's amplification of eight states. If we apply another rotation, the theoretical probability would decrease.

The 3-puzzle quantum production system highlighted the principles of quantum tree search and quantum production systems. It does not give any true computational speed up due to the simplicity of the problem.

## CHAPTER 10

8 Puzzle

The n-puzzle is a classical problem for modeling algorithms. For n-puzzle there are $n + 1$ different objects: n cells and one empty cell. Each object can be coded by $\rho = \lceil \log_2 n + 1 \rceil$ qubits and a configuration of $n + 1$ objects can be represented by a register of $z := \rho \cdot (n + 1)$ qubits $|x\rangle$. The function $g(x)$ is represented a unitary operator T. T acts on the $z + 1$ qubits with $x \in B^z$ and $c \in B^1$

$$T \cdot |x\rangle|c\rangle = |x\rangle|f(x) \oplus c\rangle.$$

We indicate how to extend the 3-puzzle to the 8-puzzle resulting in a non-constant branching factor. We show that the branching factor is reduced by Grover's amplification to the square root of the average branching factor and not to the maximal branching factor. Simple experiments of the search of the depth one requires already 49 qubits. The experiments indicate that the presented methods can be extended to a search of any depth, given that more qubits are present.

10.1 REPRESENTATION

For 8-puzzle, there are 9 different objects: eight cells and one empty cell. Each object has to be represented by four 4 qubits since 3 qubits allow only to represent $2^3 = 8$ different states. The object 1 is represented by 001, 2 is represented by 010, and 3 is represented by 011, and we continue the representation as binary numbers with 8 represented as 1000. We represent the empty space x by 1111. The state is represented by 36 qubits $x_0, x_1, x_2, x_3, x_4, x_5, x_6, x_7, \cdots, x_{35}$, see Figure 10.1. The empty cell can be present in 9 different positions. The empty cell can move either up, down, left or right. The new board configuration is determined by the function p. The input of the function p is the current board configuration and two bits $m = m_1, m_2$ (qubits 46 and 47) indicating whether the blank cell should perform move right ($m = 0 = |00\rangle$), left ($m = 1 = |01\rangle$), up ($m = 2 = |10\rangle$) or down ($m = 3 = |11\rangle$). There are 36 qubits to represent the state and 9 qubits for the trace, together with the auxiliary qubit 49 qubits are represented by the quantum circuit.

```
qc = QuantumCircuit(49,2)
#State Preparation 0-35
#N3
qc.x(0)
qc.x(1)
```

DOI: 10.1201/9781003374404-10

7	8	6
0111	1000	0110
35 34 33 32	31 30 29 28	27 26 25 24
4	**X**	**5**
0100	1111	0101
23 22 21 20	19 18 17 16	15 14 13 12
1	**2**	**3**
0001	0010	0011
11 10 9 8	7 6 5 4	3 2 1 0

Figure 10.1 8-puzzle coding. The 9 objects are by a register of 36 qubits. We indicate the state, its representation and below the position of the 36 qubits. In this representation, position description (adjective) is fixed and the class descriptors move.

```
#2
#3
..
..


#Flag 36
#1St Trace 37-45
#1St Path Descriptor in superposition 46, 47
qc.h(46)
qc.h(47)
#Preparation of Aux
qc.x(48)
qc.h(48)
```

In the case the empty cell is in the center, four movements are possible. For a cell in the edge only three movements are possible, for the corner only two movements are possible

```
def if_rules():
    qc = QuantumCircuit(46)
    #Marke the trace indicate the rule group through trace
    gate = MCXGate(4)
    #Empty Space in corner, 2 movements
    qc.append(gate, [0, 1, 2, 3, 37])
    #Empty Space in edge, 3 movements
    qc.append(gate, [4, 5, 6, 7, 38])
    #Empty Space in corner, 2 movements
    qc.append(gate, [8, 9, 10, 11, 39])
    #Empty Space in edge, 3 movements
    qc.append(gate, [12, 13, 14, 15, 40])
    #Empty Space in center, 4 movements
    qc.append(gate, [16, 17, 18, 19, 41])
```

```
    #Empty Space in edge, 3 movements
    qc.append(gate, [20, 21, 22, 23, 42])
    #Empty Space in corner, 2 movements
    qc.append(gate, [24, 25, 26, 27, 43])
     #Empty Space in edge, 3 movements
    qc.append(gate, [28, 29, 30, 31, 44])
    #Empty Space in corner, 2 movements
    qc.append(gate, [32, 33, 34, 35, 45])
    qc.name="IF"
    return qc
```

For the empty space in the center, there are four instantiations corresponding to the four movements.

```
def rules1():
    qc = QuantumCircuit(48)
    #Flag 36
    #Path Descriptor 46, 47
    #Trace 37-45
    flag_gate = MCXGate(3)

    #If then rule move right, for empty at 16, 17, 18, 19  -> 12, 13, 14, 15
    qc.append(flag_gate, [41, 46, 47, 36])
    #Move
    qc.cswap(36,16,12)
    qc.cswap(36,17,13)
    qc.cswap(36,18,14)
    qc.cswap(36,19,15)
    #Clear Flag
    qc.append(flag_gate, [41, 46, 47, 36])

    #If then rule move left, for empty at 16, 17, 18, 19  -> 20, 21, 22, 23
    qc.x(46)
    qc.append(flag_gate, [41, 46, 47, 36])
    #Move
    qc.cswap(36,16,20)
    qc.cswap(36,17,21)
    qc.cswap(36,18,22)
    qc.cswap(36,19,23)
    #Clear Flag
    qc.append(flag_gate, [41, 46, 47, 36])
    qc.x(46)

    #If then rule move up, for empty at 16, 17, 18, 19  -> 28, 29, 30, 31
    qc.x(47)
    qc.append(flag_gate, [41, 46, 47, 36])
    #Move
    qc.cswap(36,16,28)
    qc.cswap(36,17,29)
    qc.cswap(36,18,30)
    qc.cswap(36,19,31)
    #Clear Flag
```

```
qc.append(flag_gate, [41, 46, 47, 36])

qc.x(47)

#If then rule move down, for empty at 16, 17, 18, 19  -> 4, 5, 6, 7
qc.x(46)
qc.x(47)
qc.append(flag_gate, [41, 46, 47, 36])
#Move
qc.cswap(36,16,4)
qc.cswap(36,17,5)
qc.cswap(36,18,6)
qc.cswap(36,19,7)
#Clear Flag
qc.append(flag_gate, [41, 46, 47, 36])
qc.x(47)
qc.x(46)

qc.name="R1"
return qc
```

For the empty space in the center, there are four instantiations corresponding to the four movements

- For the path descriptor 00, move right $16, 17, 18, 19 \rightarrow 12, 13, 14, 15$.

- For the path descriptor 00, move left $16, 17, 18, 19 \rightarrow 20, 21, 22, 23$.

- For the path descriptor 00, move up $16, 17, 18, 19 \rightarrow 28, 29, 30, 31$.

- For the path descriptor 00, move down $16, 17, 18, 19 \rightarrow 4, 5, 6, 7$.

For the empty space in the edge, there are four instantiations corresponding to the three movements. The representation if performed in the same way as before, in our example, the empty space is at the position $12, 13, 14, 15$.

- For the path descriptor 00, move up $12, 13, 14, 15 \rightarrow 24, 25, 26, 27$.

- For the path descriptor 01, move down $12, 13, 14, 15 \rightarrow 0, 1, 2, 3$.

- For the path descriptor 10, move left $12, 13, 14, 15 \rightarrow 16, 17, 18, 19$.

- For the path descriptor 11, move left $12, 13, 14, 15 \rightarrow 16, 17, 18, 19$.

The only difference is that the rule move left is repeated twice. For the empty space in the corner, there are four instantiations corresponding to the two movements. The representation is performed in the same way as before, in our example, the empty space is at the position $0, 1, 2, 3$.

- For the path descriptor 00, move up $0, 1, 2, 3 \rightarrow 12, 13, 14, 15$.

- For the path descriptor 01, move up $0, 1, 2, 3 \rightarrow 12, 13, 14, 15$.

- For the path descriptor 10, move left $0, 1, 2, 3 \rightarrow 4, 5, 6, 7$.

- For the path descriptor 11, move left $0, 1, 2, 3 \rightarrow 4, 5, 6, 7$.

The rule move up and the rule move left are repeated twice. The marked solution cannot be bigger than the one fourth of the present states, which is present during a deeper search. Simulating 49 qubits requires higher memory capacity, we cannot use the *statevector simulator* or a search depth of two due to memory constraints. We can measure the path descriptor after applying the function *rules1 8 puzzle*, see Figure 10.2. These constraints can be overcome by higher memory capacity.

10.2 NUMBER OF ITERATIONS

For 8-puzzle, $B_{max} = 4$, $B_{min} = 2$, and

$$B_{average} = \frac{4 \cdot 1 + 2 \cdot 4 + 3 \cdot 4}{9} = 2.6667. \tag{10.1}$$

Naively, we would assume that the branching factor is reduced by Grover's amplification to

$$\sqrt{B_{max}} = \sqrt{4} = 2 \tag{10.2}$$

However, this is not the case in our coding strategy. With growing value n, the branching factor is reduced by Grover's amplification to

$$\sqrt{B_{average}} = \sqrt{2.6667} = 1.63299 \tag{10.3}$$

For k solutions, the probability of measuring a state that represents one solution of k solutions is related to the number r of iterations of the Grover's operator. The probability of seeing one solution should be as close as possible to 1, and the number of iterations r should be as small as possible. After r iterations, the probability of measuring a solution is nearly one, with m being the number of qubits describing the path descriptor [45, 72]

$$r = \left\lfloor \frac{\pi}{4} \cdot \sqrt{\frac{2^m}{k}} - \frac{1}{2} \right\rfloor. \tag{10.4}$$

The number of iterations r is the largest integer not greater than the computed value. Simplified, we can state that

$$r = \sqrt{\frac{(B_{max})^m}{k}} \tag{10.5}$$

The value of r depends on the relation of m versus k, and k is bigger than one since we execute same rules several times. For the depth m, there are k solutions with

$$k = \left(\frac{B_{max}}{B_{average}} \right)^m \tag{10.6}$$

it follows

$$r = \sqrt{(B_{average})^m} \tag{10.7}$$

and the branching factor is reduced by Grover's amplification to $\sqrt{B_{average}}$

$$\sqrt{B_{average}} = \sqrt{2.6667} = 1.63299.$$

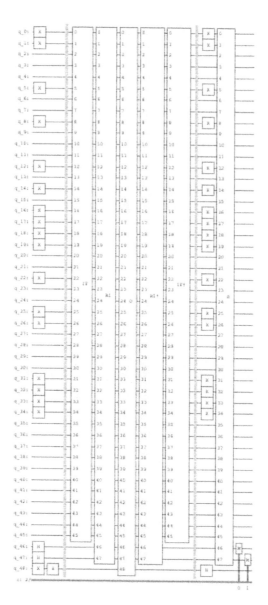

Figure 10.2 The quantum circuit for the 9-puzzle task of the depth search 1. The empty space is in the center and the desired state is represented by the empty space at top. Simulating 49 qubits requires higher memory capacity, we cannot use the *statevector simulator* or a search depth of two due to memory constraints. The path descriptor is represented by two qubits and is measured after applying the function *rules*1, which corresponds in moving the empty space up.

## CHAPTER 11

Blocks World

The blocks world is a planning domain in artificial intelligence [73]. The blocks can be placed at the table and picked up and set down on a table or another block, and the goal is to build one or more vertical stacks of blocks. Only one block may be moved at a time and any blocks that are under another block cannot be moved. There are three different types of blocks. They differ by attributes such as color (red, green, and blue) or marks, but not by form. In Artificial intelligence (AI), they are traditionally called A, B, and C blocks [61]. The simplicity of this toy problem allows to compare classical approach with quantum computing approach. We indicate how the binding of the stats is achieved through the entanglement. We indicate how to represent the states with a class descriptor and the position descriptor (adjective) and perform a search of depth one. The A, B, and C blocks planning problem results in a non-constant branching factor. We show again that the branching factor is reduced by Grover's amplification to the square root of the average branching factor and not to the maximal branching factor.

11.1 REPRESENTATION

The class descriptor is fixed and the position descriptor (adjective) moves. It is reversed as in the puzzle examples, since the reverse in this case is a more economic representation requiring 9 qubits, three qubits for each block (see Figures 11.1 and 11.2). The architecture uses 27 qubits, 9 for representation of the state, 1 for flag and 13 qubits to represent the 13 different categories of rules. The path descriptor for the depth search one is represented by three qubits, since the number of maximal instantiations is six.

```
qc = QuantumCircuit(27)
#State Preparation 0-8
# Flag 9
#1st Trace (ten) 10-22 Rule Classes
#1st Path descriptor represented by three qubit
qc.h(23)
qc.h(24)
qc.h(25)
#Preparation of Aux
qc.x(26)
```

DOI: 10.1201/9781003374404-11

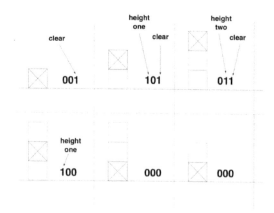

Figure 11.1 Three qubits (bits) for each block represent its state. The first qubit equaling one indicates that the block is on top of one other block. The second qubit equaling one indicates that the block is on top of two other blocks. The third qubit equaling one indicates that the block is clear with nothing on top of it.

```
qc.h(26)
```

The architecture is indicated in the Figure 11.3. All blocks on the floor are represented as:

```
def state_floor():
    qc = QuantumCircuit(9)
    #All Blocks are on floor
    #BLOCK A qubits 0-2
    qc.x(2)
    #BLOCK B qubits 3-5
    qc.x(5)
```

A		B		C		
x	2	x	5		8	clear
	1		4		7	height two
	0	x	3		6	height one

B		
C	A	001 101 000

Figure 11.2 Representing a state of A,B, and C blocks by 9 qubits (bits). The class descriptor is fixed and the position descriptor (adjective) moves (is changed). Three qubits (bits) for each block represent its state. Their value changes indicating different states. On top, we see the three blocks A, B, and C and the 9 positions of the qubits by the index from 0 to 9, x indicates that the qubit is equal to one. Below, we represent the corresponding state and the corresponding binary string.

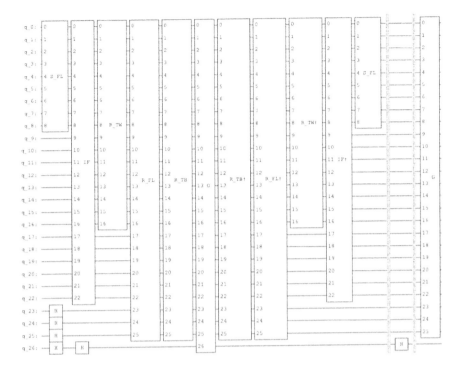

Figure 11.3 The quantum circuit for the ABC blocks task of the depth search 1. Since we are using the *statevector simulator*, we do not need any measurement since the simulator determines the exact probabilities of each qubit. The circuit's depth in the number of quantum gates is 13. The path descriptor has eight possible states represented by three qubits. One marked state results in a solution after one iteration indicated for the initial state "all blocks on the floor" in the histogram of Figure 11.7.

```
#BLOCK C qubits 6-8
  qc.x(8)
qc.name="S_FL"
return qc
```

11.1.1 Rules (Productions)

Different classes of rules are recognized during the *if_rules*() function. The class all blocks on floor has one combination (see Figure 11.4), the class tower appears in six different combinations (see Figure 11.5) as well as the class small tower and a block on table (like BC tower and block A, see Figure 11.6)

```
def if_rules():
    qc = QuantumCircuit(23)
```

A B C

Figure 11.4 The class all blocks on floor has one combination.

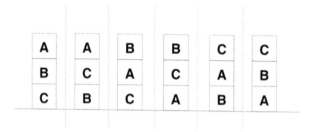

Figure 11.5 The classes tower appears in six different combinations.

```
gate = MCXGate(3)

#All blocks on table
qc.append(gate, [2, 5, 8, 10])

#ABC tower
qc.append(gate, [1, 2, 3, 11])
#ACB tower
qc.append(gate, [1, 2, 6, 12])
#BAC tower
qc.append(gate, [4, 5, 1, 13])
#BCA tower
qc.append(gate, [4, 5, 6, 14])
#CAB  tower
qc.append(gate, [1, 7, 8, 15])
#CBA tower
qc.append(gate, [4, 7, 8, 16])

#BC tower and block A
qc.append(gate, [2, 5, 3, 17])
#BA tower and block C
```

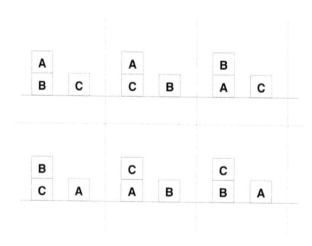

Figure 11.6 The class small tower and a block on table appears in six different combinations.

```
qc.append(gate, [8, 5, 3, 18])
#CA tower and block B
qc.append(gate, [8, 6, 5, 19])
#CB tower and block A
qc.append(gate, [8, 6, 2, 20])
#AC tower and block B
qc.append(gate, [0, 2, 5, 21])
#AB tower and block C
qc.append(gate, [0, 2, 8, 22])

qc.name="IF"
return qc
```

The class tower like for example ABC tower has just one instantiation, the class small tower and a block on table (like BC tower and block A) have three instantiations. All blocks on table have six different instantiations, for each block there are two rules.

```
def rules_floor():
    qc = QuantumCircuit(26)
     gate4 = MCXGate(4)
    qc.append(gate4, [10 ,23 ,24 ,25, 9])
    #All blocks on floor

    # Moving A
    #A on B
    qc.cswap(9,0,5)
    #Secod then part with changed descriptor
    #Reset WM (Working Memory)
    qc.append(gate4, [10 ,23 ,24 ,25, 9])
    #Fetch second superposition
    qc.x(23)
    qc.append(gate4, [10 ,23 ,24 ,25, 9])
    #A on C
    qc.cswap(9,0,8)
    #Reset WM
    qc.append(gate4, [10 ,23 ,24 ,25, 9])
    #Restore descriptor
    qc.x(23)

    # Moving B
    qc.x(24)
    qc.append(gate4, [10 ,23 ,24 ,25, 9])
    # B on A
    qc.cswap(9,2,3)
    #Secod then part with changed descriptor
    #Reset WM
    qc.append(gate4, [10 ,23 ,24 ,25, 9])
    qc.x(24)
    #Fetch second superposition
    qc.x(23)
    qc.x(24)
```

```
qc.append(gate4, [10 ,23 ,24 ,25, 9])
#B on C
qc.cswap(9,3,8)
#Reset WM
qc.append(gate4, [10 ,23 ,24 ,25, 9])
#Restore descriptor
qc.x(24)
qc.x(23)


# Moving C
qc.x(25)
qc.append(gate4, [10 ,23 ,24 ,25, 9])
#C on A
qc.cswap(9,6,2)
#Secod then part with changed descriptor
#Reset WM
qc.append(gate4, [10 ,23 ,24 ,25, 9])
qc.x(25)
#Fetch second superposition
qc.x(25)
qc.x(23)
qc.append(gate4, [10 ,23 ,24 ,25, 9])
# C on B
qc.cswap(9,6,5)
#Reset WM
qc.append(gate4, [10 ,23 ,24 ,25, 9])
#Restore descriptor
qc.x(23)
qc.x(25)


#We have only six rules, but eight possible paths!!!
#To get rid of the initial state we will move C again!!!

# Moving C Again
qc.x(24)
qc.x(25)
qc.append(gate4, [10 ,23 ,24 ,25, 9])
# A clear goes to high of B
qc.cswap(9,6,2)
#Secod then part with changed descriptor
#Reset WM
qc.append(gate4, [10 ,23 ,24 ,25, 9])
qc.x(25)
qc.x(24)
#Fetch second superposition
qc.x(23)
qc.x(24)
qc.x(25)
qc.append(gate4, [10 ,23 ,24 ,25, 9])
# C clear goes to high of B
```

```
qc.cswap(9,6,5)
#Reset WM
qc.append(gate4, [10 ,23 ,24 ,25, 9])
#Restore descriptor
qc.x(25)
qc.x(24)
qc.x(23)

qc.name="R_FL"
return qc
```

The class tower (like for example ABC tower) appears in six different combinations. For each combination there is only one instantiation that is represented through all eight states:

```
def rules_tw():
    qc = QuantumCircuit(17)
    #There is a tower (6 different towers indicated by 11,12,..,16
    qc.cswap(11,1,5)
    qc.cswap(12,1,8)
    qc.cswap(13,2,4)
    qc.cswap(14,2,8)
    qc.cswap(15,2,7)
    qc.cswap(16,5,7)
    qc.name="R_TW"
    return qc
```

There are six combinations of the class small tower and a block on table (like BC tower and block A). Each of this combination has three instantiations. Since there are eight possible states represented by the path descriptor for each combination the three instantiations are executed twice with two additional instantiations.

```
def rules_tw_bl():
    qc = QuantumCircuit(26)
    gate4 = MCXGate(4)
    #Flag 9
    #Path Descriptor 23, 24, 25

    #The three instantiations
    #BC tower and block A
    #qc.append(gate, [2, 5, 3, 17])
    #Put it on Floor
    qc.append(gate4, [17 ,23 ,24 ,25, 9])
    qc.cswap(9,3,8)
    #Clear WM
    qc.append(gate4, [17 ,23 ,24 ,25, 9])
    #Make Tower BCA
    qc.x(23)
    qc.append(gate4, [17 ,23 ,24 ,25, 9])
    qc.cswap(9,5,1)
    #Clear WM
```

```
qc.append(gate4, [17 ,23 ,24 ,25, 9])
qc.x(23)
#Move C on the other block A
qc.x(24)
qc.append(gate4, [17 ,23 ,24 ,25, 9])
qc.cswap(9,2,8)
#Clear WM
qc.append(gate4, [17 ,23 ,24 ,25, 9])
qc.x(24)


#Repeat  three instantiations  again  for the states  4-6  of the path desc
#Put it on Floor
qc.x(24)
qc.x(23)
qc.append(gate4, [17 ,23 ,24 ,25, 9])
qc.cswap(9,3,8)
#Clear WM
qc.append(gate4, [17 ,23 ,24 ,25, 9])
qc.x(24)
qc.x(23)
#Make Tower BCA
qc.x(25)
qc.append(gate4, [17 ,23 ,24 ,25, 9])
qc.cswap(9,5,1)
#Clear WM
qc.append(gate4, [17 ,23 ,24 ,25, 9])
qc.x(25)
#Move C on the other block A
qc.x(25)
qc.x(23)
qc.append(gate4, [17 ,23 ,24 ,25, 9])
qc.cswap(9,2,8)
#Clear WM
qc.append(gate4, [17 ,23 ,24 ,25, 9])
qc.x(25)
qc.x(23)


#Repeat  two instantiations again for the states 7-8 of the path descriptor
#Make Tower BCA
qc.x(25)
qc.x(24)
qc.append(gate4, [17 ,23 ,24 ,25, 9])
qc.cswap(9,5,1)
#Clear WM
qc.append(gate4, [17 ,23 ,24 ,25, 9])
qc.x(25)
qc.x(24)
#Move C on the other block A
qc.x(25)
qc.x(24)
```

```
qc.x(23)
qc.append(gate4, [17 ,23 ,24 ,25, 9])
qc.cswap(9,2,8)
#Clear WM
qc.append(gate4, [17 ,23 ,24 ,25, 9])
qc.x(25)
qc.x(24)
qc.x(23)

#In the same way
#BA tower and block C
#CA tower and block B
#CB tower and block A
#AC tower and block B
#AB tower and block C
.....
qc.name="R_TB"
return qc
```

11.1.2 Oracle

The goal states AC and B is represented by the oracle

```
def oracle():
    qc = QuantumCircuit(27)
    #Specify goal state
    gate = MCXGate(3)
    #AC  B
    qc.append(gate,[3, 5, 8, 26])
    qc.name="O"
    return qc
```

11.1.3 Architecture

The quantum circuit for the ABC blocks task of the depth search 1, (see Figure 11.3)

```
qc = QuantumCircuit(27)
#State Preparation 0-8

#Working Memory,  Flag 9

#1St Trace (ten) 10-22 Rule Classes

#1St Descriptor in superposition, one, three, six possible actions
represented by three qubit
#Possible instantiations

qc.h(23)
qc.h(24)
qc.h(25)
```

```
#Preparation of Aux
qc.x(26)
qc.h(26)

qc.append(state_floor(),range(9))
qc.append(if_rules(),range(23))
qc.append(rules_tw(),range(17))
qc.append(rules_floor(),range(26))
qc.append(rules_tw_bl(),range(26))
qc.append(oracle(),range(27))
qc.append(rules_tw_bl_inv(),range(26))
qc.append(rules_floor_inv(),range(26))
qc.append(rules_tw_inv(),range(17))
qc.append(if_rules_inv(),range(23))
qc.append(state_floor(),range(9))

qc.barrier()
qc.h(26)
qc.barrier()
qc.append(Grover(),range(26))
print("\nCirquit depth:",qc.depth())
```

11.2   EXAMPLES

One solution is marked, after one iteration of Grover's amplification, the probabilities of measuring a state using the *statevector simulator* are indicated in the Figure 11.7. Three marked states results in a solution after one iteration indicated for the initial state BC and A and the goal states AC and B, the probabilities of measuring a state using the *statevector simulator* are indicated in the Figure 11.8.

11.3   NUMBER OF ITERATIONS

For A, B, C blocks $B_{max} = 6$, $B_{min} = 1$, and

$$B_{average} = \frac{6 \cdot 1 + 1 \cdot 6 + 3 \cdot 6}{13} = 2.30769. \tag{11.1}$$

Naïvely, we would assume that the branching factor is reduced by Grover's amplification to the number 8 represented by three qubits

$$\sqrt{8} = 2.82843 \tag{11.2}$$

With growing value m, the branching factor is reduced by Grover's amplification to

$$\sqrt{B_{average}} = \sqrt{2.30769} = 1.51911 \tag{11.3}$$

For k solutions, the probability of measuring a state that represents one solution of k solutions is related to the number r of iterations of the Grover's operator. Simplified, we can state that

$$r = \sqrt{\frac{(8)^m}{k}} \tag{11.4}$$

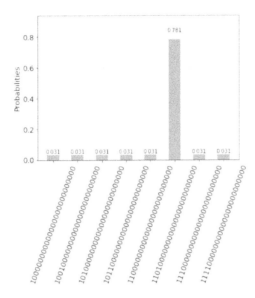

Figure 11.7 One marked state results in a solution after one iteration indicated for the initial state all blocks on the floor and the goal states AC and B. The solution is described by the path descriptor by the qubits 23, 24, and 25 with the binary value 101, the fifth branch. There are 8 branches described by 8 possible transitions $0, 1 \cdots 7$.

The value of r depends on the relation of m versus k. For the depth m

$$k = \left(\frac{8}{B_{average}} \right)^m \tag{11.5}$$

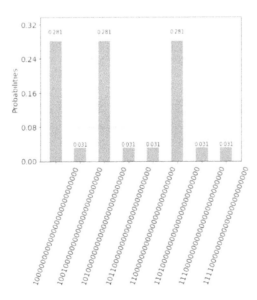

Figure 11.8 Three marked states results in a solution after one iteration indicated for the initial state BC and A and the goal states AC and B by the $statevector$ $simulator$.

it follows

$$r = \sqrt{(B_{average})^m} \tag{11.6}$$

and the branching factor is reduced by Grover's amplification to $\sqrt{B_{average}} = 1.5191$.

## CHAPTER 12

Five Pennies Nim Game

Games involving two players represent one of the classic applications of symbolic problem solving. Starting with some initial game position, the algorithm explores the tree of all legal moves down to the requested depth. An example is the *nim* game in which two players take turns removing objects from distinct piles. A simplified version is the *nim* game with no piles, the five pennies *nim* game. Two players alternate remove either one, two, or three pennies from a stack that initially contains five pennies. The player who pick up last penny loses. The five pennies *nim* game is a zero game where neither player has any legal options. The first player loses, and the second-player wins if correct moves are chosen.

We indicate the architecture for the five pennies *nim* game and indicate that a quantum tree search cannot implement the minimax-algorithm. We can determine the search path, but we cannot model the behavior of the player that choses the best move since we cannot compare different states that are described by different path descriptors.

12.1 QUANTUM CIRCUIT

In our implementation of the five pennies *nim* game we explore of legal moves to the depth of two [73]. In initial game the five pennies are represented by the qubits 0 to 4. The player A starts the game, he can remove one, two, or three pennies. The path descriptor is represented by two qubits 6 and 7. The qubit 5 is the flag that indicates the entanglement of a rule with the path descriptor. The first rule removes three pennies, the second two pennies and the third one penny. Since we have four possible paths, the rule three and four are identical. The player B has either a stack with four, three, or two pennies. Depending on the number of pennies, different rule types can be executed, either the rule of the type 1, type 2 or type 3. The correct type is identified and marked in the trace represented by the qubits 8, 9, and 10, see Figure 12.1. Each of the three rules is instantiated with the path descriptor and can be executed in parallel. The resulting states corresponding to one penny are marked by the oracle, see Figure 12.2. They correspond to the loss of player A, since the player who picks up the last penny loses.

DOI: 10.1201/9781003374404-12

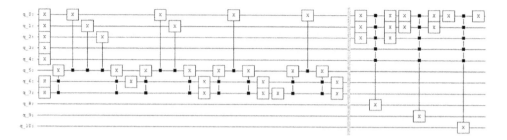

Figure 12.1 In initial game the five pennies are represented by the qubits 0 to 4. The path descriptor is represented by two qubits 6 and 7. The qubit 5 is a flag. The first rule removes three pennies, the second two pennies and the third one penny. Since we have four possible paths the rule three is executed twice in parallel. Depending of the number of pennies different rules types can be executed, either the type 1, type 2, or type 3. The correct type is identified and marked in the trace by the qubits 8, 9, and 10.

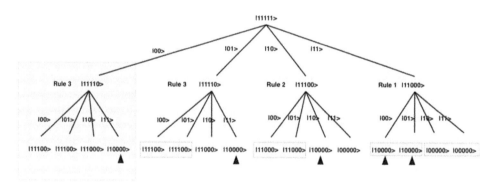

Figure 12.2 The search tree for the five pennies *nim* game of the depth two. In initial game the five pennies are present. They are represented by five qubits $|11111\rangle$. The player A starts the game, he can remove one, two, or three pennies. The path descriptors are represented by two qubits $|00\rangle$, $|01\rangle$, $|10\rangle$, $|11\rangle$. The first rule removes three pennies, the second two pennies, and the third one penny. Since we have four possible paths, the rule three and four are identical. The player B has either a stack with four, three, or two pennies. Depending of the number of pennies, different rule types can be executed, either the type 1, type 2, or type 3. Each of the three rules is instantiated with the path descriptors $|00\rangle$, $|01\rangle$, $|10\rangle$, $|11\rangle$. The resulting states corresponding to one penny $|10000\rangle$ are marked by the oracle, they are indicated in the figure by a triangle. They correspond to the loss of player A, since the player who picks up the last penny loses. Similar states and equal rules are marked by gray rectangles. We can determine the search path, but we cannot model the behavior of the player that choses the best move, since we cannot compare different states that are described by different path descriptors.

We can determine the search path, but we cannot model the behavior of the player that choses the best move since we cannot compare different states that are described by different path descriptors.

12.1.1 Representation of Rules

The first rule removes three pennies, the second two pennies and the third one penny. Since we have four possible paths, the rule three is executed twice in parallel.

```
import numpy as np
from qiskit import QuantumCircuit, transpile, Aer,assemble,execute
from qiskit.providers.aer import QasmSimulator
from qiskit.visualization import plot_histogram
from qiskit.quantum_info import Statevector
from qiskit.circuit.library import MCXGate

def rules_depth1():
    qc = QuantumCircuit(8)
    #First Rule
    #Set flag 5 dependent on the path descriptor
    qc.ccx(6,7,5)
    # Move
    qc.cx(5,0)
    qc.cx(5,1)
    qc.cx(5,2)
    #Reset flag
    qc.ccx(6,7,5)

    #Second Rule
    #Set flag 5 dependent on the path descriptor
    qc.x(6)
    qc.ccx(6,7,5)
    # Move
    qc.cx(5,0)
    qc.cx(5,1)
    #Reset flag
    qc.ccx(6,7,5)
    qc.x(6)

    #Third Rule
    #Set flag 5 dependent on the path descriptor
    qc.x(7)
    qc.ccx(6,7,5)
    # Move
    qc.cx(5,0)
    #Reset flag
    qc.ccx(6,7,5)
    qc.x(7)

    #Fourth=Third Rule
    #Set flag 5 dependent on the path descriptor
    qc.x(6)
```

```
        qc.x(7)
        qc.ccx(6,7,5)
        # Move
        qc.cx(5,0)
        #Reset flag
        qc.ccx(6,7,5)
        qc.x(7)
        qc.x(6)
        qc.name="RULES_1"
        return qc

def rules_depth1_inv():
        qc=rules_depth1()
        qc_inv=qc.inverse()
        qc_inv.name="RULES_1Ḙ"
        return qc_inv
```

Depending of the number of pennies different rule types can be executed, either the rule 1, rule 2, or rule 3. The correct rule is identified and marked in the trace represented by the qubits 8, 9, and 10.

```
def if_depth2():
        qc = QuantumCircuit(11)

        #If part of rules depth 2 marked in trace
        gate = MCXGate(5)

        #IF Rule 2 Coins
        qc.x(0)
        qc.x(1)
        qc.x(2)
        qc.append(gate, [0,1,2,3,4,8])
        qc.x(2)
        qc.x(1)
        qc.x(0)
        #IF Rule 3 Coins
        qc.x(0)
        qc.x(1)
        qc.append(gate, [0,1,2,3,4,9])
        qc.x(1)
        qc.x(0)
        #IF Rule 4 Coins
        qc.x(0)
        qc.append(gate, [0,1,2,3,4,10])
        qc.x(0)
        qc.name="IF_2"
        return qc
```

Each of the three rules is instantiated with the path descriptor represented by the qubits 11 and 12.

```
def rules_depth2():
```

```
qc = QuantumCircuit(13)
#Flag 5
#Path Descriptor 11, 12
#Trace 8-10
flag_gate = MCXGate(3)

#First Rule: trace 8

#First instantiation
qc.append(flag_gate, [8, 11, 12, 5])
# Move
qc.cx(5,3)
qc.cx(5,4)
#Clear Flag
qc.append(flag_gate, [8, 11, 12, 5])

#Second instantiation
qc.x(11)
qc.append(flag_gate, [8, 11, 12, 5])
# Move
qc.cx(5,3)
qc.cx(5,4)
#Clear Flag
qc.append(flag_gate, [8, 11, 12, 5])
qc.x(11)

#Third instantiation
qc.x(12)
qc.append(flag_gate, [8, 11, 12, 5])
# Move
qc.cx(5,3)
#Clear Flag
qc.append(flag_gate, [8, 11, 12, 5])
qc.x(12)

#Fourth instantiation
qc.x(11)
qc.x(12)
qc.append(flag_gate, [8, 11, 12, 5])
# Move
qc.cx(5,3)
#Clear Flag
qc.append(flag_gate, [8, 11, 12, 5])
qc.x(12)
qc.x(11)

#Second Rule: trace 9

#First instantiation
qc.append(flag_gate, [9, 11, 12, 5])
# Move
```

```
qc.cx(5,2)
qc.cx(5,3)
qc.cx(5,4)
#Clear Flag
qc.append(flag_gate, [9, 11, 12, 5])

#Second instantiation
qc.x(11)
qc.append(flag_gate, [9, 11, 12, 5])
# Move
qc.cx(5,2)
qc.cx(5,3)
#Clear Flag
qc.append(flag_gate, [9, 11, 12, 5])
qc.x(11)

#Third instantiation
qc.x(12)
qc.append(flag_gate, [9, 11, 12, 5])
# Move
qc.cx(5,2)
#Clear Flag
qc.append(flag_gate, [9, 11, 12, 5])
qc.x(12)

#Fourth instantiation
qc.x(11)
qc.x(12)
qc.append(flag_gate, [9, 11, 12, 5])
# Move
qc.cx(5,2)
#Clear Flag
qc.append(flag_gate, [9, 11, 12, 5])
qc.x(12)
qc.x(11)

#Third Rule: trace 10

#First instantiation
qc.append(flag_gate, [10, 11, 12, 5])
# Move
qc.cx(5,1)
qc.cx(5,2)
qc.cx(5,3)
#Clear Flag
qc.append(flag_gate, [10, 11, 12, 5])

#Second instantiation
qc.x(11)
qc.append(flag_gate, [10, 11, 12, 5])
# Move
```

```
qc.cx(5,1)
qc.cx(5,2)
#Clear Flag
qc.append(flag_gate, [10, 11, 12, 5])
qc.x(11)

#Third instantiation
qc.x(12)
qc.append(flag_gate, [10, 11, 12, 5])
# Move
qc.cx(5,1)
#Clear Flag
qc.append(flag_gate, [10, 11, 12, 5])
qc.x(12)

#Fourth instantiation
qc.x(11)
qc.x(12)
qc.append(flag_gate, [10, 11, 12, 5])
# Move
qc.cx(5,1)
#Clear Flag
qc.append(flag_gate, [10, 11, 12, 5])
qc.x(12)
qc.x(11)


qc.name="RULES_2"
return qc


def rules_depth2_inv():
    qc=rules_depth2()
    qc_inv=qc.inverse()
    qc_inv.name="RULES_2Ę"
    return qc_inv
```

12.1.2 Oracle

The states representing one penny are marked by the oracle. They correspond to the loss of player A.

```
def oracle():
    qc = QuantumCircuit(14)
    gate = MCXGate(5)
    qc.x(0)
    qc.x(1)
    qc.x(2)
    qc.x(3)
    qc.append(gate, [0, 1, 2, 3, 4, 13])
```

```
    qc.x(3)
    qc.x(2)
    qc.x(1)
    qc.x(0)

    qc.name="O"
    return qc

def Grover():

    qc = QuantumCircuit(13)
    #Diffusor 6, 7, 11, 12

    qc.h([6,7,11,12])
    qc.x([6,7,11,12])
    qc.h(6)
    gate = MCXGate(3)
    qc.append(gate, [7,11,12,6])
    qc.h(6)
    qc.x([6,7,11,12])
    qc.h([6,7,11,12])

    qc.name="G"
    return qc
```

12.1.3 Search of Depth Two

The following listing calls the defined functions. It represents the search of depth two, including the un-computing and the Grover's amplification of the marked state, see Figure 12.3.

```
qc = QuantumCircuit(14,4)

#State Preparation 0-4
qc.x(0)
qc.x(1)
qc.x(2)
qc.x(3)
qc.x(4)
#Working Memory for Flag bit 5
#1St Path descriptor 6, 7
qc.h(6)
qc.h(7)
#2th trace 8-11
#2St Path descriptor 11,12
qc.h(11)
qc.h(12)
#Auxiliary qubit 13
qc.x(13)
qc.h(13)
qc.barrier()
```

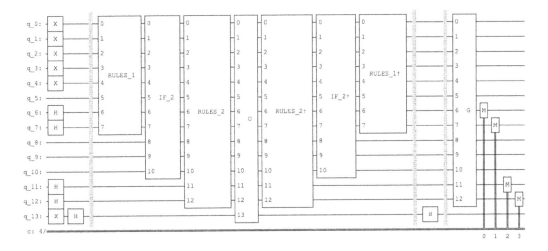

Figure 12.3 The circuit for the five pennies *nim* game representing the quantum tree search for the depth two.

```
qc.append(rules_depth1(),range(8))
qc.append(if_depth2(),range(11))
qc.append(rules_depth2(),range(13))
qc.append(oracle(),range(14))
qc.append(rules_depth2_inv(),range(13))
qc.append(if_depth2_inv(),range(11))
qc.append(rules_depth1_inv(),range(8))
qc.barrier()
qc.h(13)
qc.barrier()
qc.append(Grover(),range(13))

qc.measure(6,0)
qc.measure(7,1)
qc.measure(11,2)
qc.measure(12,3)

qc.draw(fold=200)

simulator = Aer.get_backend('qasm_simulator')
result=execute(qc,simulator,shots=1000).result()
counts = result.get_counts()
print("\nTotal count are:",counts)
plot_histogram(counts)
```

The resulting histogram represents the measured path descriptor of the depth two after one rotation of Grover's amplification of the marked states with one penny, see Figure 12.4.

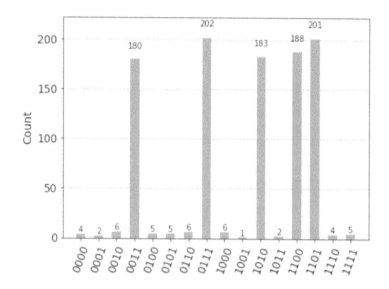

Figure 12.4 The resulting histogram represents the measured path descriptor of the depth two after one rotation of Grover's amplification of the marked states with one penny, see Figure 12.2.

12.2 LIMITATIONS OF QUANTUM TREE SEARCH

In quantum tree search we cannot use the minimax-algorithm [125], [61]. We can determine the search path, but we cannot model the behavior of the player that choses the best move, since we cannot compare different states described by different path descriptors. The comparison of alternative states is the basis of the minimax-algorithm. The minimax-algorithm explores the tree of all legal moves down to the requested depth. Scores associated with leaves of the tree are calculated using an evaluation function. A positive score indicates a good position for player A and a negative score indicates a good position for player B. For each player, the transition from one position to another is either maximized for player A or minimized for player B. By comparing the scores the players try to select the moves in a manner that will be most profitable for them.

## CHAPTER 13

Basis Encoding of Binary Vectors

Quantum encoding is a process to transform classical information into quantum states. It plays a crucial role in using quantum algorithm. Basis encoding is the most intuitive way to encode classical binary vectors into a quantum state. It encodes n-dimensional binary vector to an n-qubit quantum state represented computational basis state. We will describe two possible approaches, a method that was developed by Ventura and Martinez and the method of entanglement of binary patterns vectors with index qubits in superposition.

13.1 BINARY VECTORS

A set of binary vectors is represented by the basis encoding. A uniform superposition of binary vectors can be easily generated by Hadamard gates. For example, for two-dimensional binary vectors we generate the uniform superposition by Hadamard gates

$$H_2|00\rangle = H_1|0\rangle \otimes H_1|0\rangle = \frac{1}{\sqrt{2^2}} \sum_{x \in B^2} |x\rangle = \frac{1}{2} (|00\rangle + |01\rangle + |10\rangle + |11\rangle)$$

with the amplitude representation

$$\alpha = \begin{pmatrix} \frac{1}{2} \\ \frac{1}{2} \\ \frac{1}{2} \\ \frac{1}{2} \end{pmatrix}.$$

But how to generate the superposition

$$\frac{1}{\sqrt{3}} (|10\rangle + |01\rangle + |11\rangle)$$

with the amplitude representation

$$\alpha = \begin{pmatrix} 0 \\ \frac{1}{3} \\ \frac{1}{3} \\ \frac{1}{3} \end{pmatrix}$$

DOI: 10.1201/9781003374404-13

We will describe two possible approaches, a method that was developed by Ventura and Martinez [114, 115] and the method of entanglement of binary patterns vectors with index qubits in superposition.

13.2   SUPERPOSITIONS OF BINARY PATTERNS

To generate a superposition of m binary linear independent vectors with dimension n with $n > m$ a method was proposed by Ventura and Martinez [114, 115] and later simplified by [111]. The procedure is based on successively dividing present superposition into processing and memory branches. Into each new generated memory branch an input pattern is loaded step by step. The method is linear in the number of stored patterns and their dimension [95].

   At the initial step the system is in the basis state with load qubits, memory qubits, and the control qubits c_1, c_2.

$$|memory; c_2, c_1; load\rangle$$

We use the *qiskit* little endian notation. Note, that the original work a use big endian notation [111] $|register; c_1, c_2; memory\rangle$. The idea is to split this basis state step by step using the control register until the required superposition is present

$$\frac{1}{\sqrt{m}} \sum_{j=1}^{m} |memory; c_2, c_1; load\rangle_j$$

with the memory register in the required superposition

$$\frac{1}{\sqrt{m}} \sum_{j=1}^{m} = |memory; 0, 0; 0 \cdots 0\rangle_j = \left(\frac{1}{\sqrt{m}} \sum_{j=1}^{m} |memory\rangle_j \right) \otimes |0, 0; 0 \cdots 0\rangle,$$

also called memory branches.

   We make a distinction between a processing branch indicated by the control qubit c_2 with the value one ($c_2 = 1$) and the memory branches in superposition with the control qubit c_2 with the value zero ($c_2 = 0$). The control qubit $c_1 = 1$ indicates the split of the qubit c_2 by the operator CS_p represented by the parametrized U gate $U(\theta, \phi, \lambda) =$ with $\phi = \pi, \lambda = \pi$, and $\theta = \arcsin\left(\frac{1}{\sqrt{p}}\right) \cdot 2$

$$CS_p = CU\left(\arcsin\left(\frac{1}{\sqrt{p}}\right) \cdot 2, \pi, \pi\right) = \begin{pmatrix} 1 & 0 & 0 & 0 \\ 0 & 1 & 0 & 0 \\ 0 & 0 & \sqrt{\frac{p-1}{p}} & \frac{1}{\sqrt{p}} \\ 0 & 0 & \frac{-1}{\sqrt{p}} & \sqrt{\frac{p-1}{p}} \end{pmatrix}$$

with $CS_p|c_2, c_1\rangle$

$$CS_p|01\rangle = |01\rangle, \quad CS_p|11\rangle = \frac{1}{\sqrt{p}} \cdot |10\rangle + \sqrt{\frac{p-1}{p}} \cdot |11\rangle.$$

Since the control qubit $c_1 = 1$ is entangled with the memory register, we create the memory branch ($c_2 = 0$) with $\frac{1}{\sqrt{p}} \cdot |memory; 01\rangle$ and processing branch ($c_2 = 1$) $\sqrt{\frac{p-1}{p}} \cdot |memory; 11\rangle$ by the split operation on the preceding processing branch. We store the new pattern in the generated memory register of the new generated memory branch.

13.2.1 Storage Algorithm

The initial state is

$$|\psi\rangle_0 = |0 \cdots 0; 1, 0; pattern_p\rangle$$

with control qubit $c_2 = 1$ indicating that the state is a processing branch. In the next steps are described by a loop that stores m binary paterns

$$|pattern_m\rangle, |pattern_{m-1}\rangle, \cdots |pattern_1\rangle$$

FOR $p = m$ TO 2 STEP -1

- We load the pattern $pattern_p$ into the load register.

- IF P $= m$ THEN BEGIN

  – We invert the ground state of the memory register of the processing branch to $|11 \cdots 1\rangle$ using NOT gates.

- ELSE BEGIN

  – We copy the pattern $pattern_p$ into the memory register of the processing branch $c_2 = 1$ using ccX gate (CCNOT gate, controlled controlled not gate).

  – We copy the pattern $pattern_p$ into the memory register of the memory branch $c_2 = 0$ and processing branch $c_2 = 1$ using cX gate (CNOT gate, controlled not gate, we ignore c_2). As a result the memory register of the processing branch is in the ground state $|00 \cdots 0\rangle$, this is not the case for the memory register of memory branches where the bits are flipped.

  – We invert the ground state of the memory register of the processing branch to $|11 \cdots 1\rangle$ using NOT gates to all memory registers. Only the memory register of the processing branch represents $|11 \cdots 1\rangle$.

- The control qubit $c_1 = 1$ is entangled with the memory register $|11 \cdots 1\rangle$ by the multi-controlled X (Toffoli) gate. As a result the control qubit $c_1 = 1$ is entangled with the processing branch.

- The processing branch is split by the operator CS_p. Since the control qubit $c_1 = 1$ is entangled with the memory register we create a new memory branch and a processing branch.

- We redo the entanglement of control qubit $c_1 = 1$ with the memory register $|11 \cdots 1\rangle$.

- We redo the NOT gates operation to all memory registers.

- We apply the CNOT gate controlled by the load register ($pattern_p$) to the memory registers of all the branches. As a result:

  - The $pattern_p$ is represented in the new created memory registers of the memory branch and in the processing branch.

  - The memory registers of the already present memory branches are reconstructed by the flip back operation of the CNOT gate.

- We un-compute the memory register of the processing branch ($c_2 = 1$) to the ground state $|00 \cdots 0\rangle$ by the ccX gate.

- We reset the load register to the ground state

NEXT

We convert the processing branch into a memory branch and store the last pattern $|pattern_1\rangle$ in its memory register. We reset the load register to the ground state. As a result we represent the stored patterns in the superposition

$$|\psi\rangle = \left(\frac{1}{\sqrt{m}} \sum_{j=1}^{m} |pattern\rangle_j \right) \otimes |0,0;0\cdots0\rangle,$$

13.2.2 Qiskit Example

In this example we store three binary patterns,

$$|01\rangle_3, \quad |10\rangle_2, \quad |11\rangle_1$$

Qiskit uses little endian notation

$$|memory; c_2, c_1; register\rangle = |q_5, q_4, q_3, q_2; q_1, q_0\rangle,$$

Qubts 0 and 1 represent the load register, qubits 2 and 3 are the control qubits and the qubits 4 and 5 represent the memory register. We use the *statevector simulator* to check the value of all 6 qubits. The initial state is represented by the processing branch

$$|\psi\rangle_0 = |0,0;1,0;0,0\rangle.$$

- Figure 13.1. The qubit 3 is set to one indicating by $c_2 = 1$, that the basis state represents a processing branch. In the load register pattern $|10\rangle$ is generated and the memory register is set to $|11\rangle$. The resulting state is

$$|\psi\rangle_1 = |1,1;1,0;0,1\rangle.$$

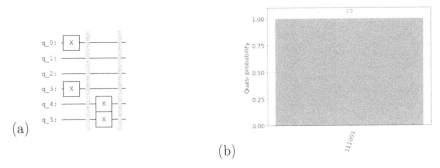

(a)

(b)

Figure 13.1 (a) The qubit 3 is set to one indicating (by $c_2 = 1$), that the basis state represents a processing branch. The pattern $|10\rangle$ is generated in the load register and the memory register is set to $|11\rangle$. (b) The resulting state is $|\psi\rangle_1 = |1, 1; 0, 1; 0, 1\rangle$.

- Figure 13.2. The control qubit 2 ($c_1 = 1$) is entangled with the memory register $|11\rangle$ by the multi-controlled X (Toffoli) gate. The processing branch is split by the operator CS_3 ($p = 3$), creating a new memory and processing branch. The resulting state is

$$|\psi\rangle_2 = \frac{1}{\sqrt{3}}|1, 1; 0, 1; 0, 1\rangle + \sqrt{\frac{2}{3}}|1, 1; 1, 1; 0, 1\rangle.$$

- Figure 13.3. We un-compute the entanglement of control qubit 2 ($c_1 = 1$) with the memory register $|11\rangle$ (using the multi-controlled X (Toffoli) gate). We apply the NOT gates operation and the controlled NOT operation (CNOT gate) to the memory register of both branches. As result we write 10 into the memory registers. The resulting state is

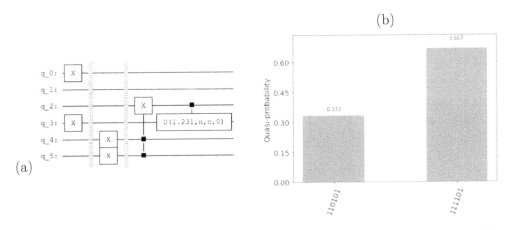

(a)

Figure 13.2 (a) The control qubit 2 ($c_1 = 1$) is entangled with the memory register $|11\rangle$ by the multi-controlled X (Toffoli) gate. The processing branch is split by the operator CS_3 ($p = 3$), creating a new memory and processing branch. (b) The resulting state is $|\psi\rangle_2 = \frac{1}{\sqrt{3}}|1, 1; 0, 1; 0, 1\rangle + \sqrt{\frac{2}{3}}|1, 1; 1, 1; 0, 1\rangle$.

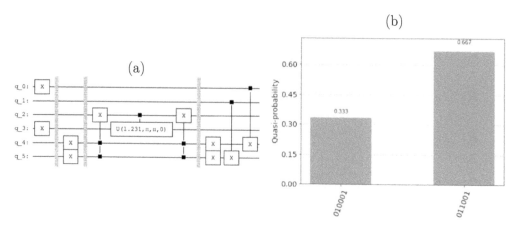

Figure 13.3 (a) We un-compute the entanglement of control qubit 2 ($c_1 = 1$) with the memory register $|11\rangle$ (using the multi-controlled X (Toffoli) gate). We apply the NOT gates operation and the controlled NOT operation (CNOT gate) to the memory register of both branches. As result we write 10 into the memory registers. (b) The resulting state is $|\psi\rangle_3 = \frac{1}{\sqrt{3}}|0, 1; 0, 0; 0, 1\rangle + \sqrt{\frac{2}{3}}|0, 1; 1, 0; 0, 1\rangle$.

$$|\psi\rangle_3 = \frac{1}{\sqrt{3}}|0, 1; 0, 0; 0, 1\rangle + \sqrt{\frac{2}{3}}|0, 1; 1, 0; 0, 1\rangle.$$

- Figure 13.4. We un-compute the memory register of the processing branch, setting it to the ground state $|00\rangle$ (the memory register before the operation is in the ground state). We use the ccX gate (CCNOT gate) controlled by the load register and the control qubit 3 ($c_2 = 1$ indicates the processing branch). We reset the load register to the ground state $|00\rangle$. The resulting state is

$$|\psi\rangle_4 = \frac{1}{\sqrt{3}}|0, 1; 0, 0; 0, 0\rangle + \sqrt{\frac{2}{3}}|0, 0; 1, 0; 0, 0\rangle.$$

- Figure 13.5. The pattern $|10\rangle$ is generated in the load register. We copy $|10\rangle$ into the memory register of the processing branch. We use the ccX gate (CCNOT gate) controlled by the load register and the control qubit 3 ($c_2 = 1$ indicates the processing branch). The resulting state is

$$|\psi\rangle_5 = \frac{1}{\sqrt{3}}|0, 1; 0, 0; 1, 0\rangle + \sqrt{\frac{2}{3}}|1, 0; 1, 0; 1, 0\rangle.$$

- Figure 13.6. We perform the controlled NOT operation controlled by the pattern $|10\rangle$ with the memory register of both branches using cX gate. As a result the memory register of the processing branch is in the ground state $|00\rangle$. This is not the case for the memory register of memory branch, where the bits are flipped leading to the state $|11\rangle$. We apply the NOT operation to the memory register of bot branches. As a result the memory register of the processing branch is

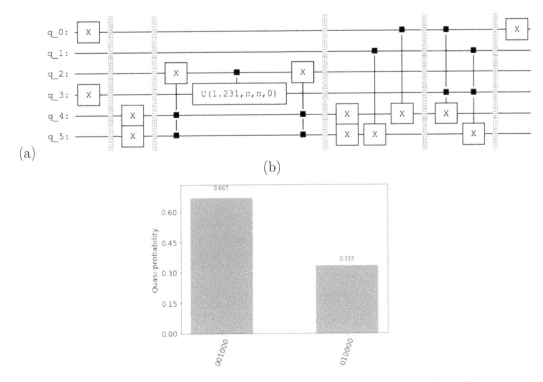

(a)

(b)

Figure 13.4 (a) We un-compute the memory register of the processing branch, setting it to the the ground state $|00\rangle$. We use the ccX gate (CCNOT gate) controlled by the load register and the control qubit 3 ($c_2 = 1$ indicates the processing branch). We reset the load register to the ground state $|00\rangle$. (b) The resulting state is $|\psi\rangle_4 = \frac{1}{\sqrt{3}}|0,1;0,0;0,0\rangle + \sqrt{\frac{2}{3}}|0,0;1,0;0,0\rangle$.

in the state $|11\rangle$. The control qubit 2 ($c_1 = 1$) is entangled with the memory register $|11\rangle$ by the multi-controlled X (Toffoli) gate. The resulting state is

$$|\psi\rangle_6 = \frac{1}{\sqrt{3}}|0,0;0,0;1,0\rangle + \sqrt{\frac{2}{3}}|1,1;1,1;1,0\rangle.$$

- Figure 13.7 The control qubit 2 ($c_1 = 1$) is entangled with the memory register $|11\rangle$ of the proscessing ranch by the multi-controlled X (Toffoli) gate. The processing branch is split by the operator CS_2 ($p = 2$), creating a new memory branch. The resulting state is

$$|\psi\rangle_7 = \frac{1}{\sqrt{3}}|0,0;0,0;1,0\rangle + \frac{1}{\sqrt{3}}|1,1;0,1;1,0\rangle + \frac{1}{\sqrt{3}}|1,1;1,1;1,0\rangle.$$

- Figure 13.8. We un-compute the entanglement of control qubit 2 ($c_1 = 1$) with the memory register $|11\rangle$ (using the multi-controlled X (Toffoli) gate). We apply the NOT gates operation and the controlled NOT operation (CNOT gate) to the memory register of the three branches. As result we un-flip (recover) the memory register of the first memory branch to $|10\rangle$ and copy $|01\rangle$ into

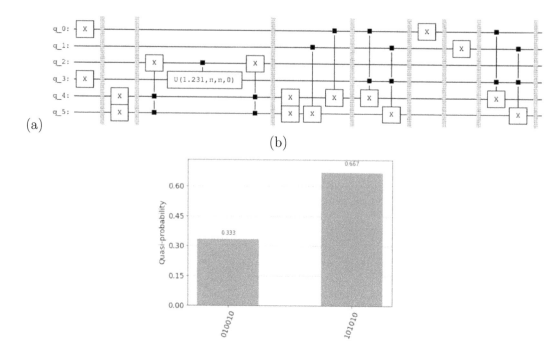

(a)

(b)

Figure 13.5 The pattern $|10\rangle$ is generated in the load register. We copy $|10\rangle$ into the memory register of the processing branch (the memory register before the operation is in the ground state). We use the ccX gate (CCNOT gate) controlled by the load register and the control qubit 3 ($c_2 = 1$ indicates the processing branch). (b) The resulting state is $|\psi\rangle_5 = \frac{1}{\sqrt{3}}|0,1;0,0;1,0\rangle + \sqrt{\frac{2}{3}}|1,0;1,0;1,0\rangle$.

the memory register of the other two branches. We un-compute the memory register of the processing branch, setting it to the the ground state $|00\rangle$. We use the ccX gate (CCNOT gate) controlled by the load register and the control qubit 3 ($c_2 = 1$ indicates the processing branch). We reset the load register to the ground state $|00\rangle$. The resulting state is

$$|\psi\rangle_8 = \frac{1}{\sqrt{3}}|0,0;1,0;0,0\rangle + \frac{1}{\sqrt{3}}|0,1;0,0;0,0\rangle + \frac{1}{\sqrt{3}}|1,0;0,0;0,0\rangle.$$

- Figure 13.9. In the load register pattern $|11\rangle$ is generated. The first qubit of the pattern $|11\rangle$, qubit 0, is entangled with the qubit 3 of control register $c_2 = 1$ using the controlled NOT gate cX.

```
qc.cx(3,0)
qc.x(1)
```

We copy $|11\rangle$ into the memory register of the processing branch by the ccX gate (CCNOT gate) controlled by the load register and the control qubit 3 ($c_2 = 1$ indicates the processing branch).

```
qc.ccx(0,3,4)
qc.ccx(1,3,5)
```

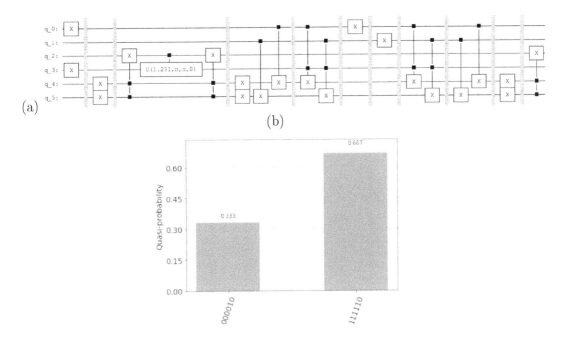

Figure 13.6 We perform the controlled NOT operation controlled by the pattern $|10\rangle$ with the memory register of both branches using cX gate. As a result the memory register of the processing branch is in the ground state $|00\rangle$. This is not the case for the memory register of memory branch, where the bits are flipped leading to the state $|11\rangle$. We apply the NOT operation to the memory register of bot branches. As a result the memory register of the processing branch is in the state $|11\rangle$. The control qubit 2 ($c_1 = 1$) is entangled with the memory register $|11\rangle$ by the multi-controlled X gate. (b) The resulting state is $|\psi\rangle_6 = \frac{1}{\sqrt{3}}|0,0;0,0;1,0\rangle + \sqrt{\frac{2}{3}}|1,1;1,1;1,0\rangle$.

We convert the processing branch into a memory branch by setting the qubit 3 of the control register c_2 to zero by the entangled qubit 0 of the pattern $|11\rangle$ (using controlled NOT gate cX).

```
qc.cx(0,3)
```

We reset the load register to the ground state $|00\rangle$. The entangled qubit in the load register is set to zero by the ccX gate (CCNOT gate) with the control qubits represented by the memory register of the stored pattern $|11\rangle$.

```
qc.ccx(4,5,0)
qc.x(1)
```

We measure the memory register: qubit 4 and 5 using the *qasm simulator* with *shots* = 10000. The results of the measurement represent the desired distribution The resulting state is

$$|\psi\rangle_9 = \frac{1}{\sqrt{3}} \cdot (|0,1\rangle + |1,0\rangle + |1,1\rangle) \otimes |0,0;0,0\rangle.$$

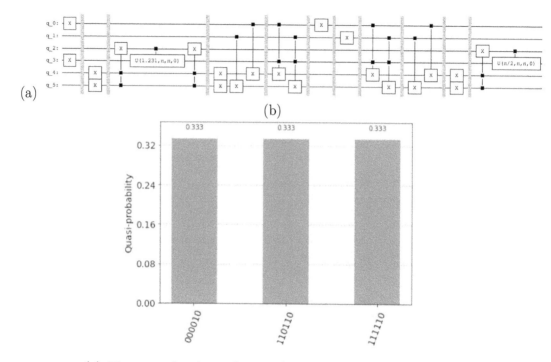

(a)

(b)

Figure 13.7 (a) The control qubit 2 ($c_1 = 1$) is entangled with the memory register $|11\rangle$ of the proscessing ranch by the multi-controlled X (Toffoli) gate. The processing branch is split by the operator CS_2 ($p = 2$), creating a new memory branch. (b) The resulting state is $|\psi\rangle_7 = \frac{1}{\sqrt{3}}|0,0;0,0;1,0\rangle + \frac{1}{\sqrt{3}}|1,1;0,1;1,0\rangle + \frac{1}{\sqrt{3}}|1,1;1,1;1,0\rangle$.

The complete circuit is defined by

```
qc = QuantumCircuit(6,2)
#0-1 loading register
#2-3 control register
#4-5 storage, memory
qc.x(3)
qc.x(0)
qc.barrier()

qc.x(4)
qc.x(5)
qc.barrier()
qc.ccx(4,5,2)
qc.cu(1.230959417340775,pi,pi,0,2,3)
qc.ccx(4,5,2)
qc.barrier()
qc.x(4)
qc.x(5)
qc.cx(1,5)
qc.cx(0,4)
#Uncompute
qc.barrier()
```

(a)

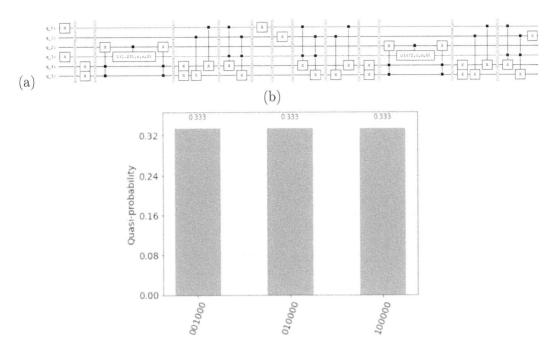

(b)

Figure 13.8 (a) We un-compute the entanglement of control qubit 2 ($c_1 = 1$) with the memory register $|11\rangle$ (*using the multi-controlled X gate*). We apply the NOT gates operation and the controlled NOT operation (CNOT gate) to the memory register of the three branches. As result we un-flip (recover) the memory register of the first memory branch to $|01\rangle$ and copy $|10\rangle$ into the memory register of the other two branches. We un-compute the memory register of the processing branch, setting it to the ground state $|00\rangle$. We use the ccX gate (CCNOT gate) controlled by the load register and the control qubit 3 ($c_2 = 1$ indicates the processing branch). We reset the load register to the ground state $|00\rangle$. (b) The resulting state is $|\psi\rangle_8 = \frac{1}{\sqrt{3}}|0,0;1,0;0,0\rangle + \frac{1}{\sqrt{3}}|0,1;0,0;0,0\rangle + \frac{1}{\sqrt{3}}|1,0;0,0;0,0\rangle$.

```
qc.ccx(0,3,4)
qc.ccx(1,3,5)

qc.barrier()
qc.x(0)

qc.barrier()
qc.x(1)
qc.barrier()

qc.ccx(0,3,4)
qc.ccx(1,3,5)
qc.barrier()
qc.cx(1,5)
qc.cx(0,4)
qc.barrier()
```

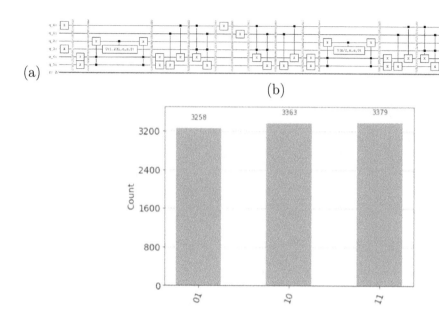

(a)

(b)

Figure 13.9 In the load register, pattern $|11\rangle$ is generated. The first qubit of the pattern $|11\rangle$, qubit 0, is entangled with the qubit 3 of control register $c_2 = 1$ using the controlled NOT gate cX. We copy $|11\rangle$ into the memory register of the processing branch by the ccX gate (CCNOT gate) controlled by the load register and the control qubit 3 ($c_2 = 1$ indicates the processing branch). We convert the processing branch into a memory branch by setting the qubit 3 of the control register c_2 to zero by the entangled qubit 0 of the pattern $|11\rangle$ (using controlled NOT gate cX). We reset the load register to the ground state $|00\rangle$. The entangled qubit in the load register is set to zero by the ccX gate (CCNOT gate) with the control qubits represented by the memory register of the stored pattern $|11\rangle$. We measure the memory register: qubit 4 and 5 using the *qasm simulator* with *shots* = 10000. (b) The results of the measurement represent the desired distribution.

```
qc.x(4)
qc.x(5)
qc.barrier()
qc.ccx(4,5,2)
qc.cu(1.5707963267948966,pi,pi,0,2,3)
qc.ccx(4,5,2)

qc.barrier()
qc.x(4)
qc.x(5)
qc.cx(1,5)
qc.cx(0,4)
#Uncompute
qc.barrier()
qc.ccx(0,3,4)
```

```
qc.ccx(1,3,5)
qc.x(1)

qc.barrier()
qc.cx(3,0)
qc.x(1)
qc.ccx(0,3,4)
qc.ccx(1,3,5)
qc.cx(0,3)
qc.ccx(4,5,0)
qc.x(1)
qc.barrier()

qc.measure(4,0)
qc.measure(5,1)

simulator = Aer.get_backend('qasm_simulator')
result=execute(qc,simulator,shots=10000).result()
counts = result.get_counts()
print("\nTotal count are:",counts)
plot_histogram(counts)
```

13.3 ENTANGLEMENT OF BINARY PATTERNS

The method is based the on the entanglement of the index qubits that are in the superposition with the patterns. To stores m binary paterns

$$|pattern_m\rangle, |pattern_{m-1}\rangle, \cdots |pattern_1\rangle$$

we entangle the index qubits using multi-controlled NOT gates (ccX gate or MCX-Gate). First, we generate $v = |log_2(m)$ index qubits using v Hadamard gates

$$H^{\otimes v}|0\rangle^{\otimes v} = \frac{1}{\sqrt{m}} \sum_{j=1}^{m} |index_j\rangle.$$

and entangle m binary pattern with the index qubits with a resulting superposition

$$|\psi\rangle = \frac{1}{\sqrt{m}} \left(\sum_{j=1}^{m} |index_j\rangle |pattern_j\rangle \right), \qquad (13.1)$$

13.3.1 *Qiskit* Example

In this example we store four binary patterns,

$$|101\rangle_4, \quad |011\rangle_3, \quad |111\rangle_2, \quad |010\rangle_1$$

by entanglement with the four index qubits $|index_j\rangle$ in superposition

$$|index_4\rangle = |11\rangle \quad |index_3\rangle = |10\rangle \quad |index_2\rangle = |01\rangle \quad |index_1\rangle = |00\rangle$$

using controlled NOT gates (ccX gates) with the circuit (see Figure 13.10):

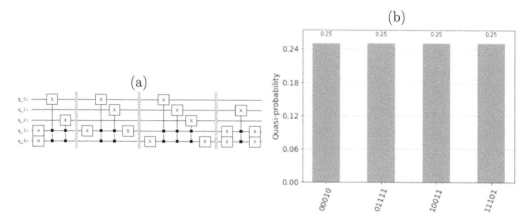

Figure 13.10 The method is based the on the entanglement of the index qubits that are in the superposition with the pattern vectors. (b) The histogram representing the superposition, qubits 0,1, and 2 represent the patterns and the qubits 4 and 5 the index qubits.

```python
from qiskit import QuantumCircuit, Aer, execute
from qiskit.visualization import plot_histogram
from qiskit.circuit.library import MCXGate

 qc = QuantumCircuit(5)
#0-2 data
#Index
#3-4
qc.h(3)
qc.h(4)

#First patern
qc.ccx(3,4,0)
qc.ccx(3,4,2)
qc.barrier()
#Second patern
qc.x(3)
qc.ccx(3,4,0)
qc.ccx(3,4,1)
qc.x(3)

qc.barrier()
#Third patern
qc.x(4)
qc.ccx(3,4,0)
qc.ccx(3,4,1)
qc.ccx(3,4,2)
qc.x(4)

qc.barrier()
#Fourth patern
```

```
qc.x(3)
qc.x(4)
qc.ccx(3,4,1)
qc.x(4)
qc.x(3)

simulator = Aer.get_backend('statevector_simulator')
result=execute(qc,simulator).result()
counts = result.get_counts()
plot_histogram(counts)
```

The superposition of patterns with their indexes is represented as

$$|\psi\rangle = \frac{1}{2} \cdot \left(|00010\rangle_1 + |01111\rangle_2 + |10011\rangle_3 + |11101\rangle_4\right).$$

We can entangle several copies of superposition binary pattern vectors that can be processed and measured independently, see Figure 13.11.

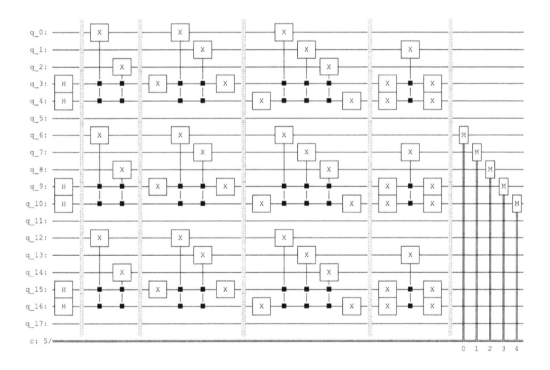

Figure 13.11 We can entangle several copies of superposition binary pattern vectors that can be processed and measured independently.

13.4   COMPARISON

The method developed by Ventura and Martinez [114, 115] leads to the superposition

$$|\psi\rangle = \left(\frac{1}{\sqrt{m}} \sum_{j=1}^{m} |pattern_j\rangle \otimes |0\cdots0; 0, 0\rangle \right),$$

while the entanglement of binary pattern vectors leads to the superposition

$$|\psi\rangle = \frac{1}{\sqrt{m}} \left(\sum_{j=1}^{m} |index_j\rangle |pattern_j\rangle \right).$$

The method of entanglement of binary pattern is easier to understand and implement an allows us to address the patterns through the index. The same pattern can be represented several times with a different index, however the dimension of the vectors in superposition is $dim(n + \log_2(m)$ compared to the dimension $dim(n)$ of Ventura and Martinez method.

## CHAPTER 14

Quantum Associative Memory

Quantum associative memory (QuAM) in the domain of quantum computation is a model with a capacity exponential in the number of neurons. Quantum Nearest Neighbor (QNN) is related to the QuAM. In QNN the binary patterns are stored by entanglement with index qubits. For Grover's amplification to the index qubits, we have to un-compute the entanglement of index qubits with the patterns. In QNN we need to un-compute. However, in QuAM we do not un-compute. In the QuAM as proposed by Venture and Martinez, a modified version of Grover's search algorithm is applied to determine the answer vector to a query vector so that instead of un-computing one can apply Grover's algorithm to all qubits. Most quantum machine learning algorithms including quantum associative memory suffer from the input destruction problem where the classical data must be read and after the measurement the superposition collapses. However, the input destruction problem is not solved till today, and usually theoretical speed ups are analyzed. We will demonstrate a simple QNN model, and a modified version of Grover's search algorithm as proposed by Venture and Martinez. Then we analyze the input destruction problem.

14.1 QUANTUM NEAREST NEIGHBOR

We store In four binary patterns,

$$|101\rangle_4, \quad |011\rangle_3, \quad |111\rangle_2, \quad |010\rangle_1$$

by entanglement with the four index qubits $|index_j\rangle$ in superposition

$$|index_4\rangle = |11\rangle \quad |index_3\rangle = |10\rangle \quad |index_2\rangle = |01\rangle \quad |index_1\rangle = |00\rangle$$

The four patterns with their indexes represented in a uniform distribution of the states

$$|\psi\rangle = \frac{1}{2} \cdot (|00010\rangle_1 + |01111\rangle_2 + |10011\rangle_3 + |11101\rangle_4).$$

We represent the patterns by the qubits 0, 1, and 2 and the index by the qubits 3 and 4. The qubit 5 represents the auxiliary qubit for the Grover's amplification (see

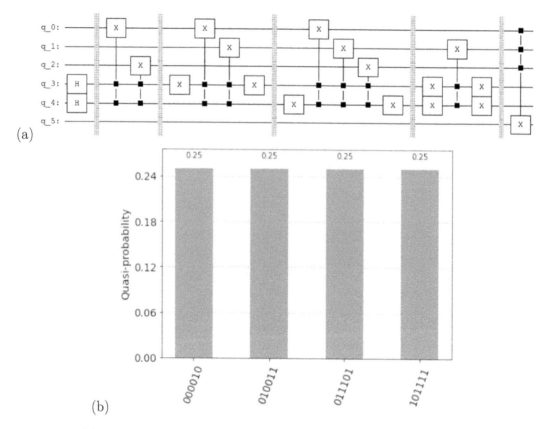

(a)

(b)

Figure 14.1 (a) The patterns are represented by the qubits 0, 1, and 2 and the index by the qubits 3 and 4. The qubit 5 represents the auxiliary qubit for the Grover's amplification. Our query vector is represented by the pattern $|111\rangle$. The ccX gate (controlled controlled not gate) marks the solution by writing a one in the qubit 5. (b) The histogram representing the four patterns and their indexes produces a uniform superposition. The solution $|111\rangle$ with the the index $|index_2\rangle = |01\rangle$ and the auxiliary qubit equal one, corresponds to the state $|01111\rangle$.

Figure 14.1 (a)). For simplicity our query vector is represented by the pattern $|111\rangle$. The quantum oracle marks the solution by writing a one in the qubit 5. The solution is the stored pattern $|111\rangle$ with the index $|index_2\rangle = |01\rangle$ (see Figure 14.1 (b)). In the next step, we perform Grover's amplification to the index qubits 3 and 4 (see Figure 14.2 (a)). However, since the index qubits are entangled with the patterns we do not get the correct results (see Figure 14.1 (b)). To apply Grover's amplification to the two index qubits, the entanglement of the index qubits with the patterns has to be un-computed (see Figure 14.3 (a)). The definition of the *qiskit* circuit:

```
import numpy as np
from qiskit import QuantumCircuit, Aer, execute
from qiskit.quantum_info import Statevector
from qiskit.visualization import plot_histogram
from qiskit.circuit.library import MCXGate
from math import pi
```

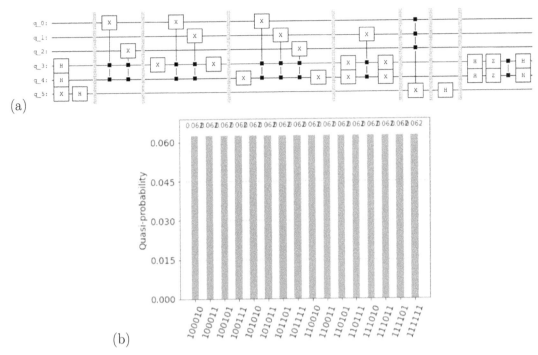

(a)

(b)

Figure 14.2 (a) Grover's amplification to the index qubits 3 and 4. (b) Since the index qubits are entangled with the patterns we do not get the correct results.

```python
def store():
    qc = QuantumCircuit(5)
    #First patern
    qc.ccx(3,4,0)
    qc.ccx(3,4,2)
    qc.barrier()
    #Second patern
    qc.x(3)
    qc.ccx(3,4,0)
    qc.ccx(3,4,1)
    qc.x(3)
    qc.barrier()
    #Third patern
    qc.x(4)
    qc.ccx(3,4,0)
    qc.ccx(3,4,1)
    qc.ccx(3,4,2)
    qc.x(4)
    qc.barrier()
    #Fourth patern
    qc.x(3)
    qc.x(4)
    qc.ccx(3,4,1)
    qc.x(4)
```

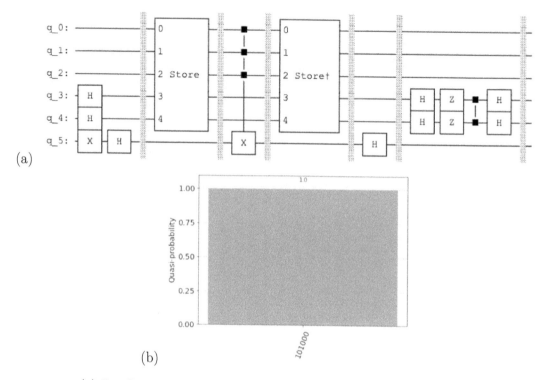

(a)

(b)

Figure 14.3 (a) For Grover's amplification to the index qubits, we have to un-compute the entanglement of index qubits are with the patterns. For the four state we require just one rotation. (b) We measure the correct result represented by one state with the $|index_2\rangle = |01\rangle$.

```
    qc.x(3)
    qc.name="Store"
    return qc

 def store_inv():
    qc=store()
    qc_inv=qc.inverse()
    qc_inv.name="StoreÉ"
    return qc_inv

qc = QuantumCircuit(6)
#0-2 data
#Index
#3-4
qc.h(3)
qc.h(4)

#Aux Bit
qc.x(5)
qc.h(5)
```

```
qc.barrier()
qc.append(store(),range(5))
qc.barrier()
#Oracle
gate = MCXGate(3)
qc.append(gate,[0, 1, 2, 5])
qc.barrier()
qc.append(store_inv(),range(5))
qc.barrier()
#Redo Aux Bit
qc.h(5)
qc.barrier()
#Diffusor
qc.h([3,4])
qc.z([3,4])
qc.cz(3,4)
qc.h([3,4])
```

For the four state we require just one rotation. We measure the correct result represented by one state with the $index_2\rangle = |10\rangle$ (see Figure 14.3 (b)). Instead of uncomputing, we would like to apply Grover's algorithm to the five qubits representing the patterns and the indexes. Measuring the states after one rotation of Grover's amplification indicates us that something wired is happening.

14.2   QUANTUM ASSOCIATIVE MEMORY (QuAM)

In the QuAM as proposed by Venture and Martinez, a modified version of Grover's search algorithm is applied to determine the answer vector to a query vector [114, 115, 110]. To prepare superposition of m binary linear independent vectors with dimension n with $n > m$, a method was proposed by Ventura and Martinez [114, 115] and later simplified by [111], with preparation cost $O(n \cdot m)$ requiring $\log_2(m)$ units. The query costs are $O(n \cdot \sqrt{m})$ compared to $O(n \cdot m)$ on a conventional computer. To understand the modified version of Grover's search algorithm and the results of Figure 14.4, we generate simple superposition

$$|\psi\rangle = \frac{1}{2} \cdot (|1100\rangle + |1001\rangle + |1111\rangle + |0110\rangle).$$

so that we can track the amplitude distribution

$$\frac{1}{2}(0, 0, 0, 1, 0, 0, 1, 0, 0, 1, 0, 0, 0, 0, 0, 1)^T.$$

We notice that the amplitude distribution is not uniform, a uniform distribution of amplitudes of four qubits would correspond to

$$\frac{1}{4}(1, 1, 1, 1, 1, 1, 1, 1, 1, 1, 1, 1, 1, 1, 1, 1)^T.$$

Could this be the cause of the problem?

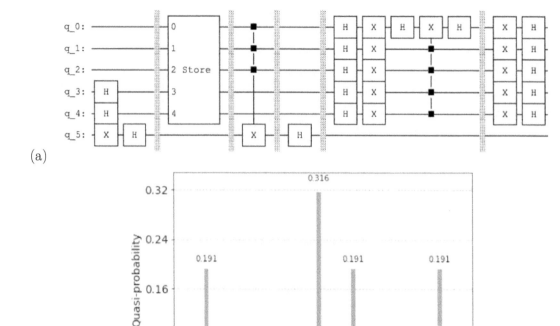

(a)

(b)

Figure 14.4 (a) Instead of un-computing, we would like to apply Grover's algorithm to the five qubits representing the patterns and the indexes. (b) Measuring the states after one rotation of Grover's amplification indicates us that something wired is happening.

14.2.1 Non-Uniform Distribution

From the initial distribution we mark the target state $|0110\rangle$ by a negative phase

$$\frac{1}{2}(0, 0, 0, 1, 0, 0, -1, 0, 0, 1, 0, 0, 0, 0, 0, 1)^T.$$

and perform a Grover's rotation with the result

$$\frac{1}{8}(-1, -1, -1, 3, -1, -1, -5, -1, -1, 3, -1, -1, -1, -1, -1, 3)^T$$

We mark again and the target state $|0110\rangle$ by a negative phase and perform a Grover's rotation with the result

$$(-0.2, -0.2, -0.2, 0.3, -0.2, -0.2, 0.6, -0.2, -0.2, 0.3, -0.2, -0.2, -0.2, -0.2, -0.2, 0.3)^T.$$

The four states that represent our distribution have high non-negative values of amplitude (the results are rounded for representation clarity). After marking the target state $|0110\rangle$ by a negative phase and a Grover's rotation

$$(0.02, 0.02, 0.02, 0.5, 0.02, 0.02, -0.4, 0.02, 0.02, 0.5, 0.02, 0.02, 0.02, 0.02, 0.02, 0.5)^T$$

all four basis states have nearly equal distribution and the information of the target state $|0110\rangle$ is negative. If we mark the target by a negative phase, the information about it will be lost. How can we deal with non-uniform distributions?

14.2.2 Ventura Martinez Trick

Venture and Martinez, proposed a modified version of Grover's search algorithm [114, 115]. As before, from the initial distribution we mark the target state $|0110\rangle$ by a negative phase

$$\frac{1}{2}(0, 0, 0, 1, 0, 0, -1, 0, 0, 1, 0, 0, 0, 0, 0, 1)^T.$$

and perform a Grover's rotation with the result

$$\frac{1}{8}(-1, -1, -1, 3, -1, -1, -5, -1, -1, 3, -1, -1, -1, -1, -1, 3)^T$$

However, now me mark all four states that represent our distribution by a negative phase and perform a Grover's rotation with the result

$$\frac{1}{8}(1, 1, 1, -1, 1, 1, 7, 1, 1, -1, 1, 1, 1, 1, 1, -1)^T$$

We mark again all four states that represent our distribution by a negative phase and perform a Grover's rotation

$$(0, 0, 0, 0, 0, 0, 1, 0, 0, 0, 0, 0, 0, 0, 0, 0)^T$$

with the amplitude one indicating the target state. The *qiskit* circuit (see Figure 14.5) is represented as:

```
import numpy as np
from qiskit import QuantumCircuit, Aer, execute
from qiskit.quantum_info import Statevector
from qiskit.visualization import plot_histogram
from qiskit.circuit.library import MCXGate
from math import pi

qc = QuantumCircuit(5)
#0-1 data
#Index
#2-3
qc.h(2)
qc.h(3)

#Aux Bit
qc.x(4)
qc.h(4)
```

```
qc.barrier()
#First patern
qc.ccx(2,3,0)
qc.ccx(2,3,1)

qc.barrier()
#Second patern
qc.x(2)
qc.ccx(2,3,0)
qc.x(2)

qc.barrier()
#Third patern
qc.x(3)
qc.ccx(2,3,1)
qc.x(3)

qc.barrier()
#Fourth patern
qc.x(2)
qc.x(3)
qc.ccx(2,3,0)
qc.ccx(2,3,1)
qc.x(3)
qc.x(2)

#Oracle
qc.barrier()
qc.x(0)
qc.x(3)
gate = MCXGate(4)
qc.append(gate, [0,1,2,3,4])
qc.x(3)
qc.x(0)
qc.barrier()
qc.h(4)
#Diffusor 0, 1, 2, 3
qc.barrier()

qc.h([0,1,2,3])
qc.x([0,1,2,3])
qc.h(0)
gate = MCXGate(3)
qc.append(gate, [1,2,3,0])
qc.h(0)
qc.x([0,1,2,3])
qc.h([0,1,2,3])

#Secend rotation
qc.barrier()
```

```
qc.h(4)
qc.barrier()

#Oracle Trick
qc.x(0)
qc.x(3)
gate = MCXGate(4)
qc.append(gate, [0,1,2,3,4])
qc.x(3)
qc.x(0)

qc.x(2)
qc.x(3)
gate = MCXGate(4)
qc.append(gate, [0,1,2,3,4])
qc.x(3)
qc.x(2)

qc.x(1)
qc.x(2)
gate = MCXGate(4)
qc.append(gate, [0,1,2,3,4])
qc.x(2)
qc.x(1)

gate = MCXGate(4)
qc.append(gate, [0,1,2,3,4])

qc.barrier()
qc.h(4)
#Diffusor 0, 1, 2, 3
qc.barrier()

qc.h([0,1,2,3])
qc.x([0,1,2,3])
qc.h(0)
gate = MCXGate(3)
qc.append(gate, [1,2,3,0])
qc.h(0)
qc.x([0,1,2,3])
qc.h([0,1,2,3])

#Third rotation
qc.barrier()
qc.h(4)
qc.barrier()

#Oracle Trick
qc.x(0)
qc.x(3)
gate = MCXGate(4)
```

```
qc.append(gate, [0,1,2,3,4])
qc.x(3)
qc.x(0)

qc.x(2)
qc.x(3)
gate = MCXGate(4)
qc.append(gate, [0,1,2,3,4])
qc.x(3)
qc.x(2)

qc.x(1)
qc.x(2)
gate = MCXGate(4)
qc.append(gate, [0,1,2,3,4])
qc.x(2)
qc.x(1)

gate = MCXGate(4)
qc.append(gate, [0,1,2,3,4])
qc.barrier()
qc.h(4)

#Diffusor 0, 1, 2, 3
qc.barrier()

qc.h([0,1,2,3])
qc.x([0,1,2,3])
qc.h(0)
gate = MCXGate(3)
qc.append(gate, [1,2,3,0])
qc.h(0)
qc.x([0,1,2,3])
qc.h([0,1,2,3])

simulator = Aer.get_backend('statevector_simulator')

result=execute(qc,simulator).result()
counts = result.get_counts()
plot_histogram(counts)
```

and to indicate the state vector (together with the auxilaiary qubit 4)

```
final_state = simulator.run(qc).result().get_statevector()
from qiskit.visualization import array_to_latex
array_to_latex(final_state,max_size=256,precision=4,prefix=
"\\text{Statevector} = ")
```

Depending on the distribution and the relation between m (the number of patterns) and n (the dimension of patterns), we have to correct by marking all present state till all states without the target state reach an uniform distribution. The correction

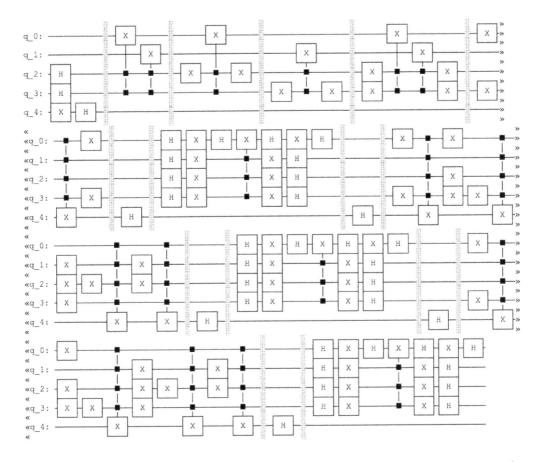

Figure 14.5 The circuit representing the three Grover's rotations with two times the cost of marking all present states.

cost influence the cost of Grover's amplification algorithm. In our case we need three Grover's rotation with two times the cost of marking all present states (see Figure 14.5). For four states in superposition and one target value, we would only need one rotation.

14.3 INPUT DESTRUCTION PROBLEM

Most quantum machine learning algorithms including quantum associative memory suffer from the input destruction problem (**ID problem**) [3, 126, 1]:

- The input (reading) problem: The amplitude distribution of a quantum state is initialized by reading n data points. Although the existing quantum algorithm requires only $O(\sqrt{n})$ steps or *less* and is faster than the classical algorithms, n data points must be read. Hence, the complexity of the algorithm does not improve and is $O(n) = O(n) + O(\sqrt{n})$.

- The destruction problem: A quantum associative memory [114, 115, 110], [111, 112] for n data points for dimension m requires only $m \cdot \log(n)$ or fewer units (quantum bits). An operator, which acts as an oracle [110] indicates the solution. However, this memory can be queried only once because of the collapse during measurement (destruction); hence, quantum associative memory does not have any advantages over classical memory.

The efficient preparation of data is possible in part for spares data [39]. However, the input destruction problem is not solved till today, and usually theoretical speed ups are analyzed [94] by ignoring the input problem, which is the main bottleneck for data encoding. We name the preparation of the input data the *sleep phase*. The query operation is extremely fast and will be called the *active phase*. The naming of the phases is in analogy to a living organism that prepares itself during the sleep for an active day. The advantage of quantum approach is present in the *active phase*.

## CHAPTER 15

Quantum Lernmatrix

We introduce quantum Lernmatrix based on Lernmatrix where n units are stored in the quantum superposition. Lernmatrix is an associative-memory-like architecture. During the retrieval phase quantum counting of ones based on Euler's formula is used for the pattern recovery as proposed by Trugenberger. We demonstrate how to represent the quantum Lernmatrix by a quantum circuit and preform experiments using *qiskit*. Then we introduce a tree-like structure that increases the measured value of correct answers. During the active phase the quantum Lernmatrices are queried and the results are estimated efficiently. The required time is much lower compared to the conventional approach or the of Grover's algorithm.

15.1 LERNMATRIX

Different associative memory models have been proposed over the years [5], [42, 49], [6, 10]. The Hopfield model represents a recurrent model of the associative memory [5], [46], [44], it is a dynamical system that evolves until it has converged to a stable state. The Lernmatrix, or Willshaw's associative memory also simply called "associative memory" (if no confusion with other models is possible [6, 10]), it was developed by Steinbuch in 1958 as a biologically inspired model from the effort to explain the psychological phenomena of conditioning [103, 104]. The goal was to produce a network that could use a binary version of Hebbian learning to form associations between pairs of binary vectors. Later this model was studied under biological and mathematical aspects mainly by Willshaw [124] and Palm [75, 76] and it was shown that this simple model has a tremendous storage capacity.

Lernmatrix is composed of a cluster of units. Each unit represents a simple model of a real biological neuron. Each unit is composed of binary weights, which correspond to the synapses and dendrites in a real neuron (see Figure. 15.1). They are described by $w_{ij} \in \{0, 1\}$ in Figure 15.2. T is the threshold of the unit. The presence of a feature is indicated by a "one" component of the vector, its absence through a "zero" component of the vector. A pair of these vectors is associated and this process of association is called learning. The first of the two vectors is called the *query vector* and the second, the *answer vector*. After learning, the query vector is presented to the associative memory and the answer vector is determined by the retrieval rule.

DOI: 10.1201/9781003374404-15

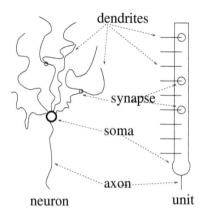

Figure 15.1 A unit is an abstract model of a biological neuron [63, 76, 44, 74, 97].

15.1.1 Learning and Retrieval

Initially, no information is stored in the associative memory. Because the information is represented in weights, all unit weights are initially set to zero. In the learning phase, pairs of binary vector are associated. Let $\mathbf{x}$ be the query vector and $\mathbf{y}$ the answer vector, the learning rule is:

$$w_{ij}^{new} = \begin{cases} 1 & if \ \ y_i \cdot x_j = 1 \\ w_{ij}^{old} & \text{otherwise.} \end{cases} \tag{15.1}$$

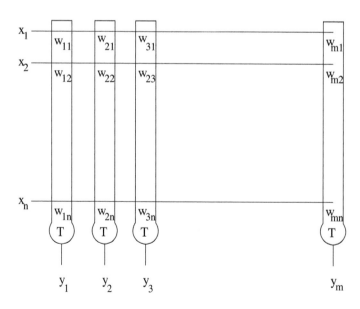

Figure 15.2 The Lernmatrix is composed of a set of units which represent a simple model of a real biological neuron. The unit is composed of weights, which correspond to the synapses and dendrites in the real neuron. In this Figure they are described by $w_{ij} \in \{0, 1\}$ where $1 \leq i \leq m$ and $1 \leq j \leq n$. T is the threshold of the unit.

This rule is called the binary Hebbian rule [75]. Every time a pair of binary vectors is stored, this rule is used.

In the *one-step* retrieval phase of the associative memory, a fault tolerant answering mechanism recalls the appropriate answer vector for a query vector $\mathbf{x}$.

The retrieval rule for the determination of the answer vector $\mathbf{y}$ is:

$$net_i = \sum_{j=1}^{n} w_{ij} x_j, \tag{15.2}$$

$$y_i = \begin{cases} 1 & \text{if} \quad net \geq T \\ 0 & \text{otherwise.} \end{cases}$$

where T is the threshold of the unit. The threshold T is set to the number of "one" components in the query vector $\mathbf{x}$, $T := |\mathbf{x}|$. If the output of the unit is 1 we say that the units fires, for the output 0 the unit does not fire. The cost of the *one-step* retrieval is $O(n \cdot m)$. The retrieval is called:

- hetero-association if both vectors are different $\mathbf{x} \neq \mathbf{y}$,

- association, if $\mathbf{x} = \mathbf{y}$, the answer vector represents the reconstruction of the disturbed query vector.

For simplicity we assume that the dimension of the query vector and the answer vector are the same, $n = m$.

Example In Figure 15.3, the vector pair $\mathbf{x}_1 = (1, 0, 0, 0, 1)$ and $\mathbf{y}_1 = (0, 1, 1, 1, 0)$ is learned. The corresponding binary weights of the associated pair are indicated by a black square. In the next step the vector pair $\mathbf{x}_2 = (0, 1, 1, 0, 1)$ and $\mathbf{y}_2 = (1, 1, 0, 0, 1)$ is learned. The corresponding binary weights of the associated pair are indicated by a black circle. In third step the retrieval phase is preformed (see Figure 15.4). The query vector $\mathbf{x}_q = (0, 1, 0, 0, 1)$ differs by one bit to the learned query vector $\mathbf{x}_2 = (0, 1, 1, 0, 1)$. The threshold T is set to the number of "one" components in the query vector $\mathbf{x}_q$, $T = 2$. The retrieved vector is the vector $\mathbf{y}_2 = (1, 1, 0, 0, 1)$ that was stored.

15.1.2 Storage Capacity

We analyze the optimal storage costs of the Lernmatrix. For an estimation of the asymptotic number L of vector pairs $(\mathbf{x}, \mathbf{y})$ that can be stored in an associative memory before it begins to make mistakes in the retrieval phase, it is assumed that both vectors have the same dimension n. It is also assumed that both vectors are composed of k ones, which are equally likely to be in any coordinate of the vector. In this case it was shown [75, 42, 102] that the optimum value for k is approximately

$$k \doteq \log_2(n/4). \tag{15.3}$$

For example, for a vector of the dimension n=1000000 only $k = 18$ ones should be used to code a pattern according to the Equation 15.3. For an optimal value for k according

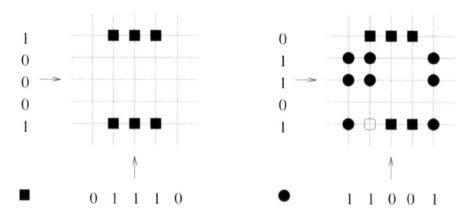

Figure 15.3 The vector pair $\mathbf{x}_1 = (1, 0, 0, 0, 1)$ and $\mathbf{y}_1 = (0, 1, 1, 1, 0)$ is learned. The corresponding binary weights of the associated pair are indicated by a black square. In the next step the vector pair $\mathbf{x}_2 = (0, 1, 1, 0, 1)$ and $\mathbf{y}_2 = (1, 1, 0, 0, 1)$ is learned. The corresponding binary weights of the associated pair are indicated by a black circle.

to the Equation 15.3 with ones equally distributed over the coordinates of the vectors, approximately L vector pairs can be stored in the associative memory [75, 42]. L is approximately

$$L \doteq (\ln 2)(n^2/k^2). \tag{15.4}$$

This value is much **greater** than n. The estimate of L is very rough because Equation 15.3 is only valid for very large networks, however the capacity increase is still

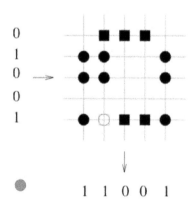

Figure 15.4 The query vector $\mathbf{x}_q = (0, 1, 0, 0, 1)$ differs by one bit to the learned query vector $\mathbf{x}_2 = (0, 1, 1, 0, 1)$. The threshold T is set to the number of "one" components in the query vector $\mathbf{x}_q$, $T = 2$. The retrieved vector is the vector $\mathbf{y}_2 = (1, 1, 0, 0, 1)$ that was stored.

considerable. The upper bound for large n is

$$I = n^2 \log 2 = n^2 \cdot 0.693 \tag{15.5}$$

the asymptotic capacity is 69.311 percent per bit which is much higher than most associative memories. This capacity is only valid for sparse equally distributed ones [75]. The promise of Willshaw's associative memory that it can store much more patterns than the number of units. The cost of loading $L = (\ln 2)(n^2/k^2)$ patterns in n units with $k = \log_2(n/4)$ is $O(n^2)$. It is much lower than storing the L patterns in a list of L units $O(n \cdot L)$ This is because $L > n$, or

$$O\left(\frac{n^2}{\log(n)^2}\right) > O(n)$$

since

$$\sqrt{n} > \log(n).$$

The Lernmatrix has a tremendous storage capacity [75, 42], it can store much more patterns then the number of units.

The description of how to generated efficiently binary sparse codes of visual patterns or other data structure is described in [122, 89, 90]. For example, real vector patterns have to binarized.

15.2 MONTE CARLO LERNMATRIX

The suggested probabilistic retrieval rule for the determination of the answer vector $\mathbf{y}$ for the query vector $\mathbf{x}$ is

$$p(y_i = 1|\mathbf{x}) = \frac{1}{n} \cdot \left(\frac{net_i}{\sum_{v=1}^{n} net_v}\right) \tag{15.6}$$

and

$$p(y_i = 0|\mathbf{x}) = \frac{1}{n} \cdot \left(1 - \frac{net_i}{\sum_{v=1}^{n} net_v}\right) \tag{15.7}$$

describing the probability of firing or not firing of one unit with

$$1 = \sum_{i=1}^{n} \left(p(y_i = 1|\mathbf{x}) + p(y_i = 0|\mathbf{x})\right). \tag{15.8}$$

During the query operation one unit is randomly sampled and either it fires or not according to the probability distribution. To determine the answer vector, we have to sample the Monte Carlo Lernmatrix several times. For the reconstructed vector, three states will be present: 1 for fired units, 0 for not fired units, and *unknown* for silent units. The Monte Carlo Lernmatrix is a close description of the quantum Lernmatrix. In quantum Lernmatrix units are represented by quantum states, sampling corresponds to the measurement.

15.3 QUANTUM COUNTING ONES

In a binary string of the length N we can represent the fraction of k ones by the simple formula k/N and of the zeros as $(N-k)/N$ resulting in a linear relation. We can interpret these numbers as probability values. We can map these linear relations into the sigmoid-like probability functions for the presence of ones using Euler's formula [111] in relation to trigonometry

$$\left(\sin\left(\frac{\pi \cdot k}{2 \cdot N}\right)\right)^2 = \left|\frac{e^{i \cdot \frac{\pi \cdot k}{2 \cdot N}} - e^{-i \cdot \frac{\pi \cdot k}{2 \cdot N}}}{2}\right|^2 \in [0,1] \tag{15.9}$$

and of zeros with

$$\left(\cos\left(\frac{\pi \cdot k}{2 \cdot N}\right)\right)^2 = \left|\frac{e^{i \cdot \frac{\pi \cdot k}{2 \cdot N}} + e^{-i \cdot \frac{\pi \cdot k}{2 \cdot N}}}{2}\right|^2 \in [0,1] \tag{15.10}$$

together with

$$\left(\sin\left(\frac{\pi \cdot k}{2 \cdot N}\right)\right)^2 + \left(\cos\left(\frac{\pi \cdot k}{2 \cdot N}\right)\right)^2 = 1$$

In the Figure 15.5 the sigmoid-like probability functions for $N = 8$ are indicated. To count the number of ones we introduced the control qubit in superposition $1/\sqrt{2} \cdot (|0\rangle + |1\rangle)$. For the superposition part represented by the control qubit 0, the phase $e^{i \cdot \frac{\pi}{2 \cdot 3}}$ is applied for each one. For the superposition part represented by the control qubit 1, the phase $e^{-i \cdot \frac{\pi}{2 \cdot 3}}$ is applied for each one.

$$\frac{1}{\sqrt{2}} \cdot |0\rangle \otimes \left(e^{i \cdot \frac{\pi}{2 \cdot 3}} \cdot |1\rangle \otimes |0\rangle \otimes e^{i \cdot \frac{\pi}{2 \cdot 3}} \cdot |1\rangle\right) +$$

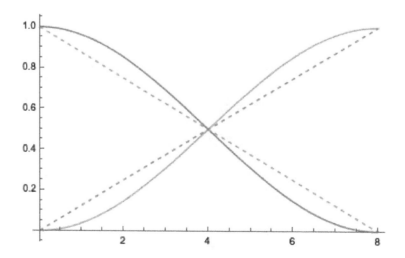

Figure 15.5 Sigmoid-like probability functions for $N = 8$ is indicated by continuous line, the linear relation by the dashed lines. The x-axis indicates the k values, the y-axis the probabilities.

$$\frac{1}{\sqrt{2}} \cdot |1\rangle \otimes \left(e^{-i \cdot \frac{\pi}{2 \cdot 3}} \cdot |1\rangle \otimes |0\rangle \otimes e^{-i \cdot \frac{\pi}{2 \cdot 3}} \cdot |1\rangle\right) = \qquad (15.11)$$

$$\frac{e^{i \cdot \frac{\pi \cdot 2}{2 \cdot 3}}}{\sqrt{2}} |0101\rangle + \frac{e^{-i \cdot \frac{\pi \cdot 2}{2 \cdot 3}}}{\sqrt{2}} |1101\rangle$$

If we apply a Hadamard gate to the control qubit [111] we get

$$(H \otimes I \otimes I \otimes I) \cdot \left(\frac{e^{i \cdot \frac{\pi \cdot 2}{2 \cdot 3}}}{\sqrt{2}} |0101\rangle + \frac{e^{-i \cdot \frac{\pi \cdot 2}{2 \cdot 3}}}{\sqrt{2}} |1101\rangle\right) =$$

$$\frac{e^{i \cdot \frac{\pi \cdot 2}{2 \cdot 3}} + e^{-i \cdot \frac{\pi \cdot 2}{2 \cdot 3}}}{2} |0101\rangle + \frac{e^{i \cdot \frac{\pi \cdot 2}{2 \cdot 3}} - e^{-i \cdot \frac{\pi \cdot 2}{2 \cdot 3}}}{2} |1101\rangle =$$

$$\cos\left(\frac{\pi \cdot 2}{2 \cdot 3}\right) \cdot |0101\rangle + i \cdot \sin\left(\frac{\pi \cdot 2}{2 \cdot 3}\right) \cdot |1101\rangle =$$

$$\left(\cos\left(\frac{\pi \cdot 2}{2 \cdot 3}\right) \cdot |0\rangle + i \cdot \sin\left(\frac{\pi \cdot 2}{2 \cdot 3}\right) \cdot |1\rangle\right) \otimes |101\rangle \qquad (15.12)$$

The probability of measuring the control qubit $|0\rangle$ is

$$p(|0\rangle) = p(|0101\rangle) = \left(\cos\left(\frac{\pi \cdot 2}{2 \cdot 3}\right)\right)^2 = 0.25$$

and the probability of measuring the control qubit $|1\rangle$ is

$$p(|1\rangle) = p(|1101\rangle) = \left(\sin\left(\frac{\pi \cdot 2}{2 \cdot 3}\right)\right)^2 = 0.75$$

indicating the presence of two ones. The representation of the circuit in *qiskit* is given by

```
from qiskit import QuantumCircuit, Aer, execute
from qiskit.visualization import plot_histogram
from math import pi

qc = QuantumCircuit(4)
#Input is |101>
qc.x(0)
qc.x(2)
qc.barrier()
qc.h(3)
qc.cp(-pi/6,0,3)
qc.cp(-pi/6,1,3)
qc.cp(-pi/6,2,3)
qc.x(3)
qc.cp(pi/6,0,3)
qc.cp(pi/6,1,3)
qc.cp(pi/6,2,3)
qc.x(3)
qc.h(3)
```

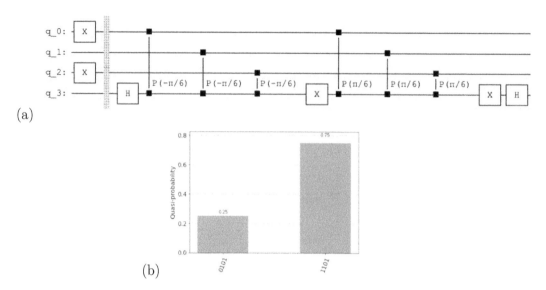

(a)

(b)

Figure 15.6 (a) Quantum counting circuit with $N = 3$ and $k = 2$. (b) $p(|0101\rangle) = 0.25$ and $p(|1101\rangle) = 0.75$.

```
simulator = Aer.get_backend('statevector_simulator')
# Run and get counts
result=execute(qc,simulator).result()
counts = result.get_counts()
plot_histogram(counts)
```

the resulting quantum circuit is represented in the Figure 15.6 (a) and the resulting histogram of the measured qubits is represented in the Figure 15.6 (b).

15.4 QUANTUM LERNMATRIX

Useful associative properties of Euler's formula result from equally distributed weights over the whole weight matrix and are only present in large matrices, in our examples. We examine toys examples as a proof of concept for future quantum associative memories.

The superposition of the weight vectors of the units is based on the entanglement of the index qubits that are in the superposition with the weight vectors. The count is represented by a unary string of qubits that controls the phase operation. It represents to the *net* value of the Lernmatrix. The phase information is the basis of the quantum counting of ones that increases the probability of measuring the correct units representing ones in the answer vector. We will represent n units in superposition by entanglement with the index qubits.

To represent four units we need two index qubits in superposition. Each index state of the qubit is entangled with a pattern by the Toffoli gate also called the ccX gate (CCNOT gate, controlled controlled not gate), by setting a corresponding qubit to one. In our example we store three patterns $\mathbf{x}_1 = (1, 0, 0, 1)$; $\mathbf{y}_1 = (1, 0, 0, 1)$, $\mathbf{x}_2 = (1, 0, 0, 0)$; $\mathbf{y}_2 = (0, 1, 0, 0)$, and $\mathbf{x}_3 = (0, 0, 1, 0)$; $\mathbf{y}_3 = (0, 0, 1, 0)$ resulting in the

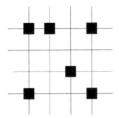

Figure 15.7 Wight matrix represented by four units after learning the correlation of the three patterns $\mathbf{x}_1 = (1, 0, 0, 1)$; $\mathbf{y}_1 = (1, 0, 0, 1)$, $\mathbf{x}_2 = (1, 0, 0, 0)$; $\mathbf{y}_2 = (0, 1, 0, 0)$ and $\mathbf{x}_3 = (0, 0, 1, 0)$; $\mathbf{y}_3 = (0, 0, 1, 0)$. The learning is identical with the learning phase of the Lernmatrix.

weight matrix represented by four units (see Figure 15.7). After the entanglement of index qubits $|index_j\rangle$ in superposition

$$|index_1\rangle = |11\rangle \quad |index_2\rangle = |10\rangle$$

$$|index_3\rangle = |01\rangle \quad |index_4\rangle = |00\rangle$$

with the weight vectors the following state is present, the state $count_j$ and $unit_j$ are represented by four qubits each for the four binary weights, with

$$|unit_j\rangle = |(w_4 w_3 w_1 w_1)_j\rangle$$

(see Figure 15.8)

$$\frac{1}{2} \cdot \left(\sum_{j=1}^{4} |index_j\rangle |count_j\rangle |unit_j\rangle \right). \tag{15.13}$$

The value $|count_j\rangle$ is the unary representation of the Lernmatrix value net_j. We include the query vector is $\mathbf{x}_q = (1, 0, 0, 1)$,

$$\frac{1}{2} \cdot \left(\sum_{j=1}^{4} |index_j\rangle |count_j\rangle |unit_j\rangle \right) \otimes |query\rangle =$$

$$\frac{1}{2} \cdot \left(\sum_{j=1}^{4} |(i_2 i_1)_j\rangle |(c_4 c_3 c_2 c_1)_j\rangle |(w_4 w_3 w_2 w_1)_j\rangle \right) \otimes |1001\rangle \tag{15.14}$$

the resulting histogram of the measured qubits is represented in the Figure 15.9. In the next steps, we describe the *active phase* (see Figure 15.10). For simplicity, we will ignore the index qubits since they are not important in the active phase. We perform quantum counting using the control bit that is set in superposition resulting in

$$\frac{1}{\sqrt{2}} \cdot (|0\rangle + |1\rangle) \otimes \frac{1}{2} \cdot \left(\sum_{j=1}^{4} |(c_4 c_3 c_2 c_1)_j\rangle |(w_4 w_3 w_2 w_1)_j\rangle \right) \otimes |1001\rangle =$$

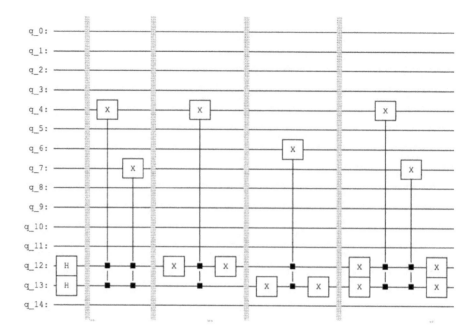

Figure 15.8 The quantum circuit that produces the *sleep phase*. The qubits 0 to 3 represent the query vector, the qubits 4 to 7 the associative memory, the qubits 8 to 11 represent the count, and the qubits 12 and 13 are the index qubits whereas the qubit 14 is the control qubit.

$$\frac{1}{2 \cdot \sqrt{2}} \cdot |0\rangle \left(\sum_{j=1}^{4} |(c_4 c_3 c_2 c_1)_j\rangle |(w_4 w_3 w_2 w_1)_j\rangle \right) \otimes |1001\rangle +$$

$$\frac{1}{2 \cdot \sqrt{2}} \cdot |1\rangle \left(\sum_{j=1}^{4} |(c_4 c_3 c_2 c_1)_j\rangle |(w_4 w_3 w_2 w_1)_j\rangle \right) \otimes |1001\rangle \qquad (15.15)$$

Applying controlled phase operation with $N = 2$ since two ones are present in the query vector and $count_j \le 2$

$$\frac{1}{2 \cdot \sqrt{2}} \cdot |0\rangle \left(\sum_{j=1}^{4} e^{i \cdot \frac{\pi \cdot count_j}{2 \cdot 2}} \cdot |(c_4 c_3 c_2 c_1)_j\rangle |(w_4 w_3 w_2 w_1)_j\rangle \right) \otimes |1001\rangle +$$

$$\frac{1}{2 \cdot \sqrt{2}} \cdot |1\rangle \left(\sum_{j=1}^{4} e^{-i \cdot \frac{\pi \cdot count_j}{2 \cdot 2}} \cdot |(c_4 c_3 c_2 c_1)_j\rangle |(w_4 w_3 w_2 w_1)_j\rangle \right) \otimes |1001\rangle \qquad (15.16)$$

and applying the Hadamard gate to the control qubit we get

$$\left(\sum_{j=1}^{4} \frac{1}{2} \cdot \left(\cos \left(\frac{\pi \cdot count_j}{2 \cdot 2} \right) \right) \cdot |0\rangle |(c_4 c_3 c_2 c_1)_j\rangle |(w_4 w_3 w_2 w_1)_j\rangle \right) \otimes |1001\rangle +$$

$$\left(\sum_{j=1}^{4} \frac{1}{2} \cdot \left(i \cdot \sin \left(\frac{\pi \cdot count_j}{2 \cdot 2} \right) \right) \cdot |1\rangle |(c_4 c_3 c_2 c_1)_j\rangle |(w_4 w_3 w_2 w_1)_j\rangle \right) \otimes |1001\rangle. \quad (15.17)$$

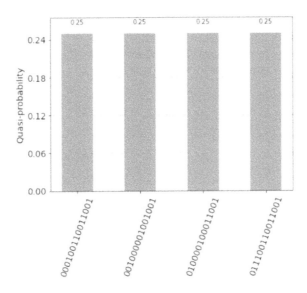

Figure 15.9 Four superposition state corresponding to the four units of the associative memory. The qubits 0 to 3 represent the query vector $\mathbf{x}_q = (1, 0, 0, 1)$, the qubits 4 to 7 the associative memory, the qubits 8 to 11 represent the count, and the qubits 12 and 13 are the index qubits whereas, the control qubit 14 is zero. Note that the units are counted in the reverse order by the index qubits: 11 first unit, 10 for the third unit, 01 for second unit, and 00 for the fourth unit.

The architecture is described by 15 qubits. The qubits 0 to 3 represent the query vector, the qubits 4 to 7 the associative memory, the qubits 8 to 11 represent the count and the qubits 12 and 13 are the index qubits, the qubit 14 is the control qubit. The count operation is done by the ccX gate (see Figures 15.8 and 15.10).

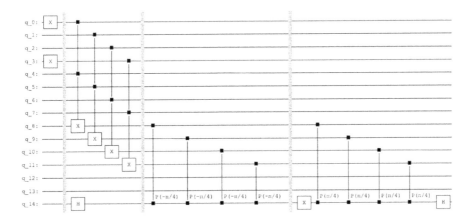

Figure 15.10 The quantum circuit that produces the *active phase*. The query and the amplification operations on the count qubits, the qubits 8 to 11. The control qubit 14.

```python
from qiskit import QuantumCircuit, Aer, execute
from qiskit.quantum_info import Statevector
from qiskit.visualization import plot_histogram
from qiskit.circuit.library import MCXGate
from math import pi

qc = QuantumCircuit(15)
#0-3 query
#4-7 data
#8-11 count
#Index Pointer
#12-13
#Aux
#14

#Sleep Phase
#Index Pointer
qc.h(12)
qc.h(13)
qc.barrier()
#1st weights
qc.ccx(12,13,4)
qc.ccx(12,13,7)
qc.barrier()
#2th weights
qc.x(12)
qc.ccx(12,13,4)
qc.x(12)
qc.barrier()
#3th weights
qc.x(13)
qc.ccx(12,13,6)
qc.x(13)
qc.barrier()
#4th weights
qc.x(12)
qc.x(13)
qc.ccx(12,13,4)
qc.ccx(12,13,7)
qc.x(13)
qc.x(12)
qc.barrier()

#Active Phase
#query
qc.x(0)
qc.x(3)
qc.barrier()
qc.ccx(0,4,8)
qc.ccx(1,5,9)
qc.ccx(2,6,10)
```

```
qc.ccx(3,7,11)
#Dividing
qc.h(14)
qc.barrier()
#Marking
qc.cp(-pi/4,8,14)
qc.cp(-pi/4,9,14)
qc.cp(-pi/4,10,14)
qc.cp(-pi/4,11,14)
qc.barrier()
qc.x(14)
qc.cp(pi/4,8,14)
qc.cp(pi/4,9,14)
qc.cp(pi/4,10,14)
qc.cp(pi/4,11,14)
qc.h(14)
qc.draw(fold=110)

simulator = Aer.get_backend('statevector_simulator')
# Run and get counts
result=execute(qc,simulator).result()
counts = result.get_counts()
plot_histogram(counts)
```

With the query vector $\mathbf{x}_q = (1,0,0,1)$ units represented by the states have following values

- The first unit has the value $count_1 = 2$ and the two corresponding states are: for the control $qubit = 1$, the value is $1 = \sin \frac{\pi}{2}$ with the measured probability $\left|\sin \frac{\pi}{2} \cdot \frac{1}{2}\right|^2 = 0.25$, and for the control $qubit = 0$, the value is $0 = \cos \frac{\pi}{2}$ with the measured probability 0.

- The second unit has the value $count_2 = 1$ and the two corresponding states are: for the control $qubit = 1$, the value is $\frac{1}{\sqrt{2}} = \sin \frac{\pi}{4}$ with the measured probability $\left|\sin \frac{\pi}{4} \cdot \frac{1}{2}\right|^2 = 0.125$, and for the control $qubit = 0$, the value is $\frac{1}{\sqrt{2}} = \cos \frac{\pi}{4}$ with the measured probability $\left|\cos \frac{\pi}{4} \cdot \frac{1}{2}\right|^2 = 0.125$.

- The third unit has the value $count_3 = 0$ and the two corresponding states are: for the control $qubit = 1$, the value is $0 = \sin 0$ with the measured probability $=0$, and for the control $qubit = 0$, the value is $1 = \cos 0$ with the measured probability $=0$.

- The fourth unit has the (decimal) value $count_4 = 2$ and the two corresponding states are: for the control $qubit = 1$, the value is $1 = \sin \frac{\pi}{2}$ with the measured probability $\left|\sin \frac{\pi}{2} \cdot \frac{1}{2}\right|^2 = 0.25$, and for the control $qubit = 0$, the value is $0 = \cos \frac{\pi}{2}$ with the measured probability 0.

There are five states with probabilities not equal to zero, see Figure 15.11. The measured probability (control $qubit = 1$) indicating a firing of the units is 0.625.

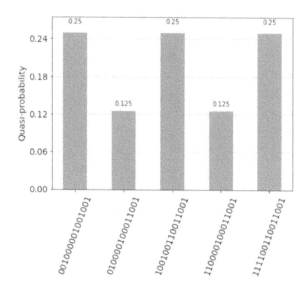

Figure 15.11 Five superposition states not equal to zero. The control qubit 14 equal to one indicates the firing of the units. The measured value is 0.625. The two probabilities 0.25 express the perfect match and the solution $(1, 0, 0, 1)$, indicated by the index qubits 12 and 13, with the values (11) for the first unit and (00) for the fourth unit. Note that the units are counted in the reverse order by the index qubits: (11) first unit, (10) for the second unit, (01) for third unit, and (00) for the fourth unit. The control qubit 14 equal to zero indicates the units that do not fire. The measured value is 0.375. The probability 0.25 with the index qubits 12 and 13, with the value (01) for the third unit indicates the most dissimilar pattern $(0, 0, 1, 0)$.

15.4.1 Generalization

We can generalize the description for n units. After the entanglement of index qubits in superposition with the weight vectors the following state is present, the state $count_j$ and $unit_j$ are represented by [111], [112],

$$\frac{1}{\sqrt{n}} \cdot \left(\sum_{j=1}^{n} |index_j\rangle |count_j\rangle |unit_j\rangle \right) \otimes |query\rangle. \tag{15.18}$$

with the cost $O(n^2)$. We apply the control qubit (ignoring the index qubits)

$$\frac{1}{\sqrt{2}} \cdot (|0\rangle + |1\rangle) \otimes \frac{1}{\sqrt{n}} \cdot \left(\sum_{j=1}^{n} |count_j\rangle |unit_j\rangle \right) \otimes |query\rangle =$$

$$\frac{1}{\sqrt{2 \cdot n}} \cdot |0\rangle \left(\sum_{j=1}^{n} |count_j\rangle |unit_j\rangle \right) \otimes |query\rangle +$$

$$\frac{1}{\sqrt{2 \cdot n}} \cdot |1\rangle \left(\sum_{j=1}^{n} |count_j\rangle |unit_j\rangle \right) \otimes |query\rangle. \tag{15.19}$$

Applying controlled phase operation with N for present ones in the query vector and $count_j \leq N$

$$\frac{1}{\sqrt{2 \cdot n}} \cdot |0\rangle \left(\sum_{j=1}^{n} e^{i \cdot \frac{\pi \cdot count_j}{2 \cdot N}} \cdot |count_j\rangle |unit_j\rangle \right) \otimes |query\rangle +$$

$$\frac{1}{\sqrt{2 \cdot n}} \cdot |1\rangle \left(\sum_{j=1}^{n} e^{-i \cdot \frac{\pi \cdot count_j}{2 \cdot N}} \cdot |count_j\rangle |unit_j\rangle \right) \otimes |query\rangle \qquad (15.20)$$

and applying the Hadamard gate to the control qubit we get the final result with

$$\left(\sum_{j=1}^{n} \frac{1}{\sqrt{n}} \cdot \left(\cos \left(\frac{\pi \cdot count_j}{2 \cdot N} \right) \right) \cdot |0\rangle |count_j\rangle |unit_j\rangle \right) \otimes |query\rangle +$$

$$\left(\sum_{j=1}^{n} \frac{1}{\sqrt{n}} \cdot \left(i \cdot \sin \left(\frac{\pi \cdot count_j}{2 \cdot N} \right) \right) \cdot |1\rangle |count_j\rangle |unit_j\rangle \right) \otimes |query\rangle \qquad (15.21)$$

The cost of one query is $O(n)$ and for $k = \log_2(n/4)$ queries $O(\log(n) \cdot n)$.

15.4.2 Example

In this example we store three patterns representing three associations: $\mathbf{x}_1 = (1, 1, 0, 0, 0, 0, 1, 0)$; $\mathbf{y}_1 = (1, 1, 0, 0, 0, 0, 1, 0)$, $\mathbf{x}_2 = (0, 1, 0, 1, 1, 0, 0, 0)$; $\mathbf{y}_2 = (0, 1, 0, 1, 1, 0, 0, 0)$ and $\mathbf{x}_3 = (0, 0, 1, 0, 0, 1, 0, 1)$; $\mathbf{y}_3 = (0, 0, 1, 0, 0, 1, 0, 1)$. The weight matrix after the learning phase is represented by eight units (see Figures 15.12 and 15.13). After the entanglement of index qubits in superposition

$$|index_1\rangle = |111\rangle \quad |index_2\rangle = |110\rangle$$

$$|index_3\rangle = |101\rangle \quad |index_4\rangle = |100\rangle$$

$$|index_5\rangle = |011\rangle \quad |index_6\rangle = |010\rangle$$

$$|index_7\rangle = |001\rangle \quad |index_8\rangle = |000\rangle$$

with the weight vectors the following state is present, the state $count_j$ and $unit_j$ are represented by eight qubits [111], [112],

$$\frac{1}{\sqrt{8}} \cdot \left(\sum_{j=1}^{8} |index_j\rangle |count_j\rangle |unit_j\rangle \right).$$

With the query vector $\mathbf{x}_q = (1, 1, 0, 0, 0, 0, 0, 0)$ we get (see Figure 15.13 (a))

$$\frac{1}{\sqrt{8}} \cdot \left(\sum_{j=1}^{8} |index_j\rangle |count_j\rangle |unit_j\rangle \right) \otimes |00000011\rangle.$$

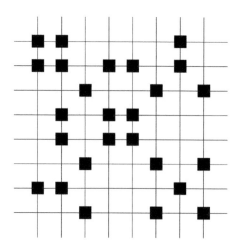

Figure 15.12 Weight matrix represented by eight units after learning the correlation of the three patterns $\mathbf{x}_1 = (1,1,0,0,0,0,1,0)$; $\mathbf{y}_1 = (1,1,0,0,0,0,1,0)$,
$\mathbf{x}_2 = (0,1,0,1,1,0,0,0)$; $\mathbf{y}_2 = (0,1,0,1,1,0,0,0)$ and $\mathbf{x}_3 = (0,0,1,0,0,1,0,1)$;
$\mathbf{y}_3 = (0,0,1,0,0,1,0,1)$. The learning is identical with the learning phase of the
Lernmatrix.

and the answer vector (ignoring the index qubits) according to

$$\left(\sum_{j=1}^{8} \frac{1}{\sqrt{8}} \cdot \left(\cos\left(\frac{\pi \cdot count_j}{2 \cdot N} \right) \right) \cdot |0\rangle |count_j\rangle |unit_j\rangle \right) \otimes |00000011\rangle +$$

$$\left(\sum_{j=1}^{8} \frac{1}{\sqrt{8}} \cdot \left(i \cdot \sin\left(\frac{\pi \cdot count_j}{2 \cdot N} \right) \right) \cdot |1\rangle |count_j\rangle |unit_j\rangle \right) \otimes |00000011\rangle$$

is $(1,1,0,0,0,0,1,0)$ (see Figure 15.14 (b)).

```
from qiskit import QuantumCircuit, Aer, execute
from qiskit.quantum_info import Statevector
from qiskit.visualization import plot_histogram
from qiskit.circuit.library import MCXGate
from math import pi

qc = QuantumCircuit(28)

#0-7 query
qc.x(0)
qc.x(1)

#qc.x(6)

#8-15 data
#16-23 net
#24-26 index
```

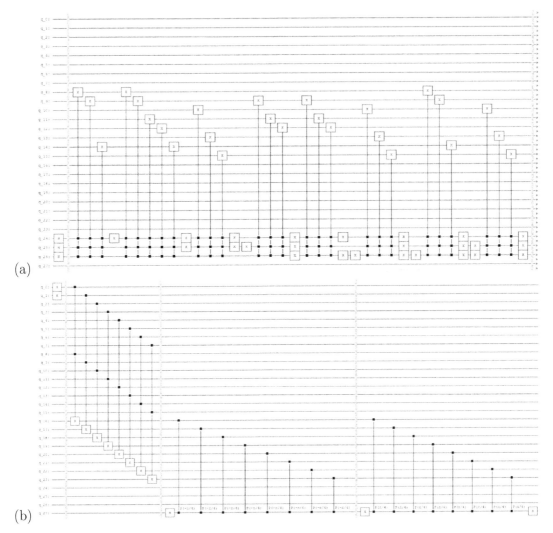

Figure 15.13 (a) The quantum circuit that produces the *sleep phase*. The qubits 0 to 7 represent the query vector, the qubits 8 to 15 the associative memory, and the qubits 16 to 23 represent the count, whereas the qubits 24, 25, and 26 are the index qubits (8 states) and the qubit 27 is the control qubit. (b) The quantum circuit that produces the *active phase*. The query and the amplification operations on the count qubits, the qubits 16 to 23 and the control qubit 27.

```
#Aux 27

#Pointer
qc.h(24)
qc.h(25)
qc.h(26)

qc.barrier()
```

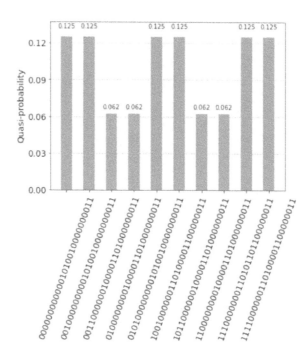

Figure 15.14 Teen superposition states not equal to zero. The qubits 24, 25, and 26 are the index qubits. Note that the units are counted in the reverse order by the index qubits: 111 first unit, 110 for the second unit, till 000 being the eighth unit. The measured value for the control qubit 27 equal to one indicates the firing of the units. The measured value is just 0.5. This happens since the weight matrix is relatively small and not homogenously filled. For the query vector $\mathbf{x}_q = (1, 1, 0, 0, 0, 0, 0, 0)$, the three values 0.125 indicate the answer vector $(1, 1, 0, 0, 0, 0, 1, 0)$ by the index qubits 24, 25, and 26; for the first unit with the value (111), the second unit (110), and seventh unit (001). The control qubit 27 equal to zero indicates the units that do not fire.

```
gate = MCXGate(3)

#1st weights
qc.append(gate, [24, 25, 26, 8])
qc.append(gate, [24, 25, 26, 9])
qc.append(gate, [24, 25, 26, 14])

#2th weights
qc.x(24)
qc.append(gate, [24, 25, 26, 8])
qc.append(gate, [24, 25, 26, 9])
qc.append(gate, [24, 25, 26, 11])
qc.append(gate, [24, 25, 26, 12])
qc.append(gate, [24, 25, 26, 14])
qc.x(24)
```

```
#3th weights
qc.x(25)
qc.append(gate, [24, 25, 26, 10])
qc.append(gate, [24, 25, 26, 13])
qc.append(gate, [24, 25, 26, 15])
qc.x(25)

#4th weights
qc.x(24)
qc.x(25)
qc.append(gate, [24, 25, 26, 9])
qc.append(gate, [24, 25, 26, 11])
qc.append(gate, [24, 25, 26, 12])
qc.x(25)
qc.x(24)

#5th weights
qc.x(26)
qc.append(gate, [24, 25, 26, 9])
qc.append(gate, [24, 25, 26, 11])
qc.append(gate, [24, 25, 26, 12])
qc.x(26)

#6th weights
qc.x(26)
qc.x(24)
qc.append(gate, [24, 25, 26, 10])
qc.append(gate, [24, 25, 26, 13])
qc.append(gate, [24, 25, 26, 15])
qc.x(24)
qc.x(26)

#7th weights
qc.x(26)
qc.x(25)
qc.append(gate, [24, 25, 26, 8])
qc.append(gate, [24, 25, 26, 9])
qc.append(gate, [24, 25, 26, 14])
qc.x(25)
qc.x(26)

#8th weights
qc.x(26)
qc.x(25)
qc.x(24)
qc.append(gate, [24, 25, 26, 10])
qc.append(gate, [24, 25, 26, 13])
qc.append(gate, [24, 25, 26, 15])
qc.x(24)
qc.x(25)
qc.x(26)
```

```
qc.barrier()
#query
qc.ccx(0,8,16)
qc.ccx(1,9,17)
qc.ccx(2,10,18)
qc.ccx(3,11,19)
qc.ccx(4,12,20)
qc.ccx(5,13,21)
qc.ccx(6,14,22)
qc.ccx(7,15,23)

#Dividing
qc.barrier()
qc.h(27)

#Marking
qc.cp(-pi/4,16,27)
qc.cp(-pi/4,17,27)
qc.cp(-pi/4,18,27)
qc.cp(-pi/4,19,27)
qc.cp(-pi/4,20,27)
qc.cp(-pi/4,21,27)
qc.cp(-pi/4,22,27)
qc.cp(-pi/4,23,27)

qc.barrier()
qc.x(27)
qc.cp(pi/4,16,27)
qc.cp(pi/4,17,27)
qc.cp(pi/4,18,27)
qc.cp(pi/4,19,27)
qc.cp(pi/4,20,27)
qc.cp(pi/4,21,27)
qc.cp(pi/4,22,27)
qc.cp(pi/4,23,27)

qc.barrier()

qc.h(27)

qc.draw(fold=210)
```

15.4.3 Applying Trugenberger Amplification Several Times

According to Trugenberger [112] applying control qubit sequential, b times results in

$$\sum_{v=0}^{b}\left(\sum_{j=1}^{n}\frac{1}{\sqrt{n}}\cdot\left(\cos\left(\frac{\pi\cdot count_j}{2\cdot N}\right)\right)^{b-v}\cdot\left(i\cdot\sin\left(\frac{\pi\cdot count_j}{2\cdot N}\right)\right)^{v}\cdot\right.$$

$$\left.\cdot|v\rangle|index_j\rangle|count_j\rangle|unit_j\rangle\right)\otimes|query\rangle. \tag{15.22}$$

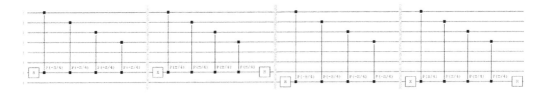

Figure 15.15 Circuit representing the application of the control qubit two times for the quantum circuit of Figure 15.8.

with $|v\rangle$ being the binary representation of the decimal value v. The idea is then to measure b control qubits b times, until the desired state is obtained. In Trugenberger identifies the inverse parameter b as temperature $t = 1/b$ and concludes that accuracy of pattern recall can be tuned by adjusting a parameter playing the role of an effective temperature [112]. In Figure 15.15, the control qubit was applied two times for quantum circuit of the Figure 15.8. Figure 15.16 represents the resulting histogram of the measured qubits. With the assumption of independence, measuring the control qubits in the sequence results in a low probability. For example, measuring the two control qubits with the value one is $0.5625 = 0.625 \cdot 0.9$.

```
qc = QuantumCircuit(23)
#0-3 query
qc.x(0)
qc.x(3)
#4-7 data agregated
#8-11 data
#12-19 net/count
#Index Pointer
#20-21
#Aux
#22
#Index Pointer
qc.h(20)
qc.h(21)

#1st weights
#OR Aggregated
qc.barrier()
qc.ccx(20,21,4)
qc.ccx(20,21,7)
#Original
qc.barrier()
qc.ccx(20,21,8)
qc.ccx(20,21,11)
#2th weights
qc.x(20)
#OR Aggregated
qc.barrier()
qc.ccx(20,21,4)
```

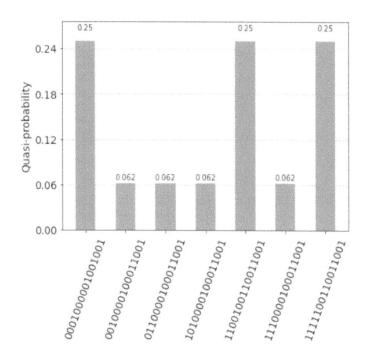

Figure 15.16 Seven superposition states not equal to zero. This is because the states with the former values 0.125 were divided into two values $0.125/2 = 0.0625$ by the two control qubits. The first control qubit 15 equal to one indicates the firing of the units. The measured value is 0.625. After measuring the first control qubit equal to one, the measured value of the second control qubit 14 equal to one is 0.9. Assuming independence, the value of measuring the two control qubits with the value one is $0.5625 = 0.625 \cdot 0.9$. As before, the two values 0.25 indicate the perfect match and the solution $(1, 0, 0, 1)$ with the values of the index qubits 12 and 13: (11) for the first unit and (00) for the fourth unit.

```
qc.ccx(20,21,7)
#Original
qc.barrier()
qc.ccx(20,21,8)
qc.x(20)
#3th weights
qc.x(21)
#OR Aggregated
qc.barrier()
qc.ccx(20,21,4)
qc.ccx(20,21,6)
qc.ccx(20,21,7)
#Original
qc.barrier()
qc.ccx(20,21,10)
qc.x(21)
```

```
#4th weights
qc.x(20)
qc.x(21)
#OR Aggregated
qc.barrier()
qc.ccx(20,21,4)
qc.ccx(20,21,6)
qc.ccx(20,21,7)
#Original
qc.barrier()
qc.ccx(20,21,8)
qc.ccx(20,21,11)
qc.x(21)
qc.x(20)
qc.barrier()
#query, counting
#OR Aggregated
qc.ccx(0,4,12)
qc.ccx(1,5,13)
qc.ccx(2,6,14)
qc.ccx(3,7,15)
#Original
qc.ccx(0,8,16)
qc.ccx(1,9,17)
qc.ccx(2,10,18)
qc.ccx(3,11,19)
#Dividing
qc.barrier()
qc.h(22)
#Marking
qc.barrier()
qc.cp(-pi/8,12,22)
qc.cp(-pi/8,13,22)
qc.cp(-pi/8,14,22)
qc.cp(-pi/8,15,22)
qc.cp(-pi/8,16,22)
qc.cp(-pi/8,17,22)
qc.cp(-pi/8,18,22)
qc.cp(-pi/8,19,22)
qc.barrier()
qc.x(22)
qc.cp(pi/8,12,22)
qc.cp(pi/8,13,22)
qc.cp(pi/8,14,22)
qc.cp(pi/8,15,22)
qc.cp(pi/8,16,22)
qc.cp(pi/8,17,22)
qc.cp(pi/8,18,22)
qc.cp(pi/8,19,22)
qc.barrier()
qc.h(22)
```

```
qc.draw()
```

15.4.4 Tree-Like Structures

We want to increase the probability of measuring the correct units representing the ones in the answer vector and decrease the probability of measuring the zeros. For example, in a sparse code with k ones, k measurements of different ones reconstruct the binary answer vector and we cannot use the idea of applying Trugenberger amplification several times as indicated before. Instead we can increase the probability of measuring a one by the introduced tree-like structure [91]. The tree-like hierarchical associative memory approach is based on aggregation neighboring units [91]. The aggregation is a Boolean OR based transform for two or three neighboring weights of units results resulting in a more dense memory, see Figure 15.17. It was shown by computer experiments that the aggregation value between two and three is an optimal one [92]. The more dense memory is copied on top or the original memory. Depending on the number of units we can repeat the process in which we aggregate groups of two to three neighboring groups of equal units. We can continue the process till we arrive in two different groups of different units, the number of possible different aggregated memories is logarithmic, with $\log(n-1)$. Since in our example only four units are present we aggregate two units resulting in a memory of four units described by 2 identical units each.

The query vector is composed of $\log(n-1)$ concatenated copies of the original

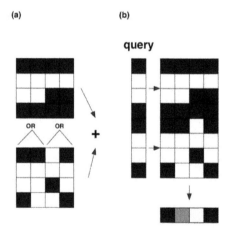

Figure 15.17 a) In our example, we store three patterns $\mathbf{x}_1 = (1,0,0,1)$, $\mathbf{y}_1 = (1,0,0,1)$; $\mathbf{x}_2 = (1,0,0,0)$, $\mathbf{y}_2 = (0,1,0,0)$ and $\mathbf{x}_3 = (0,0,1,0)$, $\mathbf{y}_3 = 0,0,1,0)$ and the query vector is $\mathbf{x}_q = (1,0,0,1)$. (b) The aggregation is a Boolean OR based transform for two neighboring weights of units results resulting in a more dense memory with $\mathbf{x}_q = (1,0,0,1,1,0,0,1)$

query vector, in our example $\mathbf{x}_q = (1, 0, 0, 1, 1, 0, 0, 1)$. We apply controlled phase operation with $N = 4$ with $count_j \leq 4$, see Figure 15.17, and the *qiskit* definition of the circuit

```
qc = QuantumCircuit(23)
#0-3 query
#4-7 data aggregated
#8-11 data
#12-19 count
#Index Pointer
#20-21
#Aux
#22

#Sleep Phase
#Index Pointer
qc.h(20)
qc.h(21)
#1st weights
#OR Aggregated
qc.barrier()
qc.ccx(20,21,4)
qc.ccx(20,21,7)
#Original
qc.barrier()
qc.ccx(20,21,8)
qc.ccx(20,21,11)
#2th weights
qc.x(20)
#OR Aggregated
qc.barrier()
qc.ccx(20,21,4)
qc.ccx(20,21,7)
#Original
qc.barrier()
qc.ccx(20,21,8)
qc.x(20)
#3th weights
qc.x(21)
#OR Aggregated
qc.barrier()
qc.ccx(20,21,4)
qc.ccx(20,21,6)
qc.ccx(20,21,7)
#Original
qc.barrier()
qc.ccx(20,21,10)
qc.x(21)
#4th weights
qc.x(20)
qc.x(21)
```

```
#OR Aggregated
qc.barrier()
qc.ccx(20,21,4)
qc.ccx(20,21,6)
qc.ccx(20,21,7)
#Original
qc.barrier()
qc.ccx(20,21,8)
qc.ccx(20,21,11)
qc.x(21)
qc.x(20)


#Active Phase
#query
qc.barrier()
qc.x(0)
qc.x(3)
qc.barrier()
#query, counting
#OR Aggregated
qc.ccx(0,4,12)
qc.ccx(1,5,13)
qc.ccx(2,6,14)
qc.ccx(3,7,15)
#Original
qc.ccx(0,8,16)
qc.ccx(1,9,17)
qc.ccx(2,10,18)
qc.ccx(3,11,19)
#Dividing
qc.barrier()
qc.h(22)
#Marking
qc.barrier()
qc.cp(-pi/8,12,22)
qc.cp(-pi/8,13,22)
qc.cp(-pi/8,14,22)
qc.cp(-pi/8,15,22)
qc.cp(-pi/8,16,22)
qc.cp(-pi/8,17,22)
qc.cp(-pi/8,18,22)
qc.cp(-pi/8,19,22)
qc.barrier()
qc.x(22)
qc.cp(pi/8,12,22)
qc.cp(pi/8,13,22)
qc.cp(pi/8,14,22)
qc.cp(pi/8,15,22)
qc.cp(pi/8,16,22)
qc.cp(pi/8,17,22)
```

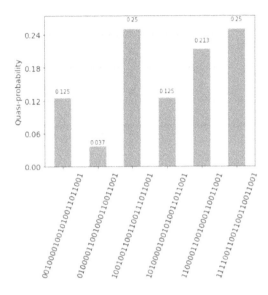

Figure 15.18 Five superposition states not equal to zero. The measured probability (control qubit equal to one) indicates the firing of the units is 0.838, the measured probability values are 0.213, 0.125, and 0.25.

```
qc.cp(pi/8,18,22)
qc.cp(pi/8,19,22)
qc.barrier()
qc.h(22)
qc.draw()
```

The measured probability (control $qubit = 1$) indicating a firing of the units is 0.838 and there are six states not equal to zero, see Figure 15.18, and compare with Figure 15.11.

15.5 CONCLUSION

The cost of the *sleep phase* and the *active phase* are the same as one of a conventional associative memory $O(n^2)$. We assume that in the *sleep phase* we have enough time to prepare several quantum Lernmatrices in superposition. The quantum Lernmatrices are kept in superposition until they are queried in the *active phase*. Each of the copies of the quantum Lernmatrix can be queried only once. We argue that the advantage to conventional associative memories is present in the *active phase* were the fast determination of information $O(\log(n) \cdot n)$ is essential by the use of quantum Lernmatrices in superposition compared to the cost of the classical Lernmatrix $O(n^2)$ or the of Grover's algorithm $O(n \cdot \sqrt{n})$ or for L sparse patttems

$$O(n \cdot \sqrt{L}) = O\left(\frac{n^2}{\log(n)}\right).$$

## CHAPTER 16

Amplitude Encoding

Amplitude encoding encodes a real or complexed value vector of the length one into the amplitudes of a quantum state. We describe the top-down strategy and indicate the algorithm step by step. Then we describe the combining states strategy. Instead of representing the binary tree by multi-control rotation gates, we can use controlled SWAP operators with simple rotation gates. The resulting circuits depth is less than top-down divide strategy, however, we require the same number of qubits as the number of rotation gates and the qubits are entangled after the operation.

Then we describe the possibility to initialize the desired states using *qiskit* commands. We cannot access the amplitudes that represent vectors, but we estimate the value of the scalar product between them using the SWAP test. We give two examples of the SWAP test.

16.1 AMPLITUDE ENCODING EXAMPLE

Amplitude encoding encodes data into the amplitudes ω_i of a quantum state.

$$|\psi\rangle = \sum_{i=1}^{N} \omega_i \cdot |x\rangle \qquad (16.1)$$

A complex normalized vector $\mathbf{x}$ (length one), for example

$$\mathbf{x} = \begin{pmatrix} \sqrt{0.03} \\ \sqrt{0.07} \\ \sqrt{0.15} \\ \sqrt{0.05} \\ \sqrt{0.1} \\ \sqrt{0.3} \\ \sqrt{0.2} \\ \sqrt{0.1} \end{pmatrix}.$$

with *qiskit* little endian ordering $|q_2 q_1 q_0\rangle$

$$|\psi\rangle = \sqrt{0.03} \cdot |000\rangle + \sqrt{0.07} \cdot |001\rangle + \sqrt{0.15} \cdot |010\rangle + \sqrt{0.05} \cdot |011\rangle +$$

$$+ \sqrt{0.1} \cdot |100\rangle + \sqrt{0.3} \cdot |101\rangle + \sqrt{0.2} \cdot |110\rangle + \sqrt{0.1} \cdot |111\rangle$$

DOI: 10.1201/9781003374404-16

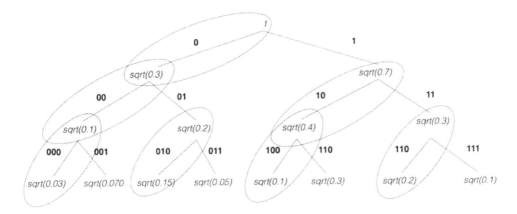

Figure 16.1 We build a top-down binary tree that divides the probability of observing $|q_2\rangle$ on the first level, to the probability of observing $|q_2 q_1\rangle$ on the second level, and finally the probability of observing $|q_2 q_1 q_0\rangle$ on the third level representing the required superposition $|\psi\rangle = \sqrt{0.03} \cdot |000\rangle + \sqrt{0.07} \cdot |001\rangle + \sqrt{0.15} \cdot |010\rangle + \sqrt{0.05} \cdot |011\rangle + \sqrt{0.1} \cdot |100\rangle + \sqrt{0.3} \cdot |101\rangle + \sqrt{0.2} \cdot |110\rangle + \sqrt{0.1} \cdot |111\rangle$. The binary tree is represented by multi-control rotation gates, the multi-control rotation gate are defined over the values indicated by the gray ellipsoids.

16.2 TOP-DOWN DIVIDE STRATEGY

We build a top-down binary tree that divides the probability of observing $|q_2\rangle$ on the first level, to the probability of observing $|q_2 q_1\rangle$ on the second level, and finally the probability of observing $|q_2 q_1 q_0\rangle$ on the third level representing the required super-position $|\psi\rangle$ [8]. The binary tree is represented by multi-control rotation gates (see Figure 16.1) and requires $\log_2 n$ qubits to represent a vector of dimension n.

16.2.1 Level 1

The probability of observing $q_2 = 0$ is $\sqrt{0.3}$;

$$\sqrt{0.03} \cdot |000\rangle + \sqrt{0.07} \cdot |001\rangle + \sqrt{0.15} \cdot |010\rangle + \sqrt{0.05} \cdot |011\rangle$$

and probability of observing $q_2 = 1$ is $\sqrt{0.7}$.

We use a parameterized RY gate

$$R_Y(\theta) = \begin{pmatrix} \cos\left(\frac{\theta}{2}\right) & -\sin\left(\frac{\theta}{2}\right) \\ \sin\left(\frac{\theta}{2}\right) & \cos\left(\frac{\theta}{2}\right) \end{pmatrix}$$

to performs a rotation of one qubit along the y-axis by the rotation angle θ (in radiants)

$$\theta_0 = 1.98231 = 2 \cdot \arccos(\sqrt{0.3}) \tag{16.2}$$

with (see Figure 16.1)

$$RY_{\theta_0}|0\rangle = \sqrt{0.3} \cdot |0\rangle + \sqrt{0.7} \cdot |1\rangle \tag{16.3}$$

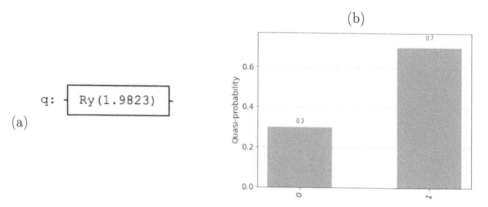

Figure 16.2 (a) Circuit representing the rotation of one qubit along the y-axis by the rotation angle θ_0. (b) The measured result representing the qubit in superposition $\sqrt{0.3} \cdot |0\rangle + \sqrt{0.7} \cdot |1\rangle$.

resulting in the circuit (see Figure 16.2),

```
from qiskit import QuantumCircuit,QuantumRegister, Aer,execute
from qiskit.visualization import plot_histogram
from qiskit.circuit.library import MCXGate
from qiskit.quantum_info import Statevector
from qiskit.circuit.library import RYGate
from math import pi

qc = QuantumCircuit(1)
#ang = Sqrt[0.3]
#ArcCos[ang]*2
qc.ry(1.98231,0)

simulator = Aer.get_backend('statevector_simulator')
result=execute(qc,simulator).result()
counts = result.get_counts()
plot_histogram(counts)
```

16.2.2 Level 2

The probability of observing $q_2q_1 = 00$ is $\sqrt{0.1}$

$$\sqrt{0.03} \cdot |000\rangle + \sqrt{0.07} \cdot |001\rangle$$

and the probability of observing $q_2q_1 = 01$ is $\sqrt{0.2}$ since both values divide the probability of observing $q_2 = 0$ $\sqrt{0.3}$. To define the angle θ_{00}, we normalize the value $\sqrt{0.1}$ by division of the probability of observing $q_2 = 0$

$$\theta_{00} = 1.91063 = 2 \cdot \arccos\left(\frac{\sqrt{0.1}}{\sqrt{0.3}}\right). \tag{16.4}$$

The rotation generates a superposition

$$RY_{\theta_{00}} \sqrt{0.3} \cdot |0\rangle \sqrt{0.1} \cdot |00\rangle + \sqrt{0.2} \cdot |01\rangle. \tag{16.5}$$

The probability of observing $q_2 q_1 = 10$ is $\sqrt{0.4}$;

$$\sqrt{0.1} \cdot |100\rangle + \sqrt{0.3} \cdot |101\rangle$$

and the probability of observing $q_2 q_1 = 11$ is $\sqrt{0.3}$ since both values divide the probability of observing $q_2 = 1$ $\sqrt{0.7}$. To define the angle θ_{10} we normalize the value $\sqrt{0.4}$ by the division of the probability of observing $q_2 = 1$

$$\theta_{10} = 1.42745 = 2 \cdot \arccos\left(\frac{\sqrt{0.4}}{\sqrt{0.7}}\right). \tag{16.6}$$

The rotation generates a superposition

$$RY_{\theta_{10}} \sqrt{0.7} \cdot |1\rangle = \sqrt{0.4} \cdot |10\rangle + \sqrt{0.3} \cdot |11\rangle. \tag{16.7}$$

Applying both rotations by two control rotation gates that are controlled by the qubit q_2 generates a superposition (see Figure 16.1)

$$RY_{\theta_{00}} \sqrt{0.3} \cdot |0\rangle + RY_{\theta_{10}} \sqrt{0.7} \cdot |1\rangle = \sqrt{0.1} \cdot |00\rangle + \sqrt{0.2} \cdot |01\rangle + \sqrt{0.4} \cdot |10\rangle + \sqrt{0.3} \cdot |11\rangle. \tag{16.8}$$

The circuit of level 1 and 2 decomposition is represented as (see Figure 16.3). Since in the circuit only the two most important qubits (from the left) $|q_2 q_1 q_0\rangle$ are represented, their identification $q_1 q_0$ corresponds to the qubits qubits $q_2 q_1$ in the final circuit of three qubits.

```
qc = QuantumCircuit(2)

#ang = Sqrt[0.3]
#ArcCos[ang]*2
qc.ry(1.98231,1)
qc.barrier()

#ang = Sqrt[0.4]/Sqrt[0.7];
#ArcCos[ang]*2
qc.cry(1.42745,1,0)
#ang = Sqrt[0.1]/Sqrt[0.3];
#ArcCos[ang]*2
qc.x(1)
qc.cry(1.91063,1,0)
qc.x(1)
```

16.2.3 Level 3

Finally we estimated eight individual values $|q_2 q_1 q_0\rangle$ by four rotations on the level three (see Figure 16.1).

$$\theta_{110} = 1.23096 = 2 \cdot \arccos\left(\frac{\sqrt{0.2}}{\sqrt{0.3}}\right), \tag{16.9}$$

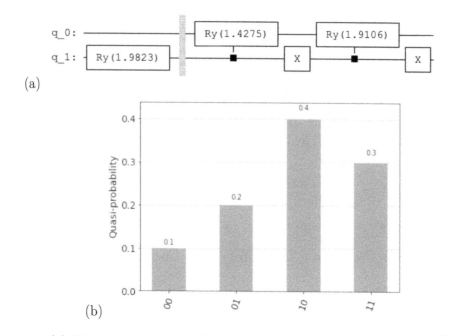

(a)

(b)

Figure 16.3 (a) Circuit representing the controlled rotation of one q qubit $\sqrt{0.7} \cdot |1\rangle$ $\theta_{10} = 1.42745$, and qubit $\sqrt{0.3} \cdot |0\rangle$ along the y-axis by the rotation angle $\theta_{00} = 1.91063$. Since in the circuit only the two most important qubits (from the left) $|q_2 q_1 q_0\rangle$ are represented, their identification $q_1 q_0$ corresponds to the qubits $q_2 q_1$ in the final circuit of three qubits. (b) The measured result representing the qubit in superposition $\sqrt{0.1} \cdot |00\rangle + \sqrt{0.2} \cdot |01\rangle + \sqrt{0.4} \cdot |10\rangle + \sqrt{0.3} \cdot |11\rangle$.

$$RY_{\theta_{110}}\sqrt{0.3} \cdot |11\rangle = \sqrt{0.2} \cdot |110\rangle + \sqrt{0.1} \cdot |111\rangle. \tag{16.10}$$

$$\theta_{100} = 2.0944 = 2 \cdot \arccos\left(\frac{\sqrt{0.1}}{\sqrt{0.4}}\right), \tag{16.11}$$

$$RY_{\theta_{100}}\sqrt{0.4} \cdot |10\rangle = \sqrt{0.1} \cdot |100\rangle + \sqrt{0.3} \cdot |101\rangle. \tag{16.12}$$

$$\theta_{010} = 1.0472 = 2 \cdot \arccos\left(\frac{\sqrt{0.15}}{\sqrt{0.2}}\right), \tag{16.13}$$

with

$$RY_{\theta_{010}}\sqrt{0.2} \cdot |01\rangle = \sqrt{0.15} \cdot |010\rangle + \sqrt{0.05} \cdot |011\rangle. \tag{16.14}$$

$$\theta_{000} = 1.98231 = 2 \cdot \arccos\left(\frac{\sqrt{0.03}}{\sqrt{0.1}}\right), \tag{16.15}$$

with

$$RY_{\theta_{000}}\sqrt{0.1} \cdot |00\rangle = \sqrt{0.03} \cdot |000\rangle + \sqrt{0.07} \cdot |001\rangle. \tag{16.16}$$

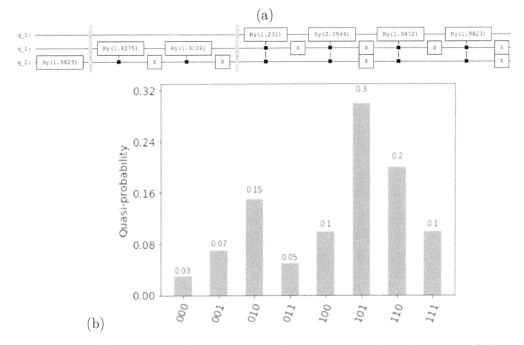

Figure 16.4 (a) The top-down binary tree divides the probability of observing $|q_2\rangle$ on the first level, to the probability of observing $|q_2q_1\rangle$ on the second level, and finally the probability of observing $|q_2q_1q_0\rangle$ on the third level representing the multi-control rotation gates. (b) The amplitudes of the superposition $|\psi\rangle$.

The four multi-control rotation gates are controlled by the qubits q_2 and q_1 resulting in the desired superposition $|\psi\rangle$, (see Figure 16.4)

$$|\psi\rangle = \sqrt{0.03} \cdot |000\rangle + \sqrt{0.07} \cdot |001\rangle + \sqrt{0.15} \cdot |010\rangle + \sqrt{0.05} \cdot |011\rangle +$$

$$+\sqrt{0.1} \cdot |100\rangle + \sqrt{0.3} \cdot |101\rangle + \sqrt{0.2} \cdot |110\rangle + \sqrt{0.1} \cdot |111\rangle$$

```
qc = QuantumCircuit(3)

#1
#ang = Sqrt[0.3] a0
#ArcCos[ang]*2
qc.ry(1.98231,2)
qc.barrier()
#2
#ang = Sqrt[0.4]/Sqrt[0.7]; a2
#ArcCos[ang]*2
qc.cry(1.42745,2,1)
#ang = Sqrt[0.1]/Sqrt[0.3]; a1
#ArcCos[ang]*2
qc.x(2)
qc.cry(1.91063,2,1)
qc.x(2)
qc.barrier()
```

```
#3
#ang = Sqrt[0.2]/(Sqrt[0.3]); a6
#ArcCos[ang]*2
ccry = RYGate(1.23096).control(2)
qc.append(ccry,[2,1,0])
#ang = Sqrt[0.1]/(Sqrt[0.4]); a5
#ArcCos[ang]*2
#ccry = RYGate(2.0944).control(2,label=None)
ccry = RYGate(2.0944).control(2)
qc.x(1)
qc.append(ccry,[2,1,0])
qc.x(1)
qc.x(2)
#ang = Sqrt[0.15]/(Sqrt[0.2]); a4
#ArcCos[ang]*2
ccry = RYGate(1.0472).control(2)
qc.append(ccry,[2,1,0])
#ang = Sqrt[0.03]/(Sqrt[0.1]); a3
#ArcCos[ang]*2
ccry = RYGate(1.98231).control(2)
qc.x(1)
qc.append(ccry,[2,1,0])
qc.x(1)
qc.x(2)
```

16.3 COMBINING STATES

Instead of representing the binary tree by multi-control rotation gates, we can use controlled SWAP operators with simple rotation gates [8].

16.3.1 Level 2

The binary tree at level two is represented by three qubits, to each qubit a rotation gate is applied. To the qubit 1 we apply the rotation $\theta_0 = 1.98231$, to the qubit 0 we apply the rotation $\theta_{10} = 1.42745$, and to qubit 2 we apply the rotation $\theta_{00} = 1.9106$. The value of the qubit 1 controls the SWAP operation and the measured tensor product of qubit 2 with qubit 1 represents the required distribution of the two qubits representing four states (see Figure 16.5)

16.3.2 Level 3

The binary tree at level three is represented by seven qubits, to each qubit a rotation gate is applied. To the qubit 3 we apply the rotation $\theta_0 = 1.98231$, to the qubit 1 we apply the rotation $\theta_{10} = 1.42745$, and to the qubit 5 we apply the rotation $\theta_{00} = 1.9106$. The value of the qubit 3 controls the SWAP operation. For the level three we apply the additional four rotations, we apply the rotation $\theta_{110} = 1.23096$ to the qubit 0, $\theta_{100} = 2.0944$ to the qubit 2, $\theta_{010} = 1.0472$ to the qubit 4, and $\theta_{000} = 1.98231$ to the qubit 6. The qubit 1 and 5 representing the level 2 control the rotation of the two sub-trees. The two sub-trees are merged with the results of level one by the controlled SWAP operation controlled by the qubit 3. The measured tensor product

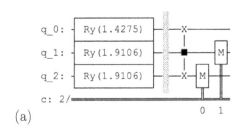

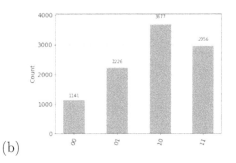

(a)

(b)

Figure 16.5 (a) The binary tree at level two is represented by three qubits, to each qubit a rotation gate is applied. To the qubit 1 we apply the rotation $\theta_0 = 1.98231$, to the qubit 0 we apply the rotation $\theta_{10} = 1.42745$, and to qubit 2 we apply the rotation $\theta_{00} = 1.9106$. The value of the qubit 1 controls the SWAP operation and the measured tensor product of qubit 1 with qubit 2 represents the required distribution of the two qubits representing four states. (b) The required distribution of the two qubits representing four states.

of qubit 3 with qubit 5 and 3 represents the required distribution of the three qubits representing eight states (see Figure 16.6)

```python
from qiskit import QuantumCircuit,QuantumRegister, Aer,execute
from qiskit.visualization import plot_histogram
from qiskit.circuit.library import MCXGate
from qiskit.quantum_info import Statevector
from qiskit.circuit.library import RYGate
from math import pi

qc = QuantumCircuit(7,3)

qc.ry(1.23096,0)
qc.ry(1.42745,1)
qc.ry(2.0944,2)
qc.ry(1.91063,3)
qc.ry(1.0472,4)
qc.ry(1.91063,5)
qc.ry(1.98231,6)
qc.barrier()
qc.cswap(1,0,2)
qc.cswap(5,4,6)
qc.barrier()
qc.cswap(3,1,5)
qc.cswap(3,2,6)
#Measuring 0 1 3
qc.measure(6,0)
qc.measure(5,1)
qc.measure(3,2)

simulator = Aer.get_backend('qasm_simulator')
result=execute(qc,simulator,shots=10000).result()
```

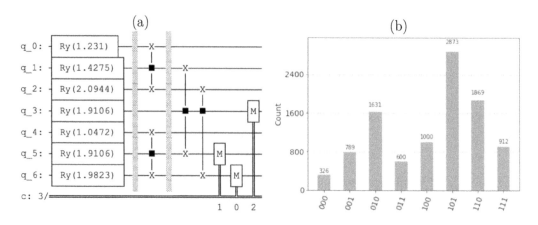

Figure 16.6 ((a) The binary tree at level three is represented by seven qubits, to each qubit a rotation gate is applied. To the qubit 3 we apply the rotation $\theta_0 = 1.98231$, to the qubit 1 we apply the rotation $\theta_{10} = 1.42745$, and to qubit 5 we apply the rotation $\theta_{00} = 1.9106$. The value of the qubit 3 controls the SWAP operation. For the level three we apply the additional four rotations, we apply the rotation $\theta_{110} = 1.23096$ to the qubit 0, $\theta_{100} = 2.0944$ to the qubit 2, $\theta_{010} = 1.0472$ to the qubit 4, and $\theta_{000} = 1.98231$ to the qubit 6. The qubit 1 and 5 representing the level 2 control the rotation of the two sub-trees. The two sub-trees are merged with the results of level one by the controlled SWAP operation controlled by the qubit 3. The measured tensor product of qubit 3 with qubit 5 and 3 represents the required distribution of the three qubits representing eight states. (b) The required distribution of the three qubits representing eight states.

```
counts = result.get_counts()
plot_histogram(counts)
```

The circuits depth is less than top-down divide strategy, however we require the same number of qubits as the rotation gates and the qubits are entangled after the operation.

16.4   QISKIT AMPLITUDE CODING

Qiskit offers through the commands *desired_state* and *initialize(desired_state, qubits)* a possibility to initialize the desired states and through the *decompose* command to indicate the resulting quantum circuit (see Figure 16.7).

```
from qiskit import QuantumCircuit,QuantumRegister, Aer,execute
from qiskit.visualization import plot_histogram
import math
from qiskit import QuantumCircuit

desired_state = [
    math.sqrt(0.03),
    math.sqrt(0.07),
    math.sqrt(0.15),
```

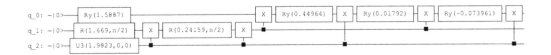

Figure 16.7 *Qiskit* offers through the commands *desired_state* and *initialize(desired_state, qubits)* a possibility to initialize the desired states and through the *decompose* command to indicate the resulting quantum circuit. The quantum circuit generating the amplitudes of the superposition $|\psi\rangle$.

```
    math.sqrt(0.05),
    math.sqrt(0.1),
    math.sqrt(0.3),
    math.sqrt(0.2),
    math.sqrt(0.1),
]
qc = QuantumCircuit(3)
qc.initialize(desired_state, [0,1,2])

qc.decompose().decompose().decompose().decompose().decompose().decompose().
draw(fold=180)

simulator = Aer.get_backend('statevector_simulator')
result=execute(qc,simulator).result()
counts = result.get_counts()
print("\nTotal count are:",counts)
plot_histogram(counts)
```

16.5 SWAP TEST

We cannot access the amplitudes that represent vectors, but we estimate $\langle x|y\rangle$ using the swap test. Each state represents a normalized vector for the dimension n represented by $m = \log_2 n$ qubits. Note that the quantum $|x\rangle$ and $|y\rangle$ are of length one in the l_2 norm,

$$\langle x|x\rangle = \||x\rangle\|_2 = 1, \quad \langle y|y\rangle = \||y\rangle\|_2 = 1.$$

The additional auxiliary qubit $|0\rangle$ generates the

$$|0\rangle \otimes |x\rangle \otimes |y\rangle = |0, x, y\rangle$$

Apply Hadamard gate on the control qubit $|0\rangle$,

$$(H \otimes I_m \otimes I_m) \cdot |0\rangle|x, y\rangle = \frac{1}{\sqrt{2}} \cdot (|0, x, y\rangle + |1, x, y\rangle) \quad (16.17)$$

Apply controlled swap operator on $|x\rangle$ and $|y\rangle$ states which swaps $|x\rangle$ and $|y\rangle$

$$|x\rangle|y\rangle \rightarrow |y\rangle|x\rangle$$

providing that the control qubit is in state $|1\rangle$ with

$$\frac{1}{\sqrt{2}} \cdot (|0, x, y\rangle + |1, x, y\rangle) \rightarrow \frac{1}{\sqrt{2}} \cdot (|0, x, y\rangle + |1, y, x\rangle) \qquad (16.18)$$

We apply another Hadamard gate on the control qubit

$$(W \otimes I_m \otimes I_m) \cdot \left(\frac{1}{\sqrt{2}} \cdot (|0, x, y\rangle + |1, y, x\rangle) \right) =$$

$$\frac{1}{2} \cdot |0\rangle \cdot (|x, y\rangle + |y, x\rangle) + \frac{1}{2} \cdot |1\rangle \cdot (|x, y\rangle - |y, x\rangle) \qquad (16.19)$$

The probability of measuring the control qubit in state $|0\rangle$ is given by

$$p(|0\rangle) = \left| \frac{1}{2} \cdot \langle 0|0\rangle \cdot (|0, x, y\rangle + |1, y, x\rangle) + \frac{1}{2} \cdot \langle 0|1\rangle \cdot (|0, x, y\rangle - |1, y, x\rangle) \right|^2$$

$$p(|0\rangle) = \frac{1}{4} \cdot |(|x\rangle|y\rangle + |y\rangle|x\rangle)|^2$$

$$p(|0\rangle) = \frac{1}{4} \cdot (\langle y|y\rangle\langle x|x\rangle + \langle y|x\rangle\langle x|y\rangle + \langle x|y\rangle\langle y|x\rangle + \langle x|x\rangle\langle y|y\rangle)$$

$$p(|0\rangle) = \frac{1}{4} \cdot (1 + \langle y|x\rangle\langle x|y\rangle + \langle x|y\rangle\langle y|x\rangle + 1)$$

$$p(|0\rangle) = \frac{1}{2} + \frac{1}{4} \cdot (\langle y|x\rangle\langle x|y\rangle + \langle x|y\rangle\langle y|x\rangle)$$

$$p(|0\rangle) = \frac{1}{2} + \frac{1}{2}|\langle x|y\rangle|^2 \qquad (16.20)$$

and

$$p(|1\rangle) = \frac{1}{2} - \frac{1}{2}|\langle x|y\rangle|^2 \qquad (16.21)$$

with

$$|\langle x|y\rangle| \approx \sqrt{2 \cdot p(|0\rangle) - 1} = \sqrt{1 - 2 \cdot p(|1\rangle)}. \qquad (16.22)$$

The probability $p(|0\rangle) = 0.5$ means that the states $|x\rangle$ and $|y\rangle$ are orthogonal, whereas the probability $p(|0\rangle) = 1$ indicates that the states are identical. We have to preform several measurements to estimate $p(|0\rangle)$ or $p((|1\rangle)$. The estimated scalar product is positive and since the vectors are normalized the inner product corresponds to the angle φ between the vectors

$$0 \le \cos \varphi = |\langle x|y\rangle| \le 1 \qquad (16.23)$$

and is usually called the cosine similarity. We can estimate the Euclidean distance as well, since the distance for normalized vectors is constrained to a unit sphere with

$$0 \le \|\mathbf{x} - \mathbf{y}\|_2 \le \sqrt{2}. \qquad (16.24)$$

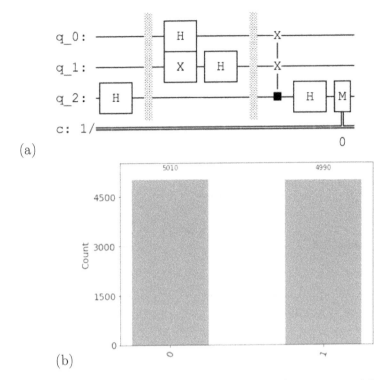

(a)

(b)

Figure 16.8 Qubit 0 represent the vector $\mathbf{x}$ and qubit 1 the vector $\mathbf{y}$. After 10000 shots we measure $p(|0\rangle) = 0.5010$.

16.5.1 Example for Two-Dimensional Vectors

$$\mathbf{x} = \begin{pmatrix} \sqrt{0.5} \\ \sqrt{0.5} \end{pmatrix}, \quad \mathbf{y} = \begin{pmatrix} \sqrt{0.5} \\ -\sqrt{0.5} \end{pmatrix}.$$

with

$$\langle \mathbf{x}|\mathbf{x}\rangle = |||\mathbf{x}\rangle||_2 = 1, \quad \langle \mathbf{y}|\mathbf{y}\rangle = |||\mathbf{y}\rangle||_2 = 1.$$

and

$$\langle \mathbf{x}|\mathbf{y}\rangle = 0$$

Qubit 0 represents the vector $\mathbf{x}$ and qubit 1 the vector $\mathbf{y}$. After 10000 shots we measure $p(|0\rangle) = 0.5010$ (see Figure 16.8)

$$|\langle \mathbf{x}|\mathbf{y}\rangle| \approx \sqrt{2 \cdot 0.501 - 1} = 0.045.$$

Note that the results are probabilistic and that they might slightly differ from run to run.

16.5.2 Example for Four-Dimensional Vectors

$$\mathbf{x} = \begin{pmatrix} \sqrt{0.1} \\ \sqrt{0.2} \\ \sqrt{0.4} \\ \sqrt{0.3} \end{pmatrix}, \quad \mathbf{y} = \begin{pmatrix} 0 \\ 0 \\ \sqrt{0.5} \\ \sqrt{0.5} \end{pmatrix}.$$

with

$$\langle \mathbf{x} | \mathbf{x} \rangle = \| |\mathbf{x} \rangle \|_2 = 1, \quad \langle \mathbf{y} | \mathbf{y} \rangle = \| |\mathbf{y} \rangle \|_2 = 1.$$

and

$$\langle \mathbf{x} | \mathbf{y} \rangle = 0.8345$$

Qubits 0 and 1 represent the vector $\mathbf{x}$ and qubits 2 and 3 the vector $\mathbf{y}$

```python
from qiskit import QuantumCircuit,QuantumRegister, Aer,execute
from qiskit.visualization import plot_histogram
from qiskit.circuit.library import MCXGate
from qiskit.quantum_info import Statevector
from qiskit.circuit.library import RYGate
from math import pi

qc = QuantumCircuit(5,1)

qc.h(4)
qc.barrier()
#vector x
#ang = Sqrt[0.3]
#ArcCos[ang]*2
qc.ry(1.98231,1)
qc.barrier()
#ang = Sqrt[0.4]/Sqrt[0.7];
#ArcCos[ang]*2
qc.cry(1.42745,1,0)
#ang = Sqrt[0.1]/Sqrt[0.3];
#ArcCos[ang]*2
qc.x(1)
qc.cry(1.91063,1,0)
qc.x(1)
qc.barrier()
#vector y
qc.h(2)
qc.x(3)
qc.barrier()
qc.cswap(4,0,2)
qc.cswap(4,1,3)
qc.h(4)
qc.measure(4,0)

simulator = Aer.get_backend('qasm_simulator')
```

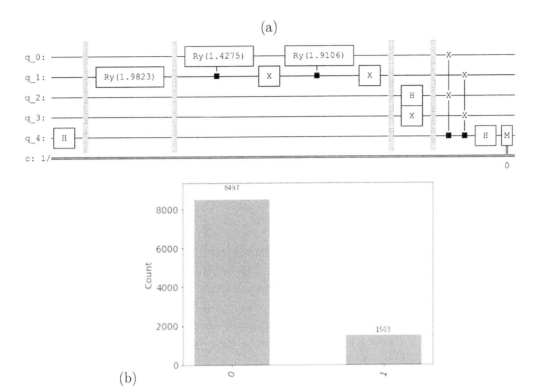

Figure 16.9 (a) Qubits 0 and 1 represent the vector **x**, qubits 2 and 3 the vector **y**. (b) after 10000 shots we measure $p(|0\rangle) = 0.8479$.

```
result=execute(qc,simulator,shots=10000).result()
counts = result.get_counts()
plot_histogram(counts)
```

See Figure 16.9 , after 10000 shots we measure $p(|0\rangle) = 0.8479$

$$|\langle \mathbf{x}|\mathbf{y}\rangle| \approx \sqrt{2 \cdot 0.8479 - 1} = 0.8345.$$

## CHAPTER 17

Quantum Kernels

A quantum computer can estimate a quantum kernel and the estimate can be used by a kernel method on a classical computer. This is because the exponential quantum advantage in evaluating inner products allows to estimate the quantum kernel directly in the higher-dimensional space. We give an example of quantum kernels and the swap test. Then we describe quantum kernels and the inversion test. Quantum feature maps encodes classical data into quantum data via a parametrized quantum circuit. Parameterized quantum circuits are based on superposition and entanglement. They are hard to simulate classically and could lead to an advantage over classical machine learning approach. The inversion test is based on the idea usual of estimating the fidelity (similarity) between two states. We describe an example using *qiskit* command *ZZFeatureMap*. Then we indicate how quantum kernel is plugged into classical kernel methods like support vector machines.

17.1   QUANTUM KERNELS

For a quantum state $|\phi(\mathbf{x})\rangle|$ and $|\phi(\mathbf{y})\rangle|$, the inner product of two such states is called a quantum kernel

$$k(\mathbf{x}, \mathbf{y}) = \langle \phi(\mathbf{x}) | \phi(\mathbf{y}) \rangle \tag{17.1}$$

with a inner product

$$\langle \mathbf{x} | \mathbf{y} \rangle = \mathbf{x}^T \cdot \mathbf{y}. \tag{17.2}$$

The absolute value of the inner product can be estimated by the swap test [95].

17.2   QUANTUM KERNELS AND SWAP TEST

A quantum computer can estimate a quantum kernel and the estimate can be used by a kernel method on a classical computer [95]. This is because the exponential quantum advantage in evaluating inner products allows to estimate the quantum kernel machines directly in the higher-dimensional space. If the result is impossible to be simulated on a classical computer, then the kernel is classically intractable [94]. We can map

$$|\phi(\mathbf{x})\rangle \rightarrow |\mathbf{x}\rangle \otimes \cdots \otimes |\mathbf{x}\rangle = |\mathbf{x}\rangle^{\otimes m} \tag{17.3}$$

DOI: 10.1201/9781003374404-17

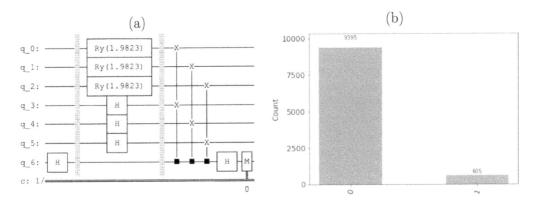

Figure 17.1 (a) Circuit representing $k(\mathbf{x}, \mathbf{y}) = (\mathbf{x}^T \cdot \mathbf{y})^3$ with the swap test. (b) After 10000 shots we measure $p(|0\rangle) = 0.9395$.

and define the homogenous polynomial kernel as

$$k(\mathbf{x}, \mathbf{y}) = \langle \phi(\mathbf{x}) | \phi(\mathbf{y}) \rangle = \langle \mathbf{x} | \mathbf{y} \rangle \otimes \cdots \otimes \langle \mathbf{x} | \mathbf{y} \rangle = (\mathbf{x}^T \cdot \mathbf{y})^m. \tag{17.4}$$

Then the absolute value of the inner product can be estimated by the swap test.

17.2.1   Example for Two-Dimensional Vectors

$$\mathbf{x} = \begin{pmatrix} \sqrt{0.3} \\ \sqrt{0.7} \end{pmatrix}, \quad \mathbf{y} = \begin{pmatrix} \sqrt{0.5} \\ \sqrt{0.5} \end{pmatrix}.$$

$$k(\mathbf{x}, \mathbf{y}) = \langle \phi(\mathbf{x}) | \phi(\mathbf{y}) \rangle = \langle \mathbf{x} | \mathbf{y} \rangle \otimes \langle \mathbf{x} | \mathbf{y} \rangle \otimes \langle \mathbf{x} | \mathbf{y} \rangle = (\mathbf{x}^T \cdot \mathbf{y})^3 \tag{17.5}$$

with the circuit (see Figure 17.1)

```
from qiskit import QuantumCircuit,QuantumRegister, Aer,execute
from qiskit.visualization import plot_histogram
from qiskit.circuit.library import MCXGate
from qiskit.quantum_info import Statevector
from qiskit.circuit.library import RYGate
from math import pi

qc = QuantumCircuit(7,1)
qc.h(6)
qc.barrier()
#ang = Sqrt[0.3]
#ArcCos[ang]*2
qc.ry(1.98231,0)
qc.ry(1.98231,1)
qc.ry(1.98231,2)
qc.h(3)
qc.h(4)
qc.h(5)
qc.barrier()
qc.cswap(6,0,3)
```

```
qc.cswap(6,1,4)
qc.cswap(6,2,5)
qc.h(6)
qc.measure(6,0)

simulator = Aer.get_backend('qasm_simulator')
result=execute(qc,simulator,shots=10000).result()
counts = result.get_counts()
print("\nTotal count are:",counts)
plot_histogram(counts)
```

Using the swap test, after 10000 shots we measure $p(|0\rangle) = 0.9395$ with

$$k(\mathbf{x}, \mathbf{y}) = |(\mathbf{x}^T \cdot \mathbf{y})^3| \approx \sqrt{2 \cdot 0.9395 - 1} = 0.93755.$$

17.3 QUANTUM KERNELS AND INVERSION TEST

Quantum feature maps encodes classical data into quantum data via a parametrized quantum circuit [40]. Instead of coding the classical feature vector $\mathbf{x}$ of dimension z by amplitudes, the feature vector defines by z parameters of the parametrized quantum circuit $U_{\phi(\mathbf{x})}$ with $z \geq m$

$$|\phi(\mathbf{x})\rangle = U_{\phi(\mathbf{x})}|0\rangle^{\otimes m} \tag{17.6}$$

with the dimension of $\phi(\mathbf{x})$ being 2^m. Parameterized quantum circuits based on superposition and entanglement are hard to simulate classically and could lead to an advantage over classical machine learning approaches. The inversion test is based on the idea usually of estimating the fidelity (similarity) between two states [40]. For an input state $|0\rangle^{\otimes m}$ if we map it by parametrized quantum circuit $U_{\phi(\mathbf{x})}$ with parameters that are defined by $\mathbf{x}$ and un-compute it by $U_{\phi(\mathbf{x})}^{\dagger}$, the inverse if the parametrized quantum circuit $U_{\phi(\mathbf{x})}$ the probability of measuring the state $|0\rangle^{\otimes m}$ is one. If we represent the quantum circuit by a matrix $U_{\phi(\mathbf{x})}$, the inverse quantum circuit represented as a matrix corresponds to the conjugate transpose $U_{\phi(\mathbf{x})}^{*}$, also written as $U_{\phi(\mathbf{x})}^{\dagger}$. If we parametrized quantum circuit U by $\mathbf{x}$ ($U_{\phi(\mathbf{x})}$) and inverse of the parametrized quantum $U^{\dagger}$ by $\mathbf{y}$ ($U_{\phi(\mathbf{y})}^{\dagger}$) and if $\mathbf{x}$ and $\mathbf{y}$ are similar, the probability of measuring $|0\rangle^{\otimes m}$ for the input $|0\rangle^{\otimes m}$ should be near 1,

$$U_{\phi(\mathbf{y})}^{\dagger} U_{\phi(\mathbf{x})} |0^{\otimes m}\rangle \tag{17.7}$$

If $\mathbf{x}$ and $\mathbf{y}$ differ a lot, this probability is smaller. The quantum kernel is represented as

$$k(\mathbf{x}, \mathbf{y}) = |\langle \phi(\mathbf{x})|\phi(\mathbf{y})\rangle|^2 = |\langle 0^{\otimes m}|U_{\phi(\mathbf{y})}^{\dagger}|U_{\phi(\mathbf{x})}|0^{\otimes m}\rangle|^2 \tag{17.8}$$

We measure the final state several times and record the number of $|0^{\otimes m}\rangle$ and estimate the value $k(\mathbf{x}, \mathbf{y})$.

(a)

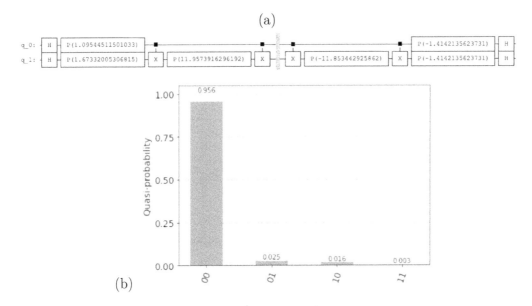

(b)

Figure 17.2 (a) Circuit representing $U_{\phi(\mathbf{y})}^{\dagger} U_{\phi(\mathbf{x})} |0^{\otimes 2}\rangle$ using the *qiskit* parameterized quantum circuit $U_{\phi(\mathbf{x})} = ZZFeatureMap$. (b) After 10000 shots we measure $p(|00\rangle) = 0.956$.

17.3.1 Example

With the same **x,y** as in the preceding example using the *qiskit* parameterized quantum circuit $U_{\phi(\mathbf{x})} = ZZFeatureMap$ [21] where the parameters are defined by the data by the command *bind_parameters* (see Figure 17.2)

```
from qiskit import QuantumCircuit,QuantumRegister, Aer,execute
from qiskit.visualization import plot_histogram
from qiskit.circuit.library import MCXGate
from qiskit.quantum_info import Statevector
from qiskit.circuit.library import RYGate
import math
from qiskit.circuit.library import ZZFeatureMap
from math import pi
import numpy as np

data = [np.sqrt(0.3), np.sqrt(0.7)]
feature_map = ZZFeatureMap(2, reps=1)
feature_map = feature_map.bind_parameters(data) # <== here

data2 = [np.sqrt(0.5), np.sqrt(0.5)]
feature_map2 = ZZFeatureMap(2, reps=1).inverse()
feature_map2 = feature_map2.bind_parameters(data2) # <== here

qc = QuantumCircuit(2)
qc.compose(feature_map, inplace=True)
qc.barrier()
qc.compose(feature_map2, inplace=True)
```

```
qc.decompose().draw(fold=180)

simulator = Aer.get_backend('statevector_simulator')
result=execute(qc,simulator).result()
counts = result.get_counts()
print("\nTotal count are:",counts)
plot_histogram(counts)
```

After 10000 shots we measure $p(|00\rangle) = 0.956$ with (see Figure 17.2 (b))

$$k(\mathbf{x}, \mathbf{y}) = |\langle 0^{\otimes m}|U^{\dagger}_{\phi(\mathbf{y})}|U_{\phi(\mathbf{x})}|0^{\otimes m}\rangle|^2 = 0.956.$$

17.3.2 Quantum Feature Maps

Quantum feature maps encodes classical data into quantum data via a parametrized quantum circuit that are hard to simulate classically and is an active area of current research. Vojtech Havlicek [40] and his collaborators propose a family of quantum Pauli feature maps that are believed to be hard to simulate classically, and can be implemented by circuit with few layers of gates. The Pauli feature maps of depth d contains layers of Hadamard gates interleaved with a circuit that contain entangling gates (such as CNOTs). The Pauli feature maps circuit of depth d is a data encoding circuit that transforms input data $\mathbf{x}$ of dimension $z = m$

$$U_{\phi(\mathbf{x})} = \prod_d U_{\phi(\mathbf{x})} \otimes H^{\otimes m}, \quad U_{\phi(\mathbf{x})} = \exp\left(i \cdot \sum_{S \subseteq [m]} \phi_S(\mathbf{x}) \prod_{j in S} P_j \right) \qquad (17.9)$$

where P_j corresponds to Pauli gates

$$P_j \in \{I, X, Y, Z\}$$

The index S indicates connectivity between different qubits represented by combination

$$S \in \left\{ \frac{m \cdot (m-1) \cdots (m-k+1)}{k \cdot (k-1) \cdots 1} \quad for \quad k \leq m \right\}$$

with

$$\phi_S(\mathbf{x}) = \begin{cases} x_i & if \quad S = \{i\} \\ (\pi - x_i) \cdot (\pi - x_j) & if \quad S = \{i,j\} \end{cases}$$

Qiskit implements these as the *PauliFeatureMap*. A special case for $k = 2$ using Z gates is called the *ZZFeatureMap*

$$U_{\phi(\mathbf{x})} = \exp\left(i \cdot \sum_{jk} \phi_{(j,k)} Z_j \otimes Z_k \right) \exp\left(i \cdot \sum_j \phi_j(\mathbf{x}) Z_j) H^{\otimes m} \right)^d \qquad (17.10)$$

represented by (Figure 17.3).

```
from qiskit.circuit.library import ZZFeatureMap
# 2 features, depth 1
map_zz = ZZFeatureMap(feature_dimension=2, reps=1)
map_zz.decompose().draw()
```

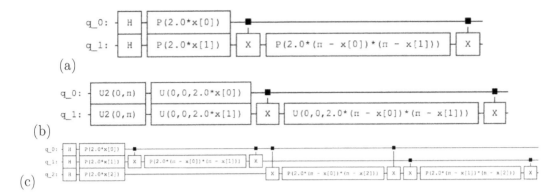

Figure 17.3 (a) The *ZZFeatureMap* with 2 features and depth 1, this is the same feature map that was used in the previous section. (b) The seme *ZZFeatureMap* indicated using twice *decompose().decompose()* comand indicating the quantum gates that are used. (c) The *ZZFeatureMap* with 3 features and depth 1.

17.4   QUANTUM SUPPORT VECTOR MACHINE

The quantum kernel is plugged into classical kernel methods like Support Vector Machine (Kernel Machine). Only the Gram matrix (kernel matrix) is determined by a quantum computer (or a simulation), the other parts of the computation are performed on a conventional computer. Either one passes a function of the quantum kernel to a conventional algorithm or one precomputes the training and testing kernel matrices. Often the actual internal representations of the quantum kernel are hidden from the outside.

qRAM

Quantum memory is proposed as an analogue to classical computer memory, like the random-access memory (RAM). RAM is a form of computer memory that can be read and changed in any order, typically used to store working data. In quantum machine learning domain, the usage of quantum random access memory ($qRAM$) is proposed to avoid input destruction problem. We demonstrate the bucket brigade architecture of $qRAM$. The method of $qRAM$ is related to the entanglement of the index qubits that are in the superposition with the patterns. We demonstrate an example of binary patterns and indicate why the representation of amplitude coding leads to the same complexity as a recall operation on a classical RAM.

18.1 QUANTUM RANDOM ACCESS MEMORY

In quantum machine learning domain, the usage of $qRAM$ [32] is proposed to avoid input destruction problem (**ID problem**) [59], [39]. A $qRAM$ copies basis states [32]. A $qRAM$ queries a register $|i\rangle$ and load the ith binary patter into the second register

$$|i\rangle|0\rangle \rightarrow |i\rangle|x^i\rangle, \tag{18.1}$$

with $|x^i\rangle$ being a basis state representing a binary vector. Such an operation can be executed in parallel with

$$\frac{1}{\sqrt{m}} \sum_{i=1}^{m} |i\rangle|0\rangle \rightarrow \frac{1}{\sqrt{n}} \sum_{i=1}^{m} |i\rangle|x^i\rangle, \tag{18.2}$$

with the time complexity ignoring the preparation cost of (due to the input problem) is $O(\log(m))$.

18.1.1 The Bucket Brigade Architecture of $qRAM$

The bucket brigade architecture of $qRAM$ is inspired by the traditional RAM architecture and consists of three main parts:

- Addressing qubits: Address for the memory cell we wish to read. In order to read a memory cell, the user has to encode the address of that memory cell on to the addressing qubits. This address can be in superposition so that several patterns can be read in one step.

DOI: 10.1201/9781003374404-18

- Routing nodes: Determine the memory cell based upon the states of the addressing qubits. Once the addressing qubits have been set the states of the routing node qubits will be effected. Whatever qubit in the routing nodes is $|1\rangle$ will lead to the memory cell that we wish to read.

- Memory cells: Store and readout patterns.

The method of $qRAM$ is related to the entanglement of the index qubits that are in the superposition with the patterns. As in the method of the entanglement of the index qubits, the qubits of $qRAM$ are entangled during the reading operation and have to be un-computed after computation. An example of the $qRAM$ (see Figure 18.1)

```
from qiskit import QuantumCircuit, Aer, execute
from qiskit.visualization import plot_histogram

qc = QuantumCircuit(9)
#address
#0-1
#Routing
#2-5
#Memory
#6-8
#address
qc.h(0) #two first elements of the memory
#Routing operation
#The addresses are ordered  00, 01, 10, 11
qc.barrier()
qc.x(0)
qc.x(1)
qc.ccx(0,1,2)
qc.x(1)
qc.x(0)
qc.barrier()
qc.x(1)
qc.ccx(0,1,3)
qc.x(1)
qc.barrier()
qc.x(0)
qc.ccx(0,1,4)
qc.x(0)
qc.barrier()
qc.ccx(0,1,5)
qc.barrier()
#Memory cells 6-8
#First memory cell
qc.barrier()
qc.cx(2,6)
qc.cx(2,8)
#Second memory cell
qc.barrier()
```

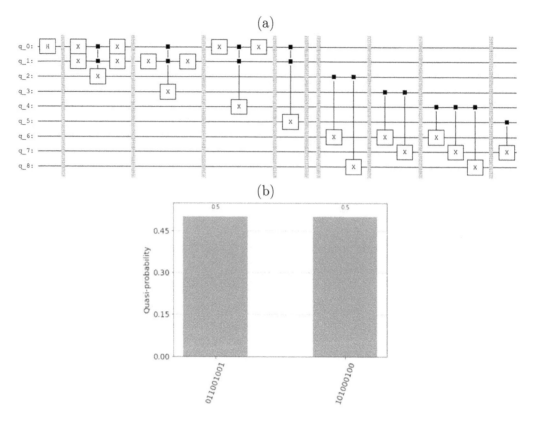

Figure 18.1 (a) $qRAM$ circuit: address is represented by qubits 0 and 1, routing by qubits 2 to 5, and the memory by qubits 6 to 8. The addresses are ordered 00, 01, 10 and for the last pattern 11. (b) The address corresponds to the first qubit in superposition, address 00 and 01. The first and the second patterns are recalled.

```
qc.cx(3,6)
qc.cx(3,7)
#Third memory cell
qc.barrier()
qc.cx(4,6)
qc.cx(4,7)
qc.cx(4,8)
#Fourth memory cell
qc.barrier()
qc.cx(5,7)

simulator = Aer.get_backend('statevector_simulator')
result=execute(qc,simulator).result()
counts = result.get_counts()
plot_histogram(counts).
```

18.1.2 Amplitude Coding

An operation that would produce a copy of an arbitrary quantum state such as $|\psi\rangle$ is not possible; we cannot copy non-basis states because of the linearity of quantum mechanics. However we can to some extent simulate the copy of non-basis states using $qRAM$, with the complexity $O(n \log(m))$ where n is the dimension of the resulting superposition vector [119]. We a convert a basis state of m qubits $|x\rangle = |01 \cdots 1\rangle$ of dimension 2^m in Hilbert space into a n-dimensional superposition

$$|01 \cdots 1\rangle \frac{1}{\sqrt{n}} \sum_{i=1}^{n} |i\rangle \rightarrow |01 \cdots 1\rangle \sum_{i=1}^{n} \alpha_i |i\rangle. \tag{18.3}$$

We divide the binary vector of the dimension 2^m into v parts, each substring representing $code_i$ a real number with $n = 2^m/v$.

$$|01 \cdots 1\rangle \frac{1}{\sqrt{n}} \sum_{i=1}^{n} |i\rangle \rightarrow |code_1 code_2 \cdots code_n\rangle \frac{1}{\sqrt{n}} \sum_{i=1}^{n} |i\rangle \tag{18.4}$$

We add an auxiliary state $|0^{\otimes n}\rangle$

$$|code_1 \cdots code_n\rangle \frac{1}{\sqrt{n}} \sum_{i=1}^{n} |i\rangle \rightarrow |code_1 \cdots code_n\rangle \frac{1}{\sqrt{n}} \sum_{i=1}^{n} |i\rangle |0^{\otimes n}\rangle \tag{18.5}$$

For each $code_i$ represents a binary representation of a fractional real number that is smaller than one

$$code_i = \alpha_i < 1.$$

For each $value_i$, we preform a controlled rotation $R(\alpha_i)$

$$\left(C \cdot \alpha_i |1\rangle + \sqrt{1 - C^2 \cdot \alpha_i^2} |0\rangle \right)$$

and preform a measurement. By measuring the corresponding auxiliary register with the result 1 we know that the resulting state is correct. We repeat the procedure at least n times with the resulting state

$$|01 \cdots 1\rangle \sum_{i=1}^{n} \alpha_i |i\rangle. \tag{18.6}$$

The resulting complexity of the routine is $O(n)$, which is the same as reading a classic information. However to read classically m vectors of dimension n, the complexity is $O(n \cdot m)$, using $qRAM$ ignoring the preparation cost it is $O(n \log(m))$. The described routine is non-reversible since it is based on measurement.

## CHAPTER 19

Quantum Fourier Transform

A periodic function can be represented in the frequency space. The frequency is the number of occurrences of a repeating event per one unit of time. If something changes rapidly, then we say that it has a high frequency. If it does not change rapidly, i.e., it changes smoothly, we say that it has a low frequency. The discrete Fourier transform (DFT) converts discrete time-based or space-based data into the frequency domain.

We describe the DFT and indicate the relation to quantum Fourier transform (QFT). The we indicate how the QFT can be factored into the tensor product of m single-qubit operations and implemented by basic quantum gates. We demonstrate examples of QFT for two, three, and four qubits. Then we indicate that the circuit for m qubits can be imported from the *qiskit* library. We analyze the QFT costs and give an simple example of its operation.

19.1 DISCRETE FOURIER TRANSFORM

The DFTs discrete time-based or space-based data into the frequency sequence-based data. Given a sequence α

$$\alpha_t : [1, 2, \cdots, n] \to C. \tag{19.1}$$

The DFT produces a sequence ω:

$$\omega_f : [1, 2, \cdots, n] \to C. \tag{19.2}$$

The DFT of $\alpha(t)$ is

$$\omega_f = \frac{1}{\sqrt{n}} \cdot \sum_{t=1}^{n} \alpha_t \cdot e^{-2\cdot\pi\cdot i\cdot(t-1)\cdot\frac{(f-1)}{n}} \tag{19.3}$$

its wave frequency is $\frac{(f-1)}{n}$ events per sample. The inverse DFT of ω_f is

$$\alpha_t = \frac{1}{\sqrt{n}} \cdot \sum_{f=1}^{n} \omega_f \cdot e^{2\cdot\pi\cdot i\cdot(t-1)\cdot\frac{(f-1)}{n}}. \tag{19.4}$$

DOI: 10.1201/9781003374404-19

DFT can be seen as a linear transform F talking the column vector α to a column

$$
\begin{pmatrix} \omega_1 \\ \omega_2 \\ \vdots \\ \omega_n \end{pmatrix} = \frac{1}{\sqrt{n}} \cdot \begin{pmatrix} e^{-2\cdot\pi\cdot i\cdot(0)\cdot\frac{(0)}{n}} & e^{-2\cdot\pi\cdot i\cdot(0)\cdot\frac{(1)}{n}} & \cdots & e^{-2\cdot\pi\cdot i\cdot(0)\cdot\frac{(n-1)}{n}} \\ e^{-2\cdot\pi\cdot i\cdot(1)\cdot\frac{(0)}{n}} & e^{-2\cdot\pi\cdot i\cdot(1)\cdot\frac{(1)}{n}} & \cdots & e^{-2\cdot\pi\cdot i\cdot(1)\cdot\frac{(n-1)}{n}} \\ \vdots & \vdots & \ddots & \vdots \\ e^{-2\cdot\pi\cdot i\cdot(n-1)\cdot\frac{(0)}{n}} & e^{-2\cdot\pi\cdot i\cdot(n-1)\cdot\frac{(1)}{n}} & \cdots & e^{-2\cdot\pi\cdot i\cdot(n)\cdot\frac{(n-1)}{n}} \end{pmatrix} \cdot \begin{pmatrix} \alpha_1 \\ \alpha_2 \\ \vdots \\ \alpha_n \end{pmatrix}
$$

$$(19.5)$$

and the IDFT can be seen as a linear transform talking the column vector ω to a column vector α

$$
\begin{pmatrix} \alpha_1 \\ \alpha_2 \\ \vdots \\ \alpha_n \end{pmatrix} = \frac{1}{\sqrt{n}} \cdot \begin{pmatrix} e^{2\cdot\pi\cdot i\cdot(0)\cdot\frac{(0)}{n}} & e^{2\cdot\pi\cdot i\cdot(0)\cdot\frac{(1)}{n}} & \cdots & e^{2\cdot\pi\cdot i\cdot(0)\cdot\frac{(n-1)}{n}} \\ e^{2\cdot\pi\cdot i\cdot(1)\cdot\frac{(0)}{n}} & e^{2\cdot\pi\cdot i\cdot(1)\cdot\frac{(1)}{n}} & \cdots & e^{2\cdot\pi\cdot i\cdot(1)\cdot\frac{(n-1)}{n}} \\ \vdots & \vdots & \ddots & \vdots \\ e^{2\cdot\pi\cdot i\cdot(n-1)\cdot\frac{(0)}{n}} & e^{2\cdot\pi\cdot i\cdot(n-1)\cdot\frac{(1)}{n}} & \cdots & e^{2\cdot\pi\cdot i\cdot(n)\cdot\frac{(n-1)}{n}} \end{pmatrix} \cdot \begin{pmatrix} \omega_1 \\ \omega_2 \\ \vdots \\ \omega_n \end{pmatrix}.
$$

$$(19.6)$$

An nth root of unity is a complex number ζ satisfying the equation

$$\zeta^n = 1 \qquad (19.7)$$

with $n = 1, 2, 3, \cdots, n-1$ being a positive integer, for example

$$\zeta_n = e^{-2\cdot\pi\cdot i\cdot\frac{1}{n}} = \cos\left(2\cdot\pi\cdot\frac{1}{n}\right) - i\cdot\sin\left(2\cdot\pi\cdot\frac{1}{n}\right) \qquad (19.8)$$

Using the nth root of unity, the matrix can be represented as a Vandermonde matrix

$$
F = \frac{1}{\sqrt{n}} \cdot \begin{pmatrix} 1 & 1 & 1 & 1 & \cdots & 1 \\ 1 & \zeta_n & \zeta_n^2 & \zeta_n^3 & \cdots & \zeta_n^{(n-1)} \\ 1 & \zeta_n^2 & \zeta_n^4 & \zeta_n^6 & \cdots & \zeta_n^{2\cdot(n-1)} \\ 1 & \zeta_n^3 & \zeta_n^6 & \zeta_n^9 & \cdots & \zeta_n^{3\cdot(n-1)} \\ \vdots & \vdots & \ddots & \vdots & \ddots & \vdots \\ 1 & \zeta_n^{(n-1)} & \zeta_n^{2\cdot(n-1)} & \zeta_n^{3\cdot(n-1)} & \cdots & \zeta_n^{(n-1)\cdot(n-1)} \end{pmatrix}.
$$

$$(19.9)$$

The matrix F, also called DFT matrix is unitary

$$F^{-1} = F^* = IF. \qquad (19.10)$$

Because F is unitary it implies that the length of a vector is preserved as stated in Parseval's theorem

$$\|\omega\| = \|F\cdot\alpha\| = \|\alpha\|. \qquad (19.11)$$

19.2 QUANTUM FOURIER TRANSFORM

QFT can be used to determine the period of a periodic function in polynomial time, see Figure 19.1. This exponentially faster than a conventional computer. It is used in the framework for the factorization algorithm on which the famous Shor's algorithm is

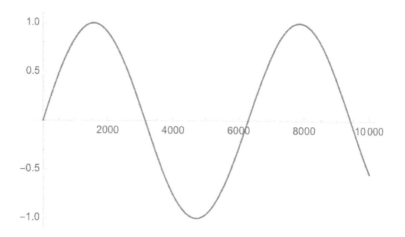

Figure 19.1 On a conventional computer we needed to compute around 10000 steps to determine the period of an unknown periodic function, on quantum computer we need only 9 to 10 steps (log 10000).

based [100], [99]. Shor's algorithm breaks conventional cryptographic codes efficiently. Such codes cannot be broken by conventional computers since the calculations would require an exponential amount of time.

The QFT on a state $|x\rangle$ of m qubits in a n-dimensional Hilbert space $H_n = H_{2^m}$ can be represented as [47]

$$|y\rangle = F_m \cdot |x\rangle = \frac{1}{\sqrt{n}} \sum_{y \in B^m} e^{2 \cdot \pi \cdot i \cdot \frac{y}{n} \cdot x} \cdot |y\rangle. \tag{19.12}$$

It is just the discrete inverse Fourier transform of $\alpha(t)$ in the bracket notation

$$\omega_f = \frac{1}{\sqrt{n}} \cdot \sum_{t=1}^{n} \alpha_t \cdot e^{2 \cdot \pi \cdot i \cdot \frac{(f-1)}{n} \cdot (t-1)}.$$

Conventions for the sign of the phase factor exponent vary; here the quantum Fourier transform has the same effect as the inverse DFT and follows the *qiskit* notation. For one qubit $m = 1$, $n = 2$

$$\zeta_2 = e^{2 \cdot \pi \cdot i \cdot \frac{1}{2}} = e^{-\pi \cdot i} = e^{\pi \cdot i} = -1$$

and the QFT F_1 is

$$F_1 = \frac{1}{\sqrt{2}} \cdot \begin{pmatrix} 1 & 1 \\ 1 & \zeta_2 \end{pmatrix} = \frac{1}{\sqrt{2}} \cdot \begin{pmatrix} 1 & 1 \\ 1 & -1 \end{pmatrix} = H_1. \tag{19.13}$$

For two qubits $m = 2$, $n = 4$

$$\zeta_4 = e^{2 \cdot \pi \cdot i \cdot \frac{1}{4}} = e^{\pi \cdot i \cdot \frac{1}{2}} = i$$

and the QFT F_2 is

$$F_2 = \frac{1}{\sqrt{4}} \cdot \begin{pmatrix} 1 & 1 & 1 & 1 \\ 1 & \zeta_4 & \zeta_4^2 & \zeta_4^3 \\ 1 & \zeta_4^2 & \zeta_4^4 & \zeta_4^6 \\ 1 & \zeta_4^3 & \zeta_4^6 & \zeta_4^9 \end{pmatrix} = \frac{1}{2} \cdot \begin{pmatrix} 1 & 1 & 1 & 1 \\ 1 & i & -1 & -i \\ 1 & -1 & 1 & -1 \\ 1 & -i & -1 & i \end{pmatrix} \tag{19.14}$$

and the inverse QFT is

$$IF_2 = F_2^* = \frac{1}{2} \cdot \begin{pmatrix} 1 & 1 & 1 & 1 \\ 1 & -i & -1 & i \\ 1 & -1 & 1 & -1 \\ 1 & i & -1 & -i \end{pmatrix}. \tag{19.15}$$

For three qubits $m = 3$, $n = 8$

$$\zeta_8 = e^{2 \cdot \pi \cdot i \cdot \frac{1}{8}} = e^{\pi \cdot i \cdot \frac{1}{4}} = \frac{1+i}{\sqrt{2}}$$

$$F_3 = \frac{1}{\sqrt{8}} \cdot \begin{pmatrix} 1 & 1 & 1 & 1 & 1 & 1 & 1 & 1 \\ 1 & e^{\frac{i\pi}{4}} & i & e^{\frac{3i\pi}{4}} & -1 & e^{-\frac{1}{4}(3i\pi)} & -i & e^{-\frac{1}{4}(i\pi)} \\ 1 & i & -1 & -i & 1 & i & -1 & -i \\ 1 & e^{\frac{3i\pi}{4}} & -i & e^{\frac{i\pi}{4}} & -1 & e^{-\frac{1}{4}(i\pi)} & i & e^{-\frac{1}{4}(3i\pi)} \\ 1 & -1 & 1 & -1 & 1 & -1 & 1 & -1 \\ 1 & e^{-\frac{1}{4}(3i\pi)} & i & e^{-\frac{1}{4}(i\pi)} & -1 & e^{\frac{i\pi}{4}} & -i & e^{\frac{3i\pi}{4}} \\ 1 & -i & -1 & i & 1 & -i & -1 & i \\ 1 & e^{-\frac{1}{4}(i\pi)} & -i & e^{-\frac{1}{4}(3i\pi)} & -1 & e^{\frac{3i\pi}{4}} & i & e^{\frac{i\pi}{4}} \end{pmatrix}. \tag{19.16}$$

The first row of F_3 is the DC average of the amplitude of the input state when measured, the following rows represent the AC (difference) of the input state amplitudes.

19.3 QFT DECOMPOSITION

The QFT can be factored into the tensor product of m single-qubit operations [47],

$$|y\rangle = F_m \cdot |x\rangle = \frac{1}{\sqrt{n}} \sum_{y \in B^m} e^{2 \cdot \pi \cdot i \cdot \frac{y}{n} \cdot x} \cdot |y\rangle =$$

$$\frac{1}{\sqrt{n}} \cdot \left(\sum_{y_m \in \{0,1\}} e^{2 \cdot \pi \cdot i \cdot y_m \cdot 0.x_1} \right) \cdot \left(\sum_{y_{m-1} \in \{0,1\}} e^{2 \cdot \pi \cdot i \cdot y_{m-1} \cdot 0.x_2 x_1} \right) \cdots$$

$$\cdots \left(\sum_{y_1 \in \{0,1\}} e^{2 \cdot \pi \cdot i \cdot y_1 \cdot 0.x_m \cdots x_2 x_1} \right) \tag{19.17}$$

$$= \frac{1}{\sqrt{n}} \cdot \left(|0\rangle + e^{2 \cdot \pi \cdot i \cdot 0.x_1} \cdot |1\rangle \right) \otimes \left(|0\rangle + e^{2 \cdot \pi \cdot i \cdot 0.x_2 x_1} \cdot |1\rangle \right) \otimes \cdots \otimes \tag{19.18}$$

$$\otimes \left(|0\rangle + e^{2 \cdot \pi \cdot i \cdot 0.x_m \cdots x_2 x_1} \cdot |1\rangle \right)$$

using the binary fractions are represented as

$$0.x_m x_{m\ 1} x_{m-2} \cdots x_2 x_1 = \frac{x_m}{2^1} + \frac{x_{m-1}}{2^2} + \cdots + \frac{x_1}{2^m}.$$

The representation involves the input in the tensor decomposition. The product of m single-qubit operations of the QFT allows us to define a quantum circuit. The circuit will use a controlled phase gate CP_k that performs following mapping on two qubits

$$CP_k|00\rangle = |00\rangle, \quad CP_k|01\rangle = |01\rangle,$$

$$CP_k|10\rangle = |10\rangle, \quad CP_k|11\rangle = e^{2\cdot\pi\cdot i/2^k} \cdot |11\rangle.$$

19.3.1 QFT for Two qubits

We demonstrate the definition of the quantum circuit on F_2

$$F_2 = \frac{1}{\sqrt{4}} \cdot \left(|0\rangle + e^{2\cdot\pi\cdot i\cdot 0.x_1} \cdot |1\rangle\right) \otimes \left(|0\rangle + e^{2\cdot\pi\cdot i\cdot 0.x_2 x_1} \cdot |1\rangle\right) \qquad (19.19)$$

on the input $|x_2 x_1\rangle$. We define the circuit recursively from the back. Because

$$e^{2\cdot\pi\cdot i\cdot 0.x_1} = e^{2\cdot\pi\cdot i\cdot \frac{x_1}{2}} = (-1)^{x_1}$$

it follows that

$$\frac{1}{\sqrt{2}} \cdot \left(|0\rangle + e^{2\cdot\pi\cdot i\cdot 0.x_1} \cdot |1\rangle\right) = \frac{1}{\sqrt{2}} \cdot (|0\rangle + (-1)^{x_1} \cdot |1\rangle)$$

can be represented by

$$(I_1 \otimes H_1) \cdot |x_2 x_1\rangle.$$

The "first" operation can be represented as

$$\frac{1}{\sqrt{2}} \cdot \left(|0\rangle + e^{-2\cdot\pi\cdot i\cdot 0.x_2 x_1} \cdot |1\rangle\right) = \frac{1}{\sqrt{2}} \cdot \left(|0\rangle + e^{-2\cdot\pi\cdot i\cdot\frac{x_2}{2^1}} \cdot e^{-2\cdot\pi\cdot i\cdot\frac{x_1}{2^2}} \cdot |1\rangle\right)$$

and can be represented as

$$CP_1 \cdot (H_1 \otimes I_1) \cdot |x_2 x_1\rangle.$$

Together we get

$$(I_1 \otimes W_1) \cdot CP_2 \cdot (W_1 \otimes I_1) \cdot |x_2 x_1\rangle =$$

$$= \frac{1}{\sqrt{4}} \cdot \left(|0\rangle + e^{-2\cdot\pi\cdot i\cdot 0.x_2 x_1} \cdot |1\rangle\right) \otimes \left(|0\rangle + e^{-2\cdot\pi\cdot i\cdot 0.x_1} \cdot |1\rangle\right) \qquad (19.20)$$

The arrangement of the bits is not correct. This is because the last qubit in the result uses the first input qubit and so on. To correct the order we have to apply swap gate $SWAP$. The decomposition is given by

$$F_2 \cdot |x_2 x_1\rangle = SWAP \cdot (I_1 \otimes W_1) \cdot CR_1 \cdot (W_1 \otimes I_1) \cdot |x_2 x_1\rangle. \qquad (19.21)$$

The circuit is represented as (see Figure 19.2)

(a)

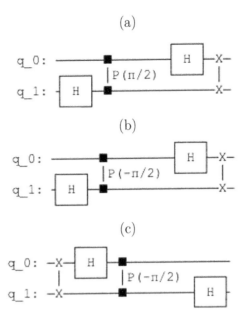

(b)

(c)

Figure 19.2 (a) QFT for two qubits. (b) Inverse QFT has a negative phase. (c) The inverse QFT after calling the command inverse, represents the un-computing of QFT with negative phase. The circuits (b) and (c) represent the same function.

```
from qiskit import QuantumCircuit, Aer, execute
from qiskit.visualization import plot_histogram
import numpy as np
from numpy import pi
qc = QuantumCircuit(2)
qc.h(1)
qc.cp(pi/2, 0, 1) # CROT from qubit 0 to qubit 1,  qc.cp(lambda, control,
target)
qc.h(0)
qc.swap(0,1)
```

We can define QFT for two qubits as a function, calling the function with the command inverse computes the inverse QFT (see Figure 19.2 (c)),

```
def qft2():
    qc = QuantumCircuit(2)
    qc.h(1)
    qc.cp(pi/2, 0, 1) # CROT from qubit 0 to qubit 1
    qc.h(0)
    qc.swap(0,1)
    qc.name="QFT_2"
    return qc

qc = QuantumCircuit(2)
qc.append(qft2().inverse(),range(2))
qc.decompose().draw(fold=130).
```

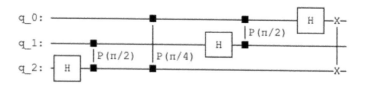

Figure 19.3 Circuit representing QFT for three qubits.

19.3.2 QFT for Three qubits

For F_3 we need to define phase gate on three qubits $|x_3x_2x_1\rangle$ and a swap operation of the first and last qubit. The swap operation is simply the swap of the value of x_1 with the value of of x_3

$$F_3 = \frac{1}{\sqrt{8}} \cdot \left(|0\rangle + e^{-2\cdot\pi\cdot i\cdot 0.x_1} \cdot |1\rangle\right) \otimes \left(|0\rangle + e^{-2\cdot\pi\cdot i\cdot 0.x_2x_1} \cdot |1\rangle\right) \otimes$$

$$\otimes \left(|0\rangle + e^{-2\cdot\pi\cdot i\cdot 0.x_3x_2x_1} \cdot |1\rangle\right) \tag{19.22}$$

The circuit is represented as (see Figure 19.3)

```
qc = QuantumCircuit(3)
qc.h(2)
qc.cp(pi/2, 1, 2) # CROT from qubit 1 to qubit 2
qc.cp(pi/4, 0, 2) # CROT from qubit 0 to qubit 2
qc.h(1)
qc.cp(pi/2, 0, 1) # CROT from qubit 0 to qubit 1
qc.h(0)
qc.swap(0,2)
```

19.3.3 QFT for Four qubits

The circuit for four qubits is represented as (see Figure 19.4)

```
qc = QuantumCircuit(4)
qc.h(3)
qc.cp(pi/2, 2, 3) # CROT from qubit 2 to qubit 3
qc.cp(pi/4, 1, 3) # CROT from qubit 1 to qubit 3
qc.cp(pi/8, 0, 3) # CROT from qubit 0 to qubit 3
qc.barrier()
qc.h(2)
qc.cp(pi/2, 1, 2) # CROT from qubit 1 to qubit 2
qc.cp(pi/4, 0, 2) # CROT from qubit 0 to qubit 2
qc.barrier()
qc.h(1)
qc.cp(pi/2, 0, 1) # CROT from qubit 0 to qubit 1
qc.barrier()
qc.h(0)
qc.barrier()
qc.swap(0,3)
qc.swap(1,2)
```

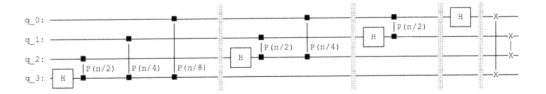

Figure 19.4 QFT for four qubits.

The circuit for m qubits can be imported from the *qiskit* library. In our example we compose a circuit of 6 qubits, (see Figure 19.5)

```
from qiskit.circuit.library import QFT
qc = QuantumCircuit(6)
#qc = qc.compose(QFT(6, inverse=True))
qc = qc.compose(QFT(6))
qc.decompose().draw(fold=200).
```

19.3.4 QFT Costs

The first term requires one Hadamard gate, the second one requires a Hadamard gate and a controlled phase gate. Each following term requires an additional controlled phase gate. Summing up

$$1 + 2 + 3 + \cdots (m - 1) + m = \frac{m \cdot (m - 1)}{2} = O(m^2).$$

The costs of a QFT are $O(m^2)$ compared to the cost of $O(2^m \cdot m)$ on a conventional computer, so the costs of QFT are exponentially less.

19.3.5 QFT

A periodic function can be represented as a superposition of qubits and their values of amplitudes (representing the probabilities). For periodic function the amplitudes representing the frequency of the function have positive value whereas all other amplitudes are zero. By measuring the register with high amplitude values, we can reconstruct the period. In our example we generate a state vector of which the DFT

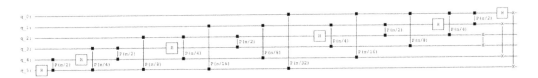

Figure 19.5 QFT for six qubits.

results in the vector

$$\alpha = \begin{pmatrix} 0 \\ 0 \\ 0 \\ 0 \\ 0 \\ 1 \\ 0 \\ 0 \end{pmatrix}.$$

```
qc = QuantumCircuit(3)
#Initialize the signal
qc.h(0)
qc.h(1)
qc.h(2)
qc.p(5*pi/4,0)
qc.p(5*pi/2,1)
qc.p(5*pi,2)
simulator = Aer.get_backend('statevector_simulator')
result=execute(qc,simulator).result()
final_state = simulator.run(qc).result().get_statevector()
from qiskit.visualization import array_to_latex
array_to_latex(final_state, max_size=16,prefix="\\text{S} = "),
```

$S = [0.35i, -0.25+0.25i, -0.35i, 0.25 +0.25i, -0.35i, 0.25 -0.25i, 0.35i, -0.25-0.25i]$

Computing the Iiverse QFT results in the binary representation of 5 (101), the amplitude representation the vector α,

```
qc = QuantumCircuit(3)
#Initialize the signal which frequency corresponds to five
qc.h(0)
qc.h(1)
qc.h(2)
qc.p(5*pi/4,0)
qc.p(5*pi/2,1)
qc.p(5*pi,2)
#And we can see this does indeed result in the Fourier state 5, 101
qc.barrier()
qc = qc.compose(QFT(3, inverse=True))
simulator = Aer.get_backend('statevector_simulator')
result=execute(qc,simulator).result()
counts = result.get_counts()
print('The result is:', counts)
```

The result is: $\{'101' : 1.0\}$.

## CHAPTER 20

Phase Estimation

The Kitaev's Phase Estimation Algorithm (also referred to as quantum eigenvalue estimation algorithm) is a quantum algorithm to estimate the phase (or eigenvalue) of an eigenvector of a unitary operator. We explain the algorithm and indicate an example of the determination of the eigenvalue of the T gate. Then we introduce the quantum counting algorithm that is based on the quantum phase estimation algorithm and on the Grover's search algorithm. Quantum counting algorithm is a quantum algorithm for counting the number of solutions for a given search problem.

20.1 KITAEV'S PHASE ESTIMATION ALGORITHM

Given a unitary operator U on m qubits with an eigenvector $|u\rangle$ with an unknown eigenvalue $e^{2\cdot\pi\cdot i\cdot\theta}$, we want to determine the phase θ [48], [47]. If we apply U to $|u\rangle$ we get

$$U \cdot |u\rangle = e^{2\cdot\pi\cdot i\cdot\theta} \cdot |u\rangle \qquad (20.1)$$

if we apply U to $|u\rangle$ w times we get

$$U^w \cdot |u\rangle = U^{w-1} \cdot \left(e^{2\cdot\pi\cdot i\cdot\theta} \cdot |u\rangle\right) = \left(e^{2\cdot\pi\cdot i\cdot\theta}\right)^w \cdot |u\rangle = e^{2\cdot\pi\cdot i\cdot\theta\cdot w} \cdot |u\rangle. \qquad (20.2)$$

However, we will not gain any information because $|u\rangle$ and $e^{2\cdot\pi\cdot i\cdot\theta\cdot w}\cdot|u\rangle$ are equivalent states and they represent the same state when a measurement is preformed. Instead of the unitary operator U^w, we use the controlled U^w operator CU^w. If the control qubit is set then U^w is applied to the target qubits, otherwise not. The operator CU^w is unitary and defines an injective mapping on two qubits that is reversible

$$CU^w \cdot |0\rangle|u\rangle = |0\rangle|u\rangle, \quad CU^w \cdot |1\rangle|u\rangle = |1\rangle \left(e^{2\cdot\pi\cdot i\cdot\theta\cdot w} \cdot |u\rangle\right) = e^{2\cdot\pi\cdot i\cdot\theta\cdot w} \cdot |1\rangle|u\rangle.$$

So with $w = 2^j$

$$CU^{2^j} \cdot \left(\left(\frac{|0\rangle + |1\rangle}{\sqrt{2}}\right) \cdot |u\rangle\right) = \left(\frac{|0\rangle + e^{2\cdot\pi\cdot i\cdot\theta\cdot 2^j}|1\rangle}{\sqrt{2}}\right) \cdot |u\rangle.$$

The QFT is represented as a tensor product of m single-qubit operations. The QFT can be factored into the tensor product of m single-qubit operations,

$$|y\rangle = F_m \cdot |x\rangle = \frac{1}{\sqrt{n}} \sum_{y\in B^m} e^{2\cdot\pi\cdot i\cdot\frac{y}{n}\cdot x} \cdot |y\rangle =$$

DOI: 10.1201/9781003374404-20

$$= \frac{1}{\sqrt{n}} \cdot \left(|0\rangle + e^{2\cdot\pi\cdot i\cdot 0.x_1} \cdot |1\rangle \right) \otimes \left(|0\rangle + e^{2\cdot\pi\cdot i\cdot 0.x_2x_1} \cdot |1\rangle \right) \otimes \cdots \otimes \qquad (20.3)$$

$$\otimes \left(|0\rangle + e^{2\cdot\pi\cdot i\cdot 0.x_m\cdots x_2x_1} \cdot |1\rangle \right).$$

If we set $\theta = 0.x_m \cdots x_2x_1$, we can rewrite the equation as

$$|y\rangle = F_m \cdot |x\rangle = \frac{1}{\sqrt{n}} \sum_{y\in B^m} e^{2\cdot\pi\cdot i\cdot y\cdot\theta} \cdot |y\rangle =$$

$$= \frac{1}{\sqrt{n}} \cdot \left(|0\rangle + e^{2\cdot\pi\cdot i\cdot\left(\theta\cdot 2^{m-1}\right)} \cdot |1\rangle \right) \otimes \left(|0\rangle + e^{2\cdot\pi\cdot i\cdot\left(\theta\cdot 2^{m-2}\right)} \cdot |1\rangle \right) \otimes \cdots \otimes \qquad (20.4)$$

$$\otimes \left(|0\rangle + e^{2\cdot\pi\cdot i\cdot\left(\theta\cdot 2^0\right)} \cdot |1\rangle \right).$$

For m control qubits, we define $C_{j+1}U^{2^j}$ in the following way. For $j \in \{0, 1, 2, \cdots, m-1\}$, the control qubit $j+1$ of the m qubits is set, then $C_{j+1}U^{2^j}$ is applied to the target $|u\rangle$, otherwise not. The initial state of the algorithm is

$$|0^{\otimes m}\rangle|u\rangle$$

with u being the eigenvector of U. In the first step of the algorithm we build a superposition of m control qubits

$$H_m \cdot |0^{\otimes m}\rangle|u\rangle = \frac{1}{\sqrt{2^m}} \sum_{x\in B^m} |x\rangle|u\rangle =$$

$$= \frac{1}{\sqrt{n}} \cdot (|0\rangle + |1\rangle) \otimes (|0\rangle + |1\rangle) \otimes \cdots \otimes (|0\rangle + |1\rangle)\, |u\rangle. \qquad (20.5)$$

In the second step we apply m $C_{j+1}U^{2^j}$ operators to the target $|u\rangle$

$$\prod_{j=0}^{m-1} C_{j+1}U^{2^j} \cdot \left(\frac{1}{\sqrt{n}} \cdot (|0\rangle + |1\rangle) \otimes (|0\rangle + |1\rangle) \otimes \cdots \otimes (|0\rangle + |1\rangle)\, |u\rangle \right) =$$

$$= \frac{1}{\sqrt{n}} \cdot \left(|0\rangle + e^{2\cdot\pi\cdot i\cdot\left(\theta\cdot 2^{m-1}\right)} \cdot |1\rangle \right) \otimes \left(|0\rangle + e^{2\cdot\pi\cdot i\cdot\left(\theta\cdot 2^{m-2}\right)} \cdot |1\rangle \right) \otimes \cdots \qquad (20.6)$$

$$\otimes \left(|0\rangle + e^{2\cdot\pi\cdot i\cdot\left(\theta\cdot 2^0\right)} \cdot |1\rangle \right) \cdot |u\rangle$$

In the third step we apply inverse QFT to the m control qubits

$$IF_m \cdot \left(\frac{1}{\sqrt{n}} \sum_{y\in B^m} e^{2\cdot\pi\cdot i\cdot y\cdot\theta} \cdot |y\rangle \right) \cdot |u\rangle =$$

$$= IF_m \cdot \left(\frac{1}{\sqrt{n}} \sum_{y\in B^m} e^{2\cdot\pi\cdot i\cdot\frac{y}{n}\cdot x} \cdot |y\rangle \right) \cdot |u\rangle = |x\rangle|u\rangle. \qquad (20.7)$$

In the fourth step we measure the first register composed of m control qubits and estimate θ

$$\theta = 0.x_m \cdots x_2x_1 = \frac{x}{n} = \frac{x}{2^m}. \qquad (20.8)$$

20.1.1 Example with T Gate

The T gate corresponds to the unitary matrix

$$T = \begin{pmatrix} 1 & 0 \\ 0 & e^{i\frac{\pi}{4}} \end{pmatrix}.$$

With the eigenvector $|1\rangle$ and the eigenvalue $e^{2\cdot\pi\cdot i\cdot\theta}$

$$U \cdot |u\rangle = T \cdot |1\rangle = e^{2\cdot\pi\cdot i\cdot\theta} \cdot |u\rangle = e^{2\cdot\pi\cdot i\cdot\theta} \cdot |1\rangle \tag{20.9}$$

with the phase is $\theta = \frac{1}{8}$ since

$$T|1\rangle = e^{2\cdot\pi\cdot i\cdot\theta} = e^{i\frac{\pi}{4}} \cdot |1\rangle = e^{2\cdot i\frac{\pi}{8}} \cdot |1\rangle.$$

The phase estimation algorithm will write the phase of T to the m qubits in the control register. The value of m determines the precision of the result. In our simple case $m = 3$

$$\theta = 0.x_3 x_2 x_1 = \frac{x}{8} = \frac{x}{2^3}.$$

The controlled T gate is represented by the controlled phase gate $CP(\lambda)$ with $\lambda = \pi/4$. The circuit is composed of 4 qubits, qubits 0, 1, 2 represent the 3 qubits in the control register. The qubit 3 represents the eigenvector $|1\rangle$. The control register is mapped into superposition by Hadamard gates and the qubit 4 is initialized to the eigenvector $|1\rangle$ with the NOT gate. The control register controls the unitary operations T applied to the target eigenvector $|1\rangle$ resulting in the Fourier basis representation of the three control qubits. To estimate the phase θ, we perform the inverse QFT to the 3 control qubits and measure the three quits and estimate θ with

$$x = |q_2 q_1 q_0\rangle$$

and

$$\theta = \frac{x}{2^3}.$$

The circuit is represented as (See Figure 20.1)

```
import numpy as np
from qiskit import QuantumCircuit, Aer, execute
from qiskit.quantum_info import Statevector
from qiskit.visualization import plot_histogram
from qiskit.circuit.library import MCXGate
from math import pi
from qiskit.circuit.library import QFT
qc = QuantumCircuit(4, 3)
qc.h(0)
qc.h(1)
qc.h(2)
qc.x(3)
#qc.cp(lambda, control, target)
qc.cp(pi/4, 0, 3)
```

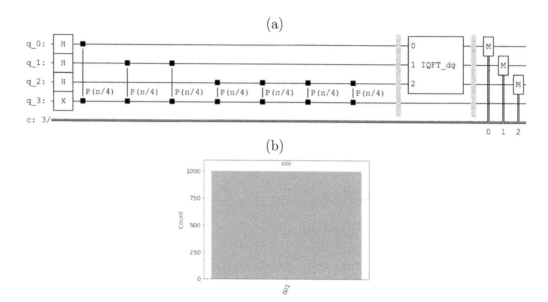

Figure 20.1 (a) Circuit estimating the phase of a T gate with accuracy of three qubits. The circuit is composed of 4 qubits, qubits 0, 1, 2 represent the control register and qubit 3 represents the eigenvector $|1\rangle$. The control register controls the unitary operations T applied to the target eigenvector $|1\rangle$. To estimate the phase θ, we perform the inverse QFT to the 3 control qubits. (b) The measured value corresponds to the binary value 001 equal to one indicating phase $\theta = 0.125 = 1/2^3$.

```
qc.cp(pi/4, 1, 3)
qc.cp(pi/4, 1, 3)
qc.cp(pi/4, 2, 3)
qc.cp(pi/4, 2, 3)
qc.cp(pi/4, 2, 3)
qc.cp(pi/4, 2, 3)
qc.barrier()
qc = qc.compose(QFT(3, inverse=True), [0,1,2])
qc.barrier()
qc.measure(0,0)
qc.measure(1,1)
qc.measure(2,2)

simulator = Aer.get_backend('qasm_simulator')
result=execute(qc,simulator,shots=1000).result()
counts = result.get_counts()
plot_histogram(counts)
```

The measured value corresponds to the binary value 001 equal to one indicating phase. The more control qubits (m) we use, the higher precision we get. However in this simple example, three control qubits lead to good estimation of the phase θ

$$\theta = \frac{1}{2^3} = \frac{1}{8}.$$

20.2 QUANTUM COUNTING

Grover's amplification is based on the unitary operator $G_{m^*} = 2 \cdot P_{m^*} - I_{m^*}$ in the computational basis with $n = 2^{m^*}$ states. (We use the notation m^* to indicate that the number of qubits used in the Grover's amplification and the number of the control qubits m do not need to be equal.) The probability of seeing one solution should be as close as possible to 1 and the number of iterations. The number of iterations r is the largest integer not greater than t^*,

$$r = \left\lfloor \frac{\pi}{4} \cdot \sqrt{\frac{n}{k}} - \frac{1}{2} \right\rfloor. \tag{20.10}$$

The value of r depends on the relation of n versus k, with k being the number of solutions. We can estimate k by quantum counting. In quantum counting, we simply use the quantum phase estimation algorithm to find an eigenvalue of a Grover search iteration.

One can represent the state $|\tau\rangle$ after t Grover's amplification by two subspaces $|\tau_{solution}\rangle$ and $|\tau_{non}\rangle$ representing the states representing the solutions and non-solutions with

$$|\tau\rangle = \alpha_t \cdot |\tau_{solution}\rangle + \beta_t \cdot |\tau_{non}\rangle \tag{20.11}$$

Quantum counting algorithm is based on the inverse QFT period algorithm to estimate the period of the sin wave period represented by the of the amplitude α_t or β_t [16], [15], [47] after t iterations (see Figure 20.2). After the amplification we get (see [119])

$$\sqrt{\frac{k}{n}} \cdot |\tau_{solution}\rangle + \sqrt{\frac{n-k}{n}} \cdot |\tau_{non}\rangle \tag{20.12}$$

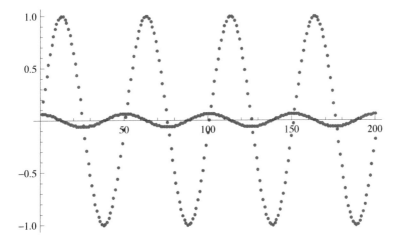

Figure 20.2 The two-dimensional subspace of amplitude and time t represents a periodic function described by α_t (the dotted curve) and β_t (the continuous curve). The x-axis indicates t and the y-axis the amplitude. The values are $n = 256$, $k = 1$, and $1 \le t \le 200$.

with

$$\sin^2 \theta = \frac{k}{n} \tag{20.13}$$

and

$$\cos^2 \theta = \frac{n-k}{n} = 1 - \frac{k}{n}. \tag{20.14}$$

We can represent the Grover's amplification matrix in the two-dimensional basis $|\tau_{solution}\rangle$ and $|\tau_{non}\rangle$

$$G = \begin{pmatrix} \cos(\theta) & -\sin(\theta) \\ \sin(\theta) & \cos(\theta) \end{pmatrix}$$

The matrix G has two eigenvectors:

$$\mathbf{u}_1 = \begin{pmatrix} \frac{i}{\sqrt{2}} \\ \frac{1}{\sqrt{2}} \end{pmatrix}, \quad \mathbf{u}_2 = \begin{pmatrix} \frac{-i}{\sqrt{2}} \\ \frac{1}{\sqrt{2}} \end{pmatrix}$$

with two eigenvalues $\lambda_1 = e^{2 \cdot i\theta}$ and $\lambda_2 = e^{-2 \cdot i\theta}$. The eigenvectors $\mathbf{u}_1$ and $\mathbf{u}_2$ are represented in the $|\tau_{solution}\rangle$ and $|\tau_{non}\rangle$ basis as

$$|\tau_1\rangle = \frac{i}{\sqrt{2}} \cdot |\tau_{solution}\rangle + \frac{1}{\sqrt{2}} \cdot |\tau_{non}\rangle$$

$$|\tau_2\rangle = \frac{i}{\sqrt{2}} \cdot |\tau_{solution}\rangle - \frac{1}{\sqrt{2}} \cdot |\tau_{non}\rangle \tag{20.15}$$

and

$$|\tau\rangle = e^{i\theta} \cdot \frac{1}{\sqrt{2}} \cdot |\tau_1\rangle + e^{-i\theta} \cdot \frac{1}{\sqrt{2}} \cdot |\tau_2\rangle \tag{20.16}$$

In the original quantum phase estimation algorithm, the required eigenvector is

$$U \cdot |u\rangle = e^{2 \cdot \pi \cdot i \cdot \theta} \cdot |u\rangle \tag{20.17}$$

However, we do not need to prepare our register in either of these eigenvectors, the register is actually in a superposition of the eigenvectors of the Grover operator

$$G \cdot |\tau\rangle = G \cdot \left(e^{i\theta} \cdot \frac{1}{\sqrt{2}} \cdot |\tau_1\rangle + e^{-i\theta} \cdot \frac{1}{\sqrt{2}} \cdot |\tau_2\rangle \right) \tag{20.18}$$

$$G \cdot |\tau\rangle = \lambda_1 \cdot \left(e^{i\theta} \cdot \frac{1}{\sqrt{2}} \cdot |\tau_1\rangle \right) + \lambda_2 \cdot \left(e^{-i\theta} \cdot \frac{1}{\sqrt{2}} \cdot |\tau_2\rangle \right) \tag{20.19}$$

Since our eigenvalues are $\lambda_1 = e^{2 \cdot i\theta}$ and $\lambda_1 = e^{-2 \cdot i\theta}$ and we have m control qubits

$$\theta = \frac{x \cdot \pi}{2^m} \tag{20.20}$$

and with n being the number of state of Grover's amplification

$$\sin^2 \theta = \frac{k}{n} \tag{20.21}$$

with

$$k = \sin^2 \theta \cdot n = \sin^2 \left(\frac{x \cdot \pi}{2^m} \right) \cdot n.$$

20.2.1 Example

The controlled Grover operator is implemented using the circuit library [21] with an oracle that marks four solutions $(k = 4)$ out of 16 states $(m^* = 4)$

```
def grover_operator():
    #Grover iteration circuit for oracle with 4/16 solutions
    from qiskit.circuit.library import Diagonal, GroverOperator
    oracle = Diagonal([1,1,-1,1,1,1,1,1,1,1,1,1,-1,-1,-1,1])
    grover_it = GroverOperator(oracle).to_gate()
    grover_it.label = "G"
    return grover_it
```

and we will use the *.control*() method to create a controlled gate from the Grover operator. The circuit is composed of 8 qubits, qubits 0, 1, 2, 3 represent the 4 qubits in the control register. The qubits 5 to 7 represent the four qubits in the computational basis representing 16 states. All qubits are mapped into superposition by Hadamard gates. The control register controls the unitary operations G by the control method *.control*() with the first qubit being the control qubit of the control register, resulting in the Fourier basis representation of the three control qubits. To estimate the phase θ, we perform the inverse QFT to the 4 control qubits and measure the four quits and estimate θ (see Figure 20.3 (a))

```
from qiskit.circuit.library import QFT
qft_dagger = QFT(4, inverse=True).to_gate()
qft_dagger.label = "QFTĘ"

import matplotlib.pyplot as plt
import numpy as np
import math
# importing Qiskit
from qiskit import QuantumCircuit,  Aer, execute
# import basic plot tools
from qiskit.visualization import plot_histogram

qc = QuantumCircuit(8, 4)

qc.h([0,1,2,3,4,5,6,7])
cgrit = grover_operator().control()

qc.append(cgrit, [0,4,5,6,7])

qc.append(cgrit, [1,4,5,6,7])
qc.append(cgrit, [1,4,5,6,7])

qc.append(cgrit, [2,4,5,6,7])
qc.append(cgrit, [2,4,5,6,7])
qc.append(cgrit, [2,4,5,6,7])
qc.append(cgrit, [2,4,5,6,7])

qc.append(cgrit, [3,4,5,6,7])
qc.append(cgrit, [3,4,5,6,7])
```

```
qc.append(cgrit, [3,4,5,6,7])
qc.append(cgrit, [3,4,5,6,7])
qc.append(cgrit, [3,4,5,6,7])
qc.append(cgrit, [3,4,5,6,7])
qc.append(cgrit, [3,4,5,6,7])
qc.append(cgrit, [3,4,5,6,7])
# Do inverse QFT on counting qubits
qc.append(qft_dagger, [0,1,2,3])
# Measure counting qubits
qc.measure([0,1,2,3], [0,1,2,3])

simulator = Aer.get_backend('qasm_simulator')
result=execute(qc,simulator,shots=1000).result()
counts = result.get_counts()
plot_histogram(counts)
```

The maximal measured value corresponds to the binary value 0011 (3 decimal) or 1101 (13 decimal), see Figure 20.3 (b). The phase is either $\theta_1 = \frac{\pi \cdot 3}{16}$ or $\theta_2 = \frac{\pi \cdot 13}{16}$ corresponding to the two eigenvalues $\lambda_1 = e^{2 \cdot i\theta}$ or $\lambda_2 = e^{-2 \cdot i\theta}$ with positive and negative phase with

$$\sin^2(\theta) = \sin^2(-\theta)$$

with approximately the correct answer

$$k = 4.9 \approx \sin^2 \left(\frac{\pi \cdot 3}{16} \right) \cdot 16 = sin^2 \left(\frac{\pi \cdot 13}{16} \right) \cdot 16.$$

The more control qubits (m) we use, the higher precision we get. In our example four control qubits lead only to an approximate estimation of the phase θ. For example if marks five solutions $(k = 5)$ out of 16 states we measure exactly the same maximal measured values 0011 (3 decimal) or 1101 (13 decimal). More control qubits would be required for less approximate result. The counts of the two maximal values indicating the phase θ_1 and θ_2 would be higher and the counts of the other states would approximate the value zero.

(a)

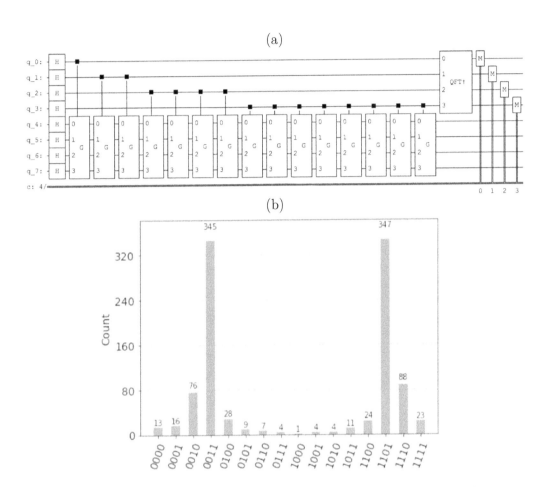

(b)

Figure 20.3 (a) The controlled Grover operator is implemented using use the circuit library with an oracle that marks four solutions ($k = 4$) out of 16 states ($m^* = 4$). The circuit is composed of 8 qubits, qubits 0, 1, 2, 3 represent the 4 qubits in the control register. The qubits 5 to 7 represents the four qubits in the computational basis representing 16 states. All qubits are mapped into superposition by Hadamard gates. The control register controls the unitary operations G resulting in the Fourier basis representation of the three control qubits. To estimate the phase θ we perform the inverse QFT to the 4 control qubits and measure the 4 qubits. (b) The maximal measured value corresponds to the binary value 0011 (3 decimal) or 1101 (13 decimal) indicating phase $\theta_1 = \pi \cdot 3/16$ or $\theta_2 = \pi \cdot 13/16$.

## CHAPTER 21

Quantum Perceptron

The classical perceptron describes an algorithm for supervised learning that considers only linearly separable problems in which groups can be separated by a line or hyperplane. The quantum perceptron does usually not include learning, instead it computes the output of a binary unit (neuron) efficiently. It is based on the Kitaev's phase estimation algorithm. A quantum perceptron can be used as building block of larger systems, it can process an arbitrary number of input vectors in parallel. We present a simple example of the quantum perceptron for two-dimensional input.

21.1 COUNTING OF ONES WITH KITAEV'S PHASE ESTIMATION ALGORITHM

The phase gate

$$P(\lambda) = \begin{pmatrix} 1 & 0 \\ 0 & e^{i \cdot \lambda} \end{pmatrix}.$$

Has tow eigenvectors $|1\rangle$ and $|0\rangle$ with the eigenvalues $e^{i \cdot \lambda}$ and 1. Setting λ to

$$\lambda = \pi \cdot \frac{net}{2^{(m-1)}}$$

results in the eigenvalue

$$e^{i \cdot \pi \cdot \frac{net}{2^{(m-1)}}}.$$

Kitaev's Phase Estimation Algorithm determines the eigenvalue using the controlled phase gate with

$$P \cdot |1\rangle = e^{2 \cdot \pi \cdot i \cdot \theta} \cdot |1\rangle = e^{2 \cdot \pi \cdot i \cdot \frac{net}{2 \cdot 2^{(m-1)}}} \cdot |1\rangle = e^{2 \cdot \pi \cdot i \cdot \frac{net}{2^m}} \cdot |1\rangle. \tag{21.1}$$

The phase estimation algorithm will write the phase of P to the m qubits in the control register

$$net = x_m \cdots x_2 x_1$$

$$\theta = 0.x_m \cdots x_2 x_1 = \frac{x}{2^m} = \frac{net}{2^m}, \tag{21.2}$$

$$\lambda = 2 \cdot \theta.$$

DOI: 10.1201/9781003374404-21

21.2 QUANTUM PERCEPTRON

The classical perceptron describes an algorithm for supervised learning that considers only linearly separable problems in which groups can be separated by a line or hyperplane. The quantum perceptron [96], [95] does usually not include learning and instead it computes efficiently the binary representation of the function *net* modulo D with $x_0 = 1$

$$net := \left(\sum_{j=0}^{D} w_j \cdot x_j \right) \bmod D = \left(\sum_{j=1}^{D} w_j \cdot x_j + w_0 \right) \bmod D = (\langle \mathbf{x} | \mathbf{w} \rangle + w_0) \bmod D$$

(21.3)

with the constraint

$$x_j \in \{0, 1\}, \quad w_j \in [-1, 1]$$

The value w_0 is called the "bias", it is a constant value that does not depend on any input value. Each dimension j is represented by a controlled phase gate CP_j with

$$\lambda = \pi \cdot \frac{w_j}{2^{(m-1)}}$$

and $D = 2^m - 2$ or $\log_2(D + 2) = m$. For $D = 2$

$$net = w_0 + w_1 \cdot x_1 + w_2 \cdot x_2$$

will be represented by three controlled phase gate that perform the following computation

$$e^{i \cdot \pi \cdot \frac{net}{2}} = e^{i \cdot \pi \cdot \frac{w_0}{2}} \cdot e^{i \cdot \pi \cdot \frac{w_1 \cdot x_1}{2}} \cdot e^{i \cdot \pi \cdot \frac{w_2 \cdot x_2}{2}}$$

(21.4)

The estimated values of *net* is represented by two control qubits in the case *net* is natural number the measured values are four possible values of the two qubits $|q_1 q_0\rangle$

$$|00\rangle, \quad |01\rangle, \quad |10\rangle, \quad |11\rangle.$$

In other case rational number value of net corresponds to a superposition of the four states. A nonlinear activation function like

$$\phi(net) := f(net) = \begin{cases} 1 & \text{if } net \geq threshold \\ 0 & \text{if } net < threshold \end{cases}$$

(21.5)

with *threshold* = 10 can be implemented reading the more important qubit, in our case the qubit q_1 which can represent the output value of the Perceptron that is either one or zero. A quantum Perceptron can be used as building block of larger systems, it can process an arbitrary number of input vectors in parallel. when the input is presented in superposition $|\psi\rangle$ representing the whole data set DB of s objects $\mathbf{x}_k$

$$\{\mathbf{x}_k \in DB \mid k \in \{1..s\}\}.$$

with

$$|\psi\rangle = \frac{1}{\sqrt{s}} \sum_{k=1}^{s} |\mathbf{x}_k\rangle$$

and then can be further processed.

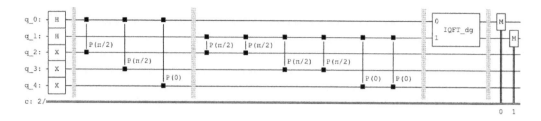

Figure 21.1 A a quantum Perceptron with $D = 2$ and two control qubits ($m = 2$) qubit 0 and qubit 1. Qubits 2 and 3 representing the input $x_1 = 1$, $x_2 = 1$ and qubit 4 the bias $x_0 = 1$ and the weights $w_0 = 0$, $w_1 = 1$ and $w_2 = 1$.

21.3 SIMPLE EXAMPLE

In this example we implement a quantum Perceptron with $D = 2$ and two control qubits ($m = 2$) qubit 0 and with qubit 2 and 3 representing the input and qubit 4 the bias $x_0 = 1$ (see Figure 21.1),

```
import numpy as np
from qiskit import QuantumCircuit, Aer, execute
from qiskit.visualization import plot_histogram
from math import pi
from qiskit.circuit.library import QFT

qc = QuantumCircuit(5, 2)

#Free Parameters set by the User
#----------------------------------
#Setting the values of weihts
w0=0
w1=1
w2=1
#Setting the Input x1=qubit 2, x2=qubit 3
qc.x(2)
qc.x(3)
#----------------------------------
#constant values with N=m-1 (m number of controll qubits)
N=1
qc.h(0)
qc.h(1)
#Bias w0 qubit 4
qc.x(4)
qc.barrier()
#qc.cp(lambda, control, target)
#w1
qc.cp(w1*pi/(2*N), 0, 2)
#w2
qc.cp(w2*pi/(2*N), 0, 3)
#w0
qc.cp(w0*pi/(2*N), 0, 4)
```

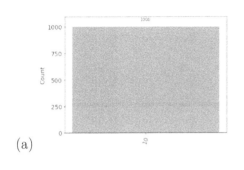
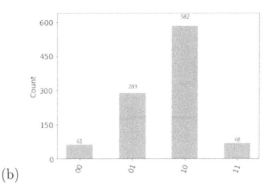

(a)

(b)

Figure 21.2 (a) The measured value of $net = 2$ for the input $x_1 = 1$, $x_2 = 1$ and the weights $w_0 = 0$, $w_1 = 1$ and $w_2 = 1$. (b) The measured value of net for the input $x_1 = 1$, $x_2 = 1$ and the weights $w_0 = 0$, $w_1 = 0.6$ and $w_2 = 1$ is in superposition between 2 and 1 ($net = 1.6$).

```
qc.barrier()
#w1
qc.cp(w1*pi/(2*N), 1, 2)
qc.cp(w1*pi/(2*N), 1, 2)
#w2
qc.cp(w2*pi/(2*N), 1, 3)
qc.cp(w2*pi/(2*N), 1, 3)
#w0
qc.cp(w0*pi/(2*N), 1, 4)
qc.cp(w0*pi/(2*N), 1, 4)
qc.barrier()
qc = qc.compose(QFT(2, inverse=True), [0,1])
qc.barrier()

qc.measure(0,0)
qc.measure(1,1)

simulator = Aer.get_backend('qasm_simulator')
result=execute(qc,simulator,shots=1000).result()
counts = result.get_counts()
plot_histogram(counts)
```

The measured value of net for the input $x_1 = 1$, $x_2 = 1$, and the weights $w_0 = 0$, $w_1 = 1$, and $w_2 = 1$ and the measured value of net for the input $x_1 = 1$, $x_2 = 1$, and the weights $w_0 = 0$, $w_1 = 0.6$, and $w_2 = 1$, see Figure 21.2.

## CHAPTER 22

HHL

The quantum algorithm for linear systems of equations for is one of the main fundamental algorithms expected to provide a speedup over their classical counterparts. In the honor of its inventors Aram Harrow, Avinatan Hassidim, and Seth Lloyd, it is called the HHL algorithm. HHL is going to be one of the most useful subroutines for any quantum machine learning algorithm because almost all machine learning uses some form of a linear system of equations. For example, in support vector machines and quantum support vector machines, maximizing the objective function with the optimum values of the Lagrange multipliers are based on solving linear equations. We describe the HHL algorithm, give an example step by step using $qiskit$ command $HamiltonianGate$, and indicate the constrains of the algorithm.

22.1 QUANTUM ALGORITHM FOR LINEAR SYSTEMS OF EQUATIONS

We see systems of linear equations in many real-life applications across a wide range of areas. For an invertible complex matrix $n \times n$ A and a complex vector $\mathbf{b}$

$$A \cdot \mathbf{x} = \mathbf{b} \tag{22.1}$$

we want to find $\mathbf{x}$. If A is Hermitian $A^* = A$ (for real matrix $A^T = A$) then A can be represented by the spectral decomposition as

$$A = \lambda_1 \cdot |u_1\rangle\langle u_1| + \lambda_2 \cdot |u_2\rangle\langle u_2| + \cdots + \lambda_n \cdot |u_n\rangle\langle u_n|. \tag{22.2}$$

and

$$A^{-1} = \frac{1}{\lambda_1} \cdot |u_1\rangle\langle u_1| + \frac{1}{\lambda_2} \cdot |u_2\rangle\langle u_2| + \cdots + \frac{1}{\lambda_n} \cdot |u_n\rangle\langle u_n|. \tag{22.3}$$

It follows

$$A^{-1} \cdot |u_j\rangle = \frac{1}{\lambda_j}|u_j\rangle \tag{22.4}$$

and writing $|b\rangle$ as a linear combination of the eigenvectors of A

$$|b\rangle = \sum_j |u_j\rangle\langle u_j|b\rangle \tag{22.5}$$

DOI: 10.1201/9781003374404-22

leads to

$$A \cdot |b\rangle = \sum_j \lambda_j |u_j\rangle \langle u_j | b\rangle \qquad (22.6)$$

and

$$|x\rangle = A^{-1} \cdot |b\rangle = \sum_j \lambda_j^{-1} |u_j\rangle \langle u_j | b\rangle. \qquad (22.7)$$

How can we estimate the eigenvalues efficiently? We know that the function $e^{i \cdot A}$ with a Hermitian A is

$$U = e^{i \cdot A} = e^{i \cdot \lambda_1} \cdot |u_1\rangle \langle u_1| + e^{i \cdot \lambda_2} \cdot |u_2\rangle \langle u_2| + \cdots + e^{i \cdot \lambda_n} \cdot |u_n\rangle \langle u_n|. \qquad (22.8)$$

and

$$U^* = U^{-1} = e^{-i \cdot A} = e^{-i \cdot \lambda_1} \cdot |u_1\rangle \langle u_1| + e^{-i \cdot \lambda_2} \cdot |u_2\rangle \langle u_2| + \cdots + e^{-i \cdot \lambda_n} \cdot |u_n\rangle \langle u_n|. \qquad (22.9)$$

with

$$U \cdot U^* = I$$

Using Kitaev's phase estimation algorithm, we could estimate then unknown eigenvalue $e^{2 \cdot \pi \cdot i \cdot \theta_j}$ If we apply U to $|u_j\rangle$ we get

$$U \cdot |u\rangle = e^{2 \cdot \pi \cdot i \cdot \theta_j} \cdot |u_j\rangle = e^{i \cdot \lambda_j} \cdot |u_j\rangle \qquad (22.10)$$

We do not want to perform the decomposition of eigenvector and eigenvalues of A since this would lead to a circular problem.

22.2 ALGORITHM

We notice that we can

- This representation is similar to the evolutionary operator $U_t = e^{-i \cdot t \cdot H}$ for $t = 1$ and $A = H$ is the Hamiltonian operator. The process of implementing a given Hamiltonian evolution on quantum computer is called Hamiltonian simulation [58]. Hamiltonian simulation can be implemented efficiently for large if the Hermitian matrix H is sparse.

- We do not need to know the eigenvector $|u_j\rangle$ of U. Since a quantum state $|b\rangle$ can be decomposed into an orthogonal basis

$$|b\rangle = \sum_j |u_j\rangle \langle u_j | b\rangle = \sum_j \beta_j |u_j\rangle \qquad (22.11)$$

22.2.1 Hamiltonian Simulation

The process of implementing a given Hamiltonian evolution on quantum computer is called Hamiltonian simulation [58]

$$|x(t)\rangle = e^{-i \cdot t \cdot H} \cdot |x(0)\rangle = U_t \cdot |x(0)\rangle. \qquad (22.12)$$

The challenge is due to the fact that the application of matrix exponentials are computationally expensive [95]. Finding reliable and accurate methods to compute the matrix exponential is difficult, and this is still a topic of considerable current research.

22.2.1.1 Diagonalization

If the matrix H is diagonal

$$H = \begin{pmatrix} a_1 & 0 & \cdots & 0 \\ 0 & a_2 & \cdots & 0 \\ \vdots & \vdots & \ddots & \vdots \\ 0 & 0 & \cdots & a_n \end{pmatrix} \tag{22.13}$$

then its exponential can be obtained by exponentiating each entry on the main diagonal

$$e^H = \begin{pmatrix} e^{a_1} & 0 & \cdots & 0 \\ 0 & e^{a_2} & \cdots & 0 \\ \vdots & \vdots & \ddots & \vdots \\ 0 & 0 & \cdots & e^{a_n} \end{pmatrix} \tag{22.14}$$

This result also allows one to exponentiate diagonalizable matrices. If

$$H = U \cdot D \cdot U^{-1} \tag{22.15}$$

and D is diagonal, then

$$e^H = U \cdot e^D \cdot U^{-1} \tag{22.16}$$

22.2.1.2 Product Formulas

If the hamiltonian H can be written as

$$H = \sum_{k=1}^{L} H_k \tag{22.17}$$

and H_k commute,

$$H_j \cdot H_k = H_k \cdot H_j, \quad for \ all \ j,k$$

then

$$e^{-i \cdot t \cdot H} = e^{-i \cdot t \cdot H_1} \cdot e^{-i \cdot t \cdot H_2} \cdots e^{-i \cdot t \cdot H_L} \quad for \ all \ t. \tag{22.18}$$

General case: For general case of non-commuting H_k

$$e^{-i \cdot t \cdot H} \neq e^{-i \cdot t \cdot H_1} \cdot e^{-i \cdot t \cdot H_2} \cdots e^{-i \cdot t \cdot H_L} \quad for \ all \ t. \tag{22.19}$$

However for non-commuting H_k the following asymptotic Suzuki-Trotter formula (Lie product formula) is true for any real t.

$$e^{-i \cdot t \cdot H} = \lim_{m \to \infty} \left(e^{-i \cdot t \cdot H_1/m} \cdot e^{-i \cdot t \cdot H_2/m} \cdots e^{-i \cdot t \cdot H_L/m} \right)^m \tag{22.20}$$

or we can write equivalently

$$e^{-i \cdot t \cdot H} = e^{-i \cdot t \cdot H_1} \cdot e^{-i \cdot t \cdot H_2} \cdots e^{-i \cdot t \cdot H_L} + O(t^2) \tag{22.21}$$

For small t the factorization is approximately valid,

$$U_t = e^{-i \cdot t \cdot H} \approx e^{-i \cdot t \cdot H_1} \cdot e^{-i \cdot t \cdot H_2} \cdots e^{-i \cdot t \cdot H_L}. \tag{22.22}$$

22.2.2 Kitaev's Phase Estimation

After applying Kitaev's phase estimation algorithm to U that we estimated by the Hamiltonian simulation for each value j, the values $\tilde{\lambda}_{k|j}$ approximate the true value λ_j. For simplicity we assume

$$\sum_{j=1}^{n} \beta_j \sum_{k=0}^{T-1} \alpha_{k|j} \cdot |\tilde{\lambda}_{k|j}|u_j\rangle \approx \sum_{j=1}^{n} \beta_j \cdot |\tilde{\lambda}_j\rangle|u_j\rangle. \tag{22.23}$$

22.2.3 Conditioned Rotation

We add an auxiliary state $|0\rangle$

$$\sum_{j=1}^{n} \beta_j \cdot |\tilde{\lambda}_j\rangle|u_j\rangle|0\rangle \tag{22.24}$$

and perform the conditioned rotation on the auxiliary state $|0\rangle$ by the operator R

$$R = \begin{pmatrix} \cos\alpha & -\sin\alpha \\ \sin\alpha & \cos\alpha \end{pmatrix}. \tag{22.25}$$

with the relation

$$\alpha = \arccos\left(\frac{C}{\tilde{\lambda}}\right) \tag{22.26}$$

with C being a constant of normalization. For each eigenvalue indicates a special rotation we have

$$\sum_{j=1}^{n} \left(\beta_j \cdot |\tilde{\lambda}_j\rangle|u_j\rangle \left(R\left(\tilde{\lambda}_j^{-1}\right)|0\rangle\right)\right) =$$

$$\sum_{j=1}^{n} \left(\beta_j \cdot |\tilde{\lambda}_j\rangle|u_j\rangle \left(\frac{C}{\tilde{\lambda}_j}|1\rangle + \sqrt{1 - \frac{C^2}{\tilde{\lambda}_j^2}}|0\rangle\right)\right). \tag{22.27}$$

22.2.4 Un-Computation

We un-compute the phase estimation procedure with $F_m = IF_m$, CU^* resulting in the state

$$|0\rangle \sum_{j=1}^{n} \left(\beta_j \cdot |u_j\rangle \left(\frac{C}{\tilde{\lambda}_j}|1\rangle + \sqrt{1 - \frac{C^2}{\tilde{\lambda}_j^2}}|0\rangle\right)\right) =$$

$$|0\rangle \sum_{j=1}^{n} \left(C \cdot \frac{\beta_j}{\tilde{\lambda}_j}|u_j\rangle|1\rangle + \sqrt{1 - \frac{C^2}{\tilde{\lambda}_j^2}} \cdot \beta_j|u_j\rangle|0\rangle\right). \tag{22.28}$$

22.2.5 Measurement

By measuring the auxiliary qubit with the result 0, we get

$$|0\rangle \sum_{j=1}^{n} \left(\sqrt{1 - \frac{C^2}{\tilde{\lambda}_j^2}} \cdot \beta_j |u_j\rangle \right) \tag{22.29}$$

and with the result 1

$$C \cdot |0\rangle \sum_{j=1}^{n} \left(\frac{\beta_j}{\tilde{\lambda}_j} |u_j\rangle \right) = C \cdot |0\rangle A^{-1}|b\rangle \approx C \cdot |0\rangle |x\rangle. \tag{22.30}$$

We have to select the outcome of the measurement 1.

$$|x\rangle = A^{-1}|b\rangle = \sum_{j=1}^{n} \frac{\beta_j}{\tilde{\lambda}_j} |u_j\rangle \tag{22.31}$$

22.2.6 Obtaining the Solution

Obtaining the required coefficient x_i from $|x\rangle$ would require at least n measurements, so the complexity of the algorithm would be $O(n)$ which problematic since the cost on a classical computer for an approximate solution for a sparse matrix via conjugate gradient descent are equivalent. Many applications are interested in the global properties of $|x\rangle$ rather than the coefficients x_i. Many features describing the vector $|x\rangle$ can be extracted efficiently, like for example values in different parts. We can as well efficiently estimate if two solutions of two different equations are the same or not [39].

22.3 EXAMPLE

$$A = \begin{pmatrix} 1 & -\frac{1}{3} \\ -\frac{1}{3} & 1 \end{pmatrix}, \quad \mathbf{b} = \begin{pmatrix} 1 \\ 0 \end{pmatrix}. \tag{22.32}$$

with eigenvectors

$$\mathbf{u}_1 = \frac{1}{\sqrt{2}} \cdot \begin{pmatrix} 1 \\ -1 \end{pmatrix}, \quad \mathbf{u}_2 = \frac{1}{\sqrt{2}} \cdot \begin{pmatrix} 1 \\ 1 \end{pmatrix}. \tag{22.33}$$

and eigenvalues

$$\lambda_1 = \frac{4}{3}, \quad \lambda_2 = \frac{2}{3}.$$

It follows

$$U = e^{i \cdot \frac{4}{3}} \cdot |u_1\rangle\langle u_1| + e^{i \cdot \frac{2}{3}} \cdot |u_2\rangle\langle u_2| = \begin{pmatrix} \frac{1}{2}e^{\frac{2i}{3}} + \frac{1}{2}e^{\frac{4i}{3}} & \frac{1}{2}e^{\frac{2i}{3}} - \frac{1}{2}e^{\frac{4i}{3}} \\ \frac{1}{2}e^{\frac{2i}{3}} - \frac{1}{2}e^{\frac{4i}{3}} & \frac{1}{2}e^{\frac{2i}{3}} + \frac{1}{2}e^{\frac{4i}{3}} \end{pmatrix} \tag{22.34}$$

and

$$U^* = e^{-i \cdot \frac{4}{3}} \cdot |u_1\rangle\langle u_1| + e^{-i \cdot \frac{2}{3}} \cdot |u_2\rangle\langle u_2| = \begin{pmatrix} \frac{1}{2}e^{\frac{-2i}{3}} + \frac{1}{2}e^{\frac{-4i}{3}} & \frac{1}{2}e^{\frac{-2i}{3}} - \frac{1}{2}e^{\frac{-4i}{3}} \\ \frac{1}{2}e^{\frac{-2i}{3}} - \frac{1}{2}e^{\frac{-4i}{3}} & \frac{1}{2}e^{\frac{-2i}{3}} + \frac{1}{2}e^{\frac{-4i}{3}} \end{pmatrix} \tag{22.35}$$

22.3.1   Kitaev's Phase Estimation to Hamiltonian Simulation

Using Kitaev's phase estimation algorithm, we get the relation

$$U \cdot |u\rangle = e^{2 \cdot \pi \cdot i \cdot \theta_j} \cdot |u_j\rangle$$

By using Hamiltonian simulation, the relation is

$$U_t \cdot |u\rangle = e^{-i \cdot t \cdot \lambda_j} \cdot |u_j\rangle.$$

We will use during Kitaev's phase estimation algorithm QFT instead of the inverse QFT to deal with the minus sign. In this case the relation becomes

$$e^{2 \cdot \pi \cdot i \cdot \theta_j} \cdot |u_j\rangle = e^{i \cdot t \cdot \lambda_j} \cdot |u_j\rangle$$

with

$$\theta_j = \frac{\lambda_j \cdot t}{2 \cdot \pi}$$

In our simulation, we will use two qubits in the control register and we chose $t = 2 \cdot \pi/8$ and we get

$$\theta_j = \frac{3}{8} \cdot \lambda_j$$

with

$$\theta_1 = \frac{3}{8} \cdot \frac{4}{3} = \frac{2}{4}, \qquad \theta_2 = \frac{3}{8} \cdot \frac{2}{3} = \frac{1}{4}$$

with measured two control qubits being $|10\rangle$ representing 2 and $|01\rangle$ representing 1

$$\theta = 0.x_2 x_1 = \frac{x}{4} = \frac{x}{2^2}.$$

We represent

$$|b\rangle = |0\rangle = \mathbf{b} = \begin{pmatrix} 1 \\ 0 \end{pmatrix}$$

with

$$|u_1\rangle = \frac{|0\rangle - |1\rangle}{\sqrt{2}}, \qquad |u_2\rangle = \frac{|0\rangle + |1\rangle}{\sqrt{2}}$$

and with

$$|b\rangle = \sum_j \beta_j |u_j\rangle = |0\rangle = \frac{1}{\sqrt{2}} \cdot |u_1\rangle + \frac{1}{\sqrt{2}} \cdot |u_2\rangle$$

$$|b\rangle = \frac{1}{\sqrt{2}} \cdot \frac{|0\rangle - |1\rangle}{\sqrt{2}} + \frac{1}{\sqrt{2}} \cdot \frac{|0\rangle + |1\rangle}{\sqrt{2}} = |0\rangle.$$

We will use *qiskit* command HamiltonianGate [21] where data is a Hermitian matrix A is represented and time $t = 2 \cdot \pi/8$ to perform Hamiltonian evolution and use QFT instead of inverse QFT (see Figure 22.1).

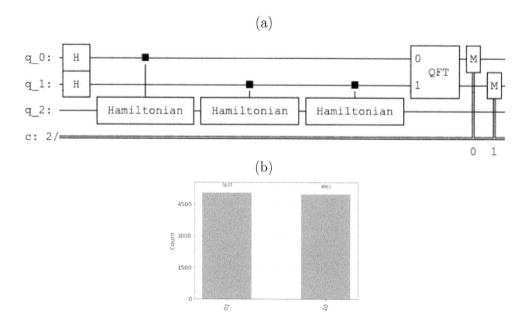

Figure 22.1 (a) Circuit estimating U_t by Hamiltonian simulation with accuracy of two qubits. The circuit is composed of 3 qubits, qubits 0, 1, represent the control register and qubit 2 represents $b = |0\rangle$. To estimate the phase θ, we perform QFT to the 2 control qubits. (b) The measured values correspond to the binary values 10 and 01.

```python
from qiskit import QuantumCircuit, Aer, execute
from qiskit.visualization import plot_histogram
from math import pi
from qiskit.quantum_info import Operator
from qiskit.extensions import HamiltonianGate

from qiskit.circuit.library import QFT
qft = QFT(2, inverse=False).to_gate()
qft.label = "QFT"

op = Operator([[1, -1/3],[-1/3, 1]])
# create gate which evolves according to exp(-i*op*3*pi/4)
gate = HamiltonianGate(op,3*pi/4).control()

qc = QuantumCircuit(3,2)
qc.h([0,1])
# apply gate to qubits [0, 1, 2] in circuit
qc.append(gate, [0,2])
qc.append(gate, [1,2])
qc.append(gate, [1,2])
# Do QFT on counting qubits
qc.append(qft, [0,1])
# Measure counting qubits
qc.measure([0,1], [0,1])
```

```
simulator = Aer.get_backend('qasm_simulator')
result=execute(qc,simulator,shots=10000).result()
counts = result.get_counts()
plot_histogram(counts)
```

22.3.2 Conditioned Rotation and Un-Computation

We perform conditioned rotation on the auxiliary state $|0\rangle$ by

$$R_Y(\alpha) = \begin{pmatrix} \cos\left(\frac{\alpha}{2}\right) & -\sin\left(\frac{\alpha}{2}\right) \\ \sin\left(\frac{\alpha}{2}\right) & \cos\left(\frac{\alpha}{2}\right) \end{pmatrix}$$

with measured two control qubits being $|10\rangle$ representing $\tilde{\lambda}_1 = 2$ and $|01\rangle$ representing $\tilde{\lambda}_2 = 1$,

$$\alpha_1 = 2 \cdot \arccos\left(\frac{1}{\tilde{\lambda}_1}\right) = 2 \cdot \arccos\left(\frac{1}{2}\right) = \frac{\pi}{3} \tag{22.36}$$

$$\alpha_2 = 2 \cdot \arccos\left(\frac{1}{\tilde{\lambda}_2}\right)) = 2 \cdot \arccos\left(\frac{1}{1}\right) = \pi \tag{22.37}$$

using a conditional RY gate controlled by $\tilde{\lambda}$ represented by qubits 1 and 2, then we un-compute. The result is represented in the qubit 3 in the case the qubit 0 is one (see Figure 22.2).

```
from qiskit import QuantumCircuit, Aer, execute
from qiskit.quantum_info import Statevector
from qiskit.visualization import plot_histogram
from math import pi
from qiskit.quantum_info import Operator
from qiskit.extensions import HamiltonianGate

from qiskit.circuit.library import QFT
qft = QFT(2, inverse=False).to_gate()
qft.label = "QFT"
qft_dagger = QFT(2, inverse=True).to_gate()
qft_dagger.label = "QFTȨ"

op = Operator([[1, -1/3],[-1/3, 1]])
#op = Operator([[1, 0],[0, 1]])
# create gate which evolves according to exp(-i*op*3*pi/4)
gate = HamiltonianGate(op,3*pi/4).control()
gate_daggar = HamiltonianGate(op,3*pi/4).inverse().control()
qc = QuantumCircuit(4)
qc.h([1,2])

# apply gate to qubits [0, 1, 2] in circuit
qc.append(gate, [1,3])

qc.append(gate, [2,3])
qc.append(gate, [2,3])
```

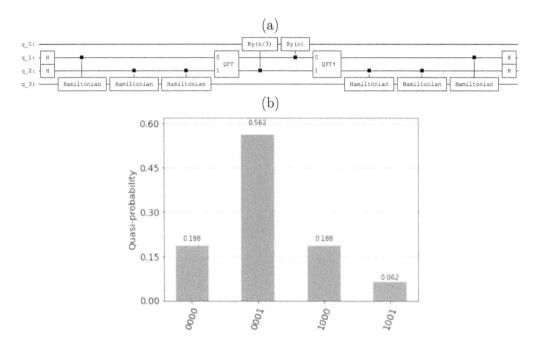

Figure 22.2 (a) The HHL circuit, we perform conditioned rotation on the auxiliary state $|0\rangle$ using a RY gate controlled by $\tilde{\lambda}$ represented by qubits 1 and 2, then we un-compute. (b) The measured result of our small HHL simulation is represented in the qubit 3 if the qubit 0 is one, with the probability values 0.562 and 0.0622.

```
# Do QFT on counting qubits
qc.append(qft, [1,2])

#rotate
#10
qc.cry(pi/3,2,0)
#01
qc.cry(pi,1,0)

#un-computing
qc.append(qft_dagger, [1,2])

qc.append(gate_daggar, [2,3])
qc.append(gate_daggar, [2,3])

qc.append(gate_daggar, [1,3])
qc.h([1,2])

simulator = Aer.get_backend('statevector_simulator')
# Run and get counts
result=execute(qc,simulator).result()
counts = result.get_counts()
plot_histogram(counts)
```

22.3.3 Obtaining the Solution

The solution to the problem

$$A = \begin{pmatrix} 1 & -\frac{1}{3} \\ -\frac{1}{3} & 1 \end{pmatrix}, \quad b = \begin{pmatrix} 1 \\ 0 \end{pmatrix}.$$

is represented by

$$A^{-1} = \begin{pmatrix} \frac{9}{8} & \frac{3}{8} \\ \frac{3}{8} & \frac{9}{8} \end{pmatrix}, \quad x = \begin{pmatrix} \frac{9}{8} \\ \frac{3}{8} \end{pmatrix}.$$

with the normalized vector being

$$x_n = \frac{x}{\|x\|} = \begin{pmatrix} 0.948683 \\ 0.316228 \end{pmatrix}.$$

The measured result of our small HHL simulation is represented in the qubit 3 in the case the qubit 0 is one (see Figure 22.2 (b))

$$x_m^2 = \begin{pmatrix} \frac{0.56}{0.562+0.0622} \\ \frac{0.0622}{0.562+0.062} \end{pmatrix}$$

with the measured value being

$$x_m = \begin{pmatrix} 0.948869 \\ 0.31567 \end{pmatrix} \approx x_n = \begin{pmatrix} 0.948683 \\ 0.316228 \end{pmatrix}.$$

Obtaining the required coefficient x_i from $|x\rangle$ would require at least n measurements, so the complexity of the algorithm would be $O(n)$ which is problematic since the cost on a classical computer for an approximate solution for a sparse matrix via conjugate gradient descent are equivalent. Many applications are interested in the global properties of $|x\rangle$ rather than the coefficients x_i. For example, we can as well efficiently estimate if two solutions of two different equations are the same or not [39].

22.4 CONSTRAINTS

In quantum we can efficiently determine the eigenvectors and eigenvalues by the Kitaev's phase estimation algorithm and the Hamiltonian simulation [39]. We will compute

$$x = A \cdot b \tag{22.38}$$

or

$$x = A^{-1} \cdot b. \tag{22.39}$$

We assume A is Hermitian. In the case A is not Hermitian, we define

$$A' = \begin{pmatrix} 0 & A \\ A^* & 0 \end{pmatrix}, \quad b' = \begin{pmatrix} 0 \\ b \end{pmatrix}, \quad x' = \begin{pmatrix} x \\ 0 \end{pmatrix}. \tag{22.40}$$

and

$$A' \cdot x' = b'. \tag{22.41}$$

with the constraints :

- The vectors $|b\rangle$, $|x\rangle$ have the length one in the l_2 norm. $|b\rangle$ is represented by $\log_2 n$ qubits with

$$|b\rangle = \frac{\sum_{i=1}^{n} b_i|i\rangle}{\|\sum_{i=1}^{n} b_i|i\rangle\|} \tag{22.42}$$

and

$$|x\rangle = \frac{\sum_{i=1}^{n} x_i|i\rangle}{\|\sum_{i=1}^{n} x_i|i\rangle\|}. \tag{22.43}$$

- $|b\rangle$ has to be prepared efficiently with the cost $\log(n)$. For example being constant with $H_{\log_2 n} \cdot |0\rangle$.

- The matrix A is sparse.

- For the output we are interested in the global properties of $|x\rangle$ rather than the coefficients x_i.

We will use the shorthand notation (Bachmann-Landau notation) since it mostly used in the related literature with

$$\tilde{O}(f(n)) = O(f(n)poly(\log(f(n)))) = O(f(n)\log(f(n))^k) \tag{22.44}$$

for some k ignoring logarithmic factors. The point of that notation is to only show the important part of the asymptotic complexity. If the constraints are fulfilled then we can find the estimate of solution in $\tilde{O}(\log n)$. Gauss elimination requires $O(n^3)$ and approximate solution for a sparse matrix via conjugate gradient descent requires $\tilde{O}(n)$ [81]. Taking into account the constraints the HHL algorithm on a quantum computer is exponentially faster than any algorithm that solves linear systems on the classical computer [39].

## CHAPTER 23

Hybrid Approaches – Variational Classification

Variational approaches are characterized using a classical optimization algorithm to iteratively update a parameterized quantum trial solution also called ansatz (from German Ansatz = approach). The parameterized quantum trial solution is defined by a parametrized quantum circuit like for example the $ZZFeatureMap$. We indicate the basic principles of a variational classifier by a simple example. Then we describe the cross entropy loss function and the Simultaneous Perturbation Stochastic Approximation (SPSA). The optimizer performs stochastic gradient approximation, which requires only two measurements of the loss function. $Qiskit$ implements the variational quantum classifier (VQC) that can be embedded in classical machine learning tasks. We indicate a simple example of the VQC classifier whose learning is based on SPSA.

23.1 VARIATIONAL CLASSIFICATION

The variational quantum classifier for a binary classification problem, with input data vectors $\mathbf{x}_k$ of dimension m and binary output labels t_k with a training set

$$D = \{(\mathbf{x}_1, t_1), (\mathbf{x}_2, t_2), \cdots, , (\mathbf{x}_N, t_N)\}, \quad t_k \in \{0, 1\}.$$

For each input data vector $\mathbf{x}_k$ a quantum feature maps encodes classical data into quantum data via a parametrized quantum circuit [95]. circuit $U_{\phi(\mathbf{x}_k)}$ with m parameters

$$U_{\phi(\mathbf{x})_k}|0\rangle^{\otimes m}. \tag{23.1}$$

Additionally, we will use a variational quantum circuits that represents the free parameter $\mathbf{w}$ that will adapt during training

$$|\psi(\mathbf{x}_k, \mathbf{w})\rangle = U_{W(\mathbf{w})} \cdot U_{\phi(\mathbf{x})_k}|0\rangle^{\otimes m}. \tag{23.2}$$

We measure the state $|\psi(\mathbf{x}_k, \mathbf{w})\rangle$ with some basis state $|q_m \cdots q_1 q_0\rangle$ representing a binary string. We define the binary output from the binary string by a parity function. A parity function is a Boolean function whose value is one if and only if the input vector has an odd number of ones. The m-variable parity function is the Boolean function $f \in \{0, 1\}$

$$f(q) = q_m \oplus q_{m-1} \oplus \cdots \oplus q_1 \oplus q_0 \tag{23.3}$$

where $\oplus$ denotes exclusive or. For each input data vector $\mathbf{x}_k$ we determine the output function $o_k \in [0, 1]$ representing the probability distribution of odd number of ones in basis state $|q_m \cdots q_1 q_0\rangle$. Alternatively we could as well try to estimate the probability of o_k the by the inversion test

$$o_k = |\langle \phi(\mathbf{x}) | \phi(\mathbf{y}) \rangle|^2 = |\langle 0^{\otimes m} | U_{\phi(\mathbf{y})}^\dagger | U_{\phi(\mathbf{x})} | 0^{\otimes m} \rangle|^2 \tag{23.4}$$

Assuming two opposite classes C_1 and C_2, we can interpret the probability of class C_1 given the input

$$p(C_1 | \mathbf{x}_k) = o_k, \quad p(C_2 | \mathbf{x}_k) = 1 - p(C_1 | \mathbf{x}_k). \tag{23.5}$$

In the training phase, we're trying to find the values for $\mathbf{w}$ using an optimizer on a classical computer.

23.1.1 Example

We use the parameterized *qiskit* quantum circuit over two qubits $U_{\phi(\mathbf{x})} = ZZFeatureMap$ [21] with repetition two where the parameter are defined by the data by the command *bind_parameters* with the two-dimensional vector $\mathbf{x}$. The variational quantum circuits that represents the free parameter $\mathbf{w}$ that will adapt during training is the *qiskit* quantum circuit $U_{W(\mathbf{w})} = TwoLocal$. The *TwoLocal* circuit is a parameterized circuit consisting of alternating rotation layers and entanglement layers. The rotation layers are single qubit gates applied on all qubits. The entanglement layer uses two-qubit gates to entangle the qubits according to the definition. In our example, we will use the rotation gates RX and RZ and the entanglement gate controlled Z rotation, CZ, with two repetitions resulting in 12 free parameters. The twelve-dimensional vector $\mathbf{w}$ defines the parameters by the *bind_parameters* command. After the operations we measure the two qubits (see Figure 23.1)

```
from qiskit import QuantumCircuit,QuantumRegister, Aer,execute
from qiskit.visualization import plot_histogram
import numpy as np
from qiskit.circuit.library import ZZFeatureMap, TwoLocal

x = [0.1, 0.1]
feature_map = ZZFeatureMap(feature_dimension=2, reps=2)
feature_map = feature_map.bind_parameters(x)
weights =np.array([3.28559355, 5.48514978, 5.13099949,
                   0.88372228, 4.08885928, 2.45568528,
                   4.92364593, 5.59032015, 3.66837805,
                   4.84632313, 3.60713748, 2.43546])
two_local = TwoLocal(2, ['ry', 'rz'],'cz', reps=2)
two_local = two_local.bind_parameters(weights)

qc = QuantumCircuit(2,2)
qc.compose(feature_map, inplace=True)
```

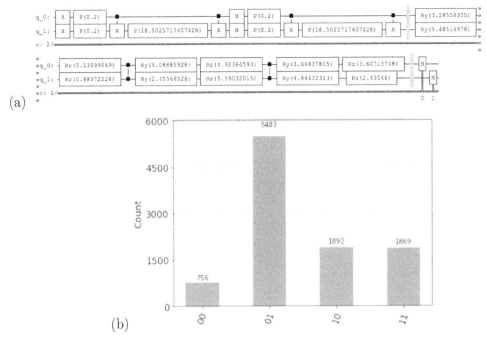

(a)

(b)

Figure 23.1 (a) We use the parameterized over two qubits $U_{\phi(\mathbf{x})} = ZZFeatureMap$ with repetition two. The $TwoLocal$ circuit is a parameterized circuit consisting of alternating rotation layers and entanglement layers. The rotation layers are single qubit gates applied on all qubits. The entanglement layer uses two-qubit gates to entangle the qubits according to the definition. In our example, we will use the rotation gates RX and RZ and the entanglement gate controlled Z rotation, CZ, with two repetitions resulting in 12 free parameters. (b) We perform 10000 shots. The string 01 appears 5483 times and the string 10 appears 1892. We define the binary output from the binary string by a parity function, $p(1) = o_k = (5483 + 1892)/1000 = 0.7375$.

```
qc.barrier()
qc.compose(two_local, inplace=True)
qc.barrier()
qc.measure(0,0)
qc.measure(1,1)

simulator = Aer.get_backend('qasm_simulator')
result=execute(qc,simulator,shots=10000).result()
counts = result.get_counts()
print("\nTotal count are:",counts)
plot_histogram(counts)
```

We define the binary output from the binary string by a parity function, see Figure 23.1 (b). We perform 10000 shots. The string 01 appears 5483 times and the string 10 appears 1892, $p(1) = o_k = (5483 + 1892)/1000 = 0.7375$.

23.2 CROSS ENTROPY LOSS FUNCTION

For a given example, we can   measure the likelihood that a variational quantum circuit, with a given set of weights has generated a given output for a given input

$$p(t_k|\mathbf{w}, \mathbf{x}_k) = Bernoulli\left(p(C_1|\mathbf{x}_k)\right) \tag{23.6}$$

$$p(t_k|\mathbf{w}, \mathbf{x}_k) = p(C_1|\mathbf{x}_k)^{t_k} \cdot (1 - p(C_1|\mathbf{x}_k))^{1-t_k} \tag{23.7}$$

Given that we know how to write the likelihood of one example [121] and if we assume that the data are independent, we can write the likelihood for the whole data set by simply multiplying the individual likelihoods

$$p(\mathbf{t}|\mathbf{x}_1, \cdots, \mathbf{x}_N, \mathbf{w}) = \prod_{k=1}^{N} p(C_1|\mathbf{x}_k)^{t_k} \cdot (1 - p(C_1|\mathbf{x}_k))^{1-t_k} \tag{23.8}$$

with

$$o_k = p(C_1|\mathbf{x}_k) = \sigma\left(\mathbf{w}^T \cdot \mathbf{x}_k\right) = \sigma(net_k), \tag{23.9}$$

we can simply write

$$p(\mathbf{t}|\mathbf{x}_1, \cdots, \mathbf{x}_N, \mathbf{w}) = \prod_{k=1}^{N} o_k^{t_k} \cdot (1 - o_k)^{1-t_k}. \tag{23.10}$$

Having the likelihood, we can estimate the weights such that the likelihood is maximized. This is equivalent to minimizing the negative log likelihood, yielding the loss function

$$L(\mathbf{w}) = -\log(p(\mathbf{t}|\mathbf{w})) = -\sum_{k=1}^{N} \left(t_k \log o_k + (1 - t_k) \log(1 - o_k)\right). \tag{23.11}$$

The resulting loss function is exactly the cross entropy between targets and output

$$H(t, p) = -\sum_{k=1}^{N} \left(t_k \cdot \log(p(C_1|\mathbf{x}_k)) + \neg t_k \cdot \log(p(C_2|\mathbf{x}_k))\right).$$

23.2.1 Multi-Class Loss Function

Assuming that the training set consists of N observations

$$X = (\mathbf{x}_1, \mathbf{x}_2, \cdots, \mathbf{x}_k, \cdots, \mathbf{x}_N)^T$$

and respective target values represented as vectors of dimension K (since t is used as an index, we will use y_{kt} to indicate the specific target)

$$Y = (\mathbf{y}_1, \mathbf{y}_2, \cdots, \mathbf{y}_k, \cdots, \mathbf{y}_N)^T.$$

During training, each variational quantum circuit is trained individually with its target value y_{kt}

$$y_{kt} \in \{0, 1\}, \quad \sum_{t=1}^{K} y_{kt} = 1$$

The resulting cross entropy loss function is given by

$$L(\mathbf{w}) = -\sum_{k=1}^{N}\sum_{t=1}^{K} y_{kt} \cdot \log o_{kt}, \tag{23.12}$$

23.3 SPSA OPTIMIZER

Simultaneous Perturbation Stochastic Approximation (SPSA) optimizer performs stochastic gradient approximation ($https://www.jhuapl.edu/SPSA/$), which requires only two measurements of the loss function, regardless of the dimension of the optimization problem [13]. The goal is to find

$$\mathbf{w}^* = \arg\min_{\mathbf{w}} L(\mathbf{w}) \tag{23.13}$$

with the gradient operator is

$$\nabla = \left[\frac{\partial}{\partial w_1}, \frac{\partial}{\partial w_2}, \cdots, \frac{\partial}{\partial w_D}\right]^T$$

$$g(\mathbf{w}) = \nabla L(\mathbf{w}) = \left[\frac{\partial L}{\partial w_1}, \frac{\partial L}{\partial w_2}, \cdots, \frac{\partial L}{\partial w_D}\right]^T.$$

SPSA use the iterative process with τ indicating the iteration starting at $\tau = 1$ with

$$\mathbf{w}_{\tau+1} = \mathbf{w}_\tau - \eta_\tau \cdot \hat{g}_\tau(\mathbf{w}_\tau) \tag{23.14}$$

with η_τ being the learning rate that converges to zero and $\hat{g}_\tau(\mathbf{w}_\tau)$ estimation of the gradient $g\tau(\mathbf{w}_\tau)$ with

$$\hat{g}_\tau = \frac{L(\mathbf{w}_\tau + c_\tau \cdot \Delta_\tau) - L(\mathbf{w}_\tau - c_\tau \cdot \Delta_\tau)}{2 \cdot c_\tau \cdot \Delta_\tau}. \tag{23.15}$$

Δ_τ is a random perturbation vector and c_τ is a small positive number that decreases with τ. The number of loss function measurements needed in the SPSA method for each is always 2, independent of the dimension. SPSA with the random search direction does not follow y the gradient path but approximates it. Ween using a variational classifier on l quantum computer SPSA is therefore the most recommended choice since it can be used in the presence of noise.

23.3.1 *Qiskit* Variational Quantum Classifier

Qiskit implements the variational quantum classifier (VQC) that can be embedded in classical machine learning tasks.

In this simple *qiskit* example, we create 10 two-dimensional training data points and 5 testing data points for two classes each. We use the same classification circuit as before. We one hot encode our labels, as required by the algorithm using cross entropy. Then, we set up our classical optimizer and the VQC algorithm using the callback function. We plot the cost function with respect to optimization step,

```
from qiskit.utils import algorithm_globals
algorithm_globals.random_seed = 3142

import numpy as np
np.random.seed(algorithm_globals.random_seed)

from qiskit_machine_learning.datasets import ad_hoc_data
TRAIN_DATA, TRAIN_LABELS, TEST_DATA, TEST_LABELS = (
    ad_hoc_data(training_size=10,
                test_size=5,
                n=2,
                gap=0.3,
                one_hot=False)
from qiskit.circuit.library import ZZFeatureMap, TwoLocal
FEATURE_MAP = ZZFeatureMap(feature_dimension=2, reps=2)
VAR_FORM = TwoLocal(2, ['ry', 'rz'], 'cz', reps=2)
AD_HOC_CIRCUIT = FEATURE_MAP.compose(VAR_FORM)

from sklearn.preprocessing import OneHotEncoder
encoder = OneHotEncoder()
train_labels_oh = encoder.fit_transform(TRAIN_LABELS.reshape(-1, 1)
                                        ).toarray()
test_labels_oh = encoder.fit_transform(TEST_LABELS.reshape(-1, 1)
                                       ).toarray()

from qiskit.algorithms.optimizers import SPSA

class OptimizerLog:
    """Log to store optimizer's intermediate results"""
    def __init__(self):
        self.evaluations = []
        self.parameters = []
        self.costs = []
    def update(self, evaluation, parameter, cost, _stepsize, _accept):
        """Save intermediate results. Optimizer passes five values
        but we ignore the last two."""
        self.evaluations.append(evaluation)
        self.parameters.append(parameter)
        self.costs.append(cost)

#initial_point = np.random.random(VAR_FORM.num_parameters)
initial_point = np.array([0.3200227 , 0.6503638 , 0.55995053,
                          0.96566328, 0.38243769, 0.90403094,
                          0.82271449, 0.26810137, 0.61076489,
                          0.82301609, 0.11789148, 0.29667125])

from qiskit_machine_learning.algorithms.classifiers import VQC
log = OptimizerLog()
vqc = VQC(feature_map=FEATURE_MAP,
          ansatz=VAR_FORM,
          loss='cross_entropy',
```

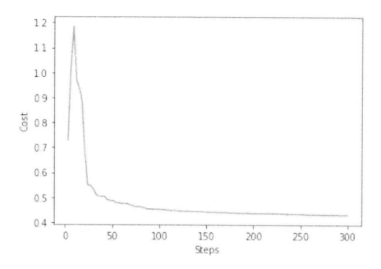

Figure 23.2 Thee cost function with respect to optimization step converges to a minimum.

```
        optimizer=SPSA(callback=log.update),
        initial_point=initial_point)

vqc.fit(TRAIN_DATA, train_labels_oh)

import matplotlib.pyplot as plt
fig = plt.figure()
plt.plot(log.evaluations, log.costs)
plt.xlabel('Steps')
plt.ylabel('Cost')
plt.show()
```

We plot the cost function with respect to optimization step, we can see it starts to converge to a minimum, see Figure 23.2. Finally we test our trained VQC classifier by score.

```
# score == accuracy
vqc.score(TEST_DATA, test_labels_oh)
```

Score indicates the mean accuracy, it determines for the test set true values, in our case the score is 0.9.

## CHAPTER 24

Conclusion

We conclude our journey with quantum artificial intelligence (QAI). A quantum computer is a computer that exploits quantum mechanical phenomena such as superposition and entanglement. The quantum advantage is based on two principles related to Grover's algorithm and the phase estimation algorithm. Quantum computing is still in its early stages, and there are many technical challenges that must be overcome before it can be used to implement QAI. However, for the quantum computing the race is on, what was a scientific dream some years ago, is becoming more real. You are now at the forefront of the revolution in quantum computing.

24.1 EPILOGUE

Quantum computation with the quantum gate model is based on principles to speed up the computation: that lead to quantum advantage

- Grover's algorithm can speed up the search quadratically for a given number of possible solutions.

- The QFT can determine the period of a wave or be the basis of the phase estimation algorithm.

- Variational Classifier can compute functions in extremely high dimensional space that cannot be done easily by conventional computers.

Most quantum machine learning algorithms suffer from the input destruction problem [1]. The efficient preparation of data is possible in part for sparse data [39]. However, the input destruction problem has not yet been solved, and theoretical speed-ups are usually analyzed [94] by ignoring the input problem, which is the main bottleneck for data encoding. The costs of data preparation, in which data points must be read, and the query time are represented by two phases that are analyzed independently; the quantum computing approach has advantages in solving such problems. Linear algebra-based quantum machine learning is based on quantum gates that describe basic quantum linear algebra subroutines. These subroutines can achieve theoretical exponential speedups over their classical counterparts and are essential for machine learning. Basic quantum linear algebra subroutines use a quantum

DOI: 10.1201/9781003374404-24

coprocessor for extensive and nontrackable computation routines in machine learning. Such "mathematical" quantum coprocessors can be used on a conventional computer.

Quantum supremacy means that programmable quantum devices can solve a problem that no classical computer can solve in any feasible amount of time. Quantum computers will dominate when enough qubits are available. Such gains in computing power could change every aspect of our lives in the future.

Even without quantum supremacy, the quantum computing approach leads to easier formulation of certain algorithms, such as certain feature maps that are difficult to handle. Quantum computing creates a new way of thinking, making it possible to perform calculations that could not be considered before. The face of the world could be changed forever.

24.2 FURTHER READING

The most important books about quantum computing which you should not miss are [72] and [47].

For a brighter mathematical coverage and the description of the adiabatic quantum computation and quantum annealing, you can consult the book [119]. Adiabatic quantum computation is an alternative approach to quantum computation and is based on the time evolution of a quantum system and is a polynomial equivalent to the quantum gate model. Quantum annealing on the other hand solves optimization problems.

Finally, if you are interested in the philosophical consequences and the interpretation of quantum physics itself motivated by the experiments that you performed on your computer, you would be maybe interested in my other book "Mind, Brain, Quantum AI, and the Multiverse" [120].

Bibliography

[1] S. Aaronson. Quantum machine learning algorithms: Read the fine print. *Nature Physics*, 11:291–293, 2015.

[2] Dorit Aharonov. *Noisy Quantum Computation*. PhD thesis, Hebrew University, July 1999.

[3] E Aïmeur, B. Brassard, and S Gambs. Quantum speed-up for unsupervised learning. *Machine Learning*, 90:261–287, 2013.

[4] Igor Aizenberg, Naum N. Aizenberg, and Joos P.L. Vandewalle. *Multi-Valued and Universal Binary Neurons*. Springer, 2000.

[5] Shun'ichi Amari. Learning patterns and pattern sequences by self-organizing nets of threshold elements. *IEEE Transactions on Computers*, C-21(11):1197–1206, 1972.

[6] James A. Anderson. *An Introduction to Neural Networks*. The MIT Press, 1995.

[7] John R. Anderson. *Cognitive Psychology and its Implications*. W. H. Freeman and Company, fourth edition, 1995.

[8] Israel F. Araujo, Daniel K. Park, Francesco Petruccione, and Adenilton J. da Silva. A divide-and-conquer algorithm for quantum state preparation. *Scientific Reports*, 11(6329), 2021.

[9] W. Aspray. *John von Neumann and the origins of modern computing*. History of computing. MIT Press, 1990.

[10] Dana H. Ballard. *An Introduction to Natural Computation*. The MIT Press, 1997.

[11] Charles H. Bennett, Ethan Bernstein, Gilles Brassard, and Umesh Vazirani. Strengths and weaknesses of quantum computing, 1997.

[12] Charles H. Bennett, Gilles Brassard, Claude Crépeau, Richard Jozsa, Asher Peres, and William K. Wootters. Teleporting an unknown quantum state via dual classical and einstein-podolsky-rosen channels. *Phys. Rev. Lett.*, 70(13):1895–1899, Mar 1993.

[13] S. Bhatnagar, H. L. Prasad, and L. A Prashanth. *Stochastic Recursive Algorithms for Optimization: Simultaneous Perturbation Methods*. Springer, 2013.

[14] Michel Boyer, Gilles Brassard, Peter Hoeyer, and Alain Tapp. Tight bounds on quantum searching. *Fortschritte der Physik*, 46:493, 1998.

[15] G. Brassard, P. Hoyer, M. Mosca, and A. Tapp. Quantum Amplitude Amplification and Estimation. *eprint arXiv:quant-ph/0005055*, May 2000.

[16] Gilles Brassard, Peter Hoyer, and Alain Tapp. Quantum counting, 1998.

[17] L. Brownston, R. Farell, E. Kant, and N. Martin. *Programming Expert Systems in OPS5: An Introduction to Rule-Based Programming.* Addison-Wesley, 1985.

[18] S. Brunak and B. Lautrup. *Neural Networks Computers with Intuition.* World Scientific, 1990.

[19] Arthur E. Bryson and Yu-Ch Ho. *Applied optimal control : optimization, estimation, and control.* Blaisdell Pub. Co., 1969.

[20] Peter Byrne. The many worlds of hugh everett. *Scientific American Magazine*, pages 98–105, December 2007.

[21] Qiskit contributors. Qiskit: An open-source framework for quantum computing. 10.5281/zenodo.2573505, 2023.

[22] T. H. Cormen, C. E. Leiserson, L. R. Rivest, and C. Stein. *Introduction to Algorithms.* Second. MIT Press, 2001.

[23] Thomas H. Cormen, Charles E. Leiserson, Ronald L. Rivest, and Clifford Stein. *Introduction to Algorithms, 2/e.* MIT Press, 2001.

[24] Corinna Cortes and Vladimir Vapnik. Support-vector networks. *Machine Learning*, 20:273–297, 1995.

[25] Rina Dechter. Learning while searching in constraint-satisfaction problems. In *AAAI-86 Proceedings*, pages 178–183, 1986.

[26] D. Deutsch and R. Jozsa. Rapid Solution of Problems by Quantum Computation. *Royal Society of London Proceedings Series A*, 439:553–558, December 1992.

[27] David Deutsch. *The Fabric of Reality.* Penguin Group, 1997.

[28] Hugh Everett. "Relative state" formulation of quantum mechanics. *Reviews of Modern Physics*, 29(3):454–462, 1957.

[29] Richard E. Fikes and Nils J. Nilsson. Strips: A new approach to the application of theorem proving. *Artificial Intelligence*, 2, 1971.

[30] C. Forgy. Ops5 user's manual cmu-cs-81-135. Technical report, Computer Science Department, Carnegie-Mellon University, Pittsburgh, Pensilvania USA, 1981.

[31] Stan Franklin. *Artificial Minds*. MIT Press, 1997.

[32] Vittorio Giovannetti, Seth Lloyd, , and Lorenzo Maccone. Quantum random access memory. *Physical Review Letters*, 100:160501, 2008.

[33] R Givan and T. Dean. Model minimization, regression, and propositional strips planning. In *15th International Joint Conference on Artificial Intelligence*, pages 1163–8, 1997.

[34] C.G. Gross and Mishkin. The neural basis of stimulus equivalence across retinal translation. In S. Harnad, R. Dorty, J. Jaynes, L. Goldstein, and Krauthamer, editors, *Lateralization in the nervous system*, pages 109–122. Academic Press, New York, 1977.

[35] Lov K. Grover. A fast quantum mechanical algorithm for database search. In *STOC '96: Proceedings of the twenty-eighth annual ACM symposium on Theory of computing*, pages 212–219, New York, NY, USA, 1996. ACM.

[36] Lov K. Grover. Quantum mechanics helps in searching for a needle in a haystack. *Physical Review Letters*, 79:325, 1997.

[37] Lov K. Grover. A framework for fast quantum mechanical algorithms. In *STOC '98: Proceedings of the thirtieth annual ACM symposium on Theory of computing*, pages 53–62, New York, NY, USA, 1998. ACM.

[38] Lov K. Grover. Quantum computers can search rapidly by using almost any transformation. *Phys. Rev. Lett.*, 80(19):4329–4332, May 1998.

[39] A. Harrow, A. Hassidim, and S. Lloyd. Quantum algorithm for solving linear systems of equations. *Physical Review Letters*, 103:150502, 2009.

[40] Vojtcch Havlicek, Antonio D. Corcoles, Kristan Temme, Aram W. Harrow, Abhinav Kandala, Jerry M. Chow, and Jay M. Gambetta. Supervised learning with quantum-enhanced feature spaces. *Nature*, 567:210–212, 2019.

[41] Simon O. Haykin. *Neural Networks and Learning Machines (3rd Edition)*. Prentice Hall, 2008.

[42] Robert Hecht-Nielsen. *Neurocomputing*. Addison-Wesley, 1989.

[43] Werner Heisenberg. *The Physical Principles of the Quantum Theory*. Courier Dover Publications, 1949.

[44] John Hertz, Anders Krogh, and Richard G. Palmer. *Introduction to the Theory of Neural Computation*. Addison-Wesley, 1991.

[45] Mika Hirvensalo. *Quantum Computing*. Springer-Verlag, Berlin Heidelberg, 2004.

[46] J. J. Hopfield. Neural networks and physical systems with emergent collective computational abilities. *Proceedings of the National Academy of Sciences of the USA*, 79(8):2554–2558, 1982.

[47] Philip R. Kaye, Raymond Laflamme, and Michele Mosca. *An Introduction to Quantum Computing*. Oxford University Press, USA, 2007.

[48] Alexei Kitaev. Quantum measurements and the abelian stabilizer problem. *Electronic Colloquium on Computational Complexity*, 3(TR96-003), 1996.

[49] Teuvo Kohonen. *Self-Organization and Associative Memory*. Springer-Verlag, 3 edition, 1989.

[50] Tamara G. Kolda and Brett W. Bader. Tensor decompositions and applications. *SIAM Review*, 51(3):455–500, 2009.

[51] Richard E. Korf. Depth-first iterative-deepening : An optimal admissible tree search. *Artificial Intelligence*, 27(1):97 – 109, 1985.

[52] Stephen M. Kosslyn. *Image and Brain, The Resolution of the Imagery Debate*. The MIT Press, 1994.

[53] Raymond Kurzweil. *The Age of Intelligent Machines*. The MIT Press, 1990.

[54] John E. Laird, Paul S. Rosenbloom, and Allen Newell. Chunking in soar: The anatomy of a general learning mechanism. *Machine Learning*, 1(1):11–46, 03 1986.

[55] John F. Laird, Allan Newell, and Paul S. Rosenbloom. SOAR: An architecture for general intelligence. *Artificial Intelligence*, 40, 1987.

[56] Yann LeCun and Yoshua Bengio. *Convolutional networks for images, speech, and time series*, pages 255–258. MIT Press, Cambridge, MA, USA, 1998.

[57] Margaret S. Livingstone. Kunst, Schein und Wahrnehmung. *Spektrum der Wissenschaft*, 10, 1988.

[58] Seth Lloyd. Universal quantum simulators. *Science*, 273(5278):1073–1078, 1996.

[59] Seth Lloyd, Masoud Mohseni, and Patrick Rebentrost. Quantum principal component analysis. *Nature Physics*, 10:631–633, 2014.

[60] George F. Luger and William A. Stubblefield. *Artificial Intelligence: Structures and Strategies for Complex Problem Solving: Second Edition*. The Benjamin/Cummings Publishing Company, Inc, Menlo Park, CA, USA, 1993.

[61] George F. Luger and William A. Stubblefield. *Artificial Intelligence, Structures and Strategies for Complex Problem Solving*. Addison-Wesley, third edition, 1998.

[62] Andrey Markov. *The theory of algorithms*. National Academy of Sciences, USSR, 1954.

[63] J.L. McClelland and A.H. Kawamoto. Mechanisms of sentence processing: Assigning roles to constituents of sentences. In J.L. McClelland and D.E. Rumelhart, editors, *Parallel Distributed Processing*, pages 272–325. The MIT Press, 1986.

[64] J.L. McClelland and D.E. Rumelhart. *Explorations in Parallel Distributed Processing - IBM version*. The MIT Press, 1986.

[65] J.L. McClelland and D.E. Rumelhart. *Explorations in the Microstructure of Cognition. Volume 1: Foundations*. The MIT Press, 1986.

[66] J.L. McClelland and D.E. Rumelhart. *Explorations in the Microstructure of Cognition. Volume 2: Psychological and Biological Models*. The MIT Press, 1986.

[67] W.S. McCulloch and W. Pitts. A logical calculus of the ideas immanent in nervous activity. *Bulletin of Mathematical Biophysics*, 5:115–133, 1943.

[68] Marvin Minsky and Seymour Papert. *Perceptrons: An Introduction to Computational Geometry*. MIT Press, 1972.

[69] T.M. Mitchell. *Machine Learning*. McGraw-Hill, 1997.

[70] A. Newell and H. Simon. Computer science as empirical inquiry: symbols and search. *Communication of the ACM*, 19(3):113–126, 1976.

[71] Allen Newell. *Unified Theories of Cognition*. Harvard University Press, 1990.

[72] Michael A. Nielsen and Isaac L. Chuang. *Quantum Computation and Quantum Information*. Cambridge University Press, Cambridge, MA, USA, 2000.

[73] Nils J. Nilsson. *Principles of Artificial Intelligence*. Springer-Verlag, 1982.

[74] OFTA. *Les Réseaux de Neurones*. Masson, 1991.

[75] Günther Palm. *Neural Assemblies, an Alternative Approach to Artificial Intelligence*. Springer-Verlag, 1982.

[76] Günther Palm. Assoziatives Gedächtnis und Gehirntheorie. In *Gehirn und Kognition*, pages 164–174. Spektrum der Wissenschaft, 1990.

[77] D. B. Parker. Learning-logic: Casting the cortex of the human brain in silicon. Technical Report Tr-47, Center for Computational Research in Economics and Management Science. MIT Cambridge, MA, 1985.

[78] J. Pearl. *Heuristics: Intelligent Strategies for Computer Problem Solving*. Addison-Wesley, 1984.

[79] Michael I. Posner and Marcus E. Raichle. *Images of Mind.* Scientific American Library, New York, 1994.

[80] E. Post. Formal reductions of the general combinatorial problem. *American Journal of Mathematics*, 65:197–268, 1943.

[81] J. H. Reif. Efficient approximate solution of sparselinear systems. *Computers Mathematical Applications*, 36(9):37–58, 1998.

[82] Eleanor Rieffel and Wolfgang Polak. *Quantum Computing - A Gentle Introduction.* The MIT Press, 2011.

[83] M. Riesenhuber and T. Poggio. Neural mechanisms of object recognition. *Current Opinion in Neurobiology*, 12:162–168, 2002.

[84] M. Riesenhuber, T. Poggio, and Hierarchical models of object recognition in cortex. Hierarchical models of object recognition in cortex. *Nature Neuroscience*, 2:1019–1025, 1999.

[85] Maximilian Riesenhuber and Tomaso Poggio. Models of object recognition. *Nat Neuroscience*, 3:1199–1204, 2000.

[86] Frank Rosenblatt. *Principles of neurodynamics: Perceptrons and the theory of brain mechanisms.* Spartan Books, 1962.

[87] S.J. Russell and P. Norvig. *Artificial intelligence: a modern approach.* Prentice Hall series in artificial intelligence. Prentice Hall, 2010.

[88] Stuart J. Russell and Peter Norvig. *Artificial intelligemce: a modern approach.* Prentice-Hall, 1995.

[89] Luis Sa-Couto and Andreas Wichert. "what-where" sparse distributed invariant representations of visual patterns. *Neural Computing and Applications*, 34:6207–6214, 2022.

[90] Luis Sa-Couto and Andreas Wichert. Competitive learning to generate sparse representations for associative memory. *ArXiv Quantum Physics e-prints*, abs/2301.02196, 2023.

[91] J. Sacramento and A. Wichert. Tree-like hierarchical associative memory structures. *Neural Networks*, 24(2):143–147, 2011.

[92] Joao Sacramento, Francisco Burnay, and Andreas Wichert. Regarding the temporal requirements of a hierarchical willshaw network. *Neural Networks*, 25:84–93, 2012.

[93] Erwin Schrödinger. Die gegenwärtige situation in der quantenmechanik. *Naturwissenschaften*, 23(807), 1935.

[94] Maria Schuld and Nathan Killoran. Quantum machine learning in feature Hilbert spaces. *Physical Review Letters*, 122, 2019.

[95] Maria Schuld and Francesco Petruccione. *Supervised Learning with Quantum Computers*. Springer, 2018.

[96] Maria Schuld, Ilya Sinayskiy, and Francesco Petruccione. Simulating a perceptron on a quantum computer. *Physics Letters A*, 379:660–663, 2014.

[97] F. Schwenker. Küntliche Neuronale Netze: Ein Überblick über die theoretischen Grundlagen. In G. Bol, G. Nakhaeizadeh, and K.H. Vollmer, editors, *Finanzmarktanalyse und -prognose mit innovativen und quantitativen Verfahren*, pages 1–14. Physica-Verlag, 1996.

[98] J. Shawe-Taylor and N. Cristianini. *Kernel Methods for Pattern Analysis*. Cambridge University Press, 2004.

[99] P. W. Shor. Polynomial-Time Algorithms for Prime Factorization and Discrete Logarithms on a Quantum Computer. *ArXiv Quantum Physics e-prints*, August 1995.

[100] P.W. Shor. Algorithms for quantum computation: discrete logarithms and factoring. In *Proceedings 35th Annual Symposium on Foundations of Computer Science*, pages 124–134, Nov 1994.

[101] Herbert A. Simon. *Models of my Life*. Basic Books, New York, 1991.

[102] Friedrich T. Sommer. *Theorie neuronaler Assoziativspeicher*. PhD thesis, Heinrich-Heine-Universität Düsseldorf, Düsseldorf, 1993.

[103] K. Steinbuch. Die Lernmatrix. *Kybernetik*, 1:36–45, 1961.

[104] Karl Steinbuch. *Automat und Mensch*. Springer-Verlag, fourth edition, 1971.

[105] Leonard Susskind. *Quantum Mechanics Theoretical Minimum*. Penguin, 2015.

[106] Luís Tarrataca and Andreas Wichert. Problem-solving and quantum computation. *Cognitive Computation*, 3:510–524, 2011.

[107] Luís Tarrataca and Andreas Wichert. Tree search and quantum computation. *Quantum Information Processing*, 10(4):475–500, 2011. 10.1007/s11128-010-0212-z.

[108] Luís Tarrataca and Andreas Wichert. Quantum iterative deepening with an application to the halting problem. *PLOS ONE*, 8(3), 2013.

[109] Alfred Tarski. *Pisma logiczno-filozoficzne. Prawda*, volume 1. Wydawnictwo Naukowe PWN, Warszawa, 1995.

[110] Nuo Tay, Chu Loo, and Mitja Perus. Face recognition with quantum associative networks using overcomplete gabor wavelet. *Cognitive Computation*, pages 1–6, 2010. 10.1007/s12559-010-9047-2.

[111] Carlo A. Trugenberger. Probabilistic quantum memories. *Physical Review Letters*, 87(6):1–4, 2001.

[112] Carlo A. Trugenberger. Quantum pattern recognition. *Quantum Information Processing*, 1(6):471–493, 2003.

[113] A.M. Turing. On computable numbers, with an application to the entscheidungsproblem. In *Proceedings of the London Mathematical Society*, volume 2, pages 260–265, 1936.

[114] D. Ventura and T. Martinez. Quantum associative memory with exponential capacity. In *Neural Networks Proceedings, 1998. IEEE World Congress on Computational Intelligence.*, volume 1, pages 509–513, 1988.

[115] D. Ventura and T. Martinez. Quantum associative memory. *Information Sciences*, 124(1):273–296, 2000.

[116] John von Neumann. First draft of a report on the edvac. Technical report, University of Pennsylvania, June 1945.

[117] Paul Werbos. *Beyond regression : new tools for prediction and analysis in the behavioral sciences*. PhD thesis, Harvard University, 1974.

[118] Andreas Wichert. *Principles of Quantum Artificial Intelligence*. World Scientific, 2013.

[119] Andreas Wichert. *Principles of Quantum Artificial Intelligence: Quantum Problem Solving and Machine Learning, 2nd Edition*. World Scientific, 2020.

[120] Andreas Wichert. *Mind, Brain, Quantum AI, and the Multiverse*. CRC Press, 2022.

[121] Andreas Wichert and Luis Sa-Couto. *Machine Learning - A Journey to Deep Learning*. World Scientific, 2021.

[122] Wayne A. Wickelgren. Context-sensitive coding, associative memory, and serial order in (speech)behavior. *Psychological Review*, 76:1–15, 1969.

[123] Norbert Wiener. *Cybernetics or Control and Communication in the Animal and the Machine, Reissue of the 1961 second edition*. The MIT Press, 2019.

[124] D.J. Willshaw, O.P. Buneman, and H.C. Longuet-Higgins. Nonholgraphic associative memory. *Nature*, 222:960–962, 1969.

[125] Partick Henry Winston. *Artificial Intelligence*. Addison-Wesley, third edition, 1992.

[126] Peter Wittek. *Quantum Machine Learning, What Quantum Computing Means to Data Mining*. Elsevier Insights. Academic Press, 2014.

Index